Date Due

LINDLEY J. STILES
Dean of the School of Education, University of Wisconsin
ADVISORY EDITOR TO DODD, MEAD & COMPANY

Theory and Practice of Supervision

Theory and Practice of Supervision

J. MINOR GWYNN

Professor of Education
The University of North Carolina

DODD, MEAD & COMPANY
New York, Toronto – 1961

EDITOR'S INTRODUCTION

FOR SOME TIME, supervision has been described as "standing at the crossroads"; yet little has been achieved to determine its choice of direction. As a consequence, those engaged in this vital instructional leadership are confronted with confused conceptions of their professional mission, conflicting and overwhelming duties, and lack of appreciation and understanding from either the teachers with whom they work or the public that employs them. Such unhappy conditions prevail at a time when the services of supervision—operating at full strength—are needed most desperately if excellence in education is to be achieved.

Theory and Practice of Supervision, prepared by one of the nation's most respected educators, J. Minor Gwynn, is a timely counteractant for the dilemmas of supervision. It offers both sound direction to the profession of educational supervision and reliable guidance to individuals engaged in instructional leadership. The author comes to grips with the critical issues, conflicts, and problems that plague the advancement of this important work in elementary and secondary schools. Out of his vision and extended scholarship emerges a clear image of what supervision should be, what it should do, and who should attempt to supervise. The picture portrayed allows no room for compromises with administrative expediency, supervisory distortions, or the professional ambitions of those who would use supervisory assignments as steppingstones to other positions. Yet, while emphasizing that supervisors are not administrators, recognition is properly given to the important fact that administrators are supervisors. In short, this book is a guide to better supervision for all who supervise, prepared by an experienced and practical scholar who understands clearly their problems and responsibilities.

Unique features of *Theory and Practice of Supervision* include the detailed suggestions the author makes to help supervisors guide the planning and work of teachers with children. A chapter on the selection and use of textbooks and other instructional materials is one of its kind in the literature of supervision. The treatment given to the unit approach offers creative suggestions and specific illustrations for helping teachers perfect this method of instruction. Up-to-date materials on audio-visual resources, including the use of educational television and instructional machines, give added value to the book. The supervision of student activities, assisting the beginning teacher, suggestions for dealing with problems peculiar to elementary, junior and senior high schools, the basic skills and controversial aspects of the school program—all are examples of the reservoir of resources this publication brings to supervisors. No less valuable are the chapters dealing with the techniques of supervision and the procedures and instruments presented for evaluating the effectiveness of instruction. The treatment of the supervisor's relationship to merit rating is particularly timely and is ably handled.

As the author points out, *Theory and Practice of Supervision* is intended both as a textbook for college courses that prepare for supervision and for the everyday reference use of supervisors at work. To achieve this dual objective, the book skillfully relates theory to practice and, also, historical development to contemporary problems. In addition, it is packed full of up-to-date illustrations, vivid examples, analytical anecdotal descriptions and case studies, useful evaluation instruments, as well as recent selected references. So comprehensive and balanced is the author's treatment, and so practical are the guides he provides for the practice of supervision, that anyone interested in improving instruction in schools, the beginning or experienced supervisor and principal, will find it invaluable.

LINDLEY J. STILES

PREFACE

SUPERVISION IN elementary and secondary schools in the United States faces another crisis in its development. Conflicting educational theories have led to a re-examination of the purposes of both education and supervision. The higher birth rate and consequent crowding of schoolrooms pose another problem. The diversity of preparation of the teachers in this period of teacher shortage focuses attention on a third problem—some individuals have had little or no professional preparation for teaching, while others are re-entering the profession after a period of homemaking. Moreover, the cumulative effects of long-continued studies of the knowledges and competencies needed by administrators and supervisors operate as a fourth major factor, one that shows clearly that adjustments must be made in the training of the supervisor because the tasks of the supervisor have changed radically.

What is the task of the supervisor in the school of today? Of what help should he be to the teacher? To the superintendent? To the principal? To the specialists on the staff? What knowledge and competencies should the supervisor possess in order to do his work effectively? What skills are needed in human relations? With what teaching materials must the supervisor be familiar? What should he know about tests? About community resources? How much responsibility does the supervisor have for school policy? For the evaluation of teaching? Does the supervisor function as an administrative official?

The majority of the problems which confront supervisors in American schools today involve both the curriculum and school organization. At the same time, changing conceptions of the supervisor's task and of how he should perform it have forced changes in

the area of supervision. This book therefore has the following purposes:

1. *To show that the main task of the supervisor is to help teach-ers attain a desirable teaching and learning situation for pupils.* Each
teacher in a school system has to solve his own teaching problems;
he can do this most effectively and quickly by creating a desirable
atmosphere for teaching. To maintain a favorable teaching and
learning situation, the teacher will have to solve problems that arise
from time to time. For example, today the problem may be to explore and select new teaching materials for a new block of work; or
it may be the selection of audio-visual aids for the work that is
planned. Tomorrow it may be how to evaluate a field trip that is to
be taken; or how to group for more effective learning; or how to
provide for the brighter pupil, or for the slow reader, or for the
retarded pupil; or how to handle a pupil who has defied authority; or
how to plan co-operatively with pupils; or how to secure and use
community resources in teaching; or how to experiment with a new
teaching method without hindering the progress and growth of the
pupils; or how to "get along" with other staff members. These are
but samples of problems that a teacher must solve if he is to maintain a desirable teaching situation. The person to whom he must
turn for help in their solution is usually the supervisor. This volume
therefore, includes a wide variety of methods which the supervisor
can use to help the teacher.

2. *To demonstrate that a major responsibility of the supervisor
is to help the administrator and other school personnel to provide
the best possible learning situation for pupils.* The teacher and supervisor alone cannot provide adequate facilities for teaching. The
modern supervisor acts as a liaison agent, maintaining communication between the teacher and the administrative and service staff.
For example, the teacher needs some new supplementary readers;
the supervisor requests them from the superintendent or principal,
who agrees to provide them; the supervisor helps the teacher to com-
pile his list of new books and follows through to see that he gets
them. Or the teacher needs a certain film for Tuesday; the supervisor
and the audio-visual director see that it is available at that time.
Or the class is working on great scientists of America; through the
supervisor's efforts the librarian lists for the pupils the materials
available in the library on these great men. In order to help the

supervisor to make maximum use of school personnel, chapters are included on effective use of texts, supplementary texts and workbooks, of supplementary materials and curricular aids, and of the workshop, group dynamics, and action research.

3. *To give evidence that the emerging concept of supervision identifies the supervisor primarily as a resource person, a teacher of teachers, of as much help to the administrator as to the teacher.* To be a teacher of teachers, the supervisor has to understand the problems of the teachers on all school levels. To be a resource person, the supervisor has to be familiar with the sources of help for teachers of all grades and school levels, for all specialists, and for the superintendent or the principal. Materials on these aspects are therefore included in this book.

4. *To provide a sourcebook for the supervisor to which he can turn and find some help or source of help on many of the problems that arise in his particular supervisory situation.* Over a period of fifteen years the author has collected from supervisors (*a*) lists of those problems on which they needed definite help and (*b*) descriptions of the kind of help or aid that they would have found useful in tackling the particular problem. This volume is designed as a resource book for the supervisor, just as the dictionary is for the newspaper editor or as *Who's Who* is for the college president or the metropolitan hotel manager. The book therefore contains materials, data, sources, examples, methods, and bibliographies in the areas of education which the supervisor might use in solving a problem in his own school community.

Part I presents the Evolution of Supervision, with a brief historical sketch of the development of supervision in the United States followed by a description of the task of the modern supervisor. The remainder of the book is organized into five parts: II. Helping Teachers to Plan Their Classwork; III. Helping Teachers to Work with Children; IV. Special Problem Areas in Supervision; V. Techniques and Methods for the Improvement of Teachers in Service; and VI. Evaluation of the Effectiveness of Instruction and the Future of Supervision.

Some chapters are pertinent to both the elementary and secondary school levels, such as Chapter 2, "Supervision Today"; Chapter 3, "How to Make Maximum Use of Textbooks and Basic Materials"; Chapters 4 and 5, "The Unit or Problems Method of

Teaching" and "The Teaching Unit"; Chapter 6, "Supplementary Materials and Curricular Aids"; Chapter 7, "Assisting Teachers with Pupil Diagnosis and Other Guidance Problems"; Chapter 8, "Supervision of Student Activities"; and Chapter 9, "Helping Teachers with Evaluation."

Chapters written especially for the secondary school supervisor are Chapter 11, "The Supervisor's Special Problems on the High School Level"; and Chapter 12, "Supervision in the Junior High School." "Special Problems in the Elementary School" are covered in Chapter 13.

Other major aspects which are presented include: suggestions for supervisors in setting up organizational arrangements for supervisory programs in current use; the devices employed in supervision, including the newer approaches for implementing a supervisory program; human relations and group processes in supervision; research, experimentation, and the scientific method in supervision; how to evaluate a supervisory program; teacher and merit rating in supervision; and a look at what supervision holds for the future. The teacher's problems and mental health are considered, too, with chapters on how to help the beginning teacher and how to aid teachers with their personal problems of various kinds.

Important resource features of the book are the bibliographies and source lists of books or materials. Chapter 2 has a special bibliography on the historical evolution of supervision; Chapter 5 has a special annotated bibliography of basic sources of information for the supervisor on resources and teaching units; Chapter 6 gives a rather complete list of types of supplementary materials and aids of different kinds; Chapter 8 likewise gives basic sources for the supervisor on group activities of pupils; Chapter 11 has a special bibliography, by subject-matter areas, for the high school supervisor; and Chapter 13 has a resource bibliography for elementary school supervisors, arranged according to subject areas. Finally, the Appendix supplies the supervisor with an annotated list of companies and organizations which supply teaching materials and equipment for schools.

At the end of each chapter there are problems for individual work and for class discussion. Each chapter also has a list of selected references where no special bibliography is included. The detailed index with cross references is designed to make the book easily and readily adaptable for reference, as well as for class use.

Throughout the volume, emphasis has been placed upon the development by the supervisor of many of the competencies of a good resource person. The supervisor of the future must develop many of these competencies and skills or fail in his task.

In preparing this book, I am indebted to many persons for their help. I want to thank particularly the students in my classes, whose co-operation for many years has made possible an extended trial of the materials; and Elizabeth M. Holbrook and Betsy Bracy, who went far beyond their research responsibilities and duties in critical reading of the manuscript and in suggesting improvements and additions; and Professor John B. Chase, Jr., for his constructive reading of the entire manuscript. Many persons and schools supplied illustrative material for the book, to whom I am most grateful, and to whom proper credit is given where they appear in the volume. I also want to thank those authors and publishers who graciously gave their permission for the use of quoted materials; special acknowledgment for this assistance is made at appropriate places in the book.

J. Minor Gwynn

Chapel Hill, North Carolina

CONTENTS

Part V. TECHNIQUES AND METHODS FOR THE IMPROVEMENT OF TEACHERS IN SERVICE

FIGURES

TABLES

Part I

HOW SUPERVISION

DEVELOPED

CHAPTER 1

The Evolution of Supervision

SUPERVISION, ONE OF THE OLDEST FORMS of educational leadership, is currently one of the most controversial. Despite the acknowledged importance of its role in the improvement of educational programs, particularly during times when competent teachers are in short supply, the field of supervision has not evolved into the kind of professional work which attracts sufficient numbers of outstanding men and women teachers. As a consequence, when leadership in supervision is most needed, many promising instructional leaders shun its opportunities, and experienced supervisors often seek transfers to other types of educational work.

Why do well-qualified people have to be coaxed into supervision? What is there about the field which makes it difficult to obtain good supervisors? Who can be a successful supervisor? What makes a supervisor successful?

The answers to these questions lie for the most part in supervision's heritage. The field was originally considered a part of school administration, and as such it was synonymous with inspection. The supervisor is no longer an inspector, however, for in the years since 1920, a number of broadened concepts of the supervisory role have gradually developed from the administrative function. Important among the concepts which evolved were those of scientific supervision and supervision as democratic educational leadership. As these views underwent synthesis, they produced the genesis of the concept of creative supervision. Allied, in turn, to the development of the concept of creative supervision were three other concepts which viewed supervision as guidance, as curriculum development, and as effective group processes.

3

The present chapter first traces supervision's administrative heritage and then describes the development of present-day concepts of supervision. The responsibilities and duties of today's supervisor must be reviewed in the light of current circumstances against the developmental background of prevailing concepts of supervision. Recognition must be given to the understanding of both the public and the professional educator as to the nature of both supervision and successful teaching. As these background factors are made clear, it becomes possible to develop the critical tasks and major responsibilities of today's supervisor as presented in Chapter 2.

Supervision's Administrative Heritage [1]

Strange as it may seem, supervision actually developed from the school superintendency and the principalship of the secondary school; yet its most successful application took place in the elementary school, where it did not start originally. In this setting, supervision developed as an adjunct to school administration. Out of this background have come conflicting ideas as to how supervision should be organized and carried on, what its relationship should be to other administrative functions in the school system, and even what the tasks of the supervisor should be.

EARLY ORIGIN

The secondary school first developed in Europe as the cathedral school, from 800–1400 A.D.; it expanded later into a similar type of institution called the grammar school. The emphasis in these schools was primarily upon religious and moral development. Close supervision from those in authority was, therefore, required. This supervisory responsibility gradually devolved upon one individual, called a *scholasticus* in England, whose duties included the selection of teachers, admission of pupils, development of courses of study, and conduct of examinations.[2]

The elementary school, on the other hand, developed after the

---

[1] The student who wishes to study in detail the historical development of supervision will find specific references in the Selected Source References at the end of Chapter 2.

[2] I. L. Kandel, *History of Secondary Education* (Boston: Houghton Mifflin Company, 1930), pp. 49-50.

establishment of the secondary school. It grew out of the Protestant Reformation to meet the demand that young people be able to read the Bible in their own language. Thus, the common, or elementary, school was designed to teach children to read and write.

When the Puritans settled in New England they established in America the same English pattern of schools for the same purposes. First, a college was organized to train ministers when Harvard College was founded in 1636. Then the Latin Grammar School was established to prepare boys for college so that they could become ministers; the Boston Latin School (1635) was the prototype for the "grammar school" set up in Massachusetts by the Law of 1647. Finally, the reading and writing school, later the school of the 3 R's, was founded; the Massachusetts Law of 1642 ordered that children should be taught to read so that they could understand the principles of religion; five years later, the Law of 1647 specified that both reading and writing should be taught. The original purpose of all these schools in New England was the same as that which had prevailed in Europe—the perpetuation of established religion.

THE DEVELOPMENT OF SUPERVISION THROUGH
THE EMERGING AMERICAN SCHOOL SYSTEM

Figure 1 shows the kinds of supervision that grew out of each major type of school or educational agency in the United States. As the local *school district* developed under the direction of a school committee or school board, certain members of the local committee were designated as a visiting committee to supervise the instruction in the schools. After 1827 this power gradually became vested in a single person, a local school superintendent, who was to administer and inspect the schools. As the free public schools emerged as an "educational ladder" during the nineteenth and twentieth centuries, the district superintendent eventually came to be the individual charged with over-all supervisory responsibilities. To assist the superintendent, other administrative officers—elementary or secondary school principals, for example—became common in the schools. Newer administrative positions were developed, including (1) non-teaching principals, (2) the "general" supervisor for the elementary or secondary schools, (3) the "special" supervisor for certain grades or for certain subjects such as music, drawing, or penmanship, and (4) assistant superintendents, men or women, in charge of instruc-

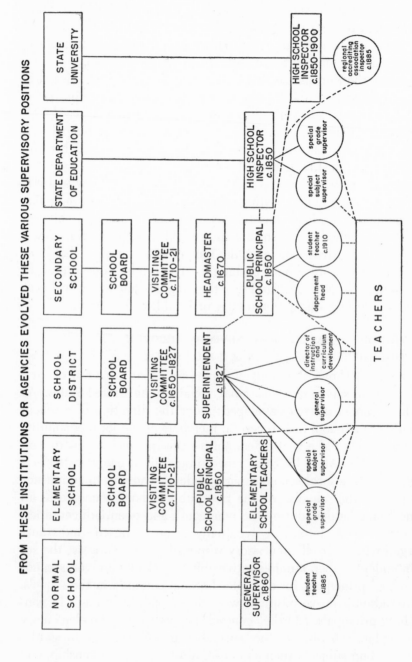

Figure 1. Historical Development of the Supervisory Position

tion or curriculum development, whose major responsibility was supervisory and instructional in nature.

A similar development occurred within the individual *secondary school* as distinct from the school district. By 1721, visiting committees were being used to investigate the work in the Latin Grammar School. Even before these committees were used, however, larger secondary schools had begun to employ assistant teachers who were under the direction of the "head" teacher, later known as the headmaster. As the public secondary school developed after 1821, the position of the principal emerged; his duties were similar to those of the headmaster. With the establishment of legal support for the secondary school (1874), and the passing of compulsory attendance laws which greatly increased secondary school attendance, experienced teachers were often used to supervise other teachers in the same subject fields; thus, the position of department head as supervisor was created.

The history of the *elementary school* principalship reflects a development similar to that of the high school principalship, but during a subsequent period. While the establishment of the free, public, elementary (or "common") school was being achieved during the first part of the nineteenth century (*c.* 1820–1860), many elementary schools developed in building units separate from high schools. From 1870 on, these new schools needed, increasingly, part-time or full-time principals. Compulsory school legislation caused considerable increases in the number of children in school, and in the building of new schools to accommodate this increase; consequently, there arose a demand for additional administrative personnel. The nonteaching principal came into being; his main task was administration and supervision of a more general type for all grades of the school.

After 1870, the rapid expansion of the *state normal school* stimulated the development of the position of general supervisor, especially in the elementary schools. The most important task of the normal school during the nineteenth century was the training of better teachers for the elementary schools; one of the ways in which they set about doing this effectively was through intensive supervision by the general supervisor of the training of teachers for all elementary school grades.

The *state department of education* also influenced the direction taken by supervision, especially at the secondary school level. Early in the twentieth century, state departments provided inspectional and supervisory services for secondary schools. After 1917 they added an increasing number of special subject supervisors whose services were required to ensure compliance with the provisions of federal grants for vocational education, such as vocational home economics and agriculture and trades and industries.

These early inspectional services of state departments, however, usually had their origin in the *state university* or in other institutions for higher education in the state or region; the main need involved was for more adequate preparation of students for college. In the Midwest especially, the state universities provided inspectional services for the secondary schools during the latter half of the nineteenth century. Once a school had satisfied the university committee with the standards of its work, the school was placed on a preferred list. A graduate of that secondary school could then be admitted to college without examination, that is, upon the basis of a transcript of his work and the recommendation of his principal. After 1885 this type of high school inspection stimulated the development of *regional college accrediting associations* whose main purpose was the improvement of private and public secondary schools to make possible better preparation for college. To carry out this purpose the associations conducted inspections of secondary schools in their regions.

The meaning of supervision in 1920. Thus, supervision in America developed through a variety of educational institutions. Each of these added a slightly different facet to the meaning of supervision. The result of such a complex heritage has been considerable confusion and misunderstanding concerning what actually constitutes supervision. However, as one looks back on the growth of supervision in American education to 1920, certain facts stand out:

1. Supervision originated as inspection of schools and continued with that as its major emphasis to about 1920.

2. Much overlapping of the responsibilities and duties of the administrator and the general supervisor communicated itself later to the office of the assistant superintendent or the special supervisor. Among educational writers and school administrators, there was

still no clear-cut distinction between the administrative and supervisory responsibilities of the supervisor.

3. Because of the confusion among administrative and supervisory officers as to their authority, teachers on both elementary and high school levels did not know whose instructions to follow. For example, should teachers follow the suggestions of the principal? Or of the supervisor?

4. Both educational theorists and practicing school men were at variance as to the functions of supervision. Such disagreements were forcing educators to define and delimit supervision.

5. Both teachers and administrators agreed in two respects—that supervision should be more than inspection and that the improvement of instruction was one of its major tasks.

Before looking at developing concepts since 1920, it is important to understand what the term *supervision* meant to the educator who used it at that time because it was upon that definition that the later concepts were built. Table 1 presents a comparison of the conceptions of supervision which were held by educational writers immediately after World War I.

One of the most significant trends which Table 1 shows is that as early as 1920 the improvement of instruction was recognized by all writers as a major function of supervision. On the other hand, it is equally significant that the administrative responsibility of rating teachers was also accepted as a major concept in supervision. The third function that was considered important was concerned with course of study construction and organization—a task which in 1920 was considered more administrative than supervisory.

Out of this background, then, a series of somewhat differing concepts of supervision developed. The following section is therefore devoted to a brief analysis of these more recent concepts.

The Development of Present-day Concepts of Supervision

Three factors have operated primarily since the turn of the twentieth century to give rise to several concepts of value to supervision: (1) changes in ideas of how children learn, (2) major advances in methods of teaching, and (3) a tremendous growth in amount and variety of textbooks and teaching materials.

In the years following 1920 educators and school personnel in

the field made a concerted effort to discover and identify the purposes and functions of supervision. The surveys, experimentation,
and research of this period operated to change supervision from an
inspectional operation into a position of instructional leadership
that demanded creative qualifications. Six concepts played major

*Table 1. Comparison of the Conceptions of Supervision, circa 1920
(adapted)*

E. P. CUBBERLEY (1916) [a]	C. A. WAGNER (1921) [b]	W. H. BURTON (1922) [c]	C. E. SCOTT (1924) [d]
Leader and helper of teachers	Improvement of instruction	Improvement of the teaching act	Stimulation of instruction
Course of study construction		Selection and organization of subject matter	Co-ordination of instruction, based on interests and experience of children
Teacher of teachers		Improvement of teachers in service	
Testing results of teaching		Testing and measuring	
Encourager of individual initiative			Encourager of experiment and scientific methods of instruction
	Visitation and observation of teaching		
Reporting on skill and success of teachers	Rating of teachers	The rating of teachers	

[a] *Public School Administration* (Boston: Houghton Mifflin Company, 1916), pp. 155-156 and ch. XIII, *passim.*
[b] *Common Sense in School Supervision* (Milwaukee: The Bruce Publishing Company, 1921), ch. II, *passim.*
[c] *Supervision and the Improvement of Teaching* (New York: D. Appleton and Company, 1922), pp. 9-10.
[d] *Educational Supervision* (Milwaukee: The Bruce Publishing Company, 1924), chs. I-II, *passim.*

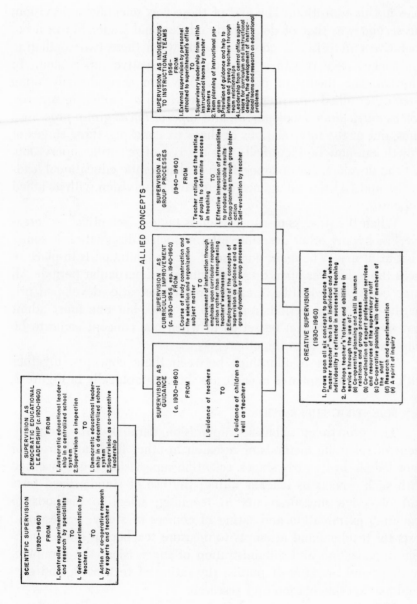

Figure 2. Various Concepts of Supervision, 1930–1960

roles in this transition. The *first* of these was scientific supervision; the *second* was that of democratic educational leadership in a cooperative enterprise. A compromise between these two conflicting approaches gave rise to a *third* concept, creative supervision. In addition, the theory of creative supervision drew heavily upon three other allied interpretations: *supervision as guidance, supervision as curriculum development,* and *supervision as group processes.* Thus, out of the interrelations of these six concepts, three stages of growth can now be identified: (1) the rise of scientific supervision, (2) the development of supervision as democratic educational leadership, and (3) the emergence of creative supervision with its allied emphases.

When the process of supervision is tagged "scientific" or "creative," or by any other descriptive term, such a designation is somewhat arbitrary. The main purpose of such a limitation is to place in focus the influences operating for change in a particular period. All three concepts—scientific, creative, and democratic—developed primarily during the period from 1925 to 1950, but one must admit that no exact date can be set as to when one concept came to be emphasized more than the other.

The complex relationships between these concepts, together with the major emphases in each, are shown graphically in Figure 2.

SCIENTIFIC SUPERVISION

The growth of scientific supervision paralleled the development of scientific methods of research in other fields and areas of knowledge. In its early stages, scientific supervision was concerned with such aspects as teacher rating; the use of standardized tests and objective measurements in teaching; scientific methods of teaching; examination and rating of courses of study; professional tests for teachers and attempts to measure teacher aptitude; scientific organization and administration of supervision; the grouping, grading, and marking of pupils; the rating of textbooks; and curriculum experimentation and research.

Now the emphasis has shifted. Instead of regarding supervision as "scientific," educators today rely on research and the scientific method as tools for improving the teaching-learning situation.[3]

---

[3] For example, read *Research for Curriculum Improvement,* 1957 Yearbook, Association for Supervision and Curriculum Development, N.E.A., *passim.* Classic

This concept accepts supervision not as a science but as a practical art, an art which employs and adapts the findings of science to its own use. Science in supervision may be looked upon as a fact-finding process, using the proper instruments to obtain pertinent data, whether it be items of information, opinions, or measures of skills. Supervision then uses these facts to improve teaching and learning.

SUPERVISION AS DEMOCRATIC EDUCATIONAL LEADERSHIP

Recently, a trend has developed toward identifying school administration as educational leadership. As a phase of this development, supervision has come to be viewed as one type of educational leadership. The successful supervisor has been described as a high type of educational leader who makes use of co-operative techniques in a democratic manner. In addition, the supervisor works for improvement of the total teaching-learning process, as well as for the improvement of teachers in service. In line with this idea, many educators have felt that supervision has as a major purpose the attainment of the purposes of education in a democracy, whether these are special purposes of the secondary school or the elementary school.

The school principal has now also been identified as a supervisor of major stature. This one development alone, coupled with the educational cutbacks of the 1930's, has caused thinking to change concerning the supervisorship; perhaps the building principal would make the better supervisor!

Finally, most authors, investigators, and practitioners have agreed in theory on one principle, whether they practiced it or not. That principle, expressed well by a teacher once in the hearing of the writer, is: "You can talk all you want about supervision, but without the co-operation of all of us, it's a dead duck!"

Public schools have grown in numbers of both pupils and teachers from 1900 to today. During this large growth many individuals became teachers who were not well prepared for teaching and who needed to improve themselves in service. During this

treatments of the subject are J. A. Rorer, *Principles of Democratic Supervision,* Contributions to Education No. 858 (New York: Teachers College, Columbia University, 1942), *passim* and especially pp. 62-79 and ch. II; and Allan C. Harman, *Supervision in Selected Secondary Schools* (Philadelphia: University of Pennsylvania, 1947), p. 5; 24 public secondary schools of various sizes and types in the Middle States Area were selected for this study.

same half-century, American schools have experienced more change in materials and methods of teaching than ever before. This change has also pointed up the need for practicing teachers to improve their instruction. The net result has been that school administrators have had to concentrate on ways and means of improving teachers' education while they were teaching.

THE EVOLUTION OF CREATIVE SUPERVISION

Discarding the old authoritarian or inspectional type of supervision, school personnel first tried to help teachers to improve their teaching by use of research and the scientific method. However, two major factors caused controversy over scientific supervision: (1) most supervisors and teachers were not trained to use the method and (2) the human factors that operate in teaching cannot all be measured scientifically. Therefore, of necessity, another concept of supervision developed, that of democratic supervision under co-operative educational leadership; this was, and is, a sound concept. But those who favored scientific supervision did not give up their fight for basing supervision on research; and they were joined by those administrators who feared that "co-operative" and "democratic" procedures in school administration would wreck sound administrative practices.

When the controversy became acute between those who advocated scientific supervision and those who supported democratic co-operative leadership, the concept of creative supervision came into its own. Offered as a compromise between democratic and scientific supervision, creative supervision was based on a simple, sound assumption with which all agreed—*that teachers need to improve their teaching while in service and that every facility and device that can make each individual into a master teacher must be available to them.*

During this evolution of creative supervision over a period of time, there were shifts in emphasis. One shift was from consideration of the supervisor as the main creative individual to the teacher as that person. Another was from the idea of "creativity" as learning to "discovering" as learning. A third change in emphasis was from the concept that a certain teaching method must be used by every teacher to the idea that different individuals use different methods effectively. Accompanying these changes in emphasis were the emergence or definite development of teacher purposes; improvements in ways of thinking and doing; efforts toward trying out new methods of teaching under proper safeguards; discoveries as to how to use new materials effectively; development of methods for directing pupil activities and activity teaching; the emergence of teaching around a center of interest, commonly called the unit method of teaching; and new emphasis on teacher-pupil planning.

Four allied concepts have also been associated with creative supervision:

1. *Supervision as skill in human relations or group processes.* This has developed rapidly since 1940. *Group dynamics* is the technical term which has been used to designate *group processes,* that is, how personalities interact democratically within an environment or situation. This theory places emphasis upon the social aspects of supervision, mainly upon social intercourse between educational personnel. The main purpose is to release those creative talents which all of us have, whether we are administrators, supervisors, teachers, students, or parents. It is easy to see that education as human relations and successful group processes is but a part of the broader concept of creative supervision.

2. *Supervision as guidance.* Guidance was named as early as 1930 as one of the four major functions of supervision.[4] The main responsibility was placed upon the principal or the supervisor for guidance of the teacher in improving and supplementing his previous training. The Department of Supervisors and Directors of Instruction of the National Education Association stated in 1940 that training youth in democratic living was the most important job of the school and that education therefore became guidance in experiences that were socially worth while. Thus, much emphasis in supervision has gradually shifted to the guidance of children as well as the guidance of teachers.[5] The evidence is clear that those authorities who believe in supervision as guidance expect such guid-

[4] "The Superintendent Surveys Supervision," Eighth Yearbook, Department of Superintendence (Washington, D. C.: National Education Association, 1930), ch. I. This volume discusses in detail the four functions of supervision under the headings of inspection, research, training, and guidance, ch. 1-2, *passim,* and especially ch. 12. This yearbook also identified three basic organizational patterns which still exist today, the line-and-staff, the dualistic, and the co-ordinate types.

[5] *Newer Instructional Practices of Promise,* Twelfth Yearbook, Department of Supervisors and Directors of Instruction (Washington, D. C.: National Education Association, 1940), Preface, and *passim.*

ance generally to result in more effective and enriched teaching; supervision as guidance should be consequently considered as one aspect of creative supervision, of which it is logically a part.

3. *Supervision as curriculum reorganization and improvement.* This concept is not new. As a matter of fact, it was listed as a major purpose by J. A. and J. H. Clement in 1930.[6] However, the concept of supervision as curriculum reorganization and improvement has developed more rapidly since 1940. The many different studies of the curriculum in the 1930's had shown the great demand for curricular revision to meet the needs of boys and girls more effectively. Harold Spears expressed this concept well. He thought of the principal as the main supervisory officer in the emerging, modern high school and defined his task in these words: [7] "In attempting to improve instruction, and thus to provide for maximum pupil development, the principal should place his attention upon curriculum reorganization rather than upon teachers' weaknesses."

In rapid succession since 1940, yearbooks of the educational organizations have indicated the trend toward acceptance of curriculum reorganization as an allied concept of creative supervision. The leader among these professional groups was the Association for Supervision and Curriculum Development of the National Education Association, and it has stressed this concept since its organization in 1943.[8] As this concept has developed it carries within it also the clearly defined ideas of human relations and group planning for improvement, of teacher and pupil guidance and planning, and of creative activity in supervision.

4. *Supervision through instructional teams.* This concept has been identified clearly only recently. It involves basically the extension of supervision and supervisory leadership to master teachers who are in charge of instructional teams, with the instructional program planned by these teams; such teams would use under this team leader other personnel such as interns, fellows, and cadet teachers and librarians and assistants in charge of materials centers. The

---

[6] J. A. Clement and J. H. Clement, *Co-operative Supervision in Grades Seven to Twelve* (New York: The Century Company, 1930), ch. XIII-XX.

[7] Harold Spears, *The Emerging High School Curriculum and Its Direction* (New York: American Book Company, 1940), p. 352. Used with permission.

[8] This newer department of the National Education Associaton was formed in 1943 by merger of the Department of Supervisors and Directors of Instruction and the Society for Curriculum Study.

central office would be responsible for curriculum and instructional designs, the development of instructional teams, and for instructional research and experimentation. Such teams are discussed later in this book (Chapters 2, 13, and 20).

Summary

Contributions have been made to supervision by research, experimentation, and the use of the scientific method in education. Action research is but another method of research, employing primarily group procedures—procedures which the modern supervisor should know how to use if he is to be successful. To be successful, he should also possess the qualities of leadership that enable him to handle a group democratically, to get them to co-operate and co-ordinate their work, and to help each teacher to develop the finest type of creative teaching. Interwoven also into the design of creative supervision are the contributions of the allied concepts of guidance, both for the teacher and for the pupil; human relations and interaction; curriculum reorganization and improvement; and the "instructional team" idea.

Problems for Individual Study and Class Discussion

1. Trace the influence of one of these writers on supervision for the period from 1920 to 1955; F. C. Ayer, A. S. Barr, W. H. Burton, C. W. Boardman, or T. H. Briggs.
2. Compare scientific methods in the natural and physical sciences with scientific methods in education. What are the differences, if any?
3. Trace the contributions of the state normal school to the growth of supervision.
4. Discuss this statement, pro or con: "There comes a time when the administrator or the supervisor must take the responsibility for making a decision and must make it, regardless of whether it conforms to the principles of democratic educational leadership."
5. In earlier days colleges and universities helped to inspect and supervise public secondary schools. Why was this practice discontinued?
6. Is inspectional supervision fostered more by a centralized or a decentralized form of school organization? Support your point of view.
7. What is the relationship between the child-centered philosophy of education and creative supervision? Explain.

8. Is the classroom teacher of today trained adequately for research? The supervisor? Give reasons for your position.
9. Should regional accrediting associations for secondary schools, such as the North Central Association, have any *supervisory* control today over their member schools? Support your stand.

Selected Source References for Problem or Unit Study

NOTE: As Chapters 1 and 2 are so closely related, the references for both have been listed at the end of Chapter 2. (Turn to p. 34.)

CHAPTER 2

Supervision Today

THE PRECEDING CHAPTER summarized the major concepts of supervision which have been operative since 1920. Two other influences on supervision have emerged also during these years: First, there have been changes in the public's conception of the responsibilities of the supervisor. Second, fundamental changes have occurred in methods of teaching. Out of an understanding of the current situation and of the historical development of supervision, the main responsibilities and tasks of the supervisor can be identified.

Changes in the Public's Concept of the Supervisor's Responsibilities

There is disagreement among both professional educators and the public as to what supervision is today. For example, some authorities would make the supervisor a strictly professional official, highly trained to do a major administrative job. Another group would go far in the opposite direction, divorcing the supervisor from administrative duties and responsibilities; this action would result in a supervisor whose main responsibility is to help teachers to meet their problems. A third group of educators would make the supervisor's position mainly that of a teacher of teachers, improving instruction through programs of in-service education. A fourth group, active and vocal, would center the emphasis around human relations; they would interpret the supervisor's responsibility as the effective use of group processes with teachers, pupils, and other school personnel. A fifth group regards supervision as a task includ-

19

ing both supervision and curriculum revision or curriculum building; in this dual role, the supervisor has to add to the responsibility of helping teachers the allied responsibility of stimulating curriculum improvement.

Still, these are not all of the various concepts of the supervisor's job that are advocated in one section or another of the country. A variety of opinion also exists concerning the responsibility of the supervisor *by type of school organization.* For instance, in many elementary schools the principal is considered to be the supervisor as well as the administrative official. In some systems, there is a supervisor for the elementary school but none for the high school. In other systems, supervision in grades 7-12 is the responsibility of special supervisors, as, for example, those in homemaking and home economics, health and physical education, music, art, and the like. In still other schools, the guidance official or personnel officer performs a type of supervision of a rather specialized nature.

In this wide-ranging disagreement concerning supervision and the task of the supervisor, a fourfold uncertainty frequently evolves which is natural under these circumstances. In the first place, the school administrator may have one concept of the supervisor's job which is not held by the supervisor, by the teacher, or by the community. In the second place, the supervisor may consider his responsibilities to be different in some respects from those expected of him by the administrator, the teacher, or the public. In the third place, the teacher's idea of how supervision can help him may differ from the ideas of the principal, the supervisor, or the parents. And finally, the community's idea of what the supervisor should be doing may not be closely related to the concept of the task held by the superintendent, the supervisor, or the teacher.

PUBLIC RELATIONS—THE COMMON FACTOR
IN SUCCESSFUL SUPERVISION

In all of these concepts of supervision one common factor is present—public relations. Now the term *public relations* has two different meanings among educators. One connotation considers public relations to be primarily those measures taken by the administrator and his staff which "inform the public" more accurately and more fully concerning the purposes, plans, program, and activities of the schools in a given community or state. The major emphasis is

upon "selling the school" and its program to the public, upon digni-
fied propaganda for the promotion of the schools. The approach is
usually through special bulletins explaining some new or proposed
departure, through columns or articles in the local press, through
pupil and school papers, through addresses and speeches by school
personnel, or through community or group meetings sponsored primarily by the school system. Through such activities as these, the
school is "advertised" to patrons, staff, and pupils alike.

The second, and newer, meaning of *public relations* centers
around the individual employee of the school system. One new
county superintendent in Florida, where superintendents are
elected by popular vote for four-year terms, gave a good illustration
of this concept. When asked why he had been successful in defeat-
ing the incumbent superintendent, he replied: "His public relations
were poor." Personal public relations have come to be recognized as
an important part of a school employee's work. How does the
teacher or supervisor "get along" with parents? Or does he? When
a mother telephones concerning the amount of homework assigned
her child, does he immediately "jump to the defense"? Or does he
endeavor to discover whether the amount of homework is excessive? When a father wonders whether his boy is mastering the three
R's in grade 5, does the teacher or supervisor ask him to come over
and discuss the type and scope of the work in fundamentals? Or
does he merely tell the father that standard tests show pretty clearly
that the achievement of the children in grade 5 in the school compares favorably with the norms for children in grade 5 the country
over?

This emerging concept of an individual school employee's public relations is influencing communities tremendously where it has
been used effectively. Basic to wise use of this idea is acceptance
of the additional concept that the schools already belong to the
people. The public does not have to be "sold" on a school system
which it already owns and supports financially. But if the public
owns the schools, it has a right to know through all kinds of school
personnel what is going on in the school; and it is the responsibility
of school employees to supply co-operatively to the public definite
and accurate information on the school and its program. The writer
once heard a wise principal tell his elementary school staff at the
opening faculty meeting in September: "Above all, remember that

we can sometimes be wrong. Therefore, *listen first*, instead of talking, when a parent questions our program or our methods of teaching."

Fundamental Changes in Methods of Teaching

These changes complicate the situation when one attempts to "blueprint" the duties and tasks of the supervisor, because we have had basic changes in teaching methods on all school levels since 1900. In turn, the tremendous increase in the knowledge and materials to be mastered in school has operated to bring about some of these fundamental changes in teaching methods.

An illustration can make this point clearer. A one-day conference of primary teachers was held recently in a Southern state to explore and analyze supplementary teaching materials in the form of texts, teachers' manuals, and workbooks. Of the teachers present, 15 had taught in the first grade for 30 years or more. The group became interested in comparing the amount of teaching materials available 30 to 40 years ago with the amount available today, the idea behind the comparison being to show parents how much more the pupil is expected to learn today and how much more materials the teacher has to be familiar with. Most of the teachers were much surprised at the results of this comparison, which was agreed upon by the 15 older teachers as typical.

Teaching Materials Available for First Grade

1919-1920	Today
1 primer	Basic texts:
1 to 2 readers	1 reading readiness book
A few (3 to 5) children's books	3 preprimers
	1 primer
	1 reader (usually 2 books)
	15 to 30 different supplementary readers
	30 to 100 children's books

The primary teachers at this same conference also agreed that the typical first grader today would read from 8 to 16 supplementary readers in the first year of school, in addition to the readiness book, preprimers, and primers; that he would complete more than one seat workbook or skilltest book based on his readers or on his work; and that he would read 10 or 12 of the interesting children's books found in every good elementary school library.

This example of the growth of materials of instruction in Grade One is typical of the increase in such texts and learning materials for pupils in all other grades, including the high school. Such a big growth in published materials to be used and learned by the pupil has necessitated basic changes in the old textbook, *memoriter* method of teaching of 50 years ago—there is a limit to the number of facts and the amount of information that one can learn in a given length of time, whether it be in one hour, in a school year, or in 12 school years. Therefore teachers and supervisors have had to make choices of *what facts, information, and knowledge* each child should master in each grade; they have also been faced with the problem of trying to meet both the *faster* learning needs of the brighter pupil and the *slower* learning needs of the slower pupil. All of these factors have forced teachers and supervisors to experiment with methods of teaching which will make for maximum use of all devices to help each individual pupil to go as far and as fast in learning in a group situation as he can.

A DESIRABLE TEACHING AND LEARNING SITUATION

Each good teacher wants the situation for his pupils which is most favorable for learning. To achieve this desirable atmosphere for his pupils, the teacher has to meet and solve satisfactorily many different kinds of problems both in and outside of the classroom from time to time. This is true because it is just as necessary for the teacher to have a desirable *teaching* situation as it is for the pupil to have a favorable *learning* situation. For example, at one time the problem may be one of grouping for most effective learning. At another time, the teacher wonders how to provide for the faster pupil. In another situation, there is lack of readiness of pupils for the work. Other good examples of the kinds of problems that the teacher will have to solve if he is to maintain such a desirable teaching situation include: helping the slow reader and retarded pupil; finding and selecting new teaching materials for a new block or unit of work; selecting effective audio-visual aids for the work that is planned; communicating with a parent whose help is needed in "getting at" a pupil's difficulties; evaluating a field trip which was taken; planning with pupils; analyzing and evaluating his own work and planning; deciding how much community work he should participate in; choosing the best instruments or tests to use in diagnosis of the case of an individual pupil; discovering and utilizing more fully the community's resources; experimenting with a new teaching method without hindering the progress and growth of the pupils; communicating troubles and problems to the principal or supervisor; and "getting along with" other staff members. These problems involve typical activities in which a normal teacher will be engaged from time to time during the school year.

TEACHERS' OPINIONS OF THE TASKS OF THE SUPERVISOR

Many factors are involved, then, in maintaining a favorable learning situation for pupils and in maintaining a desirable teaching situation for teachers. One approach to a determination of these factors is to find out what teachers themselves consider to be the job of the supervisor. During a twenty-year period (1938–1957) the author conducted surveys of opinions among the students in his classes to determine the supervisor's task as seen by the teachers. These classes represented four different sections of the country— New England, North Central, South Central, and South Atlantic. Each student was asked to list "five ways that my supervisor can help me." No limits in answering were fixed. The student could reply with as many ways as he thought of; or he could decide not to turn in a list for any reason whatsoever. No respondent was asked to sign his name; instead he was to write at the end of his list "I——(have)————(do not have) a supervisor who is supposed to work with me in my school."

A total of 521 teachers turned in lists. Of this number, 41 were supervisors, and their lists were discarded because this was a poll of teacher opinion. Lists of less than five or more ways by which the teacher could be helped were discarded as incomplete for comparative purposes; this procedure eliminated 99 more lists. The resulting net total of answers, each giving five or more ways, came to 381. When a respondent listed more than five ways, the first five were recorded as being the most important to him, since they were mentioned first. Of the 381 in the final total, only 51 listed more than five ways. Of the total, 100 were teacher candidates, mainly juniors and seniors in college who were getting ready to do their student teaching; 70 were in their first year of teaching or had just finished their first year; and 211 had had two or more years of teaching experience.

These data from teachers' opinions of the task of the supervisor are limited because of (1) arbitrary elimination of the replies of some in the interest of gaining a comparison of opinions of different groups and (2) the investigator's combination of closely similar responses under 24 main headings. Nevertheless, the responses make a most interesting, informative, and perhaps significant listing of what classroom teachers over the years consider to be responsibilities of the supervisor.

Table 2 points up two significant implications. First, teachers—whether experienced or inexperienced—believe in great majority that most of the energy and efforts of the supervisor should be devoted to helping teachers plan and carry out their teaching more effectively; secondly, teachers need the supervisor's help in solving their own problems! Otherwise, the table shows clearly that there is a wide divergence of opinion among teachers as to the tasks of the supervisor.[1]

Supervision in Today's Schools

In the historical development of supervision, the weight of evidence is clearly in favor of supervision and supervisors helping school personnel to improve the teaching-learning situation creatively. This must be achieved within the framework of the current understanding of supervision by both school people and the lay public. Since this is so, the supervisor will have to concern himself primarily with the task of helping teachers and school personnel to solve problems that arise or are concerned with a desirable learning situation for children.

[1] For the student who wishes to compare opinions of school personnel as to the duties of supervisors, the following sources are valuable: Fred C. Ayer, *Fundamentals of Instructional Supervision* (New York: Harper and Brothers, 1954), ch. VI; Harold Spears, *Improving the Supervision of Instruction* (Englewood Cliffs, N. J.: Prentice-Hall, 1953), ch. V; "The Superintendent Surveys Supervision," Eighth Yearbook, Department of Superintendence (Washington, D. C.: National Education Association, 1930), ch. III-IV; and Vernon L. Replogle, "What Help Do Teachers Want," *Instructional Leadership*, vol. VII (April, 1950), pp. 445-449.

Table 2. Teachers' Opinions of the Tasks of the Supervisor (Ranked According to Frequency of Mention)

Ways in Which Supervisor Can Help	Number of Opinions			
	Teacher Candidates	1st Year Teachers	Experienced Teachers	Totals
1. Plan classwork	83	65	190	338
2. Find teaching materials	71	60	130	261
3. With evaluation	31	53	134	218
4. With discipline	60	50	60	170
5. With my problems—professional, community, social	20	27	123	170
6. In understanding children better	12	20	80	112
7. By rating teachers and recommending promotion	40	5	40	85
8. By revising the curriculum	11		74	85
9. Plan units (long term planning)	11	11	40	62
10. Select audio-visual materials and aids	11		40	51
11. Get materials and information on the community	14	5	27	46
12. Plan with my pupils	20	7	13	40
13. By planning (handling) teachers' meetings	30	7	3	40
14. With supplementary materials	14	5	17	36
15. In working with other teachers	11	2	20	33
16. Plan and follow up field trips	5	6	20	31
17. With the course of study	20	7		27
18. Evaluate texts	10	3	14	27
19. With teachers' manuals	5	2	14	21
20. How to use the library	9	2	10	21
21. By planning my in-service courses		8	5	13
22. By planning and holding workshops	5	5	2	12
23. With my assembly program	5		1	6
24. By teaching my class while I visit	2			2

THE SUPERVISOR'S MAJOR RESPONSIBILITIES

The main responsibilities of the supervisor may now be identified as of three kinds:

1. *The responsibility to give individual help to the teacher.* A majority of the school systems in the United States today are still small. In many of these systems both the teaching principal and the individual teacher look forward regularly to the visit(s) of the supervisor, to the individual help and stimulation that he can give to each. In some cases, the teacher who is not visited each time feels that he has been slighted or has done something wrong.

2. *The responsibility to co-ordinate and make more available to all personnel the instructional services of the school.* Whether the service is concerned with the supplying of texts, supplementary materials, equipment, or supplies, or whether it is that of making available the services of the librarian, the audio-visual expert, the music or the art teacher, or the consultant from outside the school system, the supervisor is the liaison agent between these services and specialists and the principal and his staff.

3. *The responsibility to act as a resource person for the superintendent and other administrative personnel, as a special agent in training teachers in service, and as an interpreter of the school and its program both to school personnel and to the public.*

Not all supervisors or directors of instruction will have all of these responsibilities, but many of them will.

THE SUPERVISOR'S MAJOR TASKS

In order to discharge the foregoing major responsibilities in a competent fashion, the supervisor in the modern school should be well prepared to perform these major tasks:

1. *To aid the teacher and the principal in understanding children better.* Children grow at different rates; some mature more quickly, some more slowly. Their readiness for learning develops as an individual process. For example, a child's readiness for learning to read may develop during his first year in school, or it may not develop until he is in the second grade. A few are not ready to read until the third grade; yet all may be normal children.

In like manner to differences in physical growth and development, the interests of children change during childhood; they also change markedly from earlier childhood to adolescence, and still further in postadolescence. Some of their own needs are recognized by children; but the teacher has to help them recognize some needs that society emphasizes for their future welfare. The tasks which children perform to acquire fundamental skills and habits differ at the various age levels.

Since all experienced teachers have had professional courses and training in psychology and child growth and development, this text will omit detailed emphasis upon a better understanding of children as a necessary background for supervision.

2. *To help the teacher to develop and improve individually and as a co-operating member of the school staff.* This is one of the big responsibilities of the supervisor. One of the most difficult problems a human being tries to solve is how to become an accepted member of a working group. Strange as it may seem, the individual cannot succeed in being accepted as an equal by the group until he has developed a surety in his own knowledge or a sincerity in his ways of doing that draws respect from other members of the group.

3. *To assist school personnel in making more interesting and effective use of materials of instruction.* This task is one which the supervisor will be called upon to perform by both experienced and inexperienced teachers. In fact, the supervisor becomes almost a source librarian or technician at times. Here is an area in which he can be of maximum help to the beginning teacher who is insecure in his first job, anxious to succeed, and limited in his familiarity with various kinds of teaching materials. In addition, all teachers need specialized assistance in the wise choice of teaching materials and audio-visual aids for a particular purpose or block of work.

4. *To help the teacher to improve his methods of teaching.* This is another activity in which the supervisor can be of special assistance to the beginning teacher, as well as a help to the experienced one. Every good teacher grows by improving his ways of teaching. It should also be said that every good teacher develops *his own* system of teaching techniques; he may adapt to his own teaching some good idea from another teacher, but he does not adopt it per se. In this gradual improvement of teaching methods, the wise supervisor can help the teacher to see more readily interrelationships between subject-matter areas, to prepare in advance

resource materials or units, and to identify more successful and less successful methods that he employs.

5. *To make the specialized personnel in the school system of maximum assistance to the teacher.* The modern school has specially trained individuals whose contributions to the improvement of the teaching-learning situation can be important. It is up to the supervisor to see that he and the teacher make maximum and effective use of these specialists in situations demanding their special contributions. For example, the reproduction by the fourth grade of Indian life and customs might make effective use of five specialists: (1) the music teacher for Indian music and dances; (2) the art teacher for help in the painting of pictures or a frieze; (3) the shop teacher in the construction of Indian tepees or villages; (4) the physical education teacher for Indian dances; and (5) the librarian for books on Indians and Indian lore.

Other specialists have significant contributions to make at various times—among these are the guidance or personnel expert, the school psychologist or psychiatrist, the department head, the lunchroom or cafeteria manager, the visiting teacher, the school nurse, and the special education teacher.

6. *To assist the teacher in making the best possible appraisal of the student.* The writer once heard a provocative remark by a student: "Many good teachers would be master teachers if they could learn how to grade the student's work." There is much truth in this remark. In this evaluation of the progress of his pupils, the teacher should be able to obtain all kinds of help from his supervisor. The making of tests to fit the purpose of the learning is all-important. Teachers also need help in the construction of "take-home" or "open-book" types of tests. Both inexperienced and experienced teachers are calling constantly for assistance in methods or ways of evaluating such intangibles as attitudes, conduct, and co-operation. Concepts of evaluation are undergoing big changes designed to measure a pupil's growth in terms of his achievement from the point at which he started, rather than in terms of a comparison of his performance with the performance and marks of others in his class. New types of report cards to parents come under this heading, too, with their comments in written form from each teacher.

7. *To stimulate the teacher to evaluate his own planning, work,*

and progress. The ambitious teacher will turn to the effective supervisor for aid in this self-evaluation. Admittedly it is impossible for one human individual to evaluate himself and his work fairly, for too many personal factors influence him. However, it is possible for the teacher to develop instruments of various kinds that will serve as checks on his work, its strong points and its weaknesses. For example, one measure of a teacher's growth is found in the number of resource units or materials he has produced for his use in the school year. Another useful device, in spite of manifest limitations, is the check list at the end of a block or semester of work, with strong points, omissions, and repetitions of work to be checked by pupils, but with no names of students to be placed on these evaluations. Still another way a teacher may appraise his own progress is by identifying the *new* teaching methods or devices that he has learned this year.

8. *To help the teacher achieve poise and a sense of security in his work and in the community.* A sense of security in one's position or job is perhaps more conducive to success than any other one factor. The school employee is no exception to this. A salary ample enough to live on comfortably is undoubtedly a major contributor to the teacher's sense of security. But the teacher also needs help in understanding and conforming to the mores and customs of the community in which he works. Unmarried men and women tend to have more social and emotional problems than married teachers. Different communities expect different kinds of participation of teachers in community activities. There are great differences among communities in the provision of the kind of housing which makes possible normal social and community life for teachers. This is a "ticklish" area of activity for the supervisor, but one in which he cannot side-step his responsibilities.

9. *To stimulate faculty groups to plan curriculum improvements and carry them out co-operatively, and to assume a major responsibility in co-ordinating this work and in improving teacher education in service.* This is one of the newer tasks of the supervisor. Many school systems today have created a new position of "curriculum co-ordinator" or "head of the department (division) of curriculum and instruction." Whether the supervisor has one of these high-sounding titles or whether he has the old-fashioned title of "supervisor," curriculum improvement has become one of his

tasks in the modern school. Co-operative curriculum improvement involves some of the older concepts of scientific supervision and of research and also some of the newer approaches to group action and co-operative action research. The preparation and publication of resource materials, units, or course of study bulletins are also a part of this task.

10. *To acquaint the school administration, the teachers, the students, and the public with the work and progress of the school.* This service is one that is informative in nature, directed more toward groups than toward the assistance of individual school employees. The supervisor stands in a favorable position for such a service; he comes in contact with perhaps more individual school employees than any other school person except the high administrative officials. It is not difficult for him to pass along information from one group to another about the good things that are being done, the interesting new ideas that are being tried out, the progress that is being made. Also, the supervisor appears frequently before community groups of diverse nature, and these appearances provide a platform for telling the community what the school is doing. Since the supervisor is neither the teacher nor the principal of the student, he frequently has an opportunity to listen to pupils and to learn from them of other interesting events and plans at school.

Teachers, administrators, and college personnel are in fairly general agreement that the modern supervisor should be competent to perform these main tasks. The remainder of this book will attempt to offer many suggestions for the supervisor so that he may carry out these responsibilities well. In addition, the volume would not present a fair and unbiased picture of supervision unless it included analyses of several controversial issues in supervision. These include the following: (1) How far shall the school go in developing further the group activities of students? (2) What kinds of help does the beginning teacher need at the start of his career? (3) To what extent can one employ successfully the "group dynamics" technique in supervision? (4) Does teacher (merit) rating have a place in supervision? (5) How can the supervisor meet the special problems concerned with staff specialists on the elementary, the junior high, and senior high school levels? During all of this presentation, careful attention will be given to all of the devices and methods, old and new, that have proved valuable in solving supervisory problems.

Supervision and Instructional Teams

Present-day experimentation with team approaches to instruction may well modify the supervisor's relationship with individual classroom teachers. As it does, new responsibilities will be placed on those engaged in supervision to provide leadership for the organization of teaching teams and the selection and development of the professional competencies required by this co-operative approach to teaching. Undoubtedly, individual teachers will continue to function in most schools since not all will be able to function most effectively in team relationships.

The instructional team provides for experienced master teachers to provide leadership to a teaching group that is composed of individuals with various types and degrees of specialization, including both professional and noncertified personnel. In effect, such an organization for instruction provides built-in supervision for interns and beginning teachers who are included. Because team members work closely together planning the total program of instruction for a unit of students that may include as many as 200 or 300 or as few as 50 or 60, graduated professional experiences can be arranged for inexperienced and less able members. At the same time, more professional help is available from team leaders who assume in addition to master teacher responsibilities many of the duties related to the improvement of instruction that central office supervisors typically perform.[2]

In a sense the instructional team may free supervisors to devote more time and energy to top-level leadership for curriculum development and the organization and evaluation of instruction. As higher quality learning is promoted through the differentiated staff resources made available to students through instructional team arrangements, greater demands will be felt for modifications in curriculums and for the appraisal of the impact on individual students. It is possible that such developments will open doors to

[2] Lindley J. Stiles, "Individual and Team Teaching," *Wisconsin Journal of Education*, vol. 92, nos. 7-10 (January, 1960).

supervisors that permit them to exercise greater leadership for re-search—a much neglected responsibility of educational leadership.

CLARIFICATION OF SUPERVISORY TITLES

Much has been written over a long period of years concerning *who* are supervisors in the school system. As a matter of fact, supervisory and consultant resources have expanded so much and so rapidly in the public schools that a large number of titles have developed for different supervisory positions. Harold Spears illustrates well this wide range of titles, identifying a total of almost a hundred different supervisory positions.[3]

For the purposes of this volume, the term *supervisor* will be used with the connotation that a supervisor in the school is one of the personnel who spends one-third or more of his time in working to improve the teaching-learning situation. Under the limits of this definition, if he spent one-third or more of his time in this manner, the supervisor might be the elementary or high school principal; the supervisor of music, of art, of science, of guidance, or of audio-visual education; the co-ordinator of instruction, of secondary education, of curriculum, of special services, or of personnel; the director of research and guidance, of elementary education, or of special education; the consultant in reading, in curriculum, or in health education; or the general or special supervisor.

Problems for Individual Study and Class Discussion

1. Describe what you consider a desirable learning situation for grade 1. For grade 5. For work in an English class in the high school.
2. List in two parallel columns (1) the personal qualifications that a supervisor should possess as an educational leader and (2) the professional qualifications that he should possess.
3. Give your description of the duties and responsibilities of a general supervisor. Of a special supervisor.
4. Make parallel lists, one identifying the duties and responsibilities of supervision about 1890, one identifying those of 1920, and one of those of 1960.
5. Take two recent textbooks on supervision and compare the philosophy of one author in regard to supervision with the other.
6. Will beginning teachers have a concept of supervision markedly different from the concept of a teacher of 10 years or more of experience? Explain.

[3] Spears, *op. cit.*, pp. 88-89.

7. Do the duties and responsibilities of the principal as a supervisor differ from those of the general supervisor? The special supervisor? Explain.
8. Write out your creed or philosophy of supervision.
9. Are special state supervisors for the Federally-aided vocational programs in high schools warranted? Why or why not?
10. Can you distinguish clearly today between the administrative and supervisory duties of the modern school principal? Give reasons for the position that you take.
11. Can you describe some of the needs of the man teacher or the woman teacher who lists "discipline" first as an area in which he wants help from the supervisor?

Special Bibliography on the Historical Evolution of Supervision

NOTE: Some 50 books and over 100 articles in educational periodicals during the last 40 years furnished pertinent data for these historical accounts of the development of supervision. Limitations of space prevent the listing of all of them. Therefore, this bibliography is limited mostly to books and monographs, and the research student is referred to *The Reader's Guide* for the main periodical references prior to 1960. The best single source of information on developments and trends in concepts of supervision since 1943 is *Educational Leadership*, published by the Association for Supervision and Curriculum Development, National Education Association. The following six educational periodicals have presented both the pros and cons concerning scientific methodology, educational leadership, creative supervision, and action research and human relations in recent years: *Educational Administration and Supervision; Journal of Educational Psychology; Progressive Education; Review of Educational Research; School Review;* and *Teachers College Record.* Also the yearbooks of the following groups for the last 30 years are valuable sources for tracing the changes in supervision: American Association of School Administrators (formerly Department of Superintendence), N.E.A.; Association for Supervision and Curriculum Development (formerly Department of Supervisors and Directors of Instruction), N.E.A.; Department of Elementary School Principals, N.E.A.; Department of Rural Education, N.E.A.; and the National Society for the Study of Education. These writers on supervision likewise furnished basic information on developing concepts of supervision: H. P. Adams and F. G. Dickey; Harold Alberty and V. T. Thayer; F. C. Ayer; A. S. Barr; J. A. Bartky; William H. Burton; Harl R. Douglass and C. W. Boardman; Thomas H. Briggs; Ellsworth Collings; Stephen M. Corey; P. W. L. Cox; E. P. Cubberley; Inga O. Helseth and Lindley J. Stiles; J. M. Hughes and E. O. Melby; Carl A. Jessen; L. V. Koos; G. C. Kyte; C. T. McNerney; W. T. Melchior; H. W. Nutt; A. C. Roberts and E. M. Draper; S. Smith and R. K. Speer; and W. L. Uhl.

"Action Research," *Review of Educational Research,* Vol. XXIX, April, 1959, pp. 165-176, and October, 1959, pp. 378-387.

Alpren, M., "Examples of Action Research," *Bulletin of the National Association of Secondary-School Principals*, XLIII (December, 1959), 86-87.

Bent, R. K., and McCann, L. E., *Administration of Secondary Schools* (New York: McGraw-Hill Book Company, 1960), Ch. III.

The Bulletin of the National Association of Secondary-School Principals, Vol. XLV (Jan., 1961), "Seeking Improved Learning Opportunities," Parts II and III. (Team teaching and other experiments to improve instruction.)

Burton, W. H., and Brueckner, L. J., *Supervision: A Social Process*, 3rd ed. (New York: Appleton-Century-Crofts, Inc., 1955), Chs. I-III, VII.

California Journal of Secondary Education, Vol. XXXV (April, 1960), has a symposium on "The Constructive Use of Teachers' Talents," pp. 232-270 (Team Teaching).

Cramer, R. V., and Domian, O. E., *Administration and Supervision in the Elementary School* (New York: Harper and Brothers, 1960), Chs. III and XII.

Crosby, M., *Supervision as Co-operative Action* (New York: Appleton-Century-Crofts, Inc., 1957), Sections I, IV and V.

Educational Supervision—A Leadership Service, A Report of the Southern States Work Conference on Educational Problems (Tallahassee, Fla., State Department of Education, 1955), *passim.*

Elsbree, W. S., and McNally, H. J., *Elementary School Administration and Supervision*, 2nd ed. (New York: American Book Company, 1959), Chs. VII-VIII.

Franseth, J., "Improving the Curriculum and Teaching Through Action Research," *School Life*, XLII (December, 1959), 8-10.

Gulley, H. E., *Discussion, Conference, and Group Process* (New York: Henry Holt and Company, 1960), *passim.*

Hammock, R. C., and Owings, R. S., *Supervising Instruction in Secondary Schools* (New York: McGraw-Hill Book Company, Inc., 1955), Ch. II.

Hicks, H. J., *Educational Supervision in Principle and Practice* (New York: The Ronald Press Company, 1960), Parts I-III, and especially Chs. I-III.

Leadership for Improving Instruction, 1960 Yearbook, and *Research for Curriculum Improvement*, 1957, Association for Supervision and Curriculum Development (Washington, D. C.: National Education Association), *passim.*

Morse, A. D., *Schools of Tomorrow—Today!* (Garden City, N. Y.: Doubleday and Company, 1960), Chs. I, IV, and Appendix.

National Society for the Study of Education, 60th Yearbook, 1961, Part II, *Forces Influencing American Education* (Chicago: The University of Chicago Press, 1961).

Nelson, L. W., "Improvements Needed in Secondary Schools," *The Annals of the American Academy of Political and Social Science*, "American Civilization and Its Leadership Needs, 1960-1990," pp. 87-94.

Personnel Services in Education, 58th Yearbook, Part II, 1959, *passim*, and *The Dynamics of Instructional Groups*, 59th Yearbook, Part II, 1960, *passim*, National Society for the Study of Education (Chicago: University of Chicago Press).

Pierce, T. M., and Albright, A. D., *A Profession in Transition* (Auburn: Alabama Polytechnic Institute, 1960), Chs. IV, VI, and X.

Reeder, E. H., *Supervision in the Elementary School* (Boston: Houghton Mifflin Company, 1953), Chs. I-VII, XVI.

Simulation in Administrative Training (Columbus: The University Council for Educational Administration, 1960), *passim.*

The Superintendent as Instructional Leader, 35th Yearbook, American Association of School Administrators, 1957, *passim.*

Wiles, Kimball, *Supervision for Better Schools*, 1st and 2nd eds. (Englewood Cliffs, N. J.: Prentice-Hall, Inc., 1950 and 1955), Foreword and Ch. I of 1st ed., Chs. I-II of 2nd ed.

Part II

HELPING TEACHERS

TO PLAN

THEIR CLASSWORK

CHAPTER 3

How to Make Maximum Use of Textbooks

and Basic Materials

THE TEXTBOOK HAS BEEN and will continue to be one of the primary tools used by teachers in curriculum work. Since this is so, the supervisor must be able to help the teacher to make most effective use of the textbook in the modern school, especially in view of the fact that many teachers in the school today do not know how to teach children without a textbook. This chapter is devoted to the following aspects of this supervisory problem: improvements in traditional textbook presentation and teaching, standards for analysis and selection of textbooks, teachers' manuals and workbooks, and making more effective use of basal and supplementary texts.

Improvements in Traditional Textbook Presentation
and Teaching

During the last quarter of a century many improvements have been made in textbooks. The changes which catch the eye most quickly are those in format and make-up, in the introduction of color in both illustrations and type, and in greater variety in illustrations of all kinds—charts, graphs, pictures, and maps, for example. There have been several fundamental changes and improvements, however, that are of just as much importance but which can be easily overlooked. These changes involve the kinds of material which are presented, the methods of presentation, and the opportunities the text presents for the pupil to proceed at his own pace.

"WHAT ARE TEXTBOOKS FOR?" [1]

Modern authorities in education, both conservatives and progressives, see a need for the textbook in teaching. In summary form, Table 3 gives a picture of the possibilities of the use and misuse of texts.

Teachers have been heard to remark "I can't use that text—it's too poor." Or, "That text does not suit my method of teaching." When one inquires further into why the teacher thinks that the text is "poor," he usually discovers that either the teacher is referring to the text as "out of date," or not containing the latest facts and information; this could be true of subject-matter areas that change fast, such as world history in the social studies or texts in science. When the teacher thinks that the text he is supposed to use is not adapted to his "method of teaching," he may be right. Some teachers, for example, teach by the problem method, or the unit method; a text written from the chronological approach in history might not suit his way of teaching. But there are other ways in which he can get another text, ways which will be discussed later.

Actually, there are very few poor textbooks produced for the public schools. Text publishers are in business to make money; a poor text will not make money; therefore a company never knowingly turns out a poor text. As a matter of fact, most publishers today choose both the authors and editors of their individual or series textbooks, instead of the author seeking the publisher. This is a sound policy, because much of the writing today for children is specialized. For example, the writer knows of a case recently in which two authors wrote a good history—and an accurate one—for the intermediate grades; but the vocabulary range was for the junior and senior in high school, not for the seventh grader.

---

[1] This is the title of a symposium by B. R. Buckingham, Hollis L. Caswell, Donald W. Durrell, E. R. Jolie, William Kottmyer, Ullin W. Leavell, Evan Lodge, and John C. Whinnery in *The Phi Delta Kappan*, vol. XXXIII, no. 5 (January, 1952), pp. 241-247, from which Table 3 is summarized. *Cf.* also "Textbooks as Tools," by W. L. Chase, *The Instructor*, vol. LXIII (March, 1954), pp. 13, 15; and Richard M. Pearson and William E. Spaulding, "Textbook Publishers Look at Selection," *The National Elementary Principal*, vol. XXXVI (September, 1956), pp. 18-25.

Table 3. Potential Uses and Misuses of Textbooks

Textbooks, Properly Used	Textbooks, Improperly Used
Are an aid or tool in learning and teaching	Make memory work the main aim
Supply indirect experience in large and well-organized amounts	Ignore individual differences
	Form the curriculum
Supply sifted, logically arranged factual data, typical to a field or area	Become a substitute for the library and its store of knowledge
Build vocabulary upward from grade to grade	Limit the pupil to one book instead of encouraging use of many
Provide a sequential arrangement of subject matter, a core of material	Provide a crutch for inadequately trained personnel
Provide helpful hints on methods, tests, and adaptations of material	May be behind the times, out of date
Provide minimum audio-visual materials	Encourage the "page assignment" method of teaching
Save intelligent children from bad teaching	
Help beginning and substitute teachers as immediate source books	
Provide for varied learning abilities	
Provide learning for teacher as well as pupil	

In summary, the supervisor should know that some texts are more factual than others; that some cover controversial matters more adequately than others; that texts in some living, developing areas get out of date sooner than texts in more static areas, such as mathematics, Latin, and foreign languages; that competition is keen among textbook companies; that new departures and improvements are constantly being made that may suit a particular teacher's teaching methods better; that, even though some teachers may not agree with the opinion and/or the presentation of the author modern texts of interesting and provocative design catch the eye of pupils and teachers alike; that just because some texts are old, they may not be obsolete, for example, English classics, such as *Julius Caesar* or *Huckleberry Finn;* that some homes have very little reading matter in them, and a student's texts are frequently read by others in the home than the pupil; that special texts are rapidly being prepared for special purposes, such as for the interest range of the older, retarded pupil who is a slow reader and for the secondary-school pupil of more limited vocabulary; that a few textbooks are in advance of the development of new methods of teaching, but most books usually show the adoption of new methods of teaching several years later; and that new types of good texts in new subject areas have been prepared and are available.

NEW TEXTBOOKS FOR NEW OR EXPANDING
SUBJECT-MATTER AREAS

Public pressure has demanded that the school add more and more subjects to the curriculum. But it has not been possible to add them in an effective manner until resource materials have been made available. Recently such source materials in the forms of texts have been prepared for many of these new subject areas. The purpose here is to explore them with the supervisor. An additional purpose is to examine new types of texts which have come into being because of the enlargement of a subject area, such as the addition of geography and history to the field of the social studies, and reading and grammar to the language arts.

Texts on American life. Since World War II much emphasis has been placed upon teaching children in the schools the "American Way of Life," perpetuating the "private enterprise" system. American business, American labor, and the American Medical Association have gotten together in one of their rare efforts at co-operation to ballyhoo the need for perpetuating American life, institutions, and freedoms. Newer text materials have been designed primarily for the high school level for teaching about labor, industry, farming and agriculture, the family, the world of machines, public administration and public health, urban and rural living, American politics, and America's role in world affairs. Some of these materials are resource units for a shorter period of time; others are interestingly written texts for class study on one center of interest for a period of two to three months. This movement for the study of American life is closely related to the allied movement for better economic education in the schools.

Character education. Those critics who have been contending that the modern schools neglect character education should examine school textbooks. There is ample evidence from five subject areas of both materials and activities aimed directly at the development of character. English series for both elementary and high school levels stress speech and personality; the individual and his groups; facing one's problems and society; how to arrive at values; how to form sound standards for radio programs, pictures, and reading; what is success; how to get along with your age group and with older people; how to evaluate newspaper and magazine articles; how to belong to a group or club or committee; how to persuade others and how to evaluate propaganda; how to participate in discussions; and how to choose a career.

Health texts include such character education aspects as how children grow up, understand themselves, get along with others, develop good ideas of sportsmanship; how the use of alcholic beverages and drugs can have bad effects; and growth and adaptation of personality and behavior. That newcomer to the public school curriculum, psychology, looks primarily at growth, development of personality and behavior, how to get along with others, how to form standards and values, and how to study other people. Texts for the newer courses in marriage and family living for the high school emphasize personal adjustment and character development. Guidance texts for grades 7-12 stress personality growth, making friends, solving problems and making choices.

Community study. Some of the best teaching is done by teachers who center a large part of their work with their pupils around the local community. Well known are the social studies texts on civics or citizenship, problems of American democracy, and sociology. This community teaching technique does not lend itself readily to learning from texts, for no two communities are ever alike. Some attempts have been made on the elementary school level to develop series of texts in the social studies which are centered around the activities of the family and community in the primary grades; both rural and urban neighborhoods are included.

There are many new materials for the teacher. One of these texts is designed to help teachers, pupils, and citizens trace the development of their community and its resources today; it furnishes samples of instruments for use, such as questionnaires, tally sheets, and summary sheets. Another kind of source material for the teacher is found in several books which describe successful school and community programs in various sections of the United States, from kindergarten to the college and adult education level. Other books can help the teacher in regard to the problems, procedures, and techniques of community analysis. Another type presents the developing concept of the community school both as having a responsibility for improving aspects of living in the community and as being a service center for the community as well as for children.

Conservation education. Wasteful destruction and thoughtless use of America's natural resources are matters of concern to thinking educators and statesmen. Several recent developments of a national nature have focused attention sharply on conservation education. One of these is the need for a steady, constant yearly supply of wood for wood pulp and synthetic industries. Large tracts of land have been purchased by industries for tree cultivation and pulpwood production; in addition, these companies are trying to educate farmers to grow and cut logs for them in a scientific manner. Another development has been the lowering of the natural water line because of the tremendous use of water in certain industries; still another has been the soil conservation program, both to save the land and prevent floods. Another major problem now revolves around stream pollution from sewage disposal, in the attempt to conserve life and health. These are but a few of the major problems which emphasize the need for conservation education in the school. New materials have been prepared for this area, in addition to the references usually found in texts for science study and for the social studies.

Materials on consumer education. Much interest in this subject during the last decade has been caused in part by the pressure, already described, to teach about the American way of life; in part it has been stimulated by such national experiments as the Economic Education Workshops and the Citizenship Education Project.[2] The commercial teachers in high schools were the leaders years ago in introducing courses in consumer problems and economics as part of the business education program. The more recent developments have been in two directions: (1) A course for a full or one-half year in consumer education as a general elective in high school. Its content is centered around such consumer problems as income, expenditures, budgeting accounts; intelligent buying, using

2 Ch. XXI includes descriptions of these.

standards and labels; how to buy insurance and invest in yourself; consumer law; how to use advertising and consumer credit; and how to invest in insurance, your health, and in recreation. (2) A unit or a problem in some other course. For example, resource units are available on effective shopping, which might be used for a unit of six weeks in length in a regular course in arithmetic, home economics, business education, civics, or agriculture. More texts and materials have been developed on consumer education for grades 7-12 than for grades 1-6.

Economic education and economics. Economics has been primarily a course for college study until recent years. In 1940 two reports gave impetus to the study in the public schools. The Educational Policies Commission of the National Education Association and the American Association of School Administrators published its study, *Education and Economic Well-Being in American Democracy;* and the National Council for the Social Studies published its Eleventh Yearbook, *Economic Education,* devoted to the importance and methods for this subject in the public schools.

The Joint Council on Economic Education became interested in 1949 in more emphasis upon American economic life on all grade levels. Fostered by the Committee for Economic Development, the Joint Council has tried to implement the teaching of economics in the schools by means of summer workshops in different regions of the country. Teachers who are selected from all school levels are helped in these workshops (1) to understand the American economic system better and (2) to prepare teaching materials of a resource nature for use in the schools. In a small number of high schools, economics is a full course in length, as an elective for juniors and seniors. The modern trend is to teach economic education as a center of interest or a unit in each of the 12 grades, including such subjects as economic and commercial geography and consumer economics.

Newer departures in literature texts. For many years literature anthologies have emphasized the literature with which each pupil should be familiar before entering college. For this reason, the literature collections have contained more classics of all types in English literature than other selections. Now the emphasis is shifting sharply so that all children can profit from the reading, each as he makes reading a part of his life.

For example, one series for grades 3-6 makes child growth and realization the basis of the readtext series, with other main objectives being enjoyment of some of our literary heritage and the development of appreciation skills. Another series for grades 7-12 has two goals: (1) books to suit student interest in the selection of material and (2) progressive development of reading power. Still another high school series aims at adventures in reading, the setting of a liking and a love of reading; to accomplish its purposes with pupils of poor reading ability, the series includes some abridgements or simplifications of classics. In like manner, simplified or adapted editions of the great classics have been prepared for older pupils of adolescent age and interests who have reading ability of a much lower grade level. Simplified classics retain the story but simplify the vocabulary; adapted classics retain the essential story but shorten it and adapt it to a simpler vocabulary range. Abridgments are the same as adaptations of classics. It should be noted that when adapted or simplified classics are once published, their use can be continued over the years without readaptation again.

New texts are also appearing in the social studies that are pitched to a reading level several grades below a pupil's age; this is one of the ways to care for individual differences in pupils' reading and learning.

Family living, marriage, and homemaking. Good texts written for these courses in grades 9-12 have become available in the last decade. They furnish basic information on such topics as you and your family, why your family acts as it does, family understanding during dating years, and the American family; marriage customs and laws, religion and marriage; what it takes for successful marriage and successful parenthood; divorce; family income and security; parents and children; and homemaking. There are also good source texts for teachers of these subjects. Some of the school texts could be used for full-year or half-year courses; others could be used more successfully as resource materials in a unit or block of work on the family, marriage, or homemaking. Some high school psychology texts also take up some aspects of home living and marriage.

Guidance texts. The materials for guidance have grown rapidly since Margaret Bennett and Harold Hand wrote their first edition of

School and Life,[3] a handbook for the pupil on the problems he would encounter typically in his first year of high school and his orientation to them. Other texts take up self-analysis and techniques for building personality. Still others set forth the responsibilities and practices of those elected to pupil activity or school offices by their fellow students.

Educational guidance is well presented in other texts, with sections about whether to plan for college training or for a job, how to qualify for and finance college training, how to take homestudy courses, how to analyze one's self for a vocation one would like, and how to plan courses for high school graduation. Vocational guidance on a group basis has source and student texts ranging from an over-all view of vocations in an "occupations" course in grade 8 to diagnosis of characteristics that a particular job demands, getting a job, and how to hold a job.

Practically all of these materials are for junior and senior high school students. Some of these books can be used for a course; others can be used for units or problems in existing courses, such as home economics, vocational education, social studies, or health and physical fitness.

Health and physical fitness. Some of the most interesting new texts for grades 3-9 are in this area. Special attention has been devoted to health—physical and mental, personal and group, public and private. Nutrition, infection and disease, accidents and safety, adapting to weather and climate, personal appearance and grooming, how the body works, personality and family relationships, growing up, understanding community safeguards, recreation—all of these and more furnish rich materials and suggestions to teachers. The materials are adaptive to regular class work, to class problems, or to units for a shorter length of time. Illustration, charts, diagrams, drawings, and cartoons are plentiful. Materials for teaching safety education are frequently included in these texts.

International, intercultural, inter-American, and interracial materials. Several types of texts and materials have been developed. The earlier texts attempted to give elementary school pupils a better understanding of people of other nations of the world; the emphasis was on international and intercultural education. World

[3] Margaret Bennett and Harold Hand, *School and Life* (New York: McGraw-Hill Book Company, Inc., 1938).

War II turned attention sharply to our own neighbors of the Western continents. Texts were prepared on both elementary and secondary school levels about Canada and the peoples to the north; about Mexico and Central America; and about the peoples of South America. Good source books have been prepared for the teacher, too.

Recently, valuable materials have been prepared for work in intergroup relations. The Committee on Intergroup Relations of the American Council on Education sponsored Intergroup Education in Co-operating Schools (1945–1952). Publications growing out of these studies offer valuable resource materials to the teacher in the critical areas of intergroup and interracial relations.

Language arts and grammar. The specialists have collaborated to excellent effect to produce effective series of language books for pupils. The content is composed of materials, topics, and problems of interest to the age ranges involved. The appearance and design are attractive. The illustrations, many in color, are appealing and well chosen. And the devices for teaching offer many ideas for teachers on both elementary and high school levels. "Grammar can be interesting"!

Mathematics texts. This subject area, for unknown reasons, has been slow to develop interesting texts, and a field that can be so full of interest and imagination for the student deserves better tools for both pupils and teachers. Some interesting attempts have been made, mostly in texts for consumer mathematics and general mathematics. Interesting illustrations, tables, and diagrams suggest new ideas for teaching; and the problem or unit method is gradually being introduced. Improvements of a major nature are still confined largely to the materials for the intermediate grades.

Science. Science texts have improved remarkably in the last two decades. As a matter of fact, there are now well-illustrated science texts for the elementary school, series which were practically nonexistent a decade ago. These texts meet well the areas of conscious interest of the young child; they give many answers to his continual questions of "what" and "why." They also furnish ample suggestions for him to follow his natural investigative propensities, under adult guidance. For the younger years the centers of interest are plants and flowers, animals, the weather and the seasons, day and night, the earth, the sky, tools, and machines. For the later elementary years, the topics or centers of interest include airports and weather stations; conservation; inventions; advertising and warning signs; camping and science; refrigeration and air conditioning; and television, radar, and jet engines.

For the secondary school the newer biology texts and manuals have helped the good teacher to revolutionize his teaching. General science and geography texts are more interesting, with their presentation of rich resource materials in the form of units, problems, experiments, or field investigations. Chemistry has been slower to change its texts to methods adapted to adolescent learners. Physics texts, which hold the keys to the nuclear age and the intense interests of young people, give the least evidence of improvement in materials and methods for understanding and appreciating the practical applications of physics to modern life.

Psychology texts. This is a comparative newcomer to the curriculum, usually as an elective course or a half-credit course for juniors or seniors. Satisfactory texts are now available, which take up heredity and environment; learning and how to improve learning techniques; personality and personal adjustment; mental hygiene; intelligence and its measurement; and the problems of behavior in society and vocation. This new course overlaps much with the areas of character education, family living, marriage, and guidance, which have already been presented.

Radio and television. These newer subjects are becoming very popular. Since there are still comparatively few courses in these fields in public schools, materials and texts have developed slowly. One approach has been in connection with English courses on the high school level. Emphasis is on the radio or TV workshop, which covers such activities as newscasting, plays, talks, and continuity in programs. The other approach is that of teaching through radio and television; this includes such activities as broadcasting in schools and the educational radio or TV program, with programming, recording, and children's programs. Most texts for this approach are primarily for the teacher.

Regional textbooks. The widespread interest in the study of the main regions of the United States has resulted in some texts which give supplementary help to the teacher. For example, one such series of texts for youngsters includes selections from literature on the Southern region. There are both stories and poems by well-known authors, selected and edited for consistent vocabulary development. There are folk tales, stories about natural wonders, the Civil War, and great Southerners. Another series is primarily centered on frontier days and the settlement of the West.

Safety education texts. Safety education at times combines safety and health, or even health, safety, and physical education. In some states the legislation requiring instruction in these areas links them together in the statutes. Good materials of an interesting and suggestive nature are available for both the elementary and the secondary school pupil. Texts have also been prepared for the teacher, with suggestions for programs and activities. Some centers of interest and activities that were mentioned above under Health and Physical Fitness are similar to those encountered in these texts.

Sex education materials. There are few acceptable texts or supplementary books on this controversial subject. Whether sex education is primarily the duty of the home or not, children do at times ask questions of their teachers about sex; they ask them at different grade levels and in different courses. Whether a teacher is trying to teach about sex, give accurate information on sex matters, or answer questions, he needs materials graded to the child's advancement. These materials may be suggested to the parent for study or to the child, under certain conditions. Or they may be the main source of guidance for the teacher in preparing himself adequately to answer questions about sex. Simple materials, clearly written, are available on sex education. In using them, the teacher would be wise to take the parents into his confidence before he refers children to them.

New types of texts in social studies. The trend for some years has been from separate courses and texts in geography and history to work in a combination of these two, usually designated as the "social studies." This has been a natural development, since there is a close correlation between the two subjects, so close that one can hardly teach one without using the other. Some of the newer materials in social studies offer richer materials than ever before for both student and teacher.

One plan has been to emphasize in texts the child's social development in the early grades through his home, even through his school contacts, then through his neighborhood contacts, and then through his broader community contacts. Another departure is to emphasize citizenship education in social studies texts in the elementary grades. This civic education is centered around the growth of America. A newer approach has been the planning and writing of "correlated" or "unified" or "fused" texts—one text which combines both geographical and historical materials without regard to subject-matter lines. This kind of pupil text also furnishes excellent source material for the teacher who employs co-operative planning in the teaching of units in his work.

In addition, there are texts especially for the teacher on citizenship principles, programs and methods that have proved successful. These resource texts also give up-to-date bibliographical references; samples of evaluation devices, such as analysis sheets; sociometric devices; and types of teaching plans.

Summary. It is doubtful whether the many modifications and additions that have been made in text materials will be completely adequate for adjusting the curriculum of the public school to the needs of pupils and of society. Most authorities in the curriculum and in supervision believe that the key to this problem is the use the teacher makes of these vast resources. Experienced supervisors, therefore, collect and make available to their teachers selected samples of these outstanding, newer text materials for their examination and use.

Standards for Analysis and Selection of School Textbooks

The laws of the states vary concerning both free textbooks and textbook selection for public schools.[4] The trend is toward textbooks free for all children. At present the laws of the different states make textbooks free for all grades or for some grades in 30 states; in the other states the law allows school subdivisions to furnish free texts if they so decide. Textbooks are a very small item in the total cost of education, a little more than 1 per cent.

[4] See *The Phi Delta Kappan, op. cit.,* pp. 257-261 and 262-266, and *NEA Research Bulletin,* vol. XXXVII, no. 3, October, 1959 (Washington; National Education Association), p. 95.

THE SELECTION AND ADOPTION OF TEXTBOOKS

The selection and adoption of texts for schools likewise show several patterns in all of the states. Half of the states adopt texts for the whole state; the others allow local or system-wide adoptions. There are three types of textbook lists: (1) open, (2) multiple, and (3) single or basal. Open listing means free choice from all texts. Multiple listing or adoption means choice from a limited list of approved texts, usually from three to five different texts or series. Single or basal adoption means that one text or series is selected and approved for use in all schools. Nine states still practice single adoptions; however, most of these states recognize the need for more than one basic text and allow the collection of a supplementary book fee for purchase of additional texts. The trend is toward multiple or open textbook lists.

Professional educators and teachers are customarily responsible for the analysis, rating, and recommending of textbooks for adoption, but they do not usually have the power of final decision for adoption. Final selection of the textbooks to be adopted for use is usually made by laymen, not educators; the members of the official bodies that finally approve adoptions, such as state or local boards of education, are predominantly laymen. For example, the State Textbook Commission in North Carolina has a heavy majority of trained school teachers and administrators on it; but their task is to examine, screen, and recommend a certain number of texts to the State Board of Education, which makes the final decision.

Responsibility for content of texts used. In effect, the greater the freedom which school systems and teachers have in the selection of texts, the greater the responsibility; conversely, the smaller the amount of freedom, such as that granted by single or basal adoptions, the smaller is the degree of responsibility. For example, assume that you are in a state where there is freedom of choice of textbooks for the local school district or authority. An attack is made by some local or patriotic group on the social studies series in use as subversive, as not teaching democracy properly. Thus a controversy arises. In this case, the explanation and defense of the series of texts in use will fall on the local school authorities, or teachers, or both. In comparison, in a state where there is a single textbook adoption, the attack on the basal text series will have to be sustained by the state authority. The local district has had no responsibility for adoption of the basal text and cannot be held responsible for it. The only responsibility that the local authority has is for wise selection of supplementary texts and series; even in regard to these supplementary materials, some state authorities approve the lists.

Texts more likely to be attacked. The key word here is "controversial." No one can "get up a good argument" about a matter of fact; it is in the area of opinion and of conflicting opinion that disagreement thrives. There are some subject areas in which students study about current problems, controversies, conflicting theories, and history-in-the making. This is as it should be. But the textbooks which are used in these areas may not suit each segment of the population. As illustrations, the labor union may not like the way a text in problems of democracy presents the history and place of labor. Or the industrial leaders in a community may not like the light in which big business is cast in an economics text. Or the American Legion may object to the social studies series presenting communism as a type of government along with other types. Any of these groups may attack texts and appeal to the school board to throw them out. If the texts are fair, accurate, and well balanced, they will survive the attacks, as has the history series of David Saville Muzzey over a lifetime period.

The subject areas in which school textbooks are more likely to come under attack by one group or another are the social studies, especially texts in sociology, problems of American democracy, economics, government, and modern history; literature anthologies, which present selected writings of all sorts, by authors who once held political positions of influence, or who presented certain races or creeds as stereotypes; science texts, especially in biology with its explanation of reproduction and sex education; health and physical education texts, particularly in regard to some aspects of public health, sanitation, and sex education; psychology texts; and any texts which are written directly for courses or work in religious education or the Bible and in sex education.[5]

[5] Those interested in bringing themselves up to date on the textbook controversies in the mid-century period of attack and counterattack upon the schools should read: *The Phi Delta Kappan, op. cit.; Saturday Review,* "The Textbook in America: A Symposium," vol. XXXV, no. 16 (April 19, 1952), pp. 13-23, 53-57, 62-65, and "The Public School Crisis," vol. XXXIV, no. 36 (September 8, 1951), pp. 6-13, 26;

STANDARDS FOR TEXTBOOK ANALYSIS

Textbook analysis is a difficult task. There are four main reasons for this: (1) No two teachers teach alike; the materials and presentation that suit one teacher may not suit another; (2) teachers receive little or no training in textbook analysis; (3) instruments or charts for textbook analysis are hard to construct; and (4) educational authorities and text experts disagree on how to go about analysis of textbooks; some insist that each text should be analyzed in comparison with other texts written for the same purpose or course; others believe that each text should be examined against the set of standards or resources which the individual teacher has in mind.

In regard to this controversial problem, the majority opinion among the writers seems to be that each teacher should examine and select texts in the light of what his task is and the aid and resources he expects the individual text to furnish to the pupils and to himself. To do this, each teacher should write down *his own standards* for a good text and examine each text in comparison with his own desired standards. In line with this concept, suggestions are made here for the teacher and supervisor to use in setting up their own standards for examination and analysis.

Questions for Rating or Analysis of Textbooks

(Not in order of importance)

What is the copyright date? This is important for every book, and especially in ever-changing subject areas or courses, such as social studies, health, and science; not as important in some foreign languages, ancient history, grammar, or mathematics.

What of the book's format? Its shape, size, attractiveness, style? Is it interesting to me, the teacher? If so, will it be interesting to the pupil?

J. E. Heafner, "The Battle of the Books," *NEA Journal*, vol. XL (April, 1953), pp. 227-228; P. A. Knowlton, "What Is Wrong With Textbooks?" *School Executive*, vol. LXX (October, 1950), pp. 56-58; "Who's Behind the Textbook Business?" *National Parent-Teacher*, vol. XLVII (April, 1953), pp. 10-13; *101 Questions About Public Education* (Chicago: National Congress of Parents and Teachers, 1954), pp. 49-53; W. E. Spaulding, "Can Textbooks Be Subversive?" *The Educational Record*, vol. XXXIV (October, 1953), pp. 291-304; and *The American Way of Publishing—Your Safeguard Against Subversion in Textbooks*" (New York: American Textbook Publishers Institute, undated), pp. 1-8.

What effective illustrations, pictures, diagrams, charts, maps, graphs, and colors does it have?

How well are its materials correlated with other subject-matter fields that are closely related to this subject? For example, health texts have a close correlation with biology, home economics, and civics texts.

Is the content valid? Comprehensive? Does it present data and points of view on both sides of controversial issues? Are any conclusions which are drawn supported by evidence given in the text?

Is the vocabulary suited to the grade level for which it is intended?

Is the content (stories, illustrations, and the like) within the interest range of the pupils for which it is intended?

Does the author treat all groups, creeds, and races with respect?

Are the philosophy, presentation, and methods in line with those that I use? Would I get additional ideas for my teaching from it? Is it suited to the purposes for which I want to use it?

Is there provision for individual work on problems by pupils?

Is there provision or suggestion for small group or committee work on problems by pupils?

Does it give adequate supplementary references or suggestions?

Does it, if a text for grades 7-12, have a good index?

Is the author competent? The publishing company responsible?

Is it a revision, or merely a new printing?

In analyzing any text, one should keep in mind these cautions: (1) If a text is to be used by more than one teacher, more than one teacher should make an analysis of it, the supervisor should analyze it, and all analyses should be pooled as to its adequacy; (2) If only one teacher is to use the text in one class, that teacher's judgment should prevail; and (3) At no time could *all* of the items which are suggested for standards of analysis be used on a single text.[6]

Teachers' Manuals and Workbooks

There is a wide variety of these aids, ranging from the manual to help the teacher with one particular text to the self-teaching textbook or workbook. Since there is such a wide variety and since

[6] Individuals interested in evaluating texts by rating or score cards can read Ivan R. Waterman, "When You Choose a Textbook," *The Phi Delta Kappan,* vol. XXXIII (January, 1952), pp. 267-271; Floyd L. Haight, "Evaluation of Instructional Materials," *Educational Leadership,* vol. VIII (March, 1951), pp. 349-352; Abraham Tannenbaum, "Family Living in Textbook Town," *Progressive Education,* vol. XXXI (March, 1954), pp. 133-140, 166-167; and B. Everard Blanchard, "Tentative Criteria for the Selection of Textbooks," *The High School Journal,* vol. XXXVIII (May, 1955), pp. 294-296.

there is some controversy over "workbooks," they will be discussed separately.

TEACHERS' MANUALS OR GUIDES

For many years publishing companies have prepared manuals to accompany their texts, to help the teacher make most effective use of them. They set forth the purpose(s) of the textbook or series; the nature of the books and how they fit the interests and needs of pupils at that age range and grade level; suggestions for projects for slow and fast learners, for group work, for exercises for drill and mastery, for use of the library and supplementary materials, and for co-operative planning and enrichment activities. Sometimes teachers' manuals may include also keys to tests or exercises in the text, or even mastery tests.

Another kind of manual for the teacher is published separately in the form of tests for the children, based on materials in the text. These may take the form of "skilltext" manuals. In reading, for example, these may include stories, pictures, and words, with tests designed to reveal whether the pupil is understanding ideas, understanding words, studying words, interpreting and organizing ideas. In general, the tests are a drill on how well a child is reading.

Still another manual may be composed primarily of achievement tests on a certain text, such as English literature or American literature; these test books are for use by the pupil or can be of value for the teacher as he makes use of one test question or more as he desires. These tests can be essentially a form of practice book for the pupil. Or they can be merely test forms made out for the pupil to take as the teacher and pupils closely follow the book. This test book has less value than other manuals, for consistent use in this manner emphasizes textbook teaching at the expense of planning by teacher and pupils.

WORKBOOKS

The workbook as a teaching device is still a controversial issue in professional education. *The Dictionary of Education* gives this definition which is generally accepted.[7]

---

[7] Carter V. Good, ed., *The Dictionary of Education*, prepared under the auspices of Phi Delta Kappa, 2nd ed. (New York: McGraw-Hill Book Company, 1959), p. 608. Reprinted by permission.

Workbook: (1) a study or learning guide for pupils, often related to a particular textbook or to several textbooks; may contain exercises, problems, practice materials, directions for use, space for recording answers, and, frequently, means of evaluating the work done; (2) a supplementary or preparatory exercise or practice book in reading, used to give additional training not found in basic reading materials.

Types of workbooks. For more than half a century there have been workbooks in the laboratory sciences on both the high school and college levels. Different names have been given to these, such as "laboratory manuals," "laboratory guides," "laboratory exercises," and "student" or "pupil" workbooks in courses like physics, chemistry, botany, zoology, geology, biology, and general science.

The first kind of workbook in the evolution of additional learning materials for individual work was the *study* or *learning guide* for a particular textbook based primarily on exercises, practice materials, and problems for mastery of principles or laws of science as set forth in the basic text. J. G. Umstattd terms these the "old-style science laboratory manuals"; he indicated in his analysis that they were not true workbooks because they were not instructional booklets.[8]

As the workbook developed, the second type to appear was a supplementary or additional practice book for a basic text which seemed to develop in several subjects at about the same time. There is evidence to support the idea that seatwork books for arithmetic and number work in the elementary grades, supplementary practice books in reading, and English grammar workbooks for the secondary school pupil were developed about the same time, during the 1920's. These bulletins were written mostly by the teachers themselves; they endeavored to prepare materials of a self-instructive nature for the pupil. These pamphlets were therefore more of the nature of textbooks than merely practice books or laboratory manuals. Frederick Burk and Carleton Washburne among the educators and the Webster Publishing Company and the McCormick-Mathers Company among the publishers were pioneers in preparation and publication of these new instructional materials.[9] Today,

[8] *Cf.* J. G. Umstattd, *Secondary School Teaching* (Boston: Ginn and Company, 1944), p. 184. However, one who is interested in tracing the controversy over the growth of the workbook would find some interesting changes in his point of view with regard to the values of workbooks in Umstattd's 3rd ed. (1953) of this book.

[9] For the historical development of the workbook, compare A. W. Elliott, "This Workbook Craze," *School Executives Magazine,* LI (September, 1931), pp. 19-20,

an estimated 40 million workbooks are sold annually by publishers, the equivalent of about 25 per cent of the instructional budget of the nation.

A third type of workbook is identified by J. G. Umstattd as the "tablet" type, whether of exercises for practice, of tests, or other "single" educational devices.[10] Umstattd excludes this kind of classification as an instructional workbook because it is usually restricted to one feature; he likewise excludes the old-fashioned laboratory manuals in science because they are routinized in methods and lack what he terms essential features of modern workbooks.

Point of view. School personnel are gradually developing a philosophy concerning workbooks that is more in line with modern methods of teaching. For example, when the child comes to the first grade, he cannot read. But he can learn by pictures, verbal symbols, blocks, and concrete materials. The teacher therefore uses several kinds of workbooks with him which contain these readiness materials. Practically all of the texts which the beginner uses before he learns to read are really workbooks with multitudinous readiness materials in number work, science, and reading series.

When the pupil has learned to read, each at his own readiness level, he will read more and more if materials are available. And he will usually improve his basic skills of speed, vocabulary, comprehension, and reading rate in proportion as he has a tremendous volume of materials of many interesting kinds to work on; these materials are the modern skilltest books or workbooks for reading self-improvement, for each pupil at his own pace. Some of these workbooks have over 100 pages of materials for one grade.

In like manner, each child learns the fundamentals in number work and arithmetic. Some master these fundamentals faster than others; here is the need again for both a practice book and a self-

---

38; T. V. Goodrich, "Is the Workbook a Necessity or a Luxury?" *School Executive Magazine*, LI (April, 1931), pp. 359-361, 396; W. Vreeland, "A Good Workbook from the Teacher's Point of View," *Nations Schools*, XVIII (July, 1936), pp. 35-37; W. E. Spaulding and W. R. Marvin, "Should Schools Use Self-teaching Textbooks?" *School Review*, LIV (September, 1946), pp. 406-415; M. E. Kerr, "Teaching With Workbooks," *Elementary School Journal*, XLVIII (December, 1947), 218-221; W. P. Johnson, "Then Came the Workbook," *Journal of Education*, Vol. 131 (February, 1948), pp. 64-66; E. H. Mattingly, "Meet the Modern Workbook," *Illinois Education*, XXXVIII (January, 1950), pp. 190-192; A. Gray, "Lift the Workbook Cover," *The Phi Delta Kappan*, XXXIII (January, 1952), pp. 286-287; and Richard Madden, "Workbooks," *NEA Journal*, XLV (February, 1956), pp. 94-95.

10 See Umstattd, 3rd ed., *op. cit.*, p. 182.

instructing workbook. The workbooks furnished by the publishers to go with the text frequently fill this need. In this case, the more advanced pupil is not forced to repeat fundamental drill which he has already mastered; he can go on ahead at his own pace.

The modern schoolroom today in grades 1-6 may have as many as five to seven workbooks for each pupil—workbooks to accompany the texts and work in reading, language arts, spelling, arithmetic, geography and history, and science. In most cases, the workbooks will be those published by textbook companies to accompany their texts which the school is employing.

The experience of correspondence schools over a number of years in different situations adds evidence to support the worth of the self-instruction workbook or textbook. The Internationl Correspondence School (Scranton, Pa.) has given courses for years that required these materials. The United States Armed Forces Institute has likewise been successful in giving courses which required self-instruction materials.

In addition to the examples of workbooks already described for the elementary schools, there are modern, interesting workbooks in art, business education and typing, journalism, English, geometry, biology and general science, health, social studies and history and economics, homemaking, and the other vocational subjects. As a matter of fact, much of the work in agriculture, shop work, trades and industries, industrial arts, home economics, auto mechanics, and commercial education is based on individual projects; and many of the texts for carrying out these projects are of the workbook type with self-instruction features.

The supervisor or administrator who finds fault with workbooks raises a question in the mind of the listener in these days of modern textual plenty. That question is: "Does he really know about the teachers' manuals and pupil workbooks which are designed for better use of the texts that his own school has adopted?"

Making More Effective Use of Basal and Supplementary Textbook Materials

It is easy for an expert to tell teachers whom he does not know how to run their business of teaching. It is much harder to persuade them to employ his suggestions. That is where the supervisor enters the picture, to help the teacher to make better use of text materials.

There are essentially two basic problems involved in using text materials more effectively. One problem is *where* to find good text materials. To solve this for the teacher, it should be the joint responsibility of the school administration and the supervisor to furnish these materials in great variety. This will cost some money, but it will be money well spent. Two illustrations of how the classroom teacher should be equipped will make this point clear. The example in the elementary school is the fifth-grade teacher. He should have on his desk and his shelves in his room arithmetic texts for grade 5 from at least six different arithmetic series; the same number of texts for grade 5 in history and geography, or social studies; in language arts and reading; in science and nature texts; in health texts; and in spellers. He should have all of the teachers' guides and manuals that accompany these as well as pupils' workbooks for those texts. He should also have good basic source texts which are written for the teacher in a subject area, such as books on how to teach reading, arithmetic, or the social studies.

The example from the high school is the science teacher. Like the fifth-grade teacher, he should have at least six different texts for each course that he teaches, with all workbooks and manuals. He should have books on how to teach science as well as any texts that he desires in any allied fields, such as health, or home economics.

The second basic problem in learning how to use text materials more effectively is centered around the individual teacher's own methods or system of teaching. In helping the teacher to select texts, teachers' guides, and workbooks, the supervisor should know the whole range of materials well enough to suggest to a particular teacher those that will give him new ideas for his own particular way of teaching. For example, the supervisor should show the teacher who uses the unit method of teaching other texts that are written with that method of teaching as the central point of departure. On the other hand, for a good teacher of the old-fashioned "textbook type," the suggestions of the supervisor should include excellent examples of newer texts full of interesting ways of presenting practice and drill for mastery.

In the final analysis, the textbook cannot make the teacher; it is only one of the useful tools of teaching. Neither can the teacher make the textbook. But good texts, constructively used and adapted to a teacher's techniques of teaching, can help to make a much better teacher; they can also help to make an interested student instead of a bored one.

Problems for Individual Study and Class Discussion

1. Identify several ways in which textbooks have changed since you attended the second grade. The sixth grade. High school.
2. Can supervisors help teachers instill a love of reading and books in children?
3. What would be your standards as a supervisor for the selection of workbooks in arithmetic for your fourth grade? For your eighth grade?
4. If your school is planning to adopt a new textbook, what standards should you use to determine the use of Book A as the basal text, and Books B, C, and D as supplementary texts?
5. What can be done for the child who does not like to read but is proficient in other respects in his schoolwork?
6. Is it easier for the teacher to teach with one basal text or with a number of texts? Support your point of view.
7. Suppose that one of the patriotic organizations in your town has charged that your seventh-grade social studies text does not present accurately the American economic system. How would you go about a fair investigation of this charge?
8. Assume that you are the supervisor in a 20-teacher elementary school and that a fund has recently been provided by the P.T.A. for the purchase of supplementary texts. What personnel would you want on a committee with you to select these textbooks? How many people from what groups, and why?
9. Take the teachers' manuals for one basic reading series and analyze them. Then do the same with a second basic series. What differences, if any, did you discover?

Additional Selected References for Problem or Unit Study

American Council on Education, *Intergroup Relations in Teaching Materials* (Washington, D. C.: American Council on Education, 1949).

The American Textbook Publishers Institute, New York 16: *Planning Your Textbook Budget,* 1960 (The School Administrator's Guide to Realistic Budgeting); *Textbooks and Learning,* by James M. Cass; *Official Minimum Manufacturing Standards and Specifications for Textbooks,* rev., 1960.

Burton, W. H., and Brueckner, L. J., *Supervision: A Social Process* (New York: Appleton-Century-Crofts, Inc., 1955), chs. XIII and XVII.

Cronbach, L. J., ed., *Text Materials in Modern Education* (Urbana: University of Illinois Press, 1955), *passim*.

Crosby, M., *Supervision as Co-operative Action* (New York: Appleton-Century-Crofts, 1957), ch. XIV.

Dale, E., *Audio-Visual Methods in Teaching*, rev. ed. (New York: The Dryden Press, 1954), chs. III, V, XXI, XXVI, *passim*.

"Do Your Schools Have Paperback Bookstores?" *School Management*, vol. IV, No. 8 (August, 1960), pp. 39-41, 79-82.

Elsbree, W. S., and McNally, H. J., *Elementary School Administration and Supervision*, 2nd ed. (New York: American Book Company, 1959), ch. XXVII.

Feldman, D., *The Censorship of Books* (Madison: University of Wisconsin Press, 1957), *passim*.

Gwynn, J. M., *Curriculum Principles and Social Trends*, 3rd ed. (New York: The Macmillan Company, 1960), chs. VI, VIII, XVIII.

Hicks, H. J., *Educational Supervision in Principle and Practice* (New York: The Ronald Press Company, 1960), pp. 332-336.

Mehl, M. A., and others, *Teaching in Elementary School*, 2nd ed. (New York: The Ronald Press Company, 1958), ch. XI.

Michaelis, J. U., *Social Studies for Children in a Democracy*, 2nd ed. (Englewood Cliffs: Prentice-Hall, Inc., 1956), chs. I-II, VII, XII-XIII.

National Education Association, Research Division, and American Association of School Administrators, *Textbook Provisions in 624 Urban School Districts*, Education Research Service, Circular No. 6 (1959).

National Society for the Study of Education, Chicago, University of Chicago Press: 26th Yearbook, Part I: *Curriculum Making* (1927); Part II: *The Foundations of Curriculum Making* (1927); 30th Yearbook, Part II: *The Textbook in American Education* (1931); 33rd Yearbook, Part II: *The Activity Movement* (1934); 36th Yearbook, Part I: *The Teaching of Reading* (1937); 56th Yearbook, Part II: *Social Studies in the Elementary School* (1957). The textbook and its influences are discussed in all of these studies.

Wesley, E. B., and Wronski, S. P., *Teaching the Social Studies in High Schools*, 4th ed. (Boston: D. C. Heath and Company, 1958), part 3.

The Yearbook of Education, 1958, *The Secondary School Curriculum* (Yonkers-on-Hudson: World Book Company), Section III, chs. 1, 3.

CHAPTER 4

The Unit or Problems Method

of Teaching—A New

Supervisory Problem

IF ONE TRIED to pick out the *one* factor in the modern school that has complicated the task of the supervisor more than any other, he might have to decide that it is the development of the unit or "problem" approach in teaching around a "center of interest." As a matter of fact, some educators contend that the development of this approach in teaching has revolutionized the concept of the supervisor's job because (1) teaching is planned for blocks of time, instead of for one day at a time, (2) in preplanning for blocks, the teacher needs much more help with supplementary materials and references, and (3) in this type of planning one teacher may need more aid or the exclusive aid of the supervisor for several days at a time.

How Unit Teaching Developed

Unit teaching around a center of interest has developed rapidly as a sound psychological approach to instruction since 1900. It is in reality a system of teaching techniques which can be adapted to subject matter and textbook teaching or to the needs, activities, and experiences of pupils. Several steps in the improvement of teaching

63

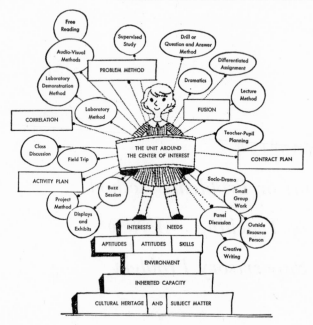

Figure 3. The Unit Method of Teaching: a "Magic Belt"

It gives teacher and pupil access to *any* teaching methods as needed. (Circles denote simpler methods; rectangles denote more complex systems of teaching techniques.)

Credit for this way of illustration to Cornelia Nixon, Charlotte, North Carolina.

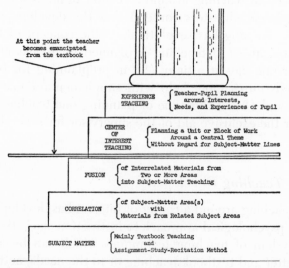

Figure 4. The Steps a Teacher Usually Takes in Going from Textbook Teaching to Teaching Around Centers of Interest by Units

Figure 5. The Effect of the Unit on the Textbook
Credit for illustration to Cornelia Nixon, Charlotte, North Carolina.

methods had to be effected before the unit method could come into its own. From textbook teaching, experimenters advanced to the utilization of the project method which involved unity of work, with the learner aware of what he was trying to accomplish, and with a carefully drawn plan for completion of the work.

The next step in this more complicated system of teaching techniques was the introduction of the "problems" approach in teaching which involves choice or decision on the part of the student and thus, in this writer's opinion, differs markedly from the project approach. An illustration may further clarify this distinction: "A Study of Our Recorder's Court" would be a project; but "Which is Better, the Local Recorder's Court or the County Recorder's Court" would be a problem because pupils would have to choose or decide which is better and then support their point of view. The natural sequel was the unit around a center of interest which is similar to both the project and problems approaches—in effect, *they are sys-*

*tems of teaching techniques where more than one method is em-
ployed in teaching a block of work.*

Three graphic illustrations serve to illuminate this discussion:
Figure 3, which shows the component parts and possibilities of the
"unit method"; Figure 4, which diagrams the probable steps of a
teacher advancing from textbook teaching to "experience" teaching;
and Figure 5, which reveals the result of unit teaching over the
previously omnipotent and omniscient textbook. For a more comprehensive and detailed description of the historical development
of the unit technique the reader is referred to several other sources.[1]

TYPES OF UNITS

Clarification is needed in regard to the kinds of units which
can be used in teaching around a center of interest. Both school
personnel and college educators have been confused at times by the
multitudinous designations which have been employed in identifying the unit. Suppose that you try to pick your concept of the unit
from the following list, taken from the educational writers of the
last quarter of a century:

Subject-matter unit: source unit; topical unit; cultural epoch unit;
activity unit; life-problem unit; common learnings unit; core unit; human
relations unit; resource unit; teaching unit; experience unit; large, or long
unit; problem unit; chronological unit; unit of adaptation; generalization
unit; functional unit; idea unit; unit based on center of interest; unit
based on pupil need; project unit; pupil-centered unit; process unit; and
broad-fields unit.

Obviously, there is a distinct need for a lucid analysis in order
to prevent confusion and misunderstanding among teaching personnel about the unit method of teaching. For the purpose of simplifi-
cation, units may be divided into two classifications: (1) according
to the teaching approach or (2) according to the organization
and/or preparation. Within these types there are subdivisions; in
regard to *the approach in teaching* there are *subject matter* units
and *experience* units; in regard to *organization and/or preparation*
there are *resource* or *source* units and *teaching* units.

---

[1] For the investigator who wishes to trace the development of the unit and
problems techniques, the basic references listed at the end of ch. 5 will be sufficient.

The Resource Unit Defined

The resource or source unit developed as a kind of compromise. Some teachers advocated the advance preparation of teaching units in subject matter; they thought that the individual teacher should do most of the planning for his pupils, even though he took into account their natural interests at that grade level as he planned. Other teachers felt strongly that most planning of units should take place as a co-operative teacher-pupil venture in the classroom; they believed that the unit should be planned around a natural center of interest, and that it should be primarily an "experience" instead of a "subject-matter" unit. After much disagreement, much experimentation, and some compromise from each camp, the resource unit developed during the second quarter of the twentieth century until it now occupies a respectable position in the minds of both conservatives and progressives in education.

With regard to definition, J. Paul Leonard has recently traced the concepts of the resource unit in the secondary school since 1940. His conclusion would be generally acceptable: [2]

Essentially, then, a resource unit is a comprehensive analysis and organization of the objectives, problems, activities, and materials which form a unit in a sequence of plans for achieving the purposes of education. It is made by teachers and is a form of preplanning designed to guide them in their selection of instructional problems and materials. Out of resource units an actual teaching unit may be built. A resource unit may be made by one teacher or by a group of teachers.

What the Supervisor Should Know About Resource Units

In brief, there are five major competencies which a good supervisor should possess in regard to resource units: (1) He should know how to construct a resource unit; (2) He should know how to work with an individual teacher in making a resource unit; (3) He should know how to lead a group of teachers in a co-operative construction of a resource unit; (4) He should know how to help a teacher analyze a resource unit which has already been produced;

[2] J. Paul Leonard, *Developing the Secondary School Curriculum*, rev. ed. (New York: Rinehart & Company, Inc., 1953), p. 477. Used with permission.

and (5) He should know how to assist the teacher in constructing a teaching unit from the resource unit.

In the long run, the supervisor has to learn first *how* to construct a resource unit by *making* one himself. There is no substitute for this learning procedure on the part of the supervisor; after he has done that, he will be able to help teachers to make, analyze, and use resource units in their work. In a text on supervision, the writer cannot have the beginning or prospective supervisor construct a resource unit under his guidance, as desirable as that might be. The next best approach is taken here, then, the presentation of a resource unit which has been prepared by a junior high school teacher. Analysis of this unit shows clearly its structural elements: I. Introduction; II. Objectives; III. Outline of Content; IV. Suggested Activities; V. Evaluation; and VI. Bibliography.

A SAMPLE RESOURCE UNIT

"Let's Go South!"

A Resource Unit on South America

7th-Grade Level

PREPARED BY ONE TEACHER [3]

I. Introduction

A unit of work on South America is valuable for students on the seventh-grade level, for, at this stage in their development, they are capable of and interested in learning about life outside their own environment. This study is particularly worthwhile because of its possibilities for producing in the pupil an appreciation and understanding of neighboring people. The emphasis throughout the unit is on the people of South America—how they live and how their living is affected by their environment and cultural heritage. It is hoped, also, that as a result of the study the students will become more sensitive to beauty in music, art, literature, and nature.

The structure of the resource unit is intended to be flexible so that the teacher can reorganize, delete, or add to the materials as necessitated by the varied interests of the students.

[3] This resource unit was prepared in 1957 by Betsy Bracy for her work as a junior high school teacher in Arkansas and North Carolina. It is used here (with the addition of some material published since 1957) with her permission.

II. *Unit Objectives*

  A. Understandings and Generalizations

    1. Differences among peoples are due to the environment in which they live and to their social and cultural heritage.

    2. All peoples have contributed to the world's culture.

    3. There is a real need for world co-operation.

    4. The interdependence of the peoples of the world is a significant factor in international affairs today.

    5. The peoples of the world must begin to think more in terms of world citizenship rather than national citizenship.

    6. The world's natural resources are widely distributed.

    7. Wise use of natural resources is important to the welfare of a country.

    8. Trade plays a significant part in international affairs.

    9. A continent can be divided into regions in various ways—topographically, culturally, or according to climate types.

    10. Climate greatly influences man's way of life.

    11. The standard of living frequently varies with different cultural groups.

    12. Education is an important factor in the development of a nation.

    13. The welfare and progress of a nation depend to a great extent upon the health of its citizens and upon its sanitation conditions.

    14. North America and South America are in many respects both similar and different.

    15. Some of the ancient Indian civilizations of South America had advanced cultures.

    16. South America was discovered as a result of Turkish control of the Mediterranean Sea.

    17. Early control of South America was largely in the hands of Spain and Portugal.

    18. The conquest of the Indians by the Europeans was neither easy nor bloodless.

    19. The colonies existed only for the benefit and enrichment of the "mother country."

    20. Peoples frequently resent foreign control and exploitation and, as a result, attempt to achieve independence by revolution.

    21. The countries of South America have many serious problems in common—education, transportation, foreign capital for industrialization, development of natural wealth, concentration of wealth in certain areas, and instability in government.

    22. The Pan American Union has done much to improve relations between the Americas.

    23. South America is characterized by a relatively small population which is concentrated in isolated clusters separated by thinly settled

areas, by racial and cultural diversity, and by diversity of the physical conditions of the land.

B. Appreciations and Attitudes

1. The pupil appreciates the value of the human being no matter how rich or poor his natural environment may be.
2. He is tolerant of manners, customs, ideas, and ideals which are different.
3. He appreciates the problems of those who are foreign to him.
4. He appreciates the contributions of different peoples to our own civilization.
5. He learns to withhold opinions in the absence of adequate information.
6. He appreciates beauty in music, art, literature, and nature.
7. He derives pleasure and satisfaction from books.
8. He develops a sense of responsibility.
9. He withholds judgment until the evidence is evaluated.
10. He realizes the destructiveness of war and has a desire for world peace.
11. He develops an attitude of interest in people outside his own environment.
12. He realizes that the people of South America are Americans just as the people of the United States are.

C. Skills and Abilities

1. The pupil increases his skill in reading both for information and for pleasure in that
   a. He learns when to scan and when to read carefully.
   b. He learns to read critically and to analyze printed matter.
   c. He becomes better able to interpret the printed word.
   d. He develops standards for the selection of reading material.
2. He improves in his ability to construct and interpret maps, charts, and cartoons.
3. He becomes more skilled in carrying on and leading a discussion.
4. He employs a variety of materials in gathering information.
5. He makes use of democratic processes in group work.
6. He improves in his ability to present material both in oral and written form.
7. He is able to follow directions.
8. He makes more effective use of library resources.
9. He displays intelligence in selection of leaders.
10. He improves in his ability to note and outline significant material.
11. He is able to form generalizations after careful study.
12. His ability in leadership and followership in group activities improves.

III. *Outline of Content*

  A. A Look at the Continent of South America

     1. Why should we be interested in South America?
       a. Is South America near the United States?
       b. Does the United States trade with South America?
       c. Are there North American business investments in South America?
       d. Has South America contributed to the world's culture through art, music, and literature?
       e. Does South America play a significant part in international affairs?
     2. How are North America and South America similar?
       a. Are the continents similar in shape?
       b. Are the major mountain ranges located in similar positions?
       c. Are the chief river systems located in similar positions?
     3. How are North America and South America different?
       a. Are the continents the same size?
       b. Does the difference in the latitudinal positions of the two continents affect the types of climates found in each?
       c. In what way are the coast lines of the continents different?
       d. Which continent has the larger population?
       e. How do the people of the continents differ?
         (1) What languages are spoken in South America?
         (2) How do the people in South America dress?
         (3) What are the predominant races of South America?
         (4) How do South Americans differ from North Americans in attitudes and beliefs?

  B. South America Yesterday

     1. Who were possibly the first inhabitants of South America?
     2. What were the names of some of the early Indian civilizations?
       a. Who were the Incas?
         (1) Where did they live?
         (2) What sort of government did they have?
         (3) What were some of their contributions to the modern world?
         (4) What brought about the destruction of the Inca Empire?
       b. Who were the Chibchas?
         (1) Where did they live?
         (2) How did their civilization differ from that of the Incas?
       c. Who were the Araucanians?
         (1) Where did they live?
         (2) Why were they more difficult to conquer than the Incas and the Chibchas?

3. How was South America discovered?
   a. Why were European merchants looking for new routes to the Far East?
   b. How did the continent come under Spanish and Portuguese control?
      (1) What areas of the New World did Columbus explore?
      (2) What areas did Cabral explore?
   c. How was control of South America divided between the Spanish and the Portuguese?
4. What was life in the early colonies like?
   a. Who were some of the outstanding *conquistadores*?
   b. What was the attitude of the Spaniards toward the Indians?
   c. What types of government did the Spanish colonies have?
      (1) What was the Council-of-the-Indies?
      (2) Who were the local rulers of the colonies?
   d. How did life in the Portuguese colony differ from that of the Spanish colonies?
      (1) What type of colonial government did Brazil have?
      (2) What was the major industry of Brazil?
5. How did the South American colonies achieve independence?
   a. Why was there discontent in the colonies?
   b. How did the United States influence the South American desire for independence?
   c. Who were the outstanding leaders in the revolution of the Spanish colonies?
      (1) Who was called the "George Washington of South America"?
      (2) What part did San Martín play in the revolution?
      (3) Who was Bernardo O'Higgins?
   d. How did Brazil achieve her independence from Portugal?
6. Are there any colonies left in South America?

C. South America Today
   1. What are the chief surface divisions of South America?
      a. What are the highlands regions?
         (1) Where are the Andes Mountains?
         (2) Where are the Brazilian Highlands?
         (3) Where are the Guiana Highlands?
      b. How do these highland regions differ?
      c. What are the major lowland and plains regions?
         (1) Where is the Amazon Basin?
            (a) How does the Amazon River compare in size with other large rivers of the world?
            (b) How large is the drainage basin of the Amazon?

    (2) Where is the Orinoco Basin?

       (*a*) How large is it?

       (*b*) How does it compare in size with the Amazon Basin?

    (3) Where is the Parana-Paraguay-Plata Basin?

       (*a*) How large is it?

       (*b*) How does it compare in size with the Amazon and Orinoco Basins?

  d. How do these lowland regions differ?

2. What variations in climate are found in South America?

  a. Does latitude affect climate?

    (1) What kind of climate is found in the Amazon Basin?

    (2) What kind of climate is found in the lowlands of Ecuador, Peru, and Colombia?

  b. Does altitude affect climate?

    (1) Is there any difference in the climate of the Peruvian lowlands and that of the Peruvian Andes?

    (2) Is the climate of the Andes different from that of the Brazilian Highlands?

  c. How do prevailing winds, ocean currents, and mountain ranges affect climate?

    (1) Why do the Guianas have such a wet climate all year?

    (2) What causes the Atacama Desert in Peru and Chile?

  d. Which two of the world's climates are not found in South America?

  e. What effect does climate have on the population?

    (1) Does climate influence where people live?

    (2) Does it affect the activities and industries of people?

    (3) Does it determine the manner of dress and type of housing?

3. What are the people of South America like?

  a. What is meant by the terms *mestizo, mulatto,* and *zambo?*

  b. Which countries are predominately white?

  c. Which countries are predominately mestizo?

  d. Which countries are predominately Indian?

  e. Which countries contain large numbers of European immigrants?

  f. How does the life of a white person in South America differ from that of an Indian, mestizo, or Negro?

    (1) In what type of location do whites and mestizos usually settle?

    (2) In what kinds of occupations do the whites and mestizos engage?

    (3) Where do most of the Indians live?

    (4) How do the Indians support themselves?

    (5) In what areas are the majority of the Negroes centered?

    (6) How do the Negroes support themselves?

    (7) What are the leading occupations of the South American people?

g. What is the educational situation in South America?
  (1) Is much of the population illiterate?
  (2) Which countries have made the most progress in the education of the people?
h. What is the predominant religion in South America?
i. What types of recreation are popular in South America?
j. What kinds of music do South Americans enjoy?
k. How are the independent republics governed?
  (1) Which countries have dictatorial governments?
  (2) Which countries have democratic governments?
  (3) Are there any noticeable differences between the countries which have democratic governments and those which have dictators?
  (4) What are the names of the capitals of the countries?
l. What are the three great South American cities of world importance?

4. What are the major products of South America? In what country or countries is each produced?

coffee	beef	petroleum
sugar	wool	iron ore
bananas	hides	bauxite
fruits	chicle	tin
cacao	rubber	gold
tropical woods	carnauba wax	platinum
corn	cotton	emeralds
wheat	copper	Panama hats
	nitrates	

a. Which countries are world leaders in the production of certain goods?
b. With which South American nations does the United States trade most?
c. Can trade affect the relations between North America and South America? How?

5. What are some of the major problems which the countries of South America have in common?
a. Are the children receiving adequate education?
b. Have all the natural resources of the continent been developed?
c. Are transportation facilities adequate throughout the continent?
d. Is the wealth fairly evenly distributed among the nations and among the people?
e. Is the standard of living high enough in South America?
f. Is there a need for foreign capital for industrialization?
g. Is there a need for improvement in government?
h. Are there problems in connection with health and sanitation?

6. How can relations between the Americas be improved?
    a. What is the Pan American Union (Office of Inter-American States)?
        (1) Why was it formed?
        (2) Who are its members?
        (3) What are its functions?
    b. How can the United States aid South America in solving its problems?

IV. Suggested Activities

A. Initiatory Activities
    1. Produce a South American atmosphere in the classroom by means of appropriate books, pictures, maps, and exhibits. Permit the pupils to browse around the room inspecting the materials. Such materials might include
        a. Pictures of
            (1) South American scenery
                (a) Andes Mountains
                (b) Angel Falls
                (c) Iguassú Falls
                (d) Amazon River
                (e) Lowland jungles
            (2) People
                (a) Indians
                (b) Gauchos
                (c) Heroes of South American history
            (3) South American industries
                (a) Coffee plantation
                (b) Sugar plantation
                (c) Tin mines in Bolivia
                (d) Oil wells in the Maracaibo Basin
            (4) South American metropolitan areas
                (a) Buenos Aires
                (b) Rio de Janeiro
                (c) São Paulo
                (d) Caracas
            (5) Early slave ships
            (6) Early Spanish weapons and armor
        b. Maps
            (1) Political
            (2) Population
            (3) Topographical
            (4) Climate
            (5) Vegetation

    c. Books

       Gill, *Manga, An Amazon Jungle Indian*

       Lansing, *Liberators and Heroes of South America*

       Quinn, *Picture Map Geography of South America*

       Quiroga, *South American Jungle Tales*

       Waldeck, *The White Panther*

       Witherspoon, *Let's See South America*

    d. Magazines

       Ross, "Chile, the Long and Narrow Land." *National Geographic Magazine,* February, 1960.

       Schultz, "Children of the Sun and Moon." *National Geographic Magazine,* March, 1959.

       Shor, "Argentina, Young Giant of the Far South." *National Geographic Magazine,* March, 1958.

    e. Play South American music

       Around the World in Music, "Latin America." Volumes I and II.

  2. Discover the special interests of the students in connection with the study of South America.

  3. Administer either oral or written pretest in order to discover the pupils' knowledge of South America.

B. Developmental Activities

  1. Reading

    a. For information

       Multiple texts for different levels of reading ability should be provided so that all pupils will be able to gain knowledge about South America. Picture books and magazines should also be available as a means of creating interest in the subject. See the bibliography. Students should be encouraged to read the daily newspapers for current news of South America.

    b. For pleasure

       An adequate supply of fiction pertaining to life in South America will aid in arousing interest. This outside reading material should consist of literature suitable to several levels of reading ability so that every pupil will have an opportunity to do other than merely assigned reading. See the bibliography.

  2. Audio-visual aids

    a. Filmstrips

      (1) *Vacation on the Pampas,* YAF, 1955, "Children of Latin America Series" (40fr., silent with text, black and white). Life in Argentina is described by means of a story.

      (2) *Chico Learns to Read,* YAF, 1955, "Children of Latin America Series" (40fr., silent with text, black and white). Life in Brazil is depicted in story form.

    (3) *Market Day at Cuzco,* YAF, 1955, "Children of Latin America Series" (40fr., silent with text, black and white). This filmstrip depicts life in Peru.

    (4) *Silver Studded Belt,* YAF, 1955 ("Children of Latin America Series" (40fr., silent with text, black and white). Life in Chile is described in story form.

  b. Films

    (1) *The Andes,* HFE (10 min., color, sound). It shows the effect of the Andes on agriculture, trade, and industry. It includes excellent maps and charts of the major geographical sectors of South America.

    (2) *Argentina—Horseman of the Pampas,* UWF (20 min., sound). It depicts the life of a gaucho on the Pampas. It stresses the geographical concept that high grass-covered plateaus are especially suited to large-scale grazing operations.

    (3) *Argentina,* EBF (11 min., sound). Shows life in the commercial, financial, and industrial center—Buenos Aires. Emphasizes the dependence of the center on the rural hinterland.

    (4) *Brazil,* OIAA (11 min., sound). Consists of a tour of Rio de Janeiro and towns on the Amazon. It stresses the vastness of Brazil's resources.

    (5) *Brazil—Tropical Lowland,* UWF (20 min., sound). A study of life in the hot, humid lowland—native families and how they live.

    (6) *Brazil,* EBF (11 min., sound). Shows Brazil as a predominantly Portuguese country. Stresses the vastness of the country and regional contrasts. Also shows a landowner, agent, and a family of pickers in their relationships to a large coffee plantation.

    (7) *Brazilian Rain Forest,* Paul Hoefler Productions (1 reel, sound, color). A general look at the vegetation, people, wildlife of two great drainage basins—Amazon and Paraguay Basins. Stresses water cycle.

    (8) *Chile,* EBF (11 min., sound). Brings out various aspects of the Chilean scene—mountains, desert, glaciers, mines, ports, agricultural and pastoral areas. Also a visit to the capital, Santiago.

    (9) *Fundo in Chile,* OIAA (20 min., sound). Contrasts the new and old farming methods. Shows the daily life of fundo workers and their families.

    (10) *Colombia—Crossroads of the Americas,* OIAA (27 min., sound). Life in Colombia from a geographic, social, and economic standpoint.

(11) *Colombia*, OIAA (10 min., sound). Visits to Barranquilla, Bogotá, and Cartagena. Also shows some of the country-side.

(12) *High Plain*, OIAA (20 min., sound). Story of the descend-ants of the Aymara tribe living on the high plain of Bolivia, and includes primitive customs and modes of working and living.

(13) *La Paz*, OIAA (20 min., sound). Journey through the "highest big city in the world." Excellent contrast between old and new South America.

(14) *This is Ecuador*, OIAA (20 min., sound). Pictures of the Galapagos Islands, of Ecuador's resources, of Quito, and of life of the Indians in the primitive rural sections.

(15) *Lima*, OIAA (17 min., sound). Includes a rich historical sketch and pictures modern life in the city.

(16) *Peru—Land of the Incas*. Paul Hoefler Productions (1 reel, sound, color). A geographical and historic overview of Peru with attention to people. Shows the industrial and cultural life, and includes pictures of a remote Inca city which was lost for 400 years.

(17) *Peru*, OIAA (20 min., sound). A study of modern social and economic life of Peru and of the attempt to meet cur-rent problems of health, poverty, and race relations.

(18) *Paraguay*, OIAA (17 min., sound). Story of the hardy and independent people of Paraguay. Depicts the Indian cul-ture and shows quebracho and maté industries.

(19) *Montevideo Family*, OIAA (19 min., sound). A study of the daily life of a middle-class family of Uruguay in the capital city. Contributes to better understanding of our neighbors.

(20) *Venezuela Moves Ahead*, OIAA (40 min., sound, color). Analysis of Venezuela from an economic, historic, and geo-graphic viewpoint. Excellent use of animated maps. Spe-cial attention to the petroleum industry.

(21) *Iron Ore from Cerro Bolivar*, United States Steel Corp. (31 min., sound, color). The discovery and development of a new mine in the equatorial wilds of Venezuela.

(22) *Good Neighbor Family*, OIAA (20 min., sound). Simi-larities and differences in Latin American and North Amer-ican family life.

(23) *Gracias Amigos*, OIAA (15 min., sound). A dramatic story of the contributions of our neighbors in winning World War II by furnishing raw materials rapidly when other sources of those supplies were cut off.

(24) *Continent of South America*, EBF (12 min., silent). Locates South America on the globe and emphasizes its tri-

angular shape. The Andes, Brazilian Highlands, La Plata Basin, Guiana Highlands, Orinoco Basin, and Amazon Basin are located, and scenes from each are shown.

3. Construction and art activities

    a. Group work to aid in the visualization of instruction

        (1) Models

            (*a*) An Inca village

            (*b*) An oil industry of the Maracaibo Basin

            (*c*) A fazenda or hacienda

        (2) Salt and flour relief maps showing the topography of

            (*a*) Individual South American countries

            (*b*) Continent of South America

        (3) Sand maps showing elevations or regions

        (4) Frieze depicting some aspect of

            (*a*) The struggle for independence

            (*b*) The colonization of South America

            (*c*) The Conquest of the Incas

        (5) Exhibit of useful articles which the United States imports from different South American countries

    b. Individual work

        (1) Charts or graphs

            (*a*) Exports

            (*b*) Imports

            (*c*) Types of colonial government

            (*d*) Trade between South America and the United States

            (*e*) Progress by individual countries in various aspects of South American life

            (*f*) Comparison of United States and individual South American countries or regions with regard to size and population

        (2) Maps

            (*a*) Individual countries and their exports, imports, and industries

            (*b*) The continent of South America and its population centers, climates, and topography

        (3) Cartoons depicting South American life

4. Dramatization

    a. Pizarro conquers the Incas

    b. Life in the colonies

    c. A trip down the Amazon

    d. A trip across the Andes

5. Drill work

    a. Map and products drill. Student stands at map, and others name products; the pupil at the map then points to the country noted for that product. When he misses, the student naming the product takes the former's place at the map.

   b. "Spelling bee" using the names of South American countries and
      their capitals
   c. Naming and locating countries and their capitals
6. Oral work
   a. Oral reports to the class on early explorers, conquerors, and
      national heroes such as

Christopher Columbus	Pedro de Mendoza
Pedro Alvares Cabral	Pedro de Valdivia
Vincente Pinzón	Simón Bolívar
Francisco de Orellana	Bernardo O'Higgins
Gonzalo de Quesada	Francisco Miranda
Francisco Pizarro	José Antonio Páez
Diego de Almagro	José de San Martín
Sebastian Cabot	Antonio José de Sucre
Dom Pedro I	Manuel Belgrano
Dom Pedro II	

   b. Book reports on outside reading
   c. General class discussion of numerous topics relating to the study
      of South America
   d. Panel discussions on subjects such as
      (1) A comparison of North America and South America
      (2) The effects of climate on the population
      (3) South American industries
      (4) The Pan American Union
      (5) The diversity of the population of South America
   e. Oral quizzes to check the progress and understanding of the
      pupils
   f. Explanation to the class by individuals of some industrial process
      such as
      (1) Drilling for oil; also, its refining and by-products
      (2) Mining and processing of bauxite
      (3) Collecting and processing rubber
      (4) Processing of coffee beans
      (5) Processing of cacao
   g. Attempts by pupils, supposedly representing travel agencies, to
      interest the class in taking vacation trips to certain areas by
      making use of posters, pictures, and literature
7. Written work
   a. Reports on early Indian civilizations
   b. Book reports on outside reading
   c. Check tests on pupil understanding and progress
   d. Recording of new words encountered in the study such as

mestizo	encomienda	siesta	gracias
mulatto	fazenda	gaucho	amigo
zambo	estancia	pampa	río
conquistador	llama	adiós	llanos

     e. Composition of class letter to the Office of Inter-American States requesting informaton on South America and the Pan American Union

     f. Noting in notebooks of significant information

     g. Outlining of important materials

     h. Brief composition by each pupil concerning his emigration to South America—where he would live and how he would support himself in that area

8. Music

     a. Listening to recordings of South American music

        (1) "Folk Songs of Brazil." (R-33), ML-2119, Columbia.

        (2) "Around the World in Music, Latin America," Vol. I, LPM-3093, Victor. Vol. II, LPT-3010, Victor.

        (3) "Bachianas Brasileiras." (R-33), LM-142, Victor.

        (4) "Folk Songs of the Americas." (A-78), E-85, Victor.

        (5) "Legend of the Sun Virgin." (By Yma Sumac). L-299, Capitol.

     b. Singing of South American folk songs

        (1) Gordon, Dorothy, *Sing It Yourself.* Contains music and folk songs of all nations.

        (2) Henius, Frank, *Songs and Games of the Americas.* Includes several songs and games native to South America.

9. Art

     a. Looking at illustrations of South American art—pottery, sculpture, architecture, and paintings. See bibliography.

10. Literature

     a. Brief study of some of the outstanding South American writers such as

José Hernández	Rubén Darío
Ricardo Guiraldes	Juan Jiménez
Horacio Quiroga	Vicente Huidobro
Leopoldo Diaz	José Silva

     b. Mention of the manner in which geography influenced the literature of South America

11. Science

     a. Research by the entire class on various aspects of climate—what causes variations in climate, etc.

     b. Class discussion concerning man's adjustment to his environment

     c. Individual research concerning the processing and use of nitrates, tin, bauxite, petroleum, platinum, and rubber

     d. Panel discussion on the health and sanitation problems of South America including possibilities for alleviation of the problems

C. Culminating Activities

1. Formation of generalizations through class discussion

     a. Chief characteristics of South America

    b. Major geographical regions of South America

    c. Similarities and differences between the South American countries

  2. Panel discussion concerning the major problems of the nations of South America

  3. Written composition comparing life in the students' community with that in a South American community

V. *Evaluation*

A. Administration of the pretest given at the beginning of the study in order to evaluate individual progress in basic understandings

B. Written examination to check on retention of the subject matter

C. Study of the individual records which have been kept by the teacher throughout the unit work and which include such items as co-operation in group work, contribution in class, industry, and attitude

D. Administration of attitude test in order to determine whether or not the pupils' attitudes toward foreign cultures have broadened

E. Sample test items

  1. Matching

a. The "George Washington of South America"	(1) Cabral
b. The conqueror of the Inca Indians of Peru	(2) O'Higgins
c. Portuguese Emperor of the colony of Brazil	(3) Bolivar
d. Liberator of Chile in the revolution	(4) San Martin
e. The explorer who claimed Brazil for Portugal	(5) Pizarro
f. The first explorer to travel the entire length of the Amazon River	
g. The Argentine general who led southern South America in the revolution	

  2. Identification

    a. Council-of-the Indies

    b. Subsistence agriculture

    c. Pampas

    d. Line of Demarcation

    e. Conquistador

  3. Multiple choice

    a. The most advanced Indian civilization in South America in the 16th century was that of the

      (1) Incas

      (2) Chibchas

      (3) Aymaras

      (4) Auracanians

    b. The *major* reason for discontent in the Spanish colonies was that

      (1) The Indians were treated cruelly

      (2) The Spanish colonists disliked living in South America

      (3) Most of the wealth from the colonies was exported to Spain

      (4) The colonies were under the rule of the King of Spain

c. Which one of the following countries was able to achieve independence without going to war?
   (1) Venezuela
   (2) Brazil
   (3) Colombia
   (4) Peru

d. Which one of the following conditions is the *major* cause of the desert in Peru?
   (1) Prevailing winds
   (2) Mountain range
   (3) Ocean currents
   (4) Latitude

e. Which one of the following countries is *not* predominately Indian?
   (1) Peru
   (2) Bolivia
   (3) Ecuador
   (4) Colombia

f. Which one of the following republics is *not* predominately white?
   (1) Chile
   (2) Argentina
   (3) Venezuela
   (4) Uruguay

g. The South American nation which leads the world in exporting petroleum is
   (1) Venezuela
   (2) Colombia
   (3) Brazil
   (4) Argentina

h. Which of the following republics does *not* have a democratic government?
   (1) Argentina
   (2) Colombia
   (3) Chile
   (4) Uruguay

i. Which one of the following leads the world in the exporting of bauxite?
   (1) Brazil
   (2) Surinam (Dutch Guiana)
   (3) French Guiana
   (4) Venezuela

j. Which one of the following nations has made the most progress in educating its citizens and raising its standard of living?
   (1) Ecuador
   (2) Peru
   (3) Bolivia
   (4) Uruguay

4. Discussion
   a. Describe the types of regions in which the whites, Indians, and Negroes usually live, and tell in what way the people of each group most frequently support themselves.
   b. Select any two of the South American republics and compare them with respect to physical features, industries, and predominant racial groups.
5. Sample questions for determining attitude
   A D 1. We of the United States are the only people who can rightfully be called "Americans."
   A D 2. There is no real need for co-operation between the United States and the nations of South America because we have everything we need within our national boundaries.
   A D 3. The United States should trade as little as possible with foreign countries so that we will not become involved in international affairs.

VI. *Bibliography*

A. Reference Books for Pupils

1. Fiction

Adams, Ruth. *Sky High in Bolivia*. Heath, 1942. Good description of Indian life in Bolivia.

Alegría, Fernando. *Lautaro*. Appleton. The adventures of an Auracanian chieftain in the fight for freedom in Chile.

Desmond, Alice C. *Soldier of the Sun*. Dodd, Mead, 1938. This story of Huascar, a page to the Inca king, takes place in and around the city of Cuzco when Pizarro was invading.

Fernald, Helen C. and Edwin M. Slocombe. *The Scarlet Fringe*. Longmans, Green, 1932. A fine story describing the Inca Indians in the 16th century.

Gill, Richard C. *Manga, an Amazon Jungle Indian*. Stokes, 1937. The story takes place in Ecuador at the headwaters of the Amazon and centers around the eldest son of an Indian chief.

——. *The Volcano of Gold*. Stokes, 1938. This story is a sequel to *Manga, an Amazon Jungle Indian* and describes a search for Inca treasure.

Henius, Frank. *Stories from the Americas*. Scribner, 1944. It includes a fascinating collection of South American folklore and Indian legends.

Hudson, W. H. *Tales of the Gaucho*. Knopf, 1946. Consists of many different tales of adventure.

Kummer, Frederic A. *Courage Over the Andes*. Winston, 1940. A story of an American boy's experiences in Chile during the War of 1812—includes much historical background.

Malkus, Alida S. *Citadel of a Hundred Stairways*. Winston, 1941. A lost gold mine, a mysterious hermit, and an adventurous journey to a Quicha Temple are included in a story of Peruvian life.

———. *Young Inca Prince*. Knopf, 1957.

Steen, Elizabeth. *Red Jungle Boy*. Harcourt, 1937. Story of a ten-year-old Indian boy living in the jungles of Brazil. Good illustrations.

Thomas, Margaret. *Paulo in the Chilean Desert*. Bobbs-Merrill, 1934. Significant information about the land and people of Chile is presented by means of a story of a small boy who works his way from an old gold mine high in the Andes to a typical seaport on the coast.

Waldeck, Theodore J. *The White Panther*. Viking, 1941. The adventures of a white panther in the jungles of British Guiana.

2. Nonfiction

Atwood, W. W. and H. G. Thomas. *The American Nations*. Ginn, 1948. Simplified description of the South American nations—good text for retarded readers.

Bailey, Bernardine. *Famous Latin-American Liberators*. Dodd, Mead, 1960. Brief biographies of ten great liberators.

Baker, Nina B. *He Wouldn't Be King*. Vanguard, 1941. Fairly accurate bibliography of Simon Bolívar written in an interesting way.

Goetz, Delia. *Other Young Americans: Latin America's Young People*. Morrow, 1948. Summary of the lives of modern young people in different parts of Latin America with respect to dress, home life, jobs, and recreation.

Hager, Alice. *Brazil: Giant to the South*. Macmillan. Numerous pictures help to tell the story of the largest Latin American republic.

Hall, Elvajean. *The Land and People of Argentina*. Lippincott, 1960. Geography, history, life, and customs—in brief.

Hamer, O. S. and others. *Exploring American Neighbors*. Follett Publishing Co., rev. ed., 1960.

———. *Exploring the New World*. Follett Publishing Co., rev. ed., 1958. Interesting account of the history and geography of South America. Excellent illustrations.

Hankins, G. C. and E. L. Thurston. *Homelands of the Americas*. New York, Chicago, Atlanta, Dallas: Iroquois Publishing Co., 1954. Particularly interesting in its comparison of North and South America—good illustrations.

Lansing, Marion F. *Liberators and Heroes of South America*. Page, 1940. Biographical sketches of many heroes such as San Martín, Bolívar, Miranda, O'Higgins, and Sucre.

Peck, A. M. *Pageant of South American History*. Longmans, Green, 1958. A history of South America from primitive to modern times.

Pendle, George. *The Lands and Peoples of Paraguay and Uruguay.* Macmillan, 1959.

———. *Argentina.* Macmillan, 1957.

Quinn, Vernon. *Picture Map Geography of South America.* 1941. The geographical story of each of the republics regarding physical features, vegetation, animals, life of the people, and some history.

Ross, "Chile, the Long and Narrow Land." *National Geographic Magazine*, February, 1960. Well illustrated description of the Republic of Chile.

Schultz, "Children of the Sun and Moon." *National Geographic Magazine*, March, 1959. Well illustrated account of Kraho Indian living deep in Brazil.

Shor, "Argentina, Young Giant of the Far South." *National Geographic Magazine*, March, 1958. 37 color illustrations.

Szulc, Tad. *New Trends in Latin America.* Foreign Policy Assoc., 1960. Survey of changes and their impact on the U.S.

Von Hagen, V. W. *South American Zoo.* Messner, 1946. A study of a variety of South American animals in the jungles, in the mountains, and on the Pampas.

Whitridge, Arnold. *Simón Bolívar, the Great Liberator.* Random House, 1954. Well-written biography of Bolívar.

Wohlrabe, Raymond A. and W. Krusch. *The Land and People of Venezuela.* Lippincott, 1959.

B. References for the Teacher

Blanksten, George. *Perón's Argentina.* University of Chicago Press, 1953. The history of an era.

Cau, J., and Bost, J. *Brazil.* Mueller, 1955. Modern account of this great country.

Herring, Hubert. *History of Latin America.* Knopf, 1955. A standard history of Latin America.

Iniguez, Diego A. *Historia del Arte Hispanoamericano.* Buenos Aires: Salvat Editores, 1945. Illustrations of all types of architecture in Colombia, Peru, Ecuador, Venezuela, Bolivia—homes, cathedrals, cloisters.

MacDonald, Austin F. *Latin American Politics and Government.* New York: Thomas Y. Crowell Co., 2nd ed., 1954. Excellent description of the politics and government of each of the South American nations.

Pagano, José L. *Historia del Arte Argentino.* Buenos Aires, 1944. Illustrations of art from primitive times to the present—pottery, paintings, architecture, and sculpture.

Pierson, W. W., and Gil, F. G. *Governments of Latin America.* McGraw-Hill, 1957. An accurate account, at the time, of these governments from the viewpoint of political economy.

Plaza, Galo. *Problems of Democracy in Latin America.* University of North Carolina Press, 1955. An account of age-old and contemporary problems.

Rippy, J. Fred. *Latin America: A Modern History.* University of Michigan Press, 1958. A good source book.

"South America." Unit of Teaching Pictures. Grand Rapids: Informative Classroom Picture Series. Excellent collection of photographs, illustrations, and information about South America; also includes a large pictorial map which visualizes customs, clothing, food, industries, natural resources, plant and animal life, topography, and climate regions.

Thomas, A. B. *Latin America.* Macmillan, 1956. Recent account of our neighbors to the South.

Williams, Mary W. *The People and Politics of Latin America.* Ginn, 4th ed., 1955. Considerable attention given to the people, history, characteristics of individual countries; some emphasis upon foreign relations.

Zalamea, Jorge. *Nueve Artistas Colombianos.* Bogotá, 1941. Seventy-seven reproductions of paintings by contemporary Colombian artists.

Problems for Individual Study and Class Discussion

The supervisor or supervisor-candidate should be concerned primarily here with securing, reading, and analyzing units which experienced teachers have developed successfully in their teaching. These samples should include as many kinds as possible—subject-matter or textbook units, problem or topical units, activity or project units, experience units, and instructional guides. The main purpose for this reading and analysis is to make the supervisor aware of the many different but successful methods that individual teachers use in planning unit work.

Additional Selected References for Problem or Unit Study

NOTE: Since both Chapters 4 and 5 are concerned with the unit, these references in annotated form will be found at the end of Chapter 5.

CHAPTER 5

The Teaching Unit

IT IS A FACT that no two teaching units will ever be the same,
even though they may be constructed for the same grade level or
for the same course. This is true because no two teachers teach
alike—and that is as it should be. It is also true because teachers
are at different stages in the development of their own teaching
methods. For example, the more experienced the teacher, the more
effectively he may employ co-operative planning with his pupils;
the less experienced the teacher, the more the tendency for him to
preplan his unit around subject-matter centers of interest rather
than around the natural centers of interest of children.

A Variety of Teaching Units Possible
from One Resource Unit

An examination of the preceding sample resource unit (Chapter 4) reveals a variety of possibilities for teaching units on the
subject covered. Suppose that two teachers are considering the resource unit for the purpose of abstracting a teaching unit based on
government. One teacher who is inclined more toward the subject-
matter approach might decide upon an examination of the "Types
of Government in South America." This block of work would probably be of two or three weeks' duration and could be accomplished
either by a study of the government in each country or by determining several general types of administration and discovering
which countries could be classified as having each kind. Although

some historical data might be included, most of the content in this unit would more than likely emphasize the current situation.

On the other hand, the more experienced teacher might utilize the news of a politically disturbed South American country to arouse interest in a unit of a problems nature such as, "Why is There Much Governmental Instability in South America?" This kind of approach lends itself readily to teacher-pupil planning and could be undertaken in many different ways. It would be of longer duration than the other unit because it would necessarily include an examination of the historical development of governments on the continent for clues as to causes of the existing turbulence. A study of this sort would be enhanced also by careful scrutiny of the people of South America—their temperament, their beliefs, their attitudes, their ambitions.

For a teacher who has been endeavoring to develop appreciation of beauty and of the value of the human being, a unit on "The Contributions of South America to the World's Culture" might prove beneficial and effective. Knowledge and enjoyment of art, music, and literature foreign to the culture of the students might result in broadening their interests and viewpoints. The scientific approach might also be used, with a unit entitled "How Do Topography and Location Affect the Development of a Continent?" In discovering reasons for the latent development of some regions and the early exploitation of others, the pupils could gain a better understanding of the great potential of South America and of North America. These four approaches should begin to give the supervisor a clearer picture of the construction and utilization of the teaching unit and its relationship to its parent, the resource unit.

Keeping Up with Resource and Teaching Materials for the Teaching Unit

The modern school possesses a tremendous number and variety of teaching materials. These include textbooks, reference books, teaching aids, and supplementary materials of all sorts. *To what extent should the supervisor be familiar with these teaching materials in order to help his teachers?* How can he keep up with new materials as they are issued? Which of them can he reasonably ask the teacher or the school librarian to evaluate for him? What new texts should he examine himself? What amount of his time should wisely be allocated to previewing new educational motion pictures, slides, filmstrips, tapes, and the like? Which readiness materials for the primary grades should he know firsthand? What reading materials should he be familiar with for those who are in the sixth grade, but who are reading at the third-grade level? What should he know about special editions for school use of popular magazines, such as those of the *Atlantic Monthly, Newsweek,* or *Readers Digest?*

These are not idle questions—they are problems which in themselves could consume all of the time of the supervisor unless he works out some system of time allocation for the examination and scanning of teaching materials. Faced thus with a problem of establishing priorities, the supervisor will give special attention to examination of these types of materials and resources:

1. Textbooks which are written in the form of "unit" presentations and which really are first-class resource units for use by both teachers and pupils.

2. Teachers' manuals and student workbooks or seatwork books, which are published to accompany texts written from the resource-unit approach.

3. Study guides or courses of study which are prepared by states, counties, or local school systems. These modern study guides are found upon examination to be more of the resource-unit type than the old-fashioned "minimum essentials."

4. Test materials and evaluative devices of all sorts—for use in subject areas, for cumulative work and achievement at the end of a unit, and for "take-home" types of tests. The supervisor should continuously collect various examples of pretests, check tests, and final tests on units; samples of handwriting, spelling, and arithmetic work as exhibits in the evaluative process; and opinions of pupils concerning the units which they have had.

5. Lists of audio-visual aids which are of particular value for unit teaching. Those types which are particularly pertinent are (1) those films or filmstrips that show pupils working co-operatively on some project in the schoolroom; (2) those films or pictures that show teacher(s) and pupils planning together; (3) trips which illustrate or illuminate the unit, such as a field trip to collect specimens or to examine an invention in science study, or a trip for a class in

problems of American democracy to watch the state legislature in session; and (4) graphs, charts, and diagrams which present much factual information in a pictorial and clear manner.

Characteristics of the Teaching Unit

Enough research and analysis have been completed in regard to the teaching unit for the following common characteristics to emerge:[1] (1) It has a central theme, and classwork and pupil activities revolve around it; (2) It employs more than one way, one method of teaching; (3) It utilizes different sorts of learning activity, including individual activity, large-group activity, and small-group activity; (4) It states its purposes, checks pupil progress toward those purposes, and makes a final evaluation of the progress of the pupils; (5) It forces careful planning and advance preparation by the teacher, with resource references and supplementary materials amply available; (6) It uses various kinds of visual and audio-visual aids and devices.

CRITERIA FOR ANALYZING AND CHECKING A UNIT

1. What are the purposes of the unit?
   a. General?
   b. Specific?
   Has it a central theme, or center of interest?
2. Does its "scope" outline relate the unit to the work already done by the class and to the work that may follow?
3. Is there a real "teaching block" of time involved or provided for?
4. Is a pretest called for by this unit? If so, is it employed?
5. Do pupils become aware of the purposes of the unit? How? Is there any opportunity for co-operative planning?
6. Are a variety of teaching methods used or suggested for the achievement of the purposes of the central theme? Can you identify each of these teaching methods?
7. Is there provision for a variety of learning activities on the part of the pupil through

[1] Although several of the authors used as basic references for this chapter have analyzed the purposes and characteristics of the teaching unit and the resource unit, the author has found no one who has tried to synthesize those characteristics that may be common to both. Therefore the writer has had to rely heavily as a source on those characteristics, in summary form, which he set forth in his *Curriculum Principles and Social Trends,* 3rd ed. (New York: The Macmillan Company, 1960), pp. 201-202.

   a. Large-group activity?
   b. Small-group activity?
   c. Individual activity?
   Can you identify provision for each one of these types of activity in
   the unit?
   8. What evidences are there of advance preparation on the part of the
   teacher, such as supplementary references for the pupils, lists of
   books or stories in the library, and audio-visual materials?
   9. What types of visual and/or audio-visual aids and materials are
   suggested, if any?
   10. Is the unit flexible enough to be lengthened or shortened if need
   arises?
   11. What provisions or suggestions are made for evaluating the work of
   the pupils in the unit? If a long unit, is there provision for a check
   test or tests on progress about the middle of the unit? Are there
   suggestions for final tests at the end of the unit, or at the end of each
   part?

   In conclusion, it should be re-emphasized that unit teaching
results in significant benefits for all concerned. The pupil profits
from the center-of-interest approach in teaching in that he is aware
of what he is trying to learn, he has some part in planning his work,
he is learning by wholes instead of by isolated parts, and he is learning to work co-operatively and successfully with other pupils. The
teacher profits in that he can preplan for his teaching in larger
blocks of work, he can adapt the unit to his way of teaching, whether
it be through subject-matter units or experience units, and he can
make provision for differentiated assignments to meet the individual differences of his pupils. In essence, the use of unit teaching
around a center of interest hastens the day when both teacher and
pupil are released from the bounds of the textbook and at last begin to use it as an aid, rather than as the end in learning.

Problems for Individual Study and Class Discussion

   1. How would a supervisor explain the unit of work around a center of interest to a visiting parent who expected to find subjects being taught to
   her child in isolated fashion?
   2. What part does the school library play in unit teaching? In what ways
   can the supervisor and the librarian co-ordinate their activities for the
   maximum benefit of teachers engaged in unit work?

3. As a practicing supervisor, can you identify the different methods of teaching that you employ in your task as a "teacher of teachers"?
4. Compare a civics textbook of 20 years ago with its modern counterpart which is written in the form of resource units for teachers. Make a similar comparison of two history texts for grade 6.
5. Are fusion and correlation in teaching really different methods, or not? Substantiate your opinion by giving examples of each.
6. What justification is there for training the supervisor to be able to identify the simpler methods of teaching that go to comprise the more complex system of teaching and learning called the "unit method"?
7. List some of the human adjustment and citizenship learnings that could come from a center of interest in the fifth grade on "The Nationalities in Our Community."
8. A teacher asks you to make clear to her the difference between the "project" and "problem" methods. As the supervisor, how will you go about this?
9. What subject-matter areas in addition to science lend themselves more readily to use of the laboratory method in teaching?
10. In order to preplan for a unit of work around a center of interest, what are some of the reliable procedures for the teacher to follow in discovering the interests of his children?
11. If a beginning teacher asked you to help him to learn how to plan a unit of work, what would be the steps that you would take?
12. Can the pupils assist in the evaluation of the results and learnings from a unit of work? Why, or why not?
13. Does unit teaching benefit the brighter student more than the slower learner? Give evidence to support your position.
14. Some writers and teachers maintain that a "subject-matter unit" is not a true unit of work, but merely another way of organizing subject matter for teaching. They maintain that a real unit involves growth and adaptation in the learner, that is, in the pupil. Take a position *pro* or *con*, and support it.
15. Is it wise to set a time limit for a unit of work? Why or why not?
16. What is a scope outline? How is it different from a unit outline?

Special Annotated Bibliography of Basic Sources of Information for the Supervisor on Resource and Teaching Units

Adams, F., *Educating America's Children*, 2nd ed. (New York: The Ronald Press Company, 1954), ch. V, and sample units or activities centered around health, science, the social studies, reading and language arts, arithmetic, music, art, and dramatic play.

Alberty, H. B., *Reorganizing the High School Curriculum*, rev. ed. (New York: The Macmillan Company, 1953), chs. XIV-XV for resource units.

Anderson, V. E., *Principles and Procedures of Curriculum Improvement* (New

York: The Ronald Press Company, 1956), part V for definition, types, co-operative planning, and evaluating the unit.

Beck, R. H., Cook, W. W., and Kearney, N. C., *Curriculum in the Modern Elementary School*, 2nd ed. (Englewood Cliffs, N. J.: Prentice-Hall, Inc., 1960), chs. XII, XIII, XV, XVII, XXI-XXIII, for the use of teaching and resource units.

Burton, W. H., *The Guidance of Learning Activities*, 2nd ed. (New York: Appleton-Century-Crofts, Inc., 1952), chs. XII-XIV for the unit method, planning and developing units, and analysis of a unit.

Dutton, W. H., and Hockett, J. A., *The Modern Elementary School: Curriculum and Methods* (New York: Rinehart and Company, 1959), ch. X.

Flaum, L. S., *The Activity High School* (New York: Harper and Brothers, 1953), chs. I-II for point of view, III-IV for the activity class and unit, and chs. VIII-IX for types of units in subject matter fields.

Giles, H. H., *The Integrated Classroom* (New York: Basic Books, 1959). A leader in the area of teacher-pupil planning here sets forth principles and examples of teaching around a center of interest.

Goetting, M. L., *Teaching in the Secondary School* (Englewood Cliffs, N. J.: Prentice-Hall, Inc., 1942), chs. XV-XX for the development of the unit 20 years ago.

Gwynn, J. M., *Curriculum Principles and Social Trends*, 3rd ed. (New York: The Macmillan Company, 1960), chs. VII-VIII for development and use of the unit, and ch. VI for growth in modern curriculum movement.

Hanna, L. A., Potter, G. L., and Hagaman, N., *Unit Teaching in the Elementary School* (New York: Rinehart and Company, Inc., 1955), parts 2 and 3 and appendix I for characteristics of the unit, preplanning for unit teaching, resource and teaching units, and teaching the unit.

Jameson, M. C., and Hicks, W. V., *Elementary School Curriculum: From Theory to Practice* (New York: American Book Company, 1960), ch. VII shows how to plan a unit in some detail.

Krug, E. A., *The Secondary School Curriculum* (New York: Harper and Brothers, 1960), ch. VIII explains the core curriculum.

Leonard, J. P., *Developing the Secondary School Curriculum*, rev. ed. (New York: Rinehart and Company, Inc., 1953), ch. X for topical, cultural, and problems types, ch. XI for correlation and fusion, ch. XIV on core courses, chs. XV-XVII on developing and organizing various types of units.

Lurry, L. L., and Alberty, E. J., *Developing a High School Core Program* (New York: The Macmillan Company, 1957), ch. VI for learning units and ch. III for large-unit ideas.

Macomber, F. G., *Teaching in the Modern Secondary School* (New York: McGraw-Hill Book Company, Inc., 1952), chs. III-VI for bases for organizing instruction around centers of interest and planning and guiding units.

Morrison, H. C., *The Practice of Teaching in the Secondary School* (Chicago: University of Chicago Press, 1926, rev. 1931). This book describes in detail the original development of the unit techniques and the types developed earlier.

Noar, G., *The Junior High School—Today and Tomorrow* (Englewood Cliffs, N. J.: Prentice-Hall, Inc., 1953), ch. XII for techniques in developing teaching and resource units, and ch. XVI for resource unit outlines.

Quillen, I. J., and Hanna, L. A., *Education for Social Competence* (Chicago: Scott, Foresman and Company, 1948), ch. V for organization of learning experiences, chs. VI-VII for chronological, topical, and problems approaches to units, preplanning, and unit development in chs. VII and VIII, and samples of resource and teaching units in appendixes.

Ragan, W. B., *Modern Elementary Curriculum* (New York: Holt, Rinehart and Winston, Inc., rev. ed., 1960), ch. VI and others for the unit concept and examples of types.

Romine, S. A., *Building the High School Curriculum* (New York: The Ronald Press Company, 1953), chs. IX-XI for definitions, types, building and using units, and their use in the core curriculum.

Saylor, J. G., and Alexander, W. M., *Curriculum Planning for Better Teaching and Learning* (New York: Rinehart and Company, Inc., 1954), chs. XII-XIV for resource units and unit plans and planning units with pupils.

Smith, B. O., Stanley, W. O., and Shores, J. H., *Fundamentals of Curriculum Development*, rev. ed. (Yonkers-on-Hudson: World Book Company, 1957), chs. XII-XIII, XVI for practices in the activity concept and centers of interest, and chs. XIV-XV for units and practices in the core curriculum.

Stratemeyer, F. B., and others, *Developing a Curriculum for Modern Living*, 2nd ed. (New York: Teachers College, Columbia University, 1957), chs. V-VI for life situations learners face, and developing curriculum from them, ch. VIII for co-operative planning with pupils, and part IV for samples of elementary and high school teacher-pupil planning.

Thut, I. N., and Gerberich, J. R., *Foundations of Method for Secondary Schools* (New York: McGraw-Hill Book Company, Inc., 1949), part II, B and C for methods based on the subject-matter and experience units.

Tippett, J. A., *Schools for a Growing Democracy* (Boston: Ginn and Company, 1936). Excellent examples of earlier units in the elementary school.

Umstattd, J. G., *Secondary School Teaching*, 3rd ed. (Boston: Ginn and Company, 1953), division II for the development features, planning, and implementation of the unit and activity plans of teaching.

The Unit in Curriculum Development and Instruction, Curriculum Research Report, Bureau of Curriculum Research, Board of Education of the City of New York (August 20, 1956; reprinted 1957), includes the teaching unit and how it is planned and developed, the resource unit, and resources for unit teaching.

Wesley, E. B., and Wronski, S. P., *Teaching the Social Studies in High Schools*, 4th ed. (Boston: D. C. Heath and Company, 1958), chs. XXII-XXIX for development of teaching methods and of the unit as a culmination of that development.

CHAPTER 6

Supplementary Materials and Curricular Aids

The Supervisor's Responsibilities to His Captive Audience

THE PUPILS IN EACH SCHOOLROOM comprise, in effect, a "captive" audience. A captive audience is usually defined as a group which has to listen or be exposed to a speech or point of view whether they like it or not; it is not within their power to leave; and they seldom have the opportunity to "answer back."

In this situation, the teacher has the opportunity to mold the thoughts and the feelings of the children under his control. His use of both texts and supplementary materials may stimulate pupils to develop as independent, thinking citizens, or as obedient, unquestioning citizens. His choice of supplementary teaching aids can help to free his captive audience, or his choice can make his audience still more captive. The supervisor, therefore, as the main resource person can operate forcefully to keep the classroom audience as "free" as a captive school audience can be and still operate effectively in the well-balanced growth and development of children.

Because this publication is also designed as a handbook or resource book for supervisors, it is pertinent here to indicate that the material in this chapter will differ from other sections of the book which furnish lists of resource and curricular materials.[1] The main

---

[1] Chs. 8, 11, and 13, and the appendix in this book list teaching and resource materials. The list at the end of ch. 8 presents annotated basic sources of informa-

emphases here will be placed upon identification of the agencies for and types of supplementary materials, how they may be appraised, and how these curricular aids may be used most effectively to supplement teaching and to enrich the curriculum.

Organized School Agencies

THE SCHOOL LIBRARY

The modern library, whether in the elementary or high school, furnishes monumental evidence of the improvement in methods of teaching and learning within recent years. For the up-to-date teacher and her pupils it is a major source of supply of all kinds of teaching materials. Most secondary school libraries now have either a full-time or part-time librarian, mainly because state and regional accrediting agencies have insisted upon this service.

The situation is different at the elementary school level. One school system may have a full-time librarian in each elementary school building; another system may have a "traveling librarian" for several elementary school buildings; and still another may have a library in each school building, but no trained person to look after it. Though library facilities and services in the elementary schools are slowly improving, the supervisor has to deal with the particular situation in which he finds himself.

The supervisor and the librarian work together to make the library the most attractive place in the school, with comfortable furniture, attractive displays of new materials and of the dust covers of new books, and open shelves of fine books suitable for all age and grade levels.

To use a library for a formal study hall defeats its main purposes and takes it "out of circulation" for a school period. The library is the main place in the modern school for the teacher and her pupils to locate, read, organize, and evaluate information. To help the library and the librarian to carry out these purposes, the supervisor has several major responsibilities. First, he helps to co-

tion for the supervisor on group activities of students. Ch. 11 includes a special bibliography of use in assisting the high school teacher, and ch. 13 gives a similar bibliography to use in helping the elementary school teacher. In addition, the appendix brings together alphabetically into one place for the supervisor and teacher an annotated list of companies and organizations which supply teaching materials and equipment for schools.

ordinate the efforts of the teaching staff in suggesting new materials which the library can provide. For example, if most teachers in the school use the unit approach in teaching, the library may have to provide more materials in the form of current maps, articles, graphs, posters, films and filmstrips, and "fugitive" materials, such as clippings and pictures pertinent to the day's happenings and curricular materials published by private concerns and businesses.

In the second place, the supervisor can help materially in the planning and scheduling of "library periods." The library period originated in the elementary school in the primary grades, a time planned far in advance and set aside for the pupils in a particular grade to go to the library, to listen to the librarian or teacher read a new book to them, and to select books and enjoy reading them individually. The books and materials for this period should be selected carefully. For example, the new book(s) used last week should be available for individual reading this week, and different books of different levels of reading difficulty should be available for examination and reading. In some elementary schools, the children in each room have one library period a week, in others, two. In schools which have no librarian, the supervisor usually develops a system of charging out books and materials to individual grade teachers, who set up in effect a library nook in the classroom, and who arrange for a library period and free-time silent reading for pleasure as a part of the regular schedule of the day or week.

Library periods in the high schools are developing slowly. The trend is toward an entire class period spent in the library; students who are working on a unit have individual or small-group assignments, and the teacher and the librarian plan in advance to have available those materials and resources that the pupils need. Another variation of the library period for the high school student is the regular assignment in the individual's schedule of one or two periods a week for "free use" of the library, whether for planned study or for leisure-time reading—"just for fun."

A third responsibility of the supervisor is to help schedule special services of the library. In larger school systems one may find a central depository or bureau for all kinds of audio-visual materials and vertical files; these would contain "fugitive" or current materials clipped from magazines and newspapers, such as accounts of interest concerning the current elections and the like.

However, other systems purchase and assign or install in each individual school building moving picture machines, record players, recorders, projectors, stereoscopes, maps, charts and globes, photographs and prints, radios or television sets, and duplicating devices of various kinds; then they encourage each school to build up its own set of vertical files, filmstrips, posters, models, charts, and consumable or fugitive materials. In many school buildings, these materials and equipment become a part of the library and its service to the school, in effect, a "materials center." Since different teachers will want to use the same materials or equipment, a planned schedule is necessary. The supervisor can help in working out such a schedule to make possible maximum use of these materials.

Another special service of the library is to make available the facilities of the public library. One way to do this is through inter-library loan; another is to arrange for a child or a group to go to the public library if its facilities on a certain unit or project are more adequate. To effect this, careful planning in advance is necessary, frequently with both teacher and supervisor pooling ideas and resources for the preparation of this kind of a teaching-learning situation.

A newer service of the library also calls for proper scheduling of special resources, for example, wise use of microfilm records. This newest refinement puts perhaps as many as 100 pages from a book on a "microcard" ($3''$ x $5''$); the one who is reading it uses an enlarger or "reader." It takes careful manipulation of students' schedules to work out a schedule for the use of this enlarger in the library, since the number of enlargers is limited.

Another responsibility of the supervisor in regard to effective use of the library revolves around a weakness in teacher training that is well known by administrators, but little talked about. A large percentage of both seasoned and new teachers do not know how to make effective use of major reference sources and lists in the library. Since they have come this far in their careers without being taught or learning how to use these basic references, they are very hesitant about asking for help, particularly from the librarian, who assumes that they already possess this competency. The supervisor can be of great help to the teacher in planning a unit with his competency in the use of such basic library tools as the *Readers Guide to Periodical Literature,* indexes to all sorts of books for various grade levels, and the standard book lists of the American Library Association. Standard reference works for school libraries are also assessed from time to time by the Association, with appraisals of such volumes as dictionaries and encyclopedias for different age and interest levels.

THE CURRICULUM LABORATORY

Other names used for this organized agency are "curriculum library," "curriculum bureau," "materials bureau," or professional library or workroom, depending upon the major emphasis in a particular school system. Many large school systems—state, city, or county—have such an agency to stimulate and help in both curriculum improvement and the in-service training of teachers. The curriculum laboratory collects and stores all kinds of materials of aid to teachers, ranging from books to be used in planning units of work to "consumable" materials in vertical files clipped from magazines, pamphlets, or newspapers and later discarded after the new information has been permanently recorded in text or reference books. Other kinds of materials that may be found in a curriculum laboratory include pictures, charts, special as well as supplementary texts, posters, maps, teachers' guides, courses of study from different parts of the country, and professional books for teachers.

FILM LIBRARIES OR DEPOSITORIES

Until recently, the curriculum laboratory served usually as a central depository or distributing agency for a whole school system; it frequently also stored, serviced, and distributed slides, films, filmstrips, and other audio-visual materials and equipment. A newer trend of the last decade has been the development of the film library, or "audio-visual depository" in large systems, to care primarily for the main audio-visual needs in teaching. Where such a film library has been established, experience has shown the need for close cooperation between the library and the audio-visual center. A new experiment has been the decentralization of many types of teaching materials in each individual school building; the reasons offered for this step are that many types of materials have continuous use in certain classes, and scientific progress has made possible the duplication of many kinds of teaching aids at small expense. Whether the system has a curriculum laboratory or an audio-visual depository, or both, individual school staffs should be encouraged to build up their own collections of teaching materials.

Types and Sources of Teaching Aids

There are many kinds of supplementary teaching materials with which the supervisor has to be familiar, for the good teacher in today's school does not confine his teaching to one textbook. As a matter of fact, most of the subject-matter areas and the activities of students are connected now indirectly or directly with swiftly moving developments of a scientific, a sociological, or economic nature. These developments, for example, may make a new text become out of date within a fast-changing course, such as physics, or economics, or problems of American democracy; the teacher and her pupils will have to bring their study up to date by using current articles and reports in periodicals, newspapers, and special bulletins.

Supplementary source materials and aids can be classified for easy reference under several heads: (1) textbooks and supplementary texts; (2) materials prepared by professional educational groups; (3) source materials issued by private groups and businesses; (4) audio-visual materials; and (5) valuable governmental publications.

TEXTBOOKS AND SUPPLEMENTARY TEXTS

Textbooks for use in schools are many; they vary widely in their organization, methodology, and content. The supervisor should help the teacher to have on his desk many different textbooks for both his subject areas and grade level. Such a variety of materials furnishes both to him and to his pupils sources of a well-illustrated nature which are valuable in many ways. In order to help the teacher in this respect, the supervisor should have available such a basic source as *The American Educational Catalogue,* annual index to textbooks and supplementary readers for all school levels.[2] For further information on textbooks, the reader should turn back to Chapter 3.

2 *The American Educational Catalogue* (New York: R. R. Bowker Company).

MATERIALS PUBLISHED BY PROFESSIONAL EDUCATIONAL GROUPS

These materials range in scope from a bibliography on supervision and curriculum and special library lists to special reports, bulletins, and handbooks for teachers. Each supervisor should be familiar with these sources. These materials include also yearbooks, special reports of experiments and investigations, resource units and curriculum guides for teachers, and professional periodicals and magazines. Prominent among the professional groups in promoting this wealth of teaching materials are:

American Association for Health, Physical Education and Recreation
American Association of School Administrators
American Council on Education
American Education Research Association
American Library Association
Association for Childhood Education
Association for Supervision and Curriculum Development
National Association of Secondary School Principals
National Council for the Social Studies
National Council of Teachers of English
National Education Association
National Science Teachers Association
National Society for the Study of Education

Many individual school systems from time to time likewise produce curriculum guides, teachers' guides, and resource units. *Source materials on use of the community.* There has been a growing trend for teachers to make more effective use of the local community and its resources in their schoolwork. The community approach to the curriculum has been presented by several writers.[3] The author discussed experiments with the community school on the local, state, regional, and national levels. William A. Yeager considered education as a co-operative process and emphasized making use of other local groups and agencies through the community survey. The Forty-Second Yearbook of the National Society

---

[3] Compare J. Minor Gwynn, *Curriculum Principles and Social Trends*, 3rd ed. (New York: The Macmillan Company, 1960), ch. XX; W. A. Yeager, *School-Community Relations* (New York: The Dryden Press, 1951), *passim; The Community School*, 42nd Yearbook of the National Society for the Study of Education (1953), part II, *passim;* and *The Modern Community School*, Association for Supervision and Curriculum Development, National Education Association (New York: Appleton-Century-Crofts, Inc., 1953), *passim.*

for the Study of Education sketched the history of the community school and presented and analyzed outstanding features. The second study of today's community school by the Association for Supervision and Curriculum Development shows the directions in which the community school is going and the types of processes and methods that have been successfully used. The bibliography of reference materials is also valuable for the supervisor.

Wide-awake professional personnel have made progress in recent years in providing two kinds of aids to help teachers utilize community resources more fully in their teaching. One type is the prepared handbook which lists for the teacher the resources of the local community. The second type might be called a source book of promising practices on how to identify the resources of a community. Standard sources of this kind are the following:

Ivey, John E., and others, *Community Resources* (Philadelphia: John C. Winston Company, 1951). A guidebook on how to search out the resources of a community. It can help school personnel to organize current materials, to plan trips for pupils out into the community, and to bring community representatives into the school and the educational program.

Olsen, Edward G., ed., *School and Community*, 2nd ed. (Englewood Cliffs, N. J.: Prentice-Hall, Inc., 1954), and *School and Community Practices* (Englewood Cliffs, N. J.: Prentice-Hall, Inc., 1949). Standard source books concerning promising and successful practices and methods.

Whitelaw, John B., *The School and Its Community*, 2nd ed. (Baltimore: Johns Hopkins University Press, 1951). How the school uses community resources.

Reports on research. Educational organizations are now preparing bulletins and reports which give supervisors and teachers the findings of research in simple, readable form. A series fostered by the Department of Classroom Teachers and the American Educational Research Association of the National Education Association may furnish a sound guide to research interpretation for school personnel in the future. These booklets present:

"What Research Says to the Teacher" (1953–   )
    No. 1. *Teaching Reading*, by Arthur I. Gates
    No. 2. *Teaching Arithmetic*, by R. L. Morton
    No. 3. *Teaching Spelling*, by Ernest Horn
    No. 4. *Teaching Handwriting*, by Frank N. Freeman
    No. 5. *Personality Adjustment of Individual Children*, by Ralph H. Ojemann

No. 6. *The Learning Process,* by William Clark Trow
No. 7. *Evaluating and Reporting Pupil Progress,* by John W. M. Rothney
No. 8. *Guided Study and Homework,* by Ruth Strang (1955)
No. 9. *Teaching High School Mathematics,* by Howard F. Fehr
No. 10. *Teaching High School Science,* by J. Darrall Bernard
No. 11. *Reading in the High School,* by Leo C. Fay
No. 12. *Science in the Elementary School,* by Gerald S. Craig
No. 13. *Class Organization for Instruction,* by J. Wayne Wrightstone
No. 14. *Audio-Visual Instruction,* by Paul R. Wendt
No. 15. *Juvenile Delinquency,* by Wm. C. Kraraceus
No. 16. *Parent-Teacher Relationships,* by Irving Wistout and Grace Langdon
No. 17. *The Gifted Child in the Elementary School,* by James J. Gallagher
No. 18. *Teaching Composition,* by Alvina T. Burrows
No. 19. *Group Processes in Elementary and Secondary Schools,* by Louis M. Smith
No. 20. *Teaching the Social Studies,* by Jonathan C. McLandon
No. 21. *Understanding Intergroup Relations,* by Jean D. Grambs

One of the better sources for the teacher on co-operative research and its reporting is *Educational Leadership,* official magazine of the Association for Supervision and Curriculum Development, National Education Association. Samples of the Association's other publications on research are *What Does Research Say About Arithmetic,* rev. ed. (1959), and *Research Helps in Teaching the Language Arts* (1955).

SOURCE MATERIALS ISSUED BY PRIVATE GROUPS
AND BUSINESSES, INCLUDING FREE MATERIALS

There is an ever growing mass of these types of materials, ranging from teaching aids of fine quality to those which are mainly propaganda for advertising purposes. Among the groups which have been issuing such materials for years are the Association of American Railroads, the Metropolitan Life Insurance Company, the Public Affairs Committee, the Motion Picture Association of America, the American Automobile Association, the American Medical Association, the General Motors Corporation, the American Red Cross, the Wheat Flour Institute, the United States Chamber of Commerce, the National Association of Manufacturers, and the information services of various countries such as England, Canada, the Netherlands, France, Spain, Argentina, Mexico, etc.

Other groups recently have spent money and have engaged

professional educators to produce teaching aids in the areas of their individual specialties. Examples of these are the American Association of Advertising Agencies, the Joint Council on Economic Education, the National Aviation Education Council and the commercial airlines, the B'nai B'rith, the Institute for Life Insurance and various life insurance companies, and radio and broadcasting companies.[4]

Newspapers and magazines with special aids for teaching or special classroom editions for student use include the *New York Times*,[5] *Time, Newsweek, Atlantic, Good Housekeeping,* and *Readers Digest.*

In addition, the supervisor should be familiar with several other kinds of miscellaneous aids for teaching which are now available. One type is illustrated by *Word Study,* published periodically during the year for teachers of English and others by the publishers of *Webster's Dictionary.*[6] Another consists of "Unit Teaching Plans" designed for use with *The World Book Encyclopedia.*[7] Another publisher of textbooks considers its notebook series of suggestions so valuable that it publishes several in different areas, such as *The Supervisor's Notebook, Language Teacher's Notebook, Social Studies Notebook,* and the like.[8] Still another is *The Rand McNally Handbook of Map and Globe Usage.*[9]

Another comprehensive source book is found in the well known annual *World Almanac and Book of Facts* and the almanacs of a similar nature published in many states of the United States. Still another type concerns itself with consumer education. Well known are *Consumer Reports,* available at newsstands or through membership in Consumers Union;[10] and *Consumer Bulletin,* available through membership in Consumers Research.[11] The *Good Housekeeping* Institute, *Parents Magazine,* and *Today's Health*

[4] Good examples of valuable resource lists developed by one group are *Resources for Citizenship: A Guide to the Selection of Teaching Materials* (1955) and *Laboratory Practices in Citizenship: Learning Experiences in the Community* (1958), both published by Citizenship Education Project, Teachers College, Columbia University.

[5] A major contribution has been J. F. Corbett and others, *Current Affairs and Modern Education* (1950).

[6] *Word Study* (Springfield, Mass.: G. & C. Merriam Company).

[7] "Unit Teaching Plans" (Chicago: Field Enterprises).

[8] Published by Scott, Foresman and Company, Chicago.

[9] Published by Rand McNally and Company, New York (1959).

[10] Published at Mt. Vernon, New York.

[11] Published at Washington, New Jersey.

(published by the American Medical Association) have featured aspects of consumer education for years. Still another kind of resource is furnished by the National Geographic Society's *Geographic School Bulletins,* which connect geography with special news events. Finally, there is the illustrated news magazine or reader for class use at different age and grade levels.[12]

Approved lists of free materials. There are quite a few lists of free and inexpensive materials, most of them annotated and classified according to teaching or unit areas. Usually, the lists have been "screened" by one group or another, but it is doubtful that any person or group used the same set of standards. These lists do, however, offer the supervisor and the teacher a variety of materials to select from, and those with which the author are famiilar are listed here:

Elementary Teachers' Guide to Free Curriculum Materials, Educators Progress Service, Randolph, Wisconsin (revised annually).

Free and Inexpensive Learning Materials, Division of Surveys and Field Services, George Peabody College for Teachers, Nashville, Tennessee (new editions published periodically).

Pepe, T. J., *Free and Inexpensive Educational Aids* (New York, Dover Publications, 1960).

Sources of Free and Inexpensive Educational Materials, Field Enterprises, Reference Library, Chicago (1955).

Sources of Free and Inexpensive Instructional Materials for Northwest Teachers, compiled periodically by the College of Education, University of Washington Press.

AUDIO-VISUAL MATERIALS

These materials have become highly developed since the 1930's. The trend has been toward whole books or yearbooks on audio-visual materials and methods, from a few lists of such aids to annual lists of varying emphasis.

General sources. Under this heading come texts on audio-visual aids and materials, on techniques and methods in teaching, on special parts of the curriculum, such as the social studies, or on the educational film. The supervisor's library should contain at least several of these basic publications on audio-visual education:

[12] The alphabetical list in the Appendix contains addresses of concerns which publish this type of source or supplementary materials.

Brown, J. W., and others, *A-V Instruction: Materials and Methods* (New York: McGraw-Hill Book Company, Inc., 1959).

Dale, Edgar, *Audio-Visual Methods in Teaching*, rev. ed. (New York: The Dryden Press, 1954).

DeKieffer, R., and Cochran, L. W., *Manual of Audio-Visual Techniques* (Englewood Cliffs, N. J.: Prentice-Hall, Inc., 2nd ed. 1961).

Erickson, C. W. H., *Administering Audio-Visual Services* (New York: the Macmillan Company, 1959).

Finn, J. D., *The Audio-Visual Equipment Manual* (New York: The Dryden Press, 1957).

Haas, Kenneth B., and Packer, H. Q., *Preparation and Use of Audio-Visual Aids*, 3rd ed. (Englewood Cliffs, N. J.: Prentice-Hall, Inc., 1955).

Holland, B. F., and others, *Audio-Visual Materials and Devices*, rev. ed. (Rogers Little Printers, Lubbock, Texas, 1960).

Kinder, J. S., *Audio-Visual Materials and Techniques*, 2nd ed. (New York: American Book Company, 1959).

Lewis, P. L., *Educational Television Handbook* (New York: McGraw-Hill Book Company, 1961).

Sands, Lester B., *Audio-Visual Procedures in Teaching* (New York: The Ronald Press Company, 1956).

Shores, L., *Instructional Materials* (New York: The Ronald Press Company, 1960).

Siepmann, C. A., *TV and Our School Crisis* (New York: Dodd, Mead and Company, 1958).

Thomas, R. M., and Swartout, S. E., *Integrated Teaching Materials* (New York: Longmans, Green and Company, 1960).

Wittich, W. A., and Shuller, C. F., *Audio-Visual Materials: Their Nature and Use*, 2nd ed. (New York: Harper and Brothers, 1957).

Types of aids. The writers in audio-visual education agree in general on the aids listed below as those most commonly employed in teaching.[13]

The textbooks in the audio-visual field also give valuable help on employing these aids on the various grade levels and in the different subject-matter areas.

Blackboard and bulletin board; duplicating devices; tack board or felt-board and display

Visual symbols; cartoons; drawings and sketches; posters; diagrams; flat maps, charts; graphs; comic strips; pictorial statistics

Dramatizations: pantomime; playlet; pageant; puppet show; shadow play

---

[13] This summary is made from an examination of the texts on audio-visual aids and is adapted in part from Gwynn, *op. cit.*, p. 563. Used with permission of The Macmillan Company.

Still pictures: (1) flat photographs, prints, and postcards; (2) projected—
opaque and daylight; slides—glass, cellophane, filmstrip, strip film,
micro-projection; tachistoscopes; (3) stereoscopes and stereographs
Models and mockups; globes; objects; specimens; exhibits; museums;
planetariums; demonstrations; dioramas; sand tables, and miniature
sets; flash cards
Motion pictures—silent and sound; television; films—educational, theatrical, documentary
Phonographs: records; recordings, transcriptions
Radio, television, dictaphone, loud speaker (public address and inter-
communicating)
Trips, journeys, tours, visits, community study

Newspapers, magazines, picture magazines, books, recordings,
transcriptions, motion pictures, radio, and television comprise the
so-called "mass media of communication." Together these methods
of communication furnish each child at least half of his informal
learning and education; separately, each medium can and does contribute to the improvement of our "communication arts," or ways of
communicating intelligently with one another and with other nations.

The picture newsmagazine, the picture-storybook, and television emphasize the education possibilities of picturization.[14] One
large community, Cincinnati, has made a fair assessment of its
comic books over a period of years, using definite standards for
evaluation and employing a large number of people from every
walk of life to help in the estimates.[15]

Films. Most schools now have available projectors and screens
for utilizing films of both the silent and sound types. Many investigations have been made, and much material has been published on
the educational film. Its use for educational purposes has become
so extensive that larger school systems today may have a trained
person for full time for this service. His title may be "director of
audio-visual education," "director of the film library," or "supervisor

---

[14] Good examples of the picture newsmagazine are *Life* and *Look*. The educational possibilities of the picture storybook are illustrated in the "Bingo Stories,
Books to Stretch On," a series published by Row, Peterson and Company, Evanston,
Illinois; and *Miss Frances' Ding Dong School Book* and storybooks to accompany
it, published by Rand McNally and Company, Chicago).

[15] Write to The Committee on Evaluation of Comic Books, Box 1486, Cincinnati,
Ohio.

of audio-visual materials"; and his duties may range from purchasing, storing, repairing, and scheduling education films and filmstrips to securing, previewing, and scheduling films for teachers from a rental or central film library. Film libraries are common in school systems large enough to warrant the capital outlay and operating budget necessary for effective use. Universities or colleges frequently run rental film libraries or bureaus for smaller schools.

The supervisor's major responsibilities in this area involve: (1) familiarity with annotated annual or serial lists of these educational film materials, (2) familiarity with critical sources which list "theatrical" films suitable and valuable for school use, (3) knowledge of the resources of the film library from which many of these film materials may be secured, (4) previewing a film for or with a teacher, upon request, and (5) a schedule sheet for satisfactory use of these materials by more than one teacher.

The educational film or filmstrip is made primarily for use in schools by private companies, the Federal government, the National Education Association and its departments, or the state or local school system. The theatrical film is prepared by private motion picture companies for commercial use in theaters for profit; some of these from time to time can be used advantageously in teaching. The following regular sources of information can help the supervisor to discharge his responsibility in this area:

Audio-Visual Instruction, published ten times a year by the Department of Audio-Visual Instruction of the National Education Association. Deals with the whole field.

Business Screen Magazine (combined with *See and Hear Magazine*), issued eight times a year. Deals with the audio-visual industry and films produced by business for educational purposes. Also publishes *The Projectionist's Handbook,* a manual for the training of the student operator.

Educational Film Guide and *Filmstrip Guide,* published quarterly, with cumulative yearly and supplementary services, by the H. W. Wilson Company. An outstanding current service in this area.

Educational Motion Pictures, and Supplements, published from time to time by the Audio-Visual Center, Indiana University, Bloomington. A good example of a lending or rental film library.

Educational Screen and Audio-Visual Guide, published monthly except July and August, devoted primarily to articles for the classroom teacher.

Educators Guide to Free Films

Educators Guide to Free Filmstrips

Educators Guide to Free Tapes, Scripts, and Transcriptions. These are annual
lists published by Educators Progress Service, Randolph, Wis.

Filmstrips: A Descriptive Index and Users Guide, by Vera M. Falconer (New
York: McGraw-Hill Book Company, Inc., 1948).

Motion Pictures for the Classroom, films available from Teaching Film Custodians, Inc., 25 West 43rd, New York 36. These are recommended by
committees of teachers of social studies, English, music, health and physical education, home economics, science, and vocations.

Motion Pictures on Child Life: A List of 16mm Films, Federal Security Agency,
Children's Bureau, compiled by Inex D. Lohr, 1952. Supplements from
time to time.

The News Letter, monthly information for the teacher about motion pictures,
radio, television, and the press, Bureau of Educational Research, Ohio
State University, Columbus.

Teaching Tools: The Manual of Classroom Tested Techniques, Ver Halen Publications, Los Angeles, California, published four times each school year. It
acts as the official publication of the Audio-Visual Education Association in
a number of states; each issue contains a 4-page insert of the individual
State news letter.

*3434 U. S. Government Films: Motion Pictures, Filmstrips, Sets of Slides
Available for Public Use in the United States,* Office of Education, Bulletin
No. 21, 1951, U. S. Government Printing Office.

U. S. Government Films for Public Educational Use, No. 1, 1955, U. S. Office of
Education Bulletin, U. S. Government Printing Office.

Other sources of aids. The National Education Association has
made a number of excellent films in recent years, some for improving teachers in service, some for better understanding of children,
some for more effective public relations purposes, and some for
more intelligent interpretation to the public of what the schools are
doing. A number of state education associations and some city
schools have developed their own films or filmstrips with scripts appropriate to accompany them. In a similar way, some schools have
developed their own slides for showing by projection, in color, with
or without accompanying scripts.

Radio and television. Devices for sound recordings are available in the modern school, either for the transcription of a regular
radio program for educational purposes or for recording a local program. Particularly can the tape recorder be of value to the teacher
and the supervisor as its recording of a class period is played back
for analysis of teaching techniques, pupil responses, and high and
low "spots." Central program-distribution sound systems are usu-

ally "built in" now as part of the normal equipment of schools. Through this new sound equipment, teachers or school personnel can record broadcasts or any type of program and use it later at any appropriate time.

Use of television in schools.[16] Television has been used for several years as a means of enriching the curriculum by bringing specialists to many schools at one time. In this instance, television is used as an audio-visual aid to supplement the work of the classroom teacher. For example, a field trip by television can be a means of taking a group, vicariously, to some remote spot or to an area in which there might be considerable danger for a visiting group of students.

One of the earliest uses of television for educational purposes was as a public relations medium. To interpret the work of the school to the public, the television program may be set up to feature a panel of educators discussing a problem. At other times there may be a demonstration of a teaching technique which has been used in the schools.

Direct teaching by television has been used in some areas of instruction for some time, especially in medicine and dentistry. Institutions of higher education have provided instruction by television for large groups of students as, for example, at Pennsylvania State University and Chicago City Junior College. The National Program in the Use of Television in the Public Schools, sponsored by the Fund for the Advancement of Education, has been an experiment to determine the practicability of using television for the instruction of large classes. This experiment involved instruction at both the elementary and the secondary school levels.

Both closed-circuit and open-circuit television have been used for instructional purposes. Hagerstown, Maryland, and Evanston, Illinois, have provided closed-circuit instruction. The North Carolina In-School Television Experiment is an illustration of open-circuit television. Part of the classroom instruction, usually 20 to 30

[16] This section on the use of television in education is based on material prepared for the author by Professor Donald G. Tarbet of the School of Education faculty, University of North Carolina, Chapel Hill. He has had experience in most phases of educational TV since World War II, and is well known in the field. His book, *Television and Our Schools*, was published in 1961 by The Ronald Press Company.

minutes, is presented by means of television. In most cases a team approach is used for instructional purposes; a studio teacher is responsible for part of the instruction, and the remainder of the teaching is done by the classroom teacher. In large classes of 100 or more students, the other members of the team may be specialists, teachers' assistants, or interns who handle certain routine matters such as records, attendance, the scoring of objective tests, and similar matters. Team teaching involves much planning at workshops and in other group sessions.

Very often the programs are presented "live," but in some cases kinescopes or video tapes are used. Both kinescopes and video tapes are means of reproducing programs and presenting them at a later time. The first involves a film process and results in a film which may be run on a 16mm sound projector. The latter is a 2-inch magnetic tape which reproduces both picture and sound.

The success or failure of televised instruction depends to a considerable extent upon the work of the classroom teacher before and after the televised lesson. Much study has been given to this problem by workshop directors and it is considered desirable to have an organizational pattern which provides for a 5- to 10-minute introduction before the telecast and for a 20- to 25-minute follow-up period after the telecast for further discussion and class activities. Reports, films, panel discussions, and many other activities may be used in addition to group discussion. The plan of the course may be modified to some extent by the size of the class, whether it be of 30 or 200 students.

Most teachers have not been prepared for the use of television as a part of the instructional process. Many have had little preparation for the use of audio-visual aids other than in in-service training. The supervisor needs to help his or her teachers meet this phase of instruction and may do so in a number of ways. Faculty meetings and workshops may be used to provide the teachers with opportunities to hear speakers who have had experience in the use of television in their classrooms. Visitation to schools using television can be very helpful. In-service education programs within the school can be of real service. Television itself can be employed to help teachers to use this means of education. Teachers often need help in planning their follow-up activities when television is used for direct instruction. If it is used for enrichment, they should know how to use it as another audio-visual aid.

Such publications as the *Educational Teleguide,* issued by the United States Department of Health, Education, and Welfare, may be of service in locating information on television teaching.

No one knows yet what television may bring in enrichment of teaching materials, methods, and aids. But it has possibilities of contributing the combined values of both the radio and the motion picture to education.

Children and TV: Making the Most of It is one of the more comprehensive, brief analyses of this controversial issue, covering research over a four-year period in the same metropolitan area on family problems and television as well as the teacher's role in television.[17] *How to Use Television in School and Home* is a valuable survey.[18] The National Council of Teachers of English reports on aspects of television from time to time, as in *Education and Mass Media of Communication.*[19] *Mass Media and Education,* Fifty-third Yearbook of the National Society for the Study of Education, contains a thorough presentation of the issues and what the schools can do about them.[20] From the standpoint of the public schools and teacher in-service education, two recent studies are informative, *Teacher In-Service Education by Television* and *The Public Schools and Television.*[21]

It is difficult to select for the supervisor those most helpful sources or aids in this vast area of the mass media of communication and the communication arts. The Department of Audio-Visual Instruction of the National Education Association has people constantly at work; one recent series in booklet form is entitled "Planning Schools for Use of Audio-Visual Materials."[22] The Yearbook of the Department is usually pertinent for the supervisor, for exam-

[17] Association for Childhood Education, Washington, D. C. (1954).
[18] Metropolitan School Study Council, 525 West 120th Street, New York (1953; mimeographed).
[19] A research bulletin (Chicago 21; 1950).
[20] Part II (1954).
[21] By Donald G. Tarbet (School of Education, University of North Carolina, 1958); and by the Southern States Work Conference (Tallahassee: Florida State Department of Education, 1959), respectively.
[22] No. 1, *Classrooms,* 2nd ed.; No. 2, *Auditorium;* and No. 3, *The Resource Center* (Instructional Materials Resource Center).

114 HELPING TEACHERS TO PLAN THEIR CLASSWORK

ple, *The School Administrator and His Audio-Visual Program;* [23] the Department also issues *Film Guides*[24] and a monthly journal, *Audio-Visual Instruction.*

Special editions of professional education magazines appear from time to time, as, for example, "Audio-Visual Aids in the Secondary School" [25] and "Audio-Visual Education in City School Systems." [26] The Institute for Education by Radio publishes its annual yearbook, *Education on the Air.*[27] *The Public Opinion Quarterly* in its main task of public opinion research devotes much of its space to the mass media of communication.[28] Two popular magazines have valuable material at times: *Radio and Television News* looks more at the technical side of radio, TV, and audio-electronics; in contrast, *Film World and AV World Magazine* publishes an educational edition for school people.

GOVERNMENTAL PUBLICATIONS

In addition to the list of government films,[29] there are many materials published by divisions and subdivisions of the Federal government. Some of these publications are of value as source materials for teachers or pupils, and a big task of the supervisor is to help the teacher choose those that can be of real help in teaching.

L. F. Schmeckebier's *Government Publications and Their Use* [30] is still a valuable guide for supervisor, librarian, and teacher. It is the main source which discusses, comprehensively, all of the kinds of publications of the Federal government and their classifications.

The United States Government Organization Manual may be considered the official handbook of the Federal government. It gives data on the various branches of the government and on the quasi-official agencies; it also provides a list of representative publications released by departments, agencies, and commissions of the

---

23 (National Education Association, 1954).
24 *Guide to Films in Human Relations, Guide to Films in Economic Education,* and *National Tape Recording Catalog.*
25 *The High School Journal,* vol. XXXIV (January, 1951).
26 *National Education Association Research Bulletin,* vol. XXIV (December, 1946).
27 Ohio State University Press, Columbus, Ohio.
28 Princeton University, Princeton, New Jersey.
29 Reference on p. 110, *ante.*
30 The Brookings Institution, 3rd ed. (1961).

Federal government. Another regular source concerning government publications is the biweekly list of "Selected United States Government Publications," obtainable from the Superintendent of Documents upon request.

Another resource is *Independent Commissions in the Federal Government*.[31] Although this book is old, librarians still consider it a basic reference to 1940. There are studies and data on the Federal Communications Commission (FCC), the Interstate Commerce Commission (ICC), the Federal Trade Commission (FTC), the Security and Exchange Commission (SEC), the Federal Power Commission (FPC), the National Labor Relations Board (NLRB), the Employees Compensation Commission (ECC), the National Bituminous Coal Commission, the U. S. Maritime Commission, the Social Security Board, the National Mediation Board, the U. S. Tariff Commission, and the Board of Governors of the Federal Reserve System. The powers and duties of these independent commissions in the national government are explained clearly.

The data from the United States Census every ten years form many volumes; some of these reports give teachers and pupils accurate information of a current nature on the population, its jobs, its homes, its income, and living levels.

A sample of government information on consumer education is found in the reports of the Food and Drug Administration.

Finally, the supervisor has to keep up with the "Bulletins" of the Office of Education in the Department of Health, Education, and Welfare. Representative examples of valuable aids in these bulletins are:

Extra-class Activities for All Pupils, by E. Tompkins, 1950.
Place of Subjects in the Curriculum, Bulletin No. 12, 1949, and
How Children Use Arithmetic, Bulletin No. 7, 1951.
How Children Learn About Human Rights, Bulletin No. 9, 1951.
How Children Learn to Think, Bulletin No. 10, 1951.
How Children Learn to Read, Bulletin No. 7, 1952.
How Children and Teacher Work Together, Bulletin No. 14, 1952.
How Children Learn to Write, Bulletin No. 2, 1953.
How Children Can Be Creative, Bulletin No. 12, 1954.
Schools at Work in 48 States: A Study of Elementary School Practices, Bulletin No. 13, 1952.

[31] By William K. Doyle (University of North Carolina Press, 1939).

With Focus on Family Living, by Muriel W. Brown, Vocational Division Bulletin No. 249, Home Economics Education Series No. 28, 1953.
Foreign Language Laboratories in Schools and Colleges, Bulletin No. 3, 1959.

Standards for Selection of Supplementary and Free Materials

What standards should the supervisor help the teacher to establish for the selection of supplementary and free materials? When confronted with the task of appraising source materials, one has to develop principles for sifting those which are most valuable from the tremendous mass of materials now available. In summary form, here are some guide lines for this task.[32]

1. Will these materials contribute positively to the fundamental educational purposes of the school?
2. Do the materials give accurate factual information on the problem or unit of learning?
3. Do the materials give both sides, in case they deal with a controversial area or issue?
4. Are the materials "up to date"?
5. Are they prepared as supplementary to the curriculum, not substitutionary for it?
6. Are they flexible-adaptable to what the teacher and the class are doing and learning?
7. Do the materials tend to include or to exclude other materials of similar nature?
8. Are the materials the best of this sort that can be obtained?
9. Are the materials as good as or, in some cases, better than those prepared for regular school use?
10. Does the material actually enrich the study and not merely add to it?

Vertical Files for the Supervisor

As one reads this chapter of suggestions for helping the teacher with supplementary teaching materials, he recognizes the supervisor's need of a vertical filing system to care for sources of this sort

[32] Consult *Choosing Free Materials for Use in Our Schools* (Washington, D. C.: The American Association of School Administrators, 1955); *Using Free Materials in the Classroom* (Association for Supervision and Curriculum Development, N.E.A., 1953); Henry Harap, "The Use of Free and Inexpensive Materials in the Classroom," *School Review,* vol. LXIII (October, 1955), pp. 378-383; and Hanne J. Hicks, *Educational Supervision in Principle and Practice,* New York: The Ronald Press Company, ch. XII.

in some orderly fashion. The teacher, also, has to learn to build his own vertical files of curricular materials of a "consumable" nature.[33]

Each of you who plans to build vertical files must first set up your own classifications or categories for filing your materials. This is necessary because only *your own classifications will be easy* for *you* to use; those of another person or commercial firm will seldom help you to find that classification under which your own brain placed a certain item. In the second place, file your materials preferably in manila folders, unmounted. Do this because your vertical files are for materials that get out of date rapidly or soon become available in permanent book form. The vertical file is meant to include only temporary aids and resources, not permanent ones; the permanent sources or aids should perhaps be mounted and placed on regular file in the library. Thirdly, write the classification of each group of materials on the folder, and file it in *alphabetical* order in a drawer of your steel filing cabinet in your office. Fourthly, go through your vertical files once every year and throw away any bulletins, lists, pictures, clippings, or materials for which you have later information or better or more improved illustrations; this keeps your files up to date.

Finally, these materials are supplementary aids for you with which to help teachers. If they are worth the trouble and time of collecting and filing, they are worth careful preparation for use with teachers. So pick out and look over again carefully those that you are going to use at any particular time with a particular teacher.

Problems for Individual Study and Class Discussion

1. Make a list of some 30 classifications or categories for your own vertical files for your work in supervision.
2. The school camp is one of education's newer mediums for learning. What learnings are available at a school camp that are not practicable on school grounds?
3. Make out a list of popular magazines and newspapers that would keep a supervisor abreast of local, state, national, and international happenings. Of a list of professional magazines and organizations to which he should subscribe or belong.

[33] *Cf.*, J. M. Gwynn, "The Vertical File in Curricular Work," *The High School Journal*, vol. XXVIII (November-December, 1945), pp. 287-290.

4. How can the supervisor and the librarian co-operate to make supplementary materials and aids easily available to the teacher?

5. The English teacher has asked your advice on using classroom editions of *Time* and the *Readers Digest* in her senior class. What study and investigation would you make before you advised her on this matter?

6. How would you proceed in establishing an in-service program in your school, which would train every teacher and a selected group of boys and girls to operate the projector, the stereoscope, the motion picture machine, the record changers, and the wire and tape recording machines?

7. How would you help a teacher to plan an experiment with her children on listening to and evaluating TV programs in the community in late afternoon or early evening hours?

8. Make out a form which your teachers could use in requesting that you order a new type of aid, book, supply, or materials.

9. How can you evaluate the effectiveness of your audio-visual program? Your library?

10. Do you believe that aesthetic materials are important in the high school as well as in the primary and intermediate grades? What could high school rooms display in lieu of growing flowers, fish tanks, sand tables, crayon art, and the like?

Special Bibliography of Additional Supplementary Materials

I. SOURCE MATERIALS PUBLISHED BY PROFESSIONAL EDUCATIONAL GROUPS

BIBLIOGRAPHIES AND LISTS

Arranged by organizations alphabetically, these are samples of major sources of this type. See latest editions.

American Education Research Association, N.E.A., Washington, D. C.: Bibliographical research survey every three years of such areas and aspects as special subject matter fields; education for work, citizenship, and leisure; general aspects of instruction, learning, teaching, and the curriculum; child growth and development; educational and psychological testing; and guidance and counseling.

American Library Association, Chicago: For example, *Standards for School Library Programs* is the latest revision in 1960 of one of a series of valuable basic reference lists for the supervisor which are revised periodically. Others pertinent here are:

A Basic Book Collection for Elementary Grades

A Basic Book Collection for High Schools

A Basic Book Collection for Junior High Schools, by E. R. Berner and M. Sacra

Administering Library Service in the Elementary Schools, by J. Gardiner

Guide to Reference Books, by B. C. M. Winchell
The Library in the School, by L. F. Fargo
Periodicals for Small and Medium-Sized Libraries, by E. R. Topping, ed.
Teacher-Librarian's Handbook, by M. P. Douglas
Association for Supervision and Curriculum Development, N.E.A., Washington, D. C.:
    Selected Bibliography for Curriculum Workers (1960)
    Books and Materials for Curriculum Workers: An Annual Bibliography
    Curriculum Materials (1961). Usually an annual list
Educational Press Association of America, N.E.A., Washington, D. C.: *America's Education Press, a Classified List of Educational Publications Issued in the United States* (published yearly).
National Council for the Social Studies, N.E.A., Washington, D. C.:
    Historical Fiction and Other Reading References for Classes in Junior and Senior High Schools, by Hannah Logasa, latest edition (published by McKinley Publishing Company, Philadelphia)
    Social Understanding Through Literature
National Council of Teachers of English, Chicago:
    Learning to Live in 1953: Basic Relationships of Life, a book list for children and young people
    Sources of Free and Inexpensive Material for Teachers of English, by J. R. Searles (1955)
    Your Reading: A Book List for Junior High School (1954)
National Education Association, Washington, D. C.:
    NEA Handbook for Local, State, and National Associations
    "Outstanding Education Books" of the Year, a list usually found in the *NEA Journal* for May
    School Health Services, a guide to provisions for disease control, health examinations and counseling, special education for handicapped children, emergency care, evaluation, and the like, prepared by the Joint Committee on Health Problems in Education of the N.E.A. and the American Medical Association.
    "Magazines in the Classroom" *NEA Research Bulletin* (February, 1960)
Secondary Education Board, Milton, Mass.:
    Current Books, Senior Book List
    Current Books, Junior Book List

OTHER SOURCE MATERIALS

Adult Education Association of the U.S.A., Washington, D. C.: *The Leaders' Digest,* a manual for the leader (1954).
American Association for Health, Physical Education, and Recreation, Washington, D. C.: *Physical Education for High School Students* (1955).
American Association of School Administrators:
    Choosing Free Materials for Use in the Schools (1955).
    Staff Relations in School Administration, 1955 Yearbook.

American Council on Education, Washington, D. C.:
> *Characteristics of Teachers: Their Description, Comparison, and Appraisal,* by David G. Ryans (1960)
> *Reading Ladders for Human Relations* (rev. 1955), by Margaret Heaton, and others
> *Sociometry in Human Relations: A Manual for Teachers* (2nd ed. 1955), by Helen H. Jenkins
> *The Study of Religion in the Public Schools,* edited by N. C. Brown, 1958

Association for Childhood Education, Washington, D. C.: Lists of books published regularly in the special bulletins of the Association.

Associated Public School Systems: *Know-How,* quarterly report on interesting practices in administration and supervision

Association for Supervision and Curriculum Development, Washington, D. C.:
> *Leadership for Improving Instruction* (1960)
> *Educating for Economic Competence* (1960)
> *Foreign Language Teaching in Elementary Schools* (1958)
> *Instructional Leadership in Small Schools* (1951)
> *Creating a Good Environment for Learning* (1954)
> *Reporting Is Communicating* (1956)

Department of Elementary School Principals, N.E.A., Washington, D. C.:
> *Science for Today's Children,* 32nd Yearbook (1953)
> *Instructional Materials for Elementary Schools,* 35th Yearbook (1956)
> *Parents and the Schools* (1957)

Lumsdaine, A. A., and Glaser, R. (eds.), *Teaching Machines and Programmed Learning: A Source Book* (Washington: National Education Association, 1960).

Metropolitan School Study Council: *Exchange,* a bimonthly report for exchange of promising practices in schools.

National Association of Secondary School Principals, *The Bulletin;* special issues such as:
> "Science in Secondary Schools Today," vol. XXXVII (January, 1953)
> "A Speech Program for the Secondary School" and "New Developments in Secondary School Mathematics," vol. XLIII (May, 1959, January and May, 1959, respectively)
> "Human Relations in Secondary Education," vol. XXXIX (March, 1955)
> "Music—A Vital Force in Today's Secondary Schools," vol. XLIII (March, 1959)
> "Advanced Placement Programs in Secondary Schools," vol. XLII (December, 1958)
> "Health, Physical Education, and Recreation in the Secondary School," vol. XLIV (May, 1960)

National Council for the Social Studies, Washington, D. C.:
> "Curriculum Series" (revised from time to time)
> No. 4, *Social Education of Young Children*
> No. 5, *Social Studies for Older Children*

No. 6, *Social Studies for Young Adolescents*
No. 7, *Social Studies in the Senior High School*
"Bibliography of Textbooks in the Social Studies," *Social Education,* annually, usually in the December issue
The resource unit type of bulletin also, such as No. 27, *World Trade,* Economic Life Series No. 1, with Teaching Aids
National Council of Teachers of English, Chicago, Ill.:
    Censorship and Controversy, 1953, on censorship of teaching materials
    Education and the Mass Media of Communication (1950)
National Council of Teachers of Mathematics, Washington, D. C.: *The Learning of Mathematics, Its Theory and Practice,* 21st Yearbook (1953)
National School Public Relations Association, Washington, D. C.:
    Janie Learns to Read
    Let's Go to Press: Guide to Better School News Reporting
    Pebbles: Successful Public Relations Ideas That Start with the Teacher in the Classroom and Reach into Every Room (1960)
National Society for the Study of Education, Chicago, Ill.:
    The Dynamics of Instructional Groups, 59th Yearbook (1960), part II
    Rethinking Science Education, 59th Yearbook (1960), part I
    Personnel Services in Education, 58th Yearbook (1959), part II
    Social Studies in the Elementary School, 56th Yearbook (1957), part II
    The Community School, 52nd Yearbook (1953), part II
National Science Teachers Association, Washington, D. C.: *Combating Prejudice Through Science Teaching;* and regular bibliographies of reference books for elementary and secondary school science
National Vocational Guidance Association, Washington, D. C.: Guidance information review service and *Bibliography of Current Occupational Literature*

TEACHERS GUIDES OR UNITS

States, counties, and many local systems produce these periodically. Good samples of the various types are listed.

Baltimore Public Schools:
    Living and Learning in the Kindergarten (1958)
    Home Economics in Junior High Schools (1958)
    Mathematics—Junior High School Special Curriculum (1959)
Bloomfield, New Jersey:
    Homemaking Guide (for Junior High Schools) (1959)
    Language Arts Guide (for Junior High Schools) (1959)
    Related Arts Guide, I and II (for Junior High Schools) (1959)
Florida State Board of Education:
    A Guide to Teaching in Florida Elementary Schools (1958)
    Arithmetic in Florida Elementary Schools (1959)
Grosse Pointe, Michigan, Public Schools:
    Physical Education (1959)
    Science—A Guide for the Elementary Schools, 1-2, 3-4 (1958)

Indianapolis Public Schools:
  *Annotated Bibliography of Selected Books with High Interest and Low Vo-
    cabulary Level* (1954)
Long Beach Public Schools:
  Teachers guides and bulletins are produced regularly and kept up to date.
Los Angeles Public Schools:
  Audio-Visual Handbook for Secondary Schools (1959)
  Instructional Guide for Spanish in the Elementary Schools (1957)
  Books to Enjoy in the Elementary Schools (1958)
New York City Public Schools:
  English Language Arts, Grades 7-8-9 (1959)
  Modern Languages and Latin, Grades 8-12 (1959)
North Carolina, State Board of Education: Guides to Curriculum Study:
  Guidance Services, by Kate Parks Kitchen (1960)
  Industrial Arts, by I. Hostetler and T. B. Young (1959)
  Science, Grades 1-12, by John B. Chase, Jr. (1959)
  The Library and Library Services, by Mary Peacock Douglas (1960)
Prince George's County Public Schools (Maryland):
  Arithmetic Bulletin (1957)
  Resource Units for core curriculum work:
    You and Your World, Grade 7 (1959)
    You and Your Heritage, Grade 8 (1959)
    You and Your Future, Grade 9 (1959)

SPECIAL ISSUES OF EDUCATIONAL MAGAZINES

Supervisors should be alert for special issues of educational magazines
which are devoted to source materials or which carry special lists or bibliographies from time to time. Good samples are listed:

"Better Aids for Learning," *Educational Leadership,* vol. IX (April, 1952),
  pp. 402-477.
"A Bibliography: Selected and Annotated," by E. C. Cieslak, *Phi Delta Kappan,*
  vol. XXXV (May, 1954), pp. 349-356 (on intercultural relations)
"Sources of Teaching Materials," by C. M. Williams, *Educational Research
  Bulletin,* vol. XXXIV (May 11, 1955), pp. 113-140

SOURCE MATERIALS ON USE OF THE COMMUNITY

Illustrations of various types are listed.

Chicago (Chicago: King Company, 1951). A source book concerning the city
  for junior high school pupils, developed by the Chicago schools.
The Community School and the Intermediate Unit (Washington, D. C.: Department of Rural Education, N.E.A., 1954).
*Denver Serves Its Children: A Handbook of School and Community Resources
  for the Use of Parents and Teachers* (Denver Public Schools, 1948).

The Elementary School in the Community, 19th Yearbook, California Elementary Principals Association (1947).

Evaluative Criteria: 1960 Edition (Washington: National Study of Secondary School Evaluation, American Council on Education). The instruments for the evaluation of a secondary school program obtain much information on the community and its resources.

Evaluating the Elementary School: A Guide for Co-operative Study, Commission on Research and Service, Southern Association of Colleges and Secondary Schools. Part of Sections B, C, D, and E give the supervisor many ideas on how to accumulate data on community resources and how to make a community survey.

Family Life Education in School and Community, by Elizabeth McHose (New York: Teachers College, Columbia University, 1952).

II. MISCELLANEOUS SOURCES AND TYPES

The Appendix at the end of this book contains a detailed, annotated list of all kinds of teaching aids, with the addresses of the organizations or business concerns which produce them.

Part III

HELPING TEACHERS TO WORK

WITH CHILDREN

CHAPTER 7

Assisting Teachers with

Pupil Diagnosis and

Other Guidance Problems

NOT TOO LONG AGO schools served primarily one clientele—the school was a rural school, or a small-town school, or a city school. In like manner, the typical school was small—each pupil and each teacher knew everyone—and problems were easier to solve in this setting. Even if the school was large, the pupils were from the same general backgrounds; and in this situation the teacher had also the help of specialists, such as guidance personnel, psychologists, research people, the visiting teacher, and health authorities.

The Different Needs of Pupils
Within the Consolidated School

School consolidation on a large scale has made the teacher's task in guidance much more complex, for today the school may, and frequently does, bring together pupils of three distinct backgrounds. There may be a large segment of farm children, whose parentage and training are predominantly rural. There may be a large number of children of industrial or textile workers, whose parents work in town but live in the rural or urban-fringe neighborhood; the problems of these pupils originate from a background different from that of the farm pupils. The third group in this consolidated school may be distinctly urban, living in the area of school consolidation but with their roots in the city and their customs conditioned primarily by city life. A further complication may be the *location* of this consolidated school. If it is built in the country, the rural group will feel more "at home"; if the school is consolidated with the town school "in town," the urban pupils will feel more at home. In each case of consolidation, the school program may tend to become more like the curriculum of the school *where* it may be established, unless great care is taken; such a tendency would fail to provide adequately for the different needs of pupils who did not live at the place of consolidation.[1]

THAT "AT HOME" FEELING

The teacher has a major responsibility in the establishment of the "at home" feeling among his pupils. The atmosphere of the school can help, too; but the pupil will usually feel at home mainly because the teacher and the other pupils make him feel that way. This feeling on the part of the pupil must be established before the teacher can operate effectively in individual diagnosis of the student, before he can help the student to solve his problems.

There are various administrative devices for the establishment of the feeling of being at home. On the elementary school level, the classroom is usually "self-contained" for grades 1-6. A self-contained classroom has the same teacher with the same group of pupils for most of the day; most of the work and activities are carried on by one teacher and the same group of children, except for some special activities, such as music, physical education, foreign language, or library periods. This kind of situation gives the teacher ample opportunity to learn to know his pupils individually, to get them to work together as a group, and to help them to solve their problems.

GOING UP WITH THE GRADE

In order to give better guidance to very young children, some schools have adopted the device of "the teacher's going up with the grade." For example, the second grade teacher would have the same pupils in the third grade that she had just taught for a year in

[1] P. Woodring, "Are Consolidated Schools Shortchanging the Country Child?" *Country Gentleman*, vol. CXXIV (March, 1954), pp. 119, 155-157.

the second. This practice has seemed to work well in cases where few "personality conflicts" develop between a teacher and a group of pupils. Where such conflicts do develop, it is perhaps better for these children to be placed in another section of the same grade or for the grade to have a new teacher for the next year. Again, in some cases there is the danger of too much identification of the teacher with the pupil and the pupil with the teacher; the pupil might get more new ideas from another teacher.

The "homeroom" on the high school level is simply an administrative device for *one teacher* to get to know a particular group of boys and girls well enough to give them the guidance that they need. In one school the homeroom period may come every day for a comparatively short length of time; in another it may come in the schedule twice or once a week for a longer period of time. The primary purpose of the homeroom is to give the teacher and his group of students time for individual and group guidance, not merely to keep study hall or check attendance. Some secondary schools have experimented with a teacher's "going up with his homeroom"—the same teacher has the same group of boys and girls in his homeroom the current year as he had the preceding year. As in the elementary school, this arrangement makes it possible for the teacher as adviser and guide to come to know his students better and thus help them to solve their problems more effectively.

Whether on the elementary or high school level, the supervisor has to be familiar with various ways of helping the teacher to organize his classroom for most effective teaching and guidance of his children. Once the feeling of being at home has been established in the pupil, there are many methods that school personnel employ for individual diagnosis and help. These may be classified under four main headings: diagnostic tests with which supervisors and teachers should be familiar; the modified "casework" technique with an individual pupil; other devices for acceleration or remedial work with children; and helping pupils to study effectively.

Diagnostic Tests with Which Supervisors
and Teachers Should Be Familiar

It is obvious that classroom teachers cannot be expected to be experts in all kinds of testing. Neither can one expect the super-

visor to be as expert in this important area as the guidance specialist or the school psychologist. What are the limits within which the
supervisor should operate as a practitioner and interpreter in the
area of diagnostic tests? Reducing these limits to the simplest terms,
the supervisor should be familiar with intelligent administration,
scoring, and interpretation of:

1. Mental tests (tests of mental ability; intelligence)

2. Achievement tests (commonly thought of as measurement
of aims and objectives, of mechanics and skills, and of achievement
in the subject-matter areas or courses)

3. Tests of readiness and interests, attitudes and aptitudes, and
personality.[2]

MENTAL TESTS

The Intelligence Quotient (I.Q.) is a number derived by formula to indicate the nature of intelligence; it indicates the ratio between a person's chronological age and mental age. For example,
the formula for deriving it is: $\text{I.Q.} = \dfrac{\text{M.A.}}{\text{C.A.}} \times 100$. It is derived
from the mental test and the person's rate of growth, which help
us to identify intelligent behavior. These intelligence tests are used
to improve the teaching-learning situation, as well as to identify
and provide for brighter and slower pupils.

With regard to tests of mental ability the supervisor should be
prepared to:

Administer, score, and tabulate intelligently group tests of
mental ability.

Establish norms for these tests for an individual school—for
those who attend school over a period of time in the same building,
in the same neighborhood, over a like number of years.

Interpret the results of group mental tests to teachers and to
individual pupils with the main ideas in mind that these tests are:

1. Primarily diagnostic in character.

---

[2] For complete information on sound analyses of instruments of measure-
ment and testing, consult O. K. Buros, ed., *Fifth Mental Measurements Yearbook*
(Highland Park, N. J.: The Gryphon Press, 1960); A. M. Jordan, *Measurement in
Education* (New York: McGraw-Hill Book Company, Inc., 1953), parts I-III; and
"Educational and Psychological Testing," *Review of Educational Research*, vol. XXIX,
no. 1 (February, 1959), part I, and *passim*.

2. Primarily designed to discover what a child can do, instead of what he cannot do.
3. Heavily weighted with the verbal factor, that is, the better the vocabulary of the child, the higher he is likely to score—unless the test is given orally or is designed to be free of culture factors.
4. Designed to point out individual differences in word (verbal) concepts, concepts of form and size, reasoning and discriminating ability, language ability, and reading comprehension.
5. Usually speed tests, requiring completion of the test in a specified time limit, as contrasted with power tests, which allow pupils all of the time they want to complete the tests. There is still a question as to whether this factor operates against good performance on the part of the slow worker.
6. Of many different kinds (authors) and of many forms. For example, if several individuals score lower than the teacher thinks they should on a group test of mental ability, there are other forms of the same test that can be administered to these same pupils later; or an entirely different group mental test can be administered as a check.
7. Not easily comparable as to results. If comparisons are going to be made of the results of a test of mental ability, *those comparisons should be with the norms established in that particular school over a number of years—involving comparison only with pupils of the same age, sex, and grade level, to show how many of these later passed the grade and were promoted, or how long they were retarded.*
8. Devised to help children to improve their work and capacities, as well as to assist teachers to teach children more effectively. Therefore, the pupil should be shown the results of his mental test, and the results should be interpreted to him only by a teacher or supervisor who has learned how to establish local norms for the particular school and its grade levels.

ACHIEVEMENT TESTS

The supervisor should be familiar with achievement test batteries of a standardized nature. Those batteries are commonly divided by measurement experts into two kinds or groups:

1. *Complete batteries,* frequently called survey batteries. Some of these batteries, like the Metropolitan Achievement Tests, include tests for grades 1-9; others, like the Stanford Achievement Test, include tests for grades 3-9. Most of these complete achievement batteries sample the greater portion of what is considered the basic

METROPOLITAN ACHIEVEMENT TESTS
ADVANCED BATTERY — COMPLETE: FORM S

Name... *Craig Smith* ....Boy. X .Girl.....

Teacher... *Mrs. Waite* Grade. *7.2* ...School. *P.S. #3* ...

City *Wintertown* County... *Jones* ....State. *Arizona*

Test	Stand-ard Score	Grade Equiva-lent			
				1946 *11* *20*	
1. Reading	*215*	*8.2*	*65*	Year Month Day	
				Date of Testing	
2. Vocabulary	*215*	*8.0*	*65*		
Average Reading	✕	*8.1*	*	*1933* *10* *19*	
3. Arithmetic Fundamentals	*178*	*5.4*	*5+*	Year Month Day	
4. Arithmetic Problems	*194*	*6.0*	*25-*	Date of Birth	
Average Arithmetic	✕	*5.7*	*		
5. English	Include only *one* English score in finding Ave. Achv't–either Parts			Age .. *13* ... yrs. ... *1* ... mos.	
I. Language Usage	I and II or Parts I, II, and III.				
II. Punct. and Cap. Total (Parts I and II)	*216*	*8.0*	*65+*		
III. Grammar Total (Parts I, II, and III)	*225*	*8.5*	*75+*		
6. Literature	*214*	*7.9*	*65-*		
7. Social Studies: Hist.	*228*	*10.1*	*85-*		
8. Social Studies: Geog.	*214*	*8.1*	*65-*		
Average Social Studies	✕	*9.1*	*		
9. Science	*202*	*6.6*	*40-*		
10. Spelling	*193*	*5.9*	*20-*		
Average Achievement	✕	*7.5*			

*Do not include when figuring average achievement.

Figure 6. Completed Title Page for the Metropolitan Achievement Tests, Advanced Battery—Complete: Form S

Reproduced by permission of Harcourt, Brace & World, Inc., Tarrytown, New York. Record for Craig Smith taken with permission from A. M. Jordan, *Measurements in Education* (New York: McGraw-Hill Book Company, 1953), p. 74.

FORM B

ADVANCED
BATTERY
COMPLETE

Metropolitan Achievement Tests

NAME_____
                        Last Name   First Name·   Initial

BOY ☐   GIRL ☐   GRADE_____TEACHER_____

SCHOOL_____DATE OF TESTING_____
                                                                                            Year   Month   Day

CITY OR TOWN_____DATE OF BIRTH_____
                                                                                            Year   Month   Day

STATE_____AGE_____
                                                                                            Years   Months

SCORE BOX

TEST	WORD KNOW.	READ- ING	SPELL- ING	PART A USAGE	PART B PUNC. & CAP.	PART C KINDS OF SENT.	PART D PARTS OF SPEECH— GRAM.	TOTAL PARTS A—D	LANG. STUDY SKILLS	ARITH. COMP.	ARITH. PROB. SOLV. & CONCEPTS	SOCIAL STUDIES INFOR- MATION	SOCIAL STUDIES STUDY SKILLS	SCI- ENCE
				LANGUAGE										
RAW SCORE														
STAND. SCORE														
STANINE														
GRADE EQUIV.														
%-ILE RANK														

World Book Company

Figure 6A. *1960 Version of the Title Page for the Metropolitan Achievement Tests, Advanced Battery Complete: Form B (formerly Form S)*

Reproduced by permission of Harcourt, Brace & World, Inc., Tarrytown, New York.

elementary school curriculum. For example, they include vocabulary and reading, arithmetic computation and reasoning, language usage, English and literature, geography and history, spelling, and elementary science.

2. *Batteries of fundamentals.* These batteries concentrate on testing those fundamentals in education which most people agree upon as necessary for all pupils to acquire. These batteries limit their testing, then, to reading and language use, arithmetic, spelling, work-study skills, and perhaps writing. Examples of this type of test are the Iowa Every-Pupil Test of Basic Skills and the California Achievement Tests.[3]

In considering achievement tests, one should hold constantly in mind that there are two types or kinds: (1) teacher-made tests, whether of the objective or essay type, and (2) standardized tests. Teacher-made tests may be objective in nature, frequently just as much so as standardized tests, but they have not been standardized. To be standardized, a test must have been administered to a large number of people or pupils in widely differing sections so that norms have been established for it; it must be highly *reliable*, that is, it will produce almost identical results on two successive administrations of the test; and it must be *valid*, that is, in proportion to what is desired to be measured, it measures it well. In this chapter we are dealing only with *standardized tests*. Teacher-made tests are considered in Chapter 9.

The results of achievement test batteries on the elementary school level and of their equivalents on the secondary school level (for example, the Cooperative Tests in subject areas) are of value in several ways. In the first place, there is a diagnostic value for the individual pupil in determining the progress he is making or can make. An examination and analysis of Figure 6 can be used as an illustration. This is the record of a single child on an achievement test.

. . . Craig Smith [in Fig. 6] is in grade 7.2, or two-tenths of the distance through the seventh grade. By looking at Average Achievement at the bottom of the table, you note that his score is 7.5. His achievement is somewhat *above* his grade standing. To interpret this score more accurately, we would need his I.Q. also. If his I.Q. were 100 this would be

---

[3] *Cf.* Jordan, *op. cit.,* ch. IV, *passim,* for example.

good; if it were 125, he would not have fully achieved up to the level of his ability. By again examining the column called Grade Equivalent, we find a variation from 5.4 in arithmetic to 10.1 in social studies. Here is a variation of over 4.5 grades. Craig undoubtedly needs special work in arithmetic. The first thing to do would be to go over his arithmetic tests with him—to discover in what processes he had made his errors and to enlist his co-operation in planning for his improvement.[4]

In like manner, Craig's science and spelling should be analyzed and co-operative efforts made to improve those areas of his work. By such analysis and use of this achievement test, efforts can be focused upon fundamentals that Craig needs, rather than upon achievements that have already placed him in advance of his grade.

A *second* sound use of achievement tests in improving instruction involves the establishment of *local norms* or standards within a school. These local norms differ from national percentile norms only in that they have been established for a single school system, or for individual schools over a period of years. For example, let us take some local norms of Liberty Ledge elementary school. Over a period of years the supervisor and the teachers have ascertained that at the end of the school year on the Stanford Achievement Test their children in the third grade have usually scored 3.3; at the end of the fourth grade, 4.4; at the end of the fifth grade, 5.3; and at the end of the sixth grade, 6.5. These local norms have been established over a period of ten years.

Now let us look at how to use these *local* norms intelligently. When a pupil transfers to Liberty Ledge school from another school, it is discovered that he has scored 5.3 at the beginning of the year in September; he is recommended at once for work in the sixth grade. On the other hand, if *national* norms were followed, he would more likely be placed in grade 5. Another use of local norms can occur when the pupils in grade 6 under a new teacher score 6.3, instead of 6.5, the local norm; there is no cause for alarm here for the principal, since the difference between the local norm and 6.3 is slight. In summary, the supervisor should remember two main points about norms: (1) grade, age, and percentile norms are those most frequently used; and (2) local or standard norms are necessary if one is to interpret achievement test scores intelligently.

[4] *Ibid.*, pp. 73, 75. Reproduced by permission of McGraw-Hill Book Company, Inc.

A *third* use of achievement test scores is for pretesting in basic subject-matter areas or on skill areas. For example, suppose that a teacher is preparing to take up with his seventh-grade pupils arithmetic problems involving reasoning, requiring use of arithmetic computation and fundamentals. One of the standard achievement test batteries, such as the Stanford or Metropolitan, can be used to discover how advanced or how slow each pupil is in reasoning in arithmetic. If John Black at the beginning of grade 7 (7.0) scores 8.4 on arithmetic problems, he is ready for advanced problem work in arithmetic, probably in the form of selfdirecting workbooks and, therefore, should not spend his time repeating the arithmetic problems of grade 7 which he has already mastered. On the other hand, if Sally White scores 6.0 she may need workbooks of sixth-grade level; and if Sam Neal scores 7.0, he may find both the texts and materials at the seventh-grade level just what he needs for his work and stage of advancement.

A *fourth* way to employ the results of achievement tests is for comparison of the achievement(s) of a school, by grades, with the national norm. This is perhaps the way in which achievement test results are most frequently used; it is likewise least productive, perhaps, of positive results for pupils and teachers, because even the test makers themselves have not yet set accurately age and grade standards for rural, town, and metropolitan areas.[5] Consequently a comparison with national norms is hardly fair, unless these types of differences are also taken into account.

TESTS OF INTERESTS, PERSONALITY, AND APTITUDES

The supervisor should be familiar with readiness tests, tests of interests, tests designed to measure attitudes and personality traits, and aptitude tests.

Tests of readiness and interests. These tests involve fundamentally two kinds of readiness—readiness for reading, primarily tests for young children, and readiness for other learning, growing from the maturing of different types of interests in the child at different age and grade levels.

What are the requirements for learning to read? What traits are necessary? What traits reflect the maturation of children?

[5] *Ibid.,* pp. 35-36.

These factors which influence and control a child's readiness to read are, in summary form: [6]

Mental age or maturity
Physical maturity
Visual perception or readiness
Cultural level of child's home or background
Emotional stability
Social maturity
Interests
Hearing (listening) or auditory readiness
Sex differences
Attitude toward reading

Self-reliance
Mastery of language, or linguistic maturity
Memory, or retention span
Association of ideas, or readiness in the perception of relationships
Informational background
Color discrimination
Motor skills, or manual competence
Responsiveness to books and storytelling

The mastery of language and linguistic concepts is difficult for the child, and his reading readiness operates as a major factor in this process: [7]

The teacher should realize that the typical six-year-old has a vocabulary of 2500 to 5000 words when he enters the first grade; that this vocabulary is made up partly of symbols, partly of concepts or meanings associated with objects, persons, occupations, or ideas; and that the child's readiness may have already been developed for reading or it may have to be stimulated and developed under the direction of the teacher. Many authors of books on reading instruction and language indicate that the mastery of language (linguistic concepts) is dependent primarily upon intelligence, listening or auditory readiness and home environment. If reading readiness has to be developed, the teacher has at hand today ample materials with which to do this, ranging from reading readiness books and storytelling to records, tape recordings, filmstrips, pictures, and the picture-story books. The more recent books on the teaching of reading give many illustrations of how reading readiness may be fostered and developed . . .

Tests of reading readiness commonly include picture directions; words or word-card matching; copying figures; recognition of letters, objects, words, and phrases; vocabulary and following in-

[6] J. M. Gwynn, *Curriculum Principles and Social Trends*, 3rd ed. (New York: The Macmillan Company, 1960), pp. 301-302. Used with permission.
[7] Gwynn, *ibid.*, p. 302. Recent research may raise these figures sharply.

structions; tracing a maze; drawing a picture; motor skills; and other visual or auditory tests. In fact, reading readiness tests may predict final achievement more accurately than intelligence tests. Supervisors can master these types of tests easily "on the job," as well as in courses of special training for supervision. Examples of such tests include: the Gates Reading Readiness Tests, the Lee-Clark Reading Readiness Tests, the Marion Monroe Reading Aptitude Tests, the Metropolitan Reading Readiness Tests, and the Stevens' Reading Readiness Tests.

The interest or preference test is another kind of readiness test. There are several ways of discovering children's interests. One is by direct questioning, the questionnaire approach, or interest inventory; Strong's Vocational Interest Blank is of this kind, one of the oldest. Another way to discover interests is through direct observation, such as A. M. Jordan's checking of the interests of children in books and magazines against their interests as expressed through a questionnaire. This method is still in the developmental state.[8] A third way to discover interests is through sampling the amount of information a child possesses; the assumption here is that the more information a child has, the greater are his interests in certain fields or areas.

In the opinion of the experts, three instruments for measuring interests have been developed which, because of their vocabulary load, are more suitable for use with Grades 7-12. These are the Cleeton Vocational Interest Inventory (Grades 9-12), the Kuder Preference Record (Grades 9-16), and the Occupational Interest Inventory, by E. A. Lee and L. P. Thorpe.

All of these interest instruments are comparatively easy to learn to use, to score, and to interpret. They are especially helpful for vocational guidance of pupils. Note that they are primarily for use in junior or senior high school. For the interests of younger children, the reader should turn to the next section on personality inventories.

Tests of attitudes and personality traits. An attitude may be defined as a *set* or *tendency*, or *predisposition*, with a feeling tone favorable or unfavorable in nature, directed toward a person, or ideal, or race, or situation. An attitude is usually the result of ex-

[8] *Cf.* Jordan, *op. cit.*, pp. 424-426.

perience and is enduring. Attitudes are also usually learned. Therefore, attitudes of children are important as a part of learning in school.

Most attitude tests are in the form of scales (or rating scales) and inventories. The work of the experts in this area from the 1920's presents interesting developments but furnishes few instruments or scales which the teacher and supervisor can use effectively to measure the amount of change in attitudes in the classroom.

In like manner, most personality inventories, rating scales, and questionnaires are somewhat questionable instruments in the hands of teachers and supervisors. This is true not because of lack of training and competence on the part of school personnel but because the traits of character and personality are so intangible, interrelated, and complex as to challenge satisfactory analysis. In this area, it is wise for the supervisor to call in the expert or clinician for the administration and interpretation of tests in case the pupil deviates markedly from the normal.

Aptitude tests. These tests involve special abilities, like music or art, and mechanical abilities. In turn, the mechanical abilities may be analyzed as manual dexterity, strength, steadiness, reaction time, and manual rhythm. There are good aptitude tests available. In general, tests of special and mechanical aptitudes should be administered by the test specialists and the interpretation made to the teacher, supervisor, and individual pupil. The tests available are constructed generally for grades 7 or 8 and up.

The Modified "Casework" Technique
with an Individual Pupil

From time immemorial man has learned by observation. Simply stated, the modified casework technique is learning about a pupil from (1) all records on him and (2) observation combined with the impersonal recording of the data from day to day or time to time. Many teachers call these recorded, running accounts of pupil behavior as it happened over a long period of time their "logs" on individual pupils. Guidance personnel, particularly for the secondary school, have developed well-defined, effective adaptations of the social worker's "case" techniques to diagnosis of pupil needs and to counseling.[9]

The purpose here is to illustrate *how* the teacher and supervisor can keep a "log" or recorded account of a pupil's growth and behavior upon which the "case history" is based. One should keep in mind all of the time that the "case history" of a pupil would contain all information, records of observations, school records, test results, and accounts of interviews—in other words, all information on the pupil, both official and anecdotal, that is available. Therefore, the log or anecdotal record of the teacher will be just a part of the total "case history."

Here are samples of good recording of a boy's actions and progress over a period of three weeks. It is an impersonal description of what occurred, with examples of co-operation or lack of it, not an account of what the teacher just thought.

BASIC INFORMATION ON BOB

Bob Leighton is almost twelve years old, and is just starting the sixth grade. He comes from a family of four. His father is a freight engineer on a big railroad line and completed high school before he went to work. His mother went to normal school for two years, and taught the first grade before she was married. He has a sister who is fifteen and who is a popular junior now in high school.

His home is in a good, older section of town, has 6 rooms, 3 downstairs and 3 upstairs. Each child has a room of his own. The house is well furnished in good taste. The family takes one daily paper, a news magazine, three women's magazines, *Life*, the *Readers Digest*, and a church magazine. There are quite a few good books in the home.

The family are all church members, and the mother and daughter are very active in the work of the church. The father is out of town three nights a week, due to his scheduled "run" on the railroad. The family

[9] The student who wishes to compare several views of the aims, types of data, and ways of collecting information for the educational case study will find the following representative: L. L. Chisholm, *Guiding Youth in the Secondary School* (New York: American Book Company, 1950), ch. XIII; H. F. Cottingham, *Guidance in Elementary Schools* (Bloomington, Ill.: McKnight and McKnight Publishing Company, 1956), ch. VI, and *passim;* E. W. Detjen and M. F. Detjen, *Elementary School Guidance* (New York: McGraw-Hill Book Company, Inc., 1952), ch. I; J. M. Gwynn, *op. cit.*, pp. 78-81; 484-486; E. G. Johnston *et al.*, *The Role of the Teacher in Guidance* (Englewood Cliffs: Prentice-Hall, 1959), Part II; D. A. Prescott, *The Child in the Educative Process* (New York: McGraw-Hill Book Company, Inc., 1957), ch. VI; and R. D. Willey, *Guidance in Elementary Education*, 2nd ed. (New York: Harper and Brothers, 1960), chs. IX-X.

apparently get along well together. Bob had a paper route last year and made quite a bit of money out of it, but he gave that up this year. He is still interested very much in constructing model airplanes and other objects—is currently working on a boat; he has a good shop in the basement of his home. His sister is music crazy, and a "hi-fi" fan deluxe. She has a good collection of long-playing records.

October 3

Bob is an interesting study of an evolving adolescent this year. I had him in the fifth grade last year, and he was co-operative, a good student, willing to help, and always in a good humor. This fall he is different—he is moody at times, like today when he fell into a brown study in the arithmetic period, and I had to speak to him three times before he heard me. He has grown 3 inches higher and weighs more—to be exact, his physical exam report shows that he weighs 17 pounds more. He has stopped studying and working on airplane models, he says; he now calls that "kid stuff." And he has not studied in school as he did last year, though it is still too early to tell whether this will seriously affect his grades. Another evidence of his "growing up" cropped up today—I heard him tell Jim to stop calling him "Bobby"—his name was "Bob."

October 10

Bob has gotten into two small scrapes this last week. First, he threatened to lick his best friend, Jim, because Jim had left him out of the gang when they went to the State Fair on Monday. Jim was about ready to fight him in the classroom, but I broke it up. Later I kept an eye out at recess and heard Jim tell him that he shouldn't believe every tale-bearer—that he (Jim) had phoned and left an invitation for Bob with Bob's sister—when he heard nothing from Bob, the crowd went on. Later Bob told me his sister forgot to give him the message.

The second scrape came off this morning. When I returned to the room after going to the audio-visual room a minute, a battle royal with erasers and chalk was going on. I asked those responsible for starting it to talk privately with me at recess—my usual procedure. Two other boys remained and told me that they started it, and were sorry, and how it happened—but they said a third boy was involved, too, who had failed to "turn himself in" (as we called our honor system!). Later Bob came in— frankly said he helped to start it when he got mad at a remark about his "poor football throwing arm"; said he was sorry. When I asked him why he failed to stay at recess with the others, he said he just forgot—he just was anxious to get first in line at the snack bar, since he had had no breakfast.

October 17

This has been a bad week for Bob. First, grade reports came out, and half of his grades were lower than last year's. I had talked with him, as is our usual practice, and told him that I had seen him study very little—he admitted that I was right. I asked if that were the best that he could do—if it were I would so indicate in the comment to his parents. He said he *could* do better, but said he did not know whether it would be worth it. He reported later that both parents were upset over his report.

Next, last Friday we had our fall picnic. We had it at the lake, as usual. Since it was still very warm, some took swim togs and went in. Though Bob was one of our life guards, considered a high honor, he spent a lot of his time "ducking" the girls in deep water, a potentially dangerous pastime. I told him to stop twice—when he disobeyed me again, I took him off the job and made him come out of the water. He has offered me no explanation of his actions, and I have asked none. I merely said that I could not delegate any more responsibility to him or allow the class to do so until he was willing to take it and use it wisely.

One bright spot! Today he brought me a late-blooming rose for the annual country club party the teachers are invited to this weekend. I shall wear it—and told him so. He also studied in school twice as much this week as I have seen him do all year.

These anecdotal records should be filed by the teacher in a folder separate from Bob's cumulative records. Then, after recording these impressions at various times during the year, at the end of the year the teacher should summarize them for the permanent record in briefer form. Such running accounts of a pupil's reactions and activities take time; but the time will be well spent for the guidance of those particular children who need more help from time to time.

Other Devices for Acceleration or Remedial Work with Children

Some of the devices for acceleration or remedial work with children will be considered here; others, like evaluation and the teacher-parent conference, which are equally valuable are considered in another section of the book (Chapter 9).

GROUPING

At times a situation beyond the control of school authorities forces attention upon a particular problem. This is true now as over-crowded schools, many with double-shift classes, force special attention upon the grouping of pupils in order to care for brighter as well as slower learners.

As the supervisor considers grouping, he should think of *grouping as a method of teaching.* In this sense, grouping means the separation of pupils into smaller or more compact units to help in learning. Grouping is based upon sound psychology. If left to do as they please, both children and adults tend to gather into groups and to operate in groups. Even though the most striking characteristic of most groups is the differences among the separate members, in each group there is a common element—this element of homogeneity may be age, interest, sex, or residence, depending on the nature of the activity.

Historically, American schools developed a system of passing pupils from grade to grade after they had mastered a satisfactory standard of achievement. Thus the first grader was "passed" to the second grade at the end of the year, or he was retained since he "failed the first grade." This system still prevails largely in the United States, for it is easy to administer. If the child passes the academic hurdles, he is promoted; if he does not pass a sufficient number or amount, he is not promoted; *and that's that.*

Research studies in recent years have added much to our information about grouping. Some schools have tried out different methods of grouping, and have reported success with them. Both the research and the experimental practices have shown one common denominator: [10]

. . . It is obvious that the term GRADE is a misnomer, that the phrase a "fourth grade" or a "fifth grade" means little, when research studies have shown that within any classroom there is a spread of at least five years in achievement, as well as a wide variation in mental age, physical size, and emotional and social development.

[10] Quoted with permission from "How Are We Grouping," *Educational Leadership*, vol. IV (March, 1947), p. 354; this whole issue is devoted to aspects of grouping. *Cf.* also John Goodlad, *The Non Graded Elementary School* (New York: Harcourt, Brace and Company, 1959), *passim.*

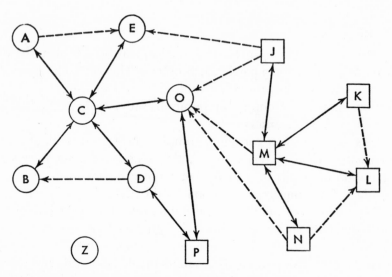

Figure 7. A Sociogram (7th Grade in a Southern Town)

NOTE: The circles represent girls and the squares represent boys. Solid arrows pointing in both directions (⟷) indicate mutual attraction; a broken arrow pointing in one direction (⟵– – or – – ⟶) indicates that one pupil likes the other pupil toward which the arrow is pointing. There were actually 30 pupils in the grade, 15 boys and 15 girls. The responses of only 6 boys and 7 girls are diagrammed, in order that the principle of constructing a sociogram may be easy to grasp.

Reproduced by permission from J. Minor Gwynn, *Curriculum Principles and Social Trends*, 3rd ed. (New York: The Macmillan Company, 1960), p. 665.

The sociogram. This device has been developed rapidly in recent years to help in more effective grouping:[11]

The sociogram is really a sociometric technique to show (in diagram form) the interpersonal relationships within a given group. [See Figure 7.] The Horace Mann-Lincoln Institute of School Experimentation studied the group behavior of boys and girls through (1) the use of the *Classroom Social Distance Scale*, and (2) constructing sociograms based on that scale. The possibilities for developing better group activities within the classroom can be grasped more clearly by analysis of a simple sociogram [Figure 7].

[11] This description is taken with permission, with a few changes, from Gwynn, *op. cit.*, pp. 664-666. For comparison, consult the reports in Ruth Cunningham and associates, *Understanding Group Behavior of Boys and Girls* (New York: Teachers College, Columbia University, 1951), *passim*, and especially ch. V for group structure and shifts in group organization.

The basic data for this sociogram were secured from unsigned responses of the boys and girls to this question: "Who are your best friends in this grade?" A partial interpretation of the sociogram would be as follows: *Among the girls:* C is liked best by other girls and likes most of them, but she is not interested in the boys yet; O attracts the interest of most of the boys, but likes only one boy, P; poor Z has no friends among either girls or boys and is isolated from all of the group. *Among the boys:* M is the best liked, and likes all of the boys except one, P; P is isolated from the boys, but likes and is liked by two girls, O and D. In summary, four of the six boys are beginning to show an interest in girls, and two of seven girls have boys as best friends; the teacher will have to work hard to get Z into some group activity where she can win friendship, and will have to keep a watchful eye on P's lack of comradeship with boys to see whether it is temporary or permanent.

Through a study of group interaction and through co-operative planning with her students, the alert teacher in the modern school uses her curriculum materials and methods to stimulate her pupils to grow in civic, group, and individual responsibility. In addition to the materials of the Horace Mann-Lincoln Institute of School Experimentation, the Association for Supervision and Curriculum Development of the National Education Association has studied teacher-pupil planning and has published materials on many aspects of it.

School levels instead of grades. There is a real trend toward broader "divisions" or "levels" in the classifications and grouping of pupils, instead of into traditional grades in the elementary school. Of 1,600 city school systems surveyed by the research division of the National Education Association at midcentury, 17 per cent practiced the larger groupings to a greater or lesser extent.[12] Earlier attempts at larger grouping substituted some larger classifications for grade levels K-8, such as kindergarten level: first and second levels; third levels; fourth and fifth levels; sixth level; and seventh and eighth levels. More recently even larger classifications have been advocated and tried out. One of the most frequently used is grouping the pupils generally in four levels: (1) kindergarten-primary level, formerly kindergarten through grades 1-3; (2) grammar grade level, formerly grades 4, 5, and 6; (3) intermediate or junior high level, formerly grades 7, 8, and 9; and (4) senior high level, grades 10, 11, and 12. Pupils in a "level" work in that

[12] "Trends in City-School Organization: 1938-1948," *National Education Association Research Bulletin,* vol. XXVII, no. 1 (February, 1949), pp. 8-9, 16-19, 20-22.

level as long as profitable and are then promoted to the next level. In case a child is a slow learner, it might take him four years to do all of the work satisfactorily for the grammar grade level, instead of the normal time of three years. But he would have a sounder basis for work on the next level, would be retarded only one year, and would not be far out of line with children of his own social maturity and physical growth.

Multiple curricula for the elementary school. Some educators are advocating differentiated curricula for the elementary grades. For example, there would be three curricula instead of one; one curriculum would be adapted to the slow pupil; another would be adapted to the typical or normal pupil; and the third would be adapted to the bright pupil. Each curriculum would be founded on learning capacity and not primarily on age or physical size or emotional maturity,[13] or health, or home conditions. Though this concept may seem far-fetched to some, it is a stimulating idea; such a program, if carefully and soundly planned, will seek out and cultivate the child of special ability. It will also furnish a challenging opportunity to each to learn according to his ability and achievement.

Ability grouping. Ability grouping has been in operation for many years. It got its major start with the title of "Grouping According to I. Q.," and had to spend the ensuing twenty years living down the bad name attached to it. Many of the earlier supervisors sectioned children by grade levels according to their mental ability alone. Thus, all children in section I of grade 3 would have I. Q.'s of 71-80; in section II of grade 3, I. Q.'s of 81-90; in section III of grade 3, I. Q.'s of 91-100; and so on up. This was called "homogeneous" grouping. Opposition soon developed to the use of the *one* standard of mental ability alone for sectioning children, and other standards were therefore added.

The four standards most commonly used now in ability grouping are: (1) a test of mental ability, (2) standard achievement test(s) on subject matter, (3) teacher's marks or grades, and (4)

---

[13] G. L. Brown, "Some Thoughts on the Elementary School Curriculum, Past and Future," *Progressive Education*, vol. XXI (November, 1953), pp. 41-43. For a clearer picture of experimental programs for the gifted, turn to *Education for the Gifted*, Fifty-seventh Yearbook of the National Society for the Study of Education (1958), Part II.

social maturity in the opinions of teachers. Little attention seems to be given to personality factors in grouping.

Small schools with an enrollment of 100-400 show little need for ability grouping or sectioning. Practically all teachers and all pupils know each other fairly well, and there are not enough pupils in any one grade to warrant more than two sections of a single grade. When pupils are sectionized without regard to special abilities and growth, this type of sectioning is labeled as "heterogeneous grouping." It is usually done simply by dividing into sections according to the calling of every other name, alphabetically, of all of those who are in the first grade, the second grade, and so on. In a small school, whether elementary or secondary, ability grouping by separate grade sections is of doubtful value, since its main purpose is to eliminate the extremely wide range of differences between pupils. Its judicious use in the large school has much to justify it.

Two main controls or checks should operate when ability grouping is employed in a school. No pupil should be compelled to join an ability group unless (1) his parents are willing for him to do so and (2) the student himself is willing to do so.

Grouping within the individual classroom. This practice is so universal among teachers in the primary grades that it is well known to all elementary school teachers. For example, a first-grade room is seldom found at midterm without three or four different reading groups composed, respectively, of (1) those yet unable to read, who are working on readiness materials, coloring figures on outline forms, or looking at picture books; (2) those who have just started reading and who are reading preprimers or primers; (3) those who are further advanced in reading and who are reading in the first readers; and (4) the fast-reading group, who have perhaps already read from six to ten different readers. Each of these four reading groups may be composed of as many as ten pupils or as few as two or three.

The purpose is to carry each pupil forward as fast in reading as he is ready and able to go. While one group reads with the teacher, the other groups work as individuals at seatwork, with workbooks, or in small groups on projects previously planned. The teacher can also group for more effective teaching and learning in other subject areas. For example, a sixth-grade teacher might have two arithmetic sections, and two language arts sections, each different in composition and based on advancement and achievement in each subject area.

It is a matter of concern to many educators that the higher the grade level, the less the grouping of pupils within the classroom for learning. Why? There seems no valid reason for less group work on the high school level than in the grades; rather, the wider variations in reading ability and achievement would seem to call for more grouping within the class.

Grouping in the whole school. This device promises much for forward-looking teachers. It is common practice in schools which have been established for those juveniles who have been judged delinquent; and it works well there. Each delinquent reports and is thoroughly tested; after that, he is assigned to a remedial school. In that school, all boys, of all ages, whether reading at the second-grade or eighth-grade level, are grouped for working together. Most of the instruction is for vocational competence; each boy who is more adept at one aspect helps another; and both young and old get on well together.

In regular schoolwork, grouping in the whole school can operate in two different ways. Method 1 involves, for example, four teachers who teach 100 children having a total age range of four years. These same children and these four teachers stay together for four years; at the end of that time the child is promoted to the *grade* or *level* for which he is prepared. There is no interruption for yearly promotions. Each teacher knows all 100 pupils well and works from time to time with all. The four-year span of work becomes a red-letter period in the school life of the child, as his individual interests, needs, and difficulties are met, as his special aptitudes and personality traits are encouraged.[14]

Method 2 is not as easy to administer in the regular type of school organization as Method 1, but it can prove to be just as effective. An example involves 200 children and eight teachers, living together for six years, all teachers teaching these same children for this span of six years, helping them to grow and develop over a space of time.

[14] *Cf.* Jeannette Veatch, "Grouping in the Whole School," *Childhood Education,* vol. XXX (October, 1953), pp. 62-64; and *A Look at Continuity in the School Program,* 1958 Yearbook, Association for Supervision and Curriculum Development, Parts II and III.

On the high school level, an interesting variation can be placement in classes and activities according to the total behavior and achievement pattern. This would work out so that one pupil in grade 10, as an illustration, would be carrying more tenth-grade class sections, perhaps one eleventh-grade section, and perhaps one ninth-grade section. Another pupil in grade 10, who should be accelerated, would be carrying two tenth-grade class sections, three eleventh-grade sections or classes, and be in grade 10 in student activities. In this scheme, no bright pupil would be retarded in two or three regular classes, and no slow pupil would be forced to work above his achievement and pace.[15]

READINESS MATERIALS

Readiness materials are of many kinds, ranging from a wealth of visual and audio-visual types to those specially prepared for reading and number readiness. Simplified reading books modified in vocabulary for slow readers were referred to in Chapter 3, as were workbooks and seatwork materials. Other readiness materials involve picture books and magazines; library periods and use of the library are also helpful. All of these kinds of materials help to "ready" the pupil for new learning and new interests, if used properly.

ACCELERATION

Acceleration, or "skipping a grade," has been employed in pupil guidance and growth for many years. This type of provision for brighter pupils is well known. Another type of acceleration found in the secondary school involves "advanced standing." The tenth grader, for example, may show on a Co-operative English Test that he is far ahead of his group on mechanics of expression (grammar). He is given advanced standing and allowed to substitute dramatic art or debating for English III. In effect, this is a type of "enrichment," instead of acceleration.

Another device for acceleration is the use by the teacher and pupils, co-operatively, of unit lesson planning. In this co-operative venture, the brighter pupils help to plan their work at times far

[15] Blanchard, B. E., "Grade Placement in Accordance to the Total Behavior Pattern of Pupils," *The Bulletin of the National Association of Secondary School Principals*, vol. XXXVII (December, 1953), pp. 140-142.

in advance of the minimum required for passing in the class. This kind of schoolwork tends to enrich the program for the brighter pupil, rather than to accelerate him so that he finishes and graduates a year or two ahead of his age and social group.

ORIENTATION AND ARTICULATION

One who delves into research will be amazed when he tries to find reports on ways for better articulation between school levels. There are few articles on means and instruments of articulation, especially in recent years. Edwin A. Juckett calls attention to the importance of this matter.[16] Prominent among the devices for better articulation are these for transition from elementary to high school (summarized by the author):

1. Joint meeting of teachers of both levels to plan better articulation
2. Exchange of teachers between levels for a few days
3. Teacher committees to work on and plan better articulation in the language arts and English curriculum; in the reading program; in regard to homework; in providing vital information on all pupils; and in reports on personality trait deviates
4. Representatives of each sixth or eighth grade to visit junior or senior high and report back
5. Visit of junior or senior high school student council to the elementary school with the student handbook
6. Programs for assembly of high school by sixth-grade or eighth-grade groups, such as a program in music

Other well-known methods that are being employed to increase better transition from one school level to another would enlarge Juckett's list by the following:

1. High school, or junior high school day—a day set aside for the sixth or eighth, or ninth grade to spend the whole time visiting the various activities and regular classes of the upper school to which they are going next year. Special assemblies and talks for the upcoming freshmen would also be planned, as well as "question sessions."
2. "Educational guidance day" in the lower school—a day during which the types of curricular programs of the high school are explained to them, including the meaning of such terms as "required" or "constant" subjects, electives, restricted electives, special interest choices,

[16] Edwin A. Juckett, "A Pleasant Bridge in the Hyde Park School," *The Clearing House*, vol. XXIX (October, 1954), pp. 81-83.

the "core" or "common learnings" program and what it means, what is involved in college preparation, and the like. Some high schools use this as the basis for preregistration.

3. Preregistration day for high school the next year, involving parents and pupils.
4. "Field day" for upper elementary grades, in which junior or senior high school boys and girls act as field judges and make awards to individual and group winners of contests.
5. "Activities" day for the lower-school pupils in the high school, a day devoted to explanation and illustration of all of the student activities on the high school level.
6. Special physical, achievement, and mental tests as information of value for guidance of the pupil as he leaves one level and goes into another.
7. Special assemblies during the last six weeks of the lower school, devoted to explanation and exploring such aspects of high school life as "the departmental system," the reasons for subject-matter and other specialists in the high school, why interscholastic competition is limited to the high school, the value and use of the library, and how to begin to explore one's life work.
8. P.T.A. meeting at junior high school for sixth-grade parents, to explain program, requirements, grading system, approved dress, and to answer questions of parents.

Supervisors and principals who want to work at it can help teachers intelligently on both elementary and high school levels to make transition from the lower to the high school level more pleasant, more profitable, and something to be anticipated pleasantly instead of a change to be feared.

Helping Pupils to Study Effectively

This is another area which could stand much well-planned research on both the public school level and the level of higher education. How does one "study"? Is any one way of studying better than another? What does one "study for"? Does the slower reader develop better study habits than the faster reader? Can a pupil learn to improve his study habits? Do "study questions" improve study habits? What is the relationship between studying and thinking, if any? Are there such differences in study habits as studying for words, for ideas and thoughts? Do bright students develop better study habits than duller students? Does it make any difference in one's studying if he is studying at one time to remember dates and at another to identify trends in change of government or of business? Does a "study hall" facilitate study? These questions indicate both the importance of learning how to study and the lack of knowledge that we have about how to develop and improve study habits.

Involved with study habits is the moot question of homework, that is, how much time the pupil should spend in study and preparation of his schoolwork at home. Even in the most traditional schools, teachers seldom require or plan for regular homestudy prior to grade four. After homework has begun to be assigned, however, teachers generally assign, and parents expect an increasing amount of homework for the student each year. How sound this theory is has not been proved from the small amount of research published in this area. An examination and analysis of the literature on "how to study" do furnish us with ideas that may be of aid in helping pupils to learn to study. For purposes of brevity, these suggestions are summarized here.[17]

1. *When is a pupil studying?* He is studying when he is getting knowledge for a purpose.
2. *Why learn to study?* For mastery of a subject, item, skill, or experience.
3. *What environment is best for effective study?* Good health, good light, a fresh mind and body, pleasant surroundings, and a reasonably cool room temperature constitute perhaps the best physical and mental surroundings for effective study.
4. *What skills does a pupil need for effective study?* Primarily these skills are ability to concentrate and shut other distractions out of his mind; planning what he has or wants to do; the ability to discover information he seeks; ability to comprehend and take in thoughts of others as he reads; ability to express himself and his own thoughts in written form; ability to organize clearly material for presentation; and the ability to identify quickly what he is looking for.
5. *How can a pupil identify his sources for study?* By checking his textbook first of all; by learning to use the library intelligently; by learning to use a book's index or glossary; by learning how to read a map;

[17] Samples of both purposes and ways to study were taken from "how to study" manuals for the last 25 years, from teachers' and educators' opinions, and from popular magazines. For a few selected references on this aspect, the reader should consult the bibliography at the end of the chapter.

by limiting the problem upon which he is working; and by asking for help and suggestions from his teacher.

6. *When shall the teacher give help to the pupil in study?* Every day, or as often as needed, in a flexible class program that allows every child ample time for both study and recitation with every teacher. The more study that is done at school in a normal learning situation under an expert (the teacher), the more meaningful the learning and the faster it takes place.

7. *Can students have different purposes in studying at different times on different types of assignments?* Certainly. To study how to write a character sketch of Prince Hal or Napoleon is a much different assignment in purpose from punctuating correctly a set of 30 sentences. Each purpose requires its own set of particular skills. A problem, such as "What Jackson really thought of Adams," would require still a different set of skills for its purpose, mainly "scanning" a lot of opinions to get at the true picture.

8. *Do schools provide desirable environments for study?* Generally the elementary schools provide better surrounding for effective study than high schools. The old-fashioned study hall in the high school is gradually giving way to the "double" or "long period" (1 hour), in which the teacher devotes part time to helping pupils in study assignments and part to regular class activities.

9. *Is ability to read and comprehend well necessary to effective study?* The better those skills, the more effectively the pupil can study. The pupil who reads and comprehends slowly can be taught by reading specialists to improve both reading rate and comprehension.

10. *How long can a pupil study without "diminishing returns" for his efforts?* Grades 4-6, about 15 minutes without a break; Grades 7-9, about 20 minutes; Grades 10-12, up to 30 minutes. Experiments have shown that concentrated study for shorter intervals of time brings better results than concentrated study over a long period of time.

Problems for Individual Study and Class Discussion

1. Explain why the supervisor, more than any other staff member, needs to be familiar with testing, its advantages and limitations, and its application to child guidance.
2. What is meant by the statement "Every teacher is a guidance person?" In what respects is a supervisor a guidance person?
3. Do you feel that unacceptable behavior should be entered in a pupil's permanent, cumulative record? Give your reasons pro or con.
4. Describe the major differences between directive and nondirective counsel-

ing. To what extent might a supervisor use these techniques in helping teachers with their problems?

5. A third-grade boy is unable to read. His parents say that it is caused by his stubbornness; the teacher feels that he is mentally handicapped; testing reveals that he has normal mentality. What would you, as a supervisor, recommend for this child as he enters the fourth grade?
6. What are the advantages of a grade teacher's continuing or going up with the same group for two or more years? The disadvantages?
7. Why is a single I.Q. measurement considered to be an unreliable index to a pupil's capacities? What other factors in addition to intelligence do modern authorities recommend testing when a child shows substandard performance?
8. Trace the development of the "homeroom" on the high school level for guidance purposes.
9. Some teachers maintain that achievement tests can be used successfully for pretesting as a teacher begins a unit. Express yourself on this statement.
10. What is a supervisor's "log" of daily happenings in a supervisor's life? What is a teacher's log? How can teacher and supervisor co-operate to use a teacher's log for improvement of his teaching?
11. Have we learned as much about teaching children successfully in large groups as we have learned about teaching them successfully in small groups? Explain.
12. List and identify the various types of ability grouping for teaching.
13. As a supervisor, have you mastered the technique of studying or reading for a particular purpose? Can you help teachers to study effectively?

Additional Selected References for Problem or Unit Study

American Education Research Association, National Education Association, Washington, D. C.: *Review of Educational Research*, vol. XXX, no. 2 (April, 1960), "Guidance and Counseling," chs. IV and V.
Armstrong, W. H., *Study Is Hard Work* (New York: Harper and Brothers, 1956), *passim.*
Association for Supervision and Curriculum Development, National Education Association, Washington, D. C.: *Creating a Good Environment for Learning*, 1954 Yearbook, chs. I-V; *Developing Programs for Young Adolescents*, 1954, *passim; A Look at Continuity in the School Program*, 1958 Yearbook, part III; *Freeing Capacity to Learn*, 1960, *passim; Human Variability and Learning*, 1961, *passim.*
Barnard, H. W., and others, *Guidance Services in Elementary Schools* (New York: Chartwell House, 1954), *passim.*
Bennett, M. E., and Johnson, C. F., *Guidance in Groups* (New York: McGraw-Hill Book Company, Inc., 1955), *passim.*
Boardman, C. W., Douglass, H. R., and Bent, R. K., *Democratic Supervision in Secondary Schools* (Boston: Houghton Mifflin Company, 1953), chs. XI-XII, XVIII.

Bonney, M. E., *Mental Health in Education* (Boston: Allyn and Bacon, 1960), *passim*. (Emphasis on the class as a group.)

The Bulletin of the National Association of Secondary School Principals, vol. XLVIII (February, 1954), "Guidance Practices in Secondary Schools," pp. 1-159.

Burton, W. H., and Brueckner, L. J., *Supervision: A Social Process* (New York: Appleton-Century-Crofts, Inc., 1955), ch. XIV.

Cutts, N. E., and Moseley, N., *Better Home Discipline* (New York: Appleton-Century-Crofts, Inc., 1952), chs. X-XII, XVI.

Elsbree, W. S., and McNally, H. J., *Elementary School Administration and Supervision*, 2nd ed. (New York: American Book Company, 1959), chs. XII-XIII, XVIII.

Goodlad, J., *The Non Graded Elementary School* (New York: Harcourt, Brace and Company, 1959), *passim*.

Gordon, I. J., *The Teacher as a Guidance Worker* (New York: Harper and Brothers, 1956), *passim*.

Greenleaf, W. J., *Occupations and Careers* (New York: McGraw-Hill Book Company, Inc., 1955), *passim*.

Johnson, M., Jr., *et al.*, *Junior High School Guidance* (New York: Harper and Brothers, 1961), *passim*.

Kelley, J. A., *Guidance and Curriculum* (Englewood Cliffs, N. J.: Prentice-Hall, Inc., 1955), *passim*.

Knapp, R. H., *Guidance in the Elementary School* (Boston: Allyn and Bacon, 1959), *passim*.

Kowitz, G. T. and Norma G., *Guidance in the Elementary Classroom* (New York: McGraw-Hill Book Company, Inc., 1959), *passim*.

Langford, L., *Guidance of the Young Child* (New York: John Wiley and Sons, Inc., 1960), *passim*.

Loughary, J. W., *Counseling in Secondary Schools* (New York: Harper and Brothers, 1960), chs. I-III, V-VI.

McCleary, L., "Homework," *Educational Leadership*, vol. XVII (January, 1960), pp. 217-220, 225.

Miller, C. H., *Foundations of Guidance* (New York: Harper and Brothers, 1960), chs. II-IV, VII, IX-X.

NEA Journal, vol. XLVIII (September, 1959), contains a special feature on "Grouping," pp. 17-28.

Phi Delta Kappan, vol. XLI (December, 1959), contains a symposium on "Discipline and Delinquency," pp. 89-117.

Reeder, E. H., *Supervision in the Elementary School* (Boston: Houghton Mifflin Company, 1953), ch. XXI.

Research Bulletin, NEA, National Education Association, Washington, D. C.: "High School Drop-outs," vol. XXXVIII, no. 1 (February, 1960), pp. 11-14.

Robinson, F. P., *Effective Study*, rev. ed. (New York: Harper and Brothers, 1960), *passim*.

Rosecrance, F. C., and Hayden, V. D., *School Guidance and Personnel Services* (Boston: Allyn and Bacon, 1960), *passim*.

Science Research Associates, Chicago. Samples of two types of materials: "Life Adjustment Booklets" and "Better Living Booklets" to assist parents, teachers, and pupils in guidance problems; and SRA Youth Inventory, to help to identify youth's problems.

Shane, H. G., "Grouping in the Elementary School," Phi Delta Kappan, vol. XLI (April, 1960), pp. 313-319.

Strang, Ruth, "What Research Says to the Teacher," Guided Study and Homework. No. 8 in the Series (Washington, D. C.; Department of Classroom Teachers and American Educational Research Association, National Education Association, 1955).

Super, D. E., Overstreet, P. L., and others, The Vocational Maturity of Ninth-Grade Boys (New York: Teachers College, Columbia University, 1960), passim.

CHAPTER 8

Supervision of Student Activities

ONE OF THE CHARACTERISTICS of American education most striking to a foreigner is the multiplicity and variety of different activities for children which are carried on under the direction of the public schools. Frequently the foreign visitor's first question is: "Why is this activity the task of the school?" An answer to this question furnishes the basis for the existence of these activities in schools.

Sound Bases for Student Activities

So-called "extracurricular," "cocurricular," or "student" activities have received more emphasis in today's schools because of the growing complexity of our society. For this reason, school authorities have attempted recently to formulate sound bases for the establishment and control of these activities. W. H. Plemmons has clearly stated these bases many times in his classes: [1]

1. Is the activity of educational value? If so:
2. What particular community agency or agencies should have the major responsibility for the establishment and direction of this activity for children of school age?
3. If this activity should be administered and controlled by the school, on what grade levels should it come, and how can it be carried out best?

[1] Formerly a member of the faculty of the University of North Carolina, and for some time prominent in the Southern Association of Colleges and Secondary Schools; now president of Appalachian State Teachers' College, Boone, N. C.

157

CHILDREN WANT "GROUND RULES" IN ACTIVITIES

Both eminent psychologists and experts who have studied specially the growth and development of children at various ages agree that children prefer consistent rules to regulate their activities. The Gesell Institute of Child Development has pointed this out repeatedly in its reports for the last twenty years. In like manner the Association for Supervision and Curriculum Development of the National Education Association has stressed this consistency in the guidance of youth in various yearbooks. Even popular magazines have published articles on it; two successive articles in a popular weekly news magazine since midcentury call attention sharply to the desire of children for discipline through consistent rules governing pupil activities.[2] Both writers indicate that children prefer a set of rules to live by, to govern their actions; both writers also make clear that *consistency* in the formulation and administration of "rules of the game" and explanations of the reasons for the rules make children feel more secure as they conform to them. "Unpredictable discipline" and "unfairness" accounted for 30 per cent of the "major sins" of parents in the eyes of their children.

THE NEED FOR STANDARDS AND REGULATIONS FOR
STUDENT ACTIVITIES

The results of a Gallup Poll in the mid-1950's showed that 65 per cent of the adults in the nation thought that current school discipline was not strict enough; six out of every ten parents of elementary and teen-age children believed that school officials should have a right to "lick" or "spank" children in serious discipline cases. This same survey showed that both size of child and size of community were important factors in the opinions held about corporal punish-

---

[2] For recent statements from psychologists and students of child growth and development, read Arnold Gesell, *et al.*, *Youth: The Years from Ten to Sixteen* (New York: Harper and Brothers, 1956), *passim*, and especially chaps. IV-VIII; and *A Look at Continuity in the School Program*, 1958 Yearbook, Parts I and II, and *Learning and the Teacher*, 1959 Yearbook, chaps. I, II, and IV, both published by Association for Supervision and Curriculum Development, National Education Association. For reference to the two popular magazine writers, turn to David Dressler, "What Does Your Child Think of You?" *This Week Magazine* (December 5, 1954), p. 11; and Charles G. Spiegler, "How to Beat Our No. 1 School Problem: Cheating," *This Week Magazine* (December 12, 1954), pp. 11-13.

ment; the smaller the child and the smaller the community, the more agreement concerning punishment; and vice versa.[3]

This public opinion poll on school discipline points up the fact that adults as well as children feel the need for consistent standards or rules under which to live. Teachers, like pupils, feel safer if they know the set of rules, the set of values, the checks and balances under which they are operating. The supervisor should help the teacher to operate under a few sound, co-operatively identified, socially approved standards rather than attempt to set up a long list of purposes, procedures, and rules. One of the most startling and alarming developments in this connection has been the growth of sentiment in favor of "antiparent" laws.[4] The positive approach to the control of pupil activities must be taken by school personnel, community agencies, parents and pupils, through the co-operative identification of fundamental bases and values in human life.

Student Activities Defined for Supervision

The term *group activities of students* is defined here as those activities of pupils which are carried on under the control and guidance of the school in addition to or other than regular classroom activities. This definition includes, therefore, all activities of an "extracurricular," "cocurricular," "extraclass," or "student group" nature under the administration of the school on both elementary and high school levels. On the other hand, this definition excludes consideration at this time of student activities which are primarily a part of regular class or subject-matter teaching.

Teacher Training for the Sponsorship and Supervision of Group Activities

There is little evidence in the literature of any systematic training of teachers for their sponsorship of student activities. The few studies of recent date re-emphasize the need for more adequate

[3] Poll of the American Institute of Public Opinion, released to newspapers in the week of November 15-20, 1954, Princeton, New Jersey.

[4] See, for example, Jack Harrison Pollack, "Should Parents Be Punished for Their Children's Wrong Doing?" *Parents' Magazine*, vol. XXX (March, 1955), pp. 50-51, 120-25.

teacher education in this area. Millard P. Burt reported his findings in regard to 242 teachers in three counties in all kinds of schools.[5] In summary form, Burt's study showed that

1. Most of the teachers recognized the educational values in the activity program.
2. Most of the teachers were willing to sponsor activities.
3. More than 80 per cent of the teachers indicated that they supervised one or more student activities.
4. A majority indicated that they had no special training to prepare them for the activities which they sponsored.
5. Most of those teachers who indicated that they had special training to sponsor the activities which they directed, sponsored activities related to their teaching fields.
6. There was a definite relationship between the activities that were sponsored and the subjects that were taught by teachers.
7. Less than one-third of the sponsors of sports activities were physical education teachers.
8. Frequently teachers sponsored activities that supported the subject-matter offerings, which indicated the use of the activity program to improve instruction in the regular academic subjects, and also indicated a close relationship between the activity program and the rest of the curriculum.

Burt's findings pointed definitely toward the need for giving teachers and prospective teachers special training for the purposes and procedures of the activity program and for the sponsorship of specific activities. He also called attention to the fact that the exploratory and orientation purposes of an activity program are not being fully met if the activities are primarily for the support of subjects in the regular curriculum.

William S. Sterner advocated that a course or work in club sponsorship should be a part of the preservice education of teachers.[6] He also listed some colleges where such work is offered in the sponsorship of activities.

[5] Millard P. Burt, A Study of Enrichment in Terms of Teacher Qualifications and Student Activities, unpublished Ph.D thesis, University of North Carolina, 1952, chs. VI-VII.
[6] William S. Sterner, "A Blind Spot in Teacher Education?" NEA Journal, vol. XL (May, 1953), pp. 301, and "Preparing Teachers to Sponsor Activities," The Bulletin of the National Association of Secondary School Principals, vol. XXXVI (February, 1952), pp. 32-42.

Responsibility of the Supervisor in Regard to In-service Training of Teachers for Group Activities

The supervisor does not usually have direct contact with pupils in the operation of their activities; neither is he the sponsor for any of them. His responsibility is primarily that of a resource person, the consultant and advisor concerning these group activities. Since most teachers come to the schoolroom with a minimum of training as to sponsoring activities, it is a duty of the supervisor both (1) to assist in the placement of the teacher over those activities in which he is most proficient himself and (2) to help him to locate and use materials and resources in the activity areas.

THE TYPES OF ACTIVITIES A TEACHER MAY HAVE TO SPONSOR

The group activities of pupils in the schools are many in number and varied in type (Table 4). Some are activities of long standing; others are relative newcomers. Some are found more frequently on the high school level, others are more characteristic of the elementary school grades; some are found on both levels. Some emphasize individual activity more, while others are centered around the interests of the group or "gang." Some are closely related to the regularly scheduled classes or subject-matter areas; others are not. Any or all may call for teacher sponsors.

Contrary to popular belief, there have not been many fundamental changes in student activities in the last 25 years. Marie Evatt showed (1) that there has been little change in objectives, except for clarification and refining of values, (2) that most of the activities in present-day schools were in existence in *some* schools a quarter of a century ago, (3) that relatively few new student activities had been added to the program, and (4) that practically no pupil activities had been entirely dropped during the 25-year period.[7]

[7] *A Study of the Growth of High School Student Activities, 1927-1952,* unpublished master's thesis, University of North Carolina, 1952, chs. VIII-IX.

Table 4. *Types and Occurrence of Student Activities** *

In the Elementary School	In the Secondary School

Older and well-established student activities:
  The school assembly
  Intramural athletic activities (including field or play day)
  Clubs, or hobby groups
  Commencement or final promotion exercises
  Contests
  Dramatic activities
  High school day
  The homeroom and class organization
  Literary activities (debating, subject contests, and awards)
  Music activities
  P.T.A.-sponsored activities
  Parties and social events
  Preschool, orientation day
  Publications (primarily the newspaper and handbook)
  Pupil council
  Special drives and campaigns
  Trips, tours
	Older and well-established student activities:
	  The assembly (also called "chapel")
	  Athletics (interscholastic)
	  Career day
	  Clubs
	  Commencement
	  Contests
	  Dramatics and dramatic arts
	  The homeroom and class organization
	  Literary activities (societies, debating, speech)
	  Music
	  National Honor Society (Senior)
	  P.T.A. and community programs
	  Parties and social events
	  Publications (newspaper, magazine, yearbook, and handbook)
	  The student council
	  Trips
	  Youth-serving organizations (Boys' Clubs, Boy Scouts, Girl Scouts, Junior Red Cross, Camp Fire Girls, Hi-Y, and Girl Reserves—now called Y-Teens)

Newer activities:
  School banking and thrift
  School camping
  Garden clubs
  Care of memorials
  School museum
  Noon-hour activities
  Pet show
  School patrols
  School store
  Store-window publicity
  Youth-serving organizations (4-H Clubs, Little Leagues, and summer activities)
	Newer activities:
	  Alumni organizations
	  School banking
	  School camping
	  Care of memorials
	  School museum
	  National { Quill and Scroll, Beta Club (type of honor society), Junior Honor Society
	  Noon-hour activities
	  School patrols
	  School store
	  Store-window publicity
	  The *long* school trip or excursion, and exchange trip between schools
	  Youth-serving organizations (4-H Clubs, Future Farmers, or Future Homemakers of America, Boys and Girls State, Future Teachers of America, Allied Youth, Youth Hostel, and youth organizations of service clubs, such as Kiwanis, Optimist, and Rotary, or American Legion Junior Baseball)

* Arranged alphabetically and based upon the sources and references found in this chapter.

Controversial Aspects of Student Activities

Since student activities first appeared in the public schools, there have been some of controversial nature. During the years, as extracurricular activities have first been tolerated and then accepted as a part of the regular school program, three kinds continue to present persistent controversial problems to school personnel. These are national contests and activities in schools, interscholastic activities, and activities in co-operation with community and youth-serving organizations. The responsibilities of school personnel in regard to pupil activities center around the application of the principle that they should supplement rather than substitute for regular classroom activities.

NATIONAL CONTESTS AND ACTIVITIES

The only representative list of approved national contests that the writer found for the guidance of administrators, supervisors, and teachers has been prepared primarily for junior and senior high school levels, the National Association of Secondary School Principals having taken the lead in the establishment of standards for screening such contests. It is to be hoped that other responsible educational groups will undertake soon the formulation of such approved lists for the elementary grades.[8]

The list is prepared annually by the Committee on National Contests and Activities of the Association, which considers requests for placement on the list from business or industrial organizations and other agencies sponsoring national contests and activities of a nonathletic nature for youth in high schools.

The Committee has established a policy that urges all secondary schools to refuse to allow participation in unapproved national contests, except where the individual state sponsors contests of its own or has its own approved list of contests. In general, student participation, when approved: (1) allows no pupil to be absent from school more than five school days for a single contest or activity; (2) allows no high school to enter more than

---

[8] Refer to *The Bulletin of the National Association of Secondary School Principals*, vol. XLIV, No. 257 (September, 1960), pp. 138-145, for a recent, complete account of the principles and standards employed in the approval of the list, and for the approved list for 1961. This list is published annually in an issue of *The Bulletin*.

two regional or two national contests per year in which ten or more pupils are involved at the beginning, except scholarship contests; (3) permits a school to participate in only one essay or forensic contest each semester (with the proviso that fewer than five pupils in each school is not considered official school participation); and (4) allows an individual student to participate in no more than one contest in each of the classifications of approved contests and activities, with the stipulation that he may participate in more than one each if scholarships are involved. The classifications of contests and activities usually are:

Art contests	Forensic contests
Essay and writing contests	Home economics and industrial arts
Examinations	Scholarships
	Miscellaneous

There is an approved list of National Activities in which no contests are included; this list is also selected by the Committee on National Contests and Activities. On this list for 1960-61 were the following:

American National Red Cross—Junior
American Poultry Industries' Fact Finding Conference
Boys' Nation
Distributive Education Clubs of America
Freedoms Foundation
Future Business Leaders of America
Future Farmers of America
Future Homemakers of America
Girls' Nation
Junior Classical League
Key Club International
Music Educators National Conference
National Association of Student Councils
National 4-H Club Conference
National Junior Vegetable Growers Association
National Scholastic Press Association
National Science Fair
New Farmers of America
New Homemakers of America
Student Traffic Safety Program, National Education Association
The Williamsburg Student Burgesses

In checking over the types of approved national contests and awards, one notes that scholarships rank high as approved awards. Thus emphasis is placed upon the natural rewards for learning and scholastic excellence. On the other hand, the Committee questions frankly the educational value of essay contests, since the winning of awards through them has tended at times to encourage the student to be dishonest and to plagiarize.

With some such list as this at hand, school personnel have a starting point for discussion whenever any new contest is proposed for the children of the school by either a local or national group. For example, some local group may wish to present a new award, annually, to "the Best Citizen," a very difficult choice to make among the pupils in a school. Reference to the Committee's approved list of national contests will show that only one contest of this sort is listed, the Good Citizen Award of the National Society of the Daughters of the American Revolution, whereas more than a dozen different contests are approved for scholarship awards for college work.

INTERSCHOLASTIC ACTIVITIES

This term includes more activities than the highly controversial area of athletics alone. Interscholastic activities on a state or national level involve contests in six major areas: (1) athletics, (2) debating or forensics, (3) dramatics or dramatic arts, (4) music, (5) publications, and (6) subject-matter areas. Of these six, quarrels and controversies have arisen more frequently in regard to interscholastic contests in athletics and music than in the other areas.

Athletics. Since World War II there has been a tremendous expansion in the scope of intercollegiate and interscholastic athletics; at the same time, an emphasis upon specialization in athletics has developed. These two movements have forced both college and high school authorities to re-examine the functions and practices of interschool competition. This re-examination has been centered primarily around these controversial issues in athletics:

1. Is there too much emphasis upon winning and too little on the development of fine ideals of fair play and sportsmanship?
2. Do athletics tend to lower pupil and school morale and to develop false standards and attitudes hostile toward all opponents, instead of developing fine ethical standards in youth?

3. Do athletics tend to exploit children, to parade them in contests for the entertainment of the public on a commercial basis?

4. Does the school tend to lose control of its interscholastic competitive program when it accepts or approves the raising and expenditure of funds by special local groups for athletics?

5. Is the athletic program tending to upset the balance that should exist in the school's educational program? In other words, is there too much emphasis upon athletics at the expense of the subject-matter learning which is the main task of the school?

6. Is specialization in athletics good for high school students? For example, should a school be allowed to have, and keep, students practicing football in spring or summer, as well as in the fall, thus preventing them from developing other interests and skills in baseball, track, golf, and the like?

Three comprehensive studies of athletic competition for school children have been completed. Each study was made by a competent group of professional educators. The findings and recommendations of these studies are available to school personnel as *Desirable Athletic Competition for Children* (1952), *School Athletics: Problems and Policies* (1954), and *Current Administrative Problems: Athletics, Health Education, Physical Education, Recreation* (1960). The supervisor should have these three reports [9] and should be thoroughly familiar with their full recommendations, which are here summarized in part:

For Children of Elementary and Junior High School Age	*For Pupils of Senior High School Age*
Instruction in physical education for all	"Meaningful" competition is desirable
Voluntary informal recreation	Intramural play and sports
Intramural activities	"Extramural" competition in games
Play days and informal games	and sports for all boys and girls
A few invitational and informal contests appropriate to the level of maturity, interests, and skills of growing children	on all levels of skill
	Play days and sports days
	Interscholastic competition for the skilled, more for boys than girls
Avoidance of high-pressure practices of interscholastic nature	
Provision for the athletic needs of both boys and girls	

[9] All available from the National Education Association. Read also Norman Schactor, "The Administrator, the Coach, and the Riot," *California Journal of Secondary Education,* vol. XXXV (March, 1960), pp. 155-160.

In addition, there is consensus among educators that (1) school authorities should establish policies for athletics, (2) athletics should be a part of the school program, (3) athletics should be supervised by competently trained school personnel, and (4) the natural awards of competition are more effective than such artificial awards as "player of the year," or "player who contributed most to team play."

Music Activities. There is controversy over music activities, too, primarily because of differing purposes and practices. For example, in one school piano instruction is given by teachers employed by the school; in another, it is given by private teachers who use school instruments and space. In one school the major emphasis is upon instrumental music and band work, which require considerable financing for instruments and uniforms from time to time; in another school the emphasis is upon vocal music. In the elementary school, rhythmics, singing, and dancing are important; in the high school the orchestra may be considered more valuable.

Much of the music instruction is expensive; when large groups participate, as they do in glee clubs, bands, and choruses, it is expensive to equip them and to transport them to all the places and functions where they are invited to perform. The supervisor's responsibilities in this controversial area can be summed up simply in answers to two questions:

1. What is the school's policy concerning extramural activities of its musical organizations?
2. In line with the policy of the school, how can this activity be supervised most effectively?

ACTIVITIES IN CO-OPERATION WITH COMMUNITY AND YOUTH-SERVING ORGANIZATIONS

This group of activities sometimes gives the supervisor his biggest headache because of the tremendous increase in demands upon the schools by outside groups and organizations. The problem of how much aid to accept for student activities from outside agencies is complicated by the facts that many of the projects are worthy and are of educational value and their sponsors offer financial resources which the school does not possess. For example, if the Junior Chamber of Commerce wants to raise $5,000 for uniforms for the members of the elementary and high school bands, it seems perfectly all right to use both bands for parties, parades, and activities connected with the fund-raising. Later, the same JC's ask the school for use of the bands for a parade for the JC State Convention. Should the school give permission for such extramural use of the band?

Here, again, the supervisor should recall the sound bases for student activities listed at the beginning of this chapter. If the activity is of sound educational value, whose responsibility is it? If it is the school's responsibility, the school personnel should be responsible for it. If it is the responsibility of some organization in the community, the supervision should be carried on by that organization, not by the school. If it is an activity sponsored jointly by the school *and* some community or national organization, the school should define its responsibility for both sponsoring and supervising and should insist that both parties fulfill their responsibilities.

Developing Trends in Group Activities

As a consultant, advisor, and resource person to the teacher on group activities of pupils, the supervisor has to keep abreast of developing trends. In summary form, and without regard to order of importance, there is evidence of the following trends in the modern public school: [10]

1. States seem to be developing high school activity associations for better control of interscholastic contests. This trend is in line with the movement at the national level for such control, as exemplified by the various committees of the National Association of Secondary School Principals and by the National Federation of State High School Athletic Associations. One example of such action is furnished by the Ohio High School Activity Association, organized in 1948 by the Ohio High School Principals Association. Its main duties are concerned with events of an interscholastic nature, except athletics, involving more than two schools. Another example is the adoption by the North Carolina State Board of Education in 1952 of "Regulations Governing Athletics in Public Schools of North Caro-

[10] Consult the special bibliography at the end of the chapter for definite references or sources of information on these trends.

lina," in effect state control of this type of interscholastic activity for boys and girls.

2. Activities of the pupil (safety) patrol now are being worked out carefully with local police and traffic officers. Such plans will prevent the placement of minors in dangerous positions of traffic enforcement for which they have insufficient training, judgment, and authority.

3. School personnel and co-operating agencies now tend to recognize "Best Citizens" each year, instead of trying to pick a single boy or girl as "Best Citizen."

4. There is less emphasis upon establishment of a "point system" for students for participation in activities. Experience has shown that careful planning, guidance, and supervision of activities, especially in large high schools, encourage students to participate up to capacity, instead of beyond individual capacity.

5. The "United Fund" idea for charity drives in schools is gaining wide approval. Under this plan, the particular school or school system carries on its own "drive" for all charities on one day in September or October; the money thus raised among the pupils is allocated to the various national and local campaigns on a percentage basis determined by a committee of both pupils and faculty.

6. The policy has become fairly well established for public schools to take little, if any, part in the celebration of "special weeks" or "days" to promote this type of business or that type of behavior. There are more than a hundred of these special weeks or days or months now, and more seem to be added each year. Exceptions to this trend are special programs for Thanksgiving, Easter, Christmas, Fire Prevention Week, American Education Week, Halloween, Armistice Day, May Day, Mother's Day, Memorial Day, and Flag Day.

7. The accounting for student activity funds now is usually under a faculty member, properly bonded; funds all go into a central account controlled by school authorities, and payments are made from them only upon proper authorization.

8. In the case of fees charged for student activities, the trend is for a fee as small as possible, in order not to drive children of the poor out of participation and membership.

9. The "activity period" in the school schedule for student activities is being used more and more for voluntary pupil activities and less and less for compulsory participation.

10. Legally, traditionally, and in fairness to all students, secret social fraternities have no place in a public school. Twenty-five states prohibit them by law.

11. The student council continues to grow as one of the best ways to develop concepts and practices of democracy and citizenship.
12. The practice of extra pay to faculty sponsors for extra work in student activities continues to grow, but such extra pay is usually confined to activities that take place after the close of regular school hours. This trend is growing in the face of questioning of its wisdom.
13. Faculty sponsors of activities are being selected primarily because of special interest in the activity, training in it, and willingness to work extra hours on it.
14. In some sections, as in California and Florida, there is a growing trend to have interscholastic athletics in the afternoon after school and to make admission free to all pupils. The parents are welcome if they want to come, but the plan places emphasis upon participation and student spectator status.
15. Evaluation of student activities is growing in popularity. Instruments are being devised for evaluation by both students and school faculties, such as questionnaires with open-end questions, check lists, and rating scales. Such evaluation tends to improve activity programs.
16. School personnel seldom give out a complete list of graduating seniors to any persons except reputable newsmen and educational authorities. This policy prevents the list of names from falling into the hands of unscrupulous racketeers who use the lists to circularize these youngsters on special commercial ventures.
17. Any funds raised by community agencies for a school activity are turned over to the regular school authorities for expenditures for the activity for which it was raised.
18. The trend among the states is to forbid, or to discourage postseason and "all-star" games.
19. "Training" periods for students who are elected to pupil activity offices are becoming more common.

Problems for Individual Study and Class Discussion

1. Why do modern educators seem to prefer the term *student activities* instead of *extracurricular activities?* In what way does this terminology reflect a newer philosophy of education?
2. At what age do children naturally become interested in clubs? What is the developmental task that children are trying to master with this urge to organize clubs?
3. A sound student activity can lose value because of the overdomination of the sponsoring teacher. Could the supervisor come to the aid of such an activity? How might he proceed?

4. How can the supervisor help students and teachers to discontinue an activity or an organization after it has served its purpose and is no longer needed?
5. Are pupils wise enough and responsible enough to plan their own activities? Why or why not?
6. Is there a difference between "student participation in school government" and "student self-government" in schools? Support your position.
7. As supervisor of a 25-teacher high school, you have five new teachers who have had no previous training in how to sponsor student activities. Each is assigned to sponsor one (different) student activity this year. How will you go about training them "on the job"?
8. Are teachers' own hobbies frequently indexes of the types of activities that they should sponsor? Why or why not?
9. Are interschool contests, such as sports, music, or dramatics, natural or artificial motivating forces for boys and girls? Explain.
10. If a new contest such as a poster contest is proposed for the children in your elementary grades, how would you and your teachers decide whether to give it your approval or not?
11. Why are interscholastic activities harder to supervise than intraschool activities? Explain.
12. Would a "co-operating community committee on school activities" be a sound idea for your school? Why or why not?
13. How rich a program of student activities would you desire for the schools you are going to supervise? Explain.
14. Should sponsorship of a student activity count as part of a teacher's load, or not? Explain.

The relative stability of types of student activities in the schools makes it a simpler matter for the supervisor to help the teacher in this area than one might think. This is true because certain writers and professional educational groups have set forth the values and prevailing practices in regard to student activities from time to time. The following Special Annotated Bibliography has therefore been prepared to provide the supervisor with a representative list of helpful books and articles.

The list is arranged alphabetically by author or source with three types of sources included: comprehensive books and bibliographies; periodicals; and books, bulletins, and handbooks on special aspects.

Special Annotated Bibliography of Basic Sources of Information for the Supervisor of Group Activities

COMPREHENSIVE BOOKS AND BIBLIOGRAPHIES

Detjen, E. W., and Detjen, M. F., *Elementary School Guidance* (New York: McGraw-Hill Book Company, Inc., 1952). They present naturally many aspects of activities in the group-guidance approach; it is especially valuable for its bibliographies.

Frederick, R. W., *The Third Curriculum: Student Activities in American Education* (New York: Appleton-Century-Crofts, Inc., 1959), presents his philosophy that this "Third Curriculum" should receive the same attention as that devoted to the required and elective curricula. Types of activities, their functions, and their management are discussed.

Gruber, F. C., and Beatty, T. B., *Secondary School Activities* (New York: Mc-Graw-Hill Book Company, Inc., 1954). Sets forth the place and justification for activities in the high school; offers specific helps for sponsors in establishing, carrying on, and evaluating student activities; its annotated bibliographies are extensive and comprehensive.

The High School Journal, School of Education, University of North Carolina, Chapel Hill. The issues of October and November, 1954 (Vol. XXXVIII, nos. 1 and 2) present a well-selected, comprehensive, annotated bibliography on all aspects of student activities, "Extraclass Activities, 1950-1953," by Ellsworth Thompkins and Walter H. Gaumnitz, of the U. S. Department of Health, Education, and Welfare, pp. 23-29 and 62-69.

Johnston, E. G., and Faunce, R. C., *Student Activities in Secondary Schools* (New York: The Ronald Press Company, 1952). A reconsideration and also a type of reappraisal of student activities; presents the point of view that classroom and out-of-classroom learnings alike enrich the pupil's program if properly tried out, administered, and evaluated. The bibliographies are annotated.

Kilzer, L. R., and others, *Allied Activities in the Secondary School* (New York: Harper and Brothers, 1956). Presents the philosophy of "allied" student activities, types, participation, and problems of financing.

McKown, H. C., *Activities in the Elementary School* (New York: McGraw-Hill Book Company, Inc., 1938). Though this book is considered "old" by many educators, its completeness and simple explanations in regard to activities on the elementary school level have perhaps not been equaled by any later publication in this area.

McKown, H. C., *Extracurricular Activities,* 3rd ed. (New York: The Macmillan Company, 1952). Presents at midcentury the author's views and research, which may be compared with his findings over the 25-year period, in his first and second editions; the list of activities is rather complete.

Miller, F. A., and others, *Planning School Activities* (Englewood Cliffs, N. J.: Prentice-Hall, Inc., 1956). Orientation to the area of the cocurriculum and representative practices from all over the country, most from junior and senior high schools.

PERIODICALS

To help the sponsoring teacher or youth-serving organization which is involved in an activity, the supervisor should be familiar with this list of magazines or publications on one activity or another. The periodicals contain helpful suggestions both for the sponsor and the pupils.

National Education Association:
Department of Elementary School Principals: Thirty-third Yearbook, *The Elementary Principal, Guidance for Today's Children* (1954). Looks at formal guidance and guidance activities in the elementary school; offers a large variety of experiences to the teacher, supervisor, and administrator, including the role of the principal and the teacher, the use of specialists, and especially guidance through pupil activities, chap. VII.
National Association of Secondary School Principals: *The Bulletin of the National Association of Secondary School Principals, Vitalizing Student Activities in the Secondary School*, vol. XXXVI, no. 184 (February, 1952). Over 200 pages devoted to problems, values, sponsorship, and types of activities, including contests and finances. This special edition of *The Bulletin* continues a service performed periodically by the Association for junior and senior high school personnel since the early 1940's.
The Allied Youth, 1709 M. Street, N. W., Washington 6, D. C. Allied Youth has worked in schools on a program of alcohol education since the 1930's. This magazine contains basic information and program suggestions for alcohol education.
American Junior Red Cross Journal (for high schools) and *American Junior Red Cross News* (for elementary schools), American Red Cross, Washington 13, D. C.
The Beta Club Journal, Spartanburg, S. C. Official magazine of the Beta Club (an honor society).
Boys' Club Bulletin, Boys' Clubs of America, 381 Fourth Avenue, New York 16, N. Y. Official organ of this national association of local clubs for boys.
Catholic School Editor, Catholic School Press Association, Marquette University, Milwaukee. Organ of this association for student publishers and publications.
Dramatics, College Hill Station, Cincinnati 24, Ohio. Official magazine of the National Thespian Society, for teachers, directors, and students of dramatic arts.
Girl Scout Leader, 155 East Forty-Fourth Street, New York 17, N. Y. Guide for the Girl Scouts.
Hi-Y Ways, 291 Broadway, New York 7, N. Y. The official magazine of the National Hi-Y Fellowship.
National 4H News, 59 East Van Buren Street, Chicago 5, Illinois. Publication of the National Committee on Boys and Girls Club Work.
Quill and Scroll, 111 West Jackson Boulevard, Chicago 4, Illinois. Official publication of the National Association of Journalism Directors and the International Honorary Society for High School Journalists.
Scholastic Corporation Magazines, 33 West Forty-Second Street, New York 36, N. Y.: *Junior Scholastic, Senior Scholastic, Scholastic Coach, Scholastic Teacher*. For teachers, supervisors, and administrators, both for some subject-matter areas and for student activities.
Scholastic Editor, University of Minnesota, Minneapolis 14, Minnesota. Official

organ of the National Scholastic Press Association, on all aspects of scholastic journalism.

School Activities, 1041 New Hampshire Street, Laurence, Kansas. Edited by H. C. McKown for 25 years, this has become known as the national extracurricular magazine for both elementary and high school.

School Press Review, Low Memorial Library, Columbia University, New York 27, N. Y. Official publication of the Columbia Scholastic Press Association.

Scouting, National Council, Boy Scouts of America, New Brunswick, N. J. This is the Scout leader's official magazine.

Student Life, 1201 Sixteenth Street, N. W., Washington 6, D. C. A magazine sponsored by the National Association of Secondary School Principals in connection with the National Honor Society and devoted to projects of service clubs in high schools.

BOOKS, BULLETINS, AND HANDBOOKS ON SPECIAL ASPECTS

There are many of these. This list, however, is limited primarily to those which are (1) written by educational authorities, (2) published by professional education groups, or (3) published by groups and youth-serving organizations generally approved by schools for co-operative work with children. The list is arranged alphabetically by titles.

The Activity Period in Public High Schools, Superintendent of Documents, Washington. Purposes, practices, and trends in scheduling and use of the activity period.

The American Citizens Handbook, National Education Association, 1201 Sixteenth Street, N. W. Washington 6, D. C. A source book for all school personnel, including pupils.

"The Assembly Program in the Secondary School," *The Bulletin of the National Association of Secondary School Principals,* vol. XXX, no. 141 (November, 1946), pp. 2-227. Whole issue is devoted to purposes, planning, practices, changes and trends, problems, materials, and ways to evaluate.

Athletics: Desirable Athletic Competition for Children (1952). National Education Association, 1201 Sixteenth Street, N. W., Washington, D. C. Joint Committee report and recommendations on athletics competition for children of elementary and junior high school age. Prepared by the American Association for Health, Physical Education, and Recreation; Society of State Directors of Health, Physical Education, and Recreation; National Council of State Consultants in Elementary Education; and Department of Elementary School Principals, N.E.A.

AYH Handbook and Hostelers Manual, American Youth Hostels, 14 West 8th Street, New York, 11, N. Y. Directed toward vacation and travel activities for youth at reasonable expense.

The Camp Counselor, by R. A. Benson and J. A. Goldberg (New York: McGraw-Hill Book Company, Inc., 1951). Responsibilities, need for preparation, types of duties and problems, standards—a book for in-service training.

"Camping and Outdoor Education," *The Bulletin of the National Association of Secondary School Principals*, vol. XXXI, no. 147 (May, 1947), pp. 5-136.

Camping Magazine, 343 South Dearborn Street, Chicago 4, Illinois. Official journal of the American Camping Association, with special issues from time to time on aspects such as reference materials and buying guides.

Developing Citizenship Through School Activities (1949), by L. M. Shufelt, ed., National Council for the Social Studies, 1201 Sixteenth Street, N. W., Washington 6, D. C.

"Dramatics in the Secondary School," *The Bulletin of the National Association of Secondary School Principals*, vol. XXXIII, no. 166 (December, 1949), pp. 4-182. The place and status of dramatic arts, materials, methods, practices, and problems.

Driver Education and Training Manual for High School Teachers, American Automobile Association, Washington, D. C. Editions revised and issued periodically.

Extraclass Activities for All Pupils, by E. Tompkins (Washington, D. C.: Superintendent of Documents, Government Printing Office, Office of Education, 1950). Responsibilities of school personnel for organization, programming, supervision, and evaluation of extraclass activities.

Future Teachers of America, Annual *Yearbook*, and *The Future Teacher*, National Education Association, 1201 Sixteenth Street, N. W., Washington 6, D. C. Source book for both teacher and pupils, and newsletter for FTA members, respectively.

Guiding Homeroom and Club Activities, by Ruth Fedder (New York: McGraw-Hill Book Company, Inc., 1949). For the teacher of younger and older adolescents, full of ideas and suggestions.

Handbook of the National Beta Club, Spartanburg, S. C. Official publication of this achievement-service organization for students in state-accredited high schools.

Handbook of the National Honor Society of Secondary Schools, National Association of Secondary School Principals, 1201 Sixteenth Street, Washington 6, D. C. Describes the history, purposes, organization, and programs of the Senior and Junior Societies.

High School Journalism, rev. ed., by H. Spears and C. H. Lawshe (New York: The Macmillan Company, Inc., 1949). A sample textbook for high school students.

Hi-Y Today, by R. C. Hamlin, A Report of the National Study of the Hi-Y and Tri-Hi-Y movement (New York: Association Press, 1955). The contributions of the Hi-Y Organization and a re-evaluation of its purposes and activities in line with the needs of youth.

Home Room Guidance, 2nd ed., by H. C. McKown (New York: McGraw-Hill Book Company, Inc., 1946). Philosophy and purposes, organization and guidance programs and activities, and evaluation.

How to Cover, Write and Edit Sports, by H. E. Heath, Jr., and L. Gelfand

(Ames: The Iowa State College Press, 1951). A "how-to-do-it" publication for the sports journalist who wants to do a good job.

Journalism and the Student Publication (New York: Harper and Brothers, 1951). Text and source book for high schools.

Manual for FTA Clubs in High Schools, National Education Association, 1201 Sixteenth Street, N. W., Washington 6, D. C. For teachers and students.

National Federation of State High School Athletic Associations Handbook, 7 South Dearborn Street, Chicago 3, Illinois. History, purposes, publications, constitution, regulations for boys and girls. Also publishes seasonally the rules for various sports sponsored and controlled by the Association for boys and girls.

The 1953 Commencement Manual, National Association of Secondary School Principals, 1201 Sixteenth Street, N. W., Washington 6, D. C. Suggestions, practices, programs, and scripts.

Public School Camping, by J. M. Clarke (Stanford: Stanford University Press, 1951). California's pilot project, purposes, administration and planning, curricula, relation to home.

Pupil Patrols in Elementary and Secondary Schools, NEA Research Bulletin, vol. XXVIII, no. 1 (February, 1950). Use, types, school liability and policies.

"The Role of Speech in the Secondary School," *The Bulletin of the National Association of Secondary School Principals*, vol. XXIX, no. 133 (November, 1945). Curricula, activities, including dramatics, motion picture, radio, and the extracurriculum program.

School Athletics: Problems and Policies (1954). Educational Policies Commission, 1201 Sixteenth Street, N. W., Washington 6, D. C. The Commission's careful three-year study of athletics, the problems involved, and types of programs recommended for elementary, junior high, and senior high school levels.

School Camping, Association for Supervision and Curriculum Development, National Education Association (1954). The movement, types of programs for pupils and for teachers, problems, and values.

School Review, University of Chicago. Selected bibliographies on the extracurriculum from time to time.

So You Were Elected! by V. Bailard and H. C. McKown (New York: McGraw-Hill Book Company, Inc., 1946). Source book for training of student officers and personnel in high school.

Spiritual Values in the Elementary School, 26th Yearbook, Department of Elementary School Principals, National Education Association, vol. XXVII, no. 1 (September, 1947). Group experiences, and relations with other organizations and institutions in this area.

The Student Council, by H. C. McKown (New York: McGraw-Hill Book Company, Inc., 1944). Complete source book for teacher and pupils.

The Student Council in the Secondary School and *Student Council Yearbook*, both published by the National Association of Student Councils, which is sponsored by the National Association of Secondary School Principals. Regular handbooks for sponsors, students, and school personnel.

Student Councils in Action, by L. A. Kirkendall and F. R. Zeran (New York: Chartwell House, 1953). A critical commentary on councils as student-participation agencies and on the basic philosophy of pupil participation as exemplified through the student council.

Student Councils for Our Times, by J. Smith (New York: Bureau of Publications, Teachers College, Columbia University, 1951). Principles, status, practices for sound work in this activity.

Vitalized Assemblies, by N. Z. Thompson (New York: E. P. Dutton and Company, Inc., 1952). Primarily for junior and senior high schools; many of the types in the 200 programs could be used in some elementary grades.

Your School Clubs, by N. Z. Thompson (New York: E. P. Dutton and Company, Inc., 1953). A guide to 500 activities for group leaders and members. For junior and senior high schools.

Youth-serving Organizations: National Nongovernmental Associations, 3rd ed., by M. M. Chambers (Washington, D. C.: American Council on Education, 1948). An indispensable source for the teacher of the types and purposes of youth organizations sponsored by community and national groups ranging in variety from service clubs and religious groups to special organizations such as the Boy Scouts or Camp Fire Girls.

CHAPTER 9

Helping Teachers with Evaluation

EVALUATION IS OF PRIME IMPORTANCE IN TEACHING, and yet, most teachers are stronger in techniques of teaching than they are in techniques of evaluation. The teacher's lack of familiarity with methods of appraising pupils' work stems from a variety of causes. In the first place, the colleges give teacher-candidates little training in appraising pupil progress. In the second place, most of the training that is given is concerned with pupil achievement in subject-matter courses, not with other aspects of growth and development, such as progress in oral expression, social adjustment, reading for enjoyment, and critical thinking. In the third place, neither the colleges nor the school systems have developed universally satisfactory instruments for measuring such intangibles. And lastly, evaluation too often still involves measurement of the achievement of one pupil in terms of the achievement of the average and the best pupils in the group, rather than in terms of how much progress the individual has made from the point at which he started.

The Purposes of Evaluation

Life tests human beings as they grow up. For example, the baby wants the bright red ball on the low stool; he cannot reach it; he tries to do so, and eventually this trying results in his crawling and reaching it. He has met the test successfully at last, after trying and failing many times to reach the ball. In like manner, life puts every boy, every girl, through a series of tests from time to time. As the children try to meet the tests, they sometimes fail; but as

178

often as they "pass the test," they tend to become more used to success and better oriented to life and its tasks. In this process of life's tests, we all fail one test or another, at one time or another; that failure is part and parcel of life's plan.

Just as life sets test after test for each one, so does the school set such tests for its pupils. The major uses of tests in evaluation might be classified for our purposes here into two types:

A. *For Diagnosis and Guidance*
  (These purposes have been discussed adequately in Chapter 7.)
  1. Diagnosis and analysis of students, including classification
  2. Basis for guidance—educational, vocational, social, and personal
  3. Prognosis—for prediction of probable success
  4. Establishment of standards, norms, or goals of achievement for a year of work, a grade, or a group

B. *For Pupil Achievement and Teacher Improvement*
  (These purposes will be analyzed and presented in this chapter.)
  1. Appraisal of pupil progress: pupil evaluation, pupil promotion and failure
  2. Promotion policies and school promotion systems
  3. Record keeping and reporting. Reports to parents, to other school personnel, and to pupils on the quality and amount of work being accomplished by students
  4. Self-evaluation of teaching, and how it can motivate the teaching-learning situation and improve the teacher's teaching

Appraisal of Pupil Progress

In order to evaluate a pupil's progress, the teacher has to have a point of departure with which he can compare the progress that the pupil has made over a period of time. That point of departure should be (1) the amount of knowledge a pupil possesses when he comes into that particular class or grade for the first time and (2) those attitudes, habits, patterns of conduct, and ideals the pupil possesses when he enters that grade or class for the first time. With information on these two aspects, the teacher can appraise pupil growth with a fair degree of accuracy. But it should be noted that neither of these two bases for appraisal—his amount of knowledge and his attitudes and habits—involves comparison of the individual pupil with the group; instead, both involve comparison with the individual himself and his growth from the point at which he entered this class. How can the teacher explain this growth to pupils? To parents? To other school personnel?

GRADING AND MARKING PUPILS

Tradition has been the prime factor controlling the marking of pupils over the centuries. In the days before much was known about how a child grows and develops, it was a simple matter for the teacher to grade a pupil on his progress in subject matter alone, especially if the basis of measurement had been established by units or figures from 1 to 100. This system of "grading a pupil's work" as 70 per cent on this scale, or 90 per cent, worked little hardship on the pupil as long as teaching remained on an individual basis. The "margin of error" was simply what is always present when one individual attempts to "rate" another—and as long as the same person continued to do the rating, this margin remained, but it remained an individual margin. When two or more teachers began to rate or mark the same pupil, however, conditions changed; whereas the idea of comparison of progress with other pupils had not entered before, it was now an important factor in assigning grades. For this reason, we have to turn to a consideration of the variability and subjectivity of school marks.

School marks as frequently given are decidedly unreliable.[1] There are reasons for this: (1) Different teachers in the same school have different bases for marking; (2) Some teachers try to measure only the actual performance of a pupil; (3) Other teachers attempt to measure performance in the light of a pupil's ability; (4) Some teachers count effort, general behavior, and attitude in evaluating a pupil's performance; (5) In some cases, emphasis is placed upon the pupil's ability to reproduce the materials of the course; in other cases, pupil initiative and ability to make applications of what has been learned are stressed; (6) Good written English is important in some tests; in others, speed is emphasized; and finally (7) School marks may vary because of the mental, physical, and emotional state of the teacher at the time of the scoring of a test or the

---

[1] For a summary of earlier research in regard to school marks, consult J. Minor Gwynn, *Curriculum Principles and Social Trends,* 3rd ed. (New York: The Macmillan Company, 1960), pp. 459-462; for evaluation as the broader concept of measurement, pp. 462-470.

giving of a grade, or they may vary according to how his standards vary from those of other teachers.

It is important for school personnel to realize that we "fell into" the easiest way of grading and marking pupils when we began to bestow school marks on the basis of comparison of the achievement of the poorest pupil with the achievement of the brightest student. This easy way of marking the progress of pupils was strengthened and more firmly established by our misapplication of the findings of the specialists in testing after 1925. These test specialists showed us from their research that *if an adequate sample of the normal pupil population were taken at any one grade level,* there would result *a normal curve of distribution* of intelligence from the very bright to the very dull. We as school personnel have sometimes used this normal distribution curve improperly as the "norm" in every class—according to which we must award a certain percentage of "A's," "B's," "C's," "D's," and "F's," regardless of the individual abilities of our very narrow sampling in a class of 25 to 40. In other words, we have adopted as the basis for our marking of pupils an *assumed normal distribution* of native ability which never exists in such a small group as 50. Therefore, our awarding of school marks by comparison on the assumption of a normal distribution in each class is an unsound procedure and should be given up for a better way of arriving at school marks or grades.

STEPS IN PUPIL EVALUATION

There are three fundamental steps in the evaluation of any pupil's progress: (1) establishing the pupil's starting point in order to determine the purposes to be accomplished in a particular group or class; (2) employment of various devices to evaluate the methods used by the teacher and the pupils in achieving their purposes; (3) making the final evaluation of pupil outcomes and growth, and checking these against the purposes that were determined.

1. Establishing the pupil's starting point in order to determine the purposes to be accomplished in a particular group or class. For many years teachers assumed that the purposes of schoolwork were well known to both parents and pupils. For example, the main purpose of the work in grade 3 was to continue and enlarge upon the work done in grade 2; or the main purposes in algebra were to master a new tool and to prepare students for college. In like manner, the teacher assumed that the pupil was prepared for grade 3 because he had passed grade 2; or that the ninth grader was ready to begin algebra because he had passed his arithmetic in grade 8.

The intelligent teacher in today's schools goes about evaluation in a different manner. Of course he "hopes" that the boy who finished the eighth grade is well enough grounded in his mathematics fundamentals to start algebra successfully; but this modern teacher wants to "make sure" that the boy has sufficient preparation, in order for him to go forward without loss of time and effort. So he prepares and administers to the boy a pretest on mathematics, including the four fundamental processes, fractions and inversion, decimals, factoring, and problems involving arithmetic reasoning as well as computation. He follows up after the pretest with a conference or two, to confirm whether the answers to the pretest were accurate. From these pretesting procedures both the teacher and the pupil have a starting point from which to measure the growth and progress of this pupil as he begins algebra. The pretests help to take the guesswork out of evaluation by furnishing a base for the measurement of achievement; they also allow a student who already knows some algebra to start from that point, instead of repeating material he has already mastered.

On the elementary school level, the teacher likewise discovers *where* the pupil is when he comes into grade 3 from grade 2. What is John's reading level? His speed in reading? His comprehension? What kind of a vocabulary does he possess? How far advanced is he in number work? How well can he write, or is he handicapped in this respect? What knowledge of natural and applied science does he have, and what interest in them? What are his health habits and concepts? Does he like music? Is he "good with his hands"? Interested in tools, drawing, and building? In one way or another the third-grade teacher discovers quickly about all of these kinds of learning and growth and marks them down as starting points for his appraisal of John's progress in grade 3. In one instance he asks John to describe his trip to Canada during the preceding summer; in another, to write down a record of the class's planning for the week; and in still another, to copy a short poem on the board. By these different methods the teacher pinpoints John's writing, John's spelling, John's difficulties or strengths in this broad area of fundamental skills. In another instance, the teacher wants to discover John's familiarity with nature and with the scientific world around him. From the sharing periods during the first weeks he finds that John is crazy about airplanes, riding them, seeing them, studying them; he is even beginning to construct them; as a matter of fact, John may be far in advance of the rest of the class in this respect, able to work alone at certain times on his airplane models. On the other hand, by observation at lunch time and recess periods, the teacher may find John to be far behind the rest of the group in good health habits, knowledge of balance in diet, and of the values of sleep and rest for a fast-growing youngster.

Gradually, in various ways, the teacher in grade 3 learns rather accurately about the status of John's development when he came to school in September. Some of these facts the teacher learned by observation; some by conversation with John; some by tests which the teacher gave; some by obtaining samples of John's work, as of his writing or vocabulary; and some from the "sharing," and "free-time" periods for the children. Also, this identification of John's stage of learning and development when he first came to grade 3 is not all done in one day. John is going to be with this teacher all year; it is important in fairness to him that the teacher make an accurate estimate of *where he was in his achievement* when he came into the grade. The teacher will therefore take two or three weeks, sometimes a month, to discover exactly where John is, using the methods which have just been described.

Supervisors are asked by teachers from time to time why standard achievement tests could not be used at the beginning of the year for the pretest purposes which have been discussed here. Achievement tests can be used, provided the teacher realizes the limitations of these tests for pretest purposes. For example, if rapport exists between the teacher and the individual pupil, standard achievement tests can give the teacher accurate, comparative information on John's reading and language skills; on his spelling and vocabulary; on his arithmetic or mathematics skills and reasoning; on his knowledge and information in social studies, science, health and safety; and on his ability to follow directions, to use reference skills, and to reason and interpret. But standard achievement tests will *not* give the teacher adequate information and data for a starting point with John on his written and his oral language; on his personality traits and attitudes; on his special, as compared to his general interests; on his environment and his cultural and social patterns; and on his characteristics as a fast or slow worker.

Another difficulty arises when a teacher attempts to employ standard achievement tests as pretests for his classwork. This difficulty stems from the different ways of teaching of different teachers, each of which can be successful in use. For example, the teacher in grade 6 may be an exponent of the value and success of teacher-pupil planning in the classroom. In the course of this planning together, the teacher and pupils may decide on a unit or center of interest for about four weeks, namely, "Transportation and Communication." The planning and carrying out of this unit may originally include primarily the development of means of transportation and communication from ancient times to the present. The pretest would consequently have been mostly on these aspects.

As the group becomes more and more interested in the unit, however, the teacher and pupils expand it to include traffic problems in a modern world, safety in transportation, the future of the railroads, and the additional possibilities of jet propulsion. For this greatly expanded unit, the original pretest would have had to be expanded as the group planned and added to it from day to day. For this sort of "teacher-pupil planned" unit the standard achievement test is not adequate either in terms of scope or the changed purposes of the unit. It may be stated fairly that standard achievement tests can be employed satisfactorily as pretests on segments or units of work in which the "content-to-be-mastered" remains the same from year to year, as is true in the "prepping" of high school students for the examinations of the College Entrance Examination Board, or for state-wide standard tests. They will be largely inadequate for the establishment of the purposes in teaching by individual teachers for meeting individual differences of pupils.

2. Employment of various devices to evaluate the methods used by the teacher and the pupils in achieving their purposes. This second fundamental step in evaluation may involve the employment of all sorts of evaluative devices, each for a particular purpose. The main idea here is to help to identify the measuring instrument which more nearly will attain the particular purpose which the teacher has in mind. In general, there are several types of devices which the teacher may use in this second step.

1. *For drill.* The main purpose of the teacher during this type

of exercise is to help the pupil to master some fundamental skill or work habit. This instrument should be selected for this particular purpose; and it should be used only to measure acquisition of that skill. For example, the teacher wants to test a child's improvement in handwriting. To do this, the test chosen should involve (1) a previous sample of the pupil's handwriting as a pattern, or standard; (2) a new sample of handwriting of the same general type, such as a description or a poem; and (3) a comparison of the two samples to note improvements in the formation of words, in cursive transition from one letter to another, in balance, and in legibility. The handwriting test is not a test of other aspects of a pupil's work in language arts and the teacher should not attempt in the same test to grade the pupil on such additional points as spelling accuracy, use of singulars and plurals, punctuation, and clarity of thought and expression; these are items to be tested with another particular kind of test.

Another example can be taken from mathematics, whether upon the elementary or secondary school level. If one is testing for mastery of fundamental processes in drill, then the test should be devised for that particular purpose, for example, a test on addition or multiplication. In this case, it is of doubtful value to compel a child (1) to solve a problem involving reasoning, and (2) to use such fundamental skills as addition and multiplication in the solution of it, and then mark the pupil off if he fails to get them correct. In this case, the teacher should set up "problem-solving" as the main purpose, rather than mastery and drill upon fundamental skills; and then the teacher should give the pupil partial credit for his computation work as far as the pupil carries it to completion.

2. *For recognition and recall.* This type of test is closely related to the old-fashioned, so-called "mastery" test. The main purpose is to see whether a pupil has mastered facts or information adequately enough to recall and identify the item when it is brought again to his mind. A sample of this kind of test would be contained in either of these questions:

Q. All of these factors except one operated to cause the War of 1861. Star (*) that factor:

( ) *a.* Slavery
( ) *b.* John Brown's raid

( ) *c.* States' Rights
( ) *d.* The admission of the State of Minnesota to the Union
( ) *e.* The labor struggle between the South and the West and North

Q. Identify these people or events during the Civil War:

a. "Stonewall" Jackson
b. Manassas
c. Jefferson Davis
d. Gettysburg
e. Sherman
f. Sheridan
g. Fort Sumter

In the recognition and recall question, the teacher is testing more for memory acquisition than for reasoning or synthesis. Therefore, the questions should be phrased so that they probe more for mastery of facts than for reasoning. For example, the following question would not be driving at the main purpose of recognition or recall and should be discarded:

Q. Discuss the main reasons for the Civil War.

As a matter of fact, this question is so vague and takes in so much ground without reasonable limits that it should either be discarded as a poor question, or else broken up into two or three more definite questions prepared for purposes of testing reasoning.

3. *For reasoning.* In order to test the pupil's ability to reason, let us recast the question just under discussion:

Former Statement of the Question:	*Restatement to Test Pupil Reasoning:*
1. Discuss the main reasons for the Civil War.	1. State four reasons why slavery was called a reason for the Civil War.
	2. Could the struggle between the industrial North and the free-labor West on the one hand and the slave South on the other have been the main cause of the Civil War? Take a position as "yes" or "no," and support your position with evidence to back it up.

The multiple-choice question is an excellent device for use in testing critical thinking. For example, reverting again to the Civil War, here is one in point:

1. The main factor causing Robert E. Lee's eventual defeat was:
   ( ) *a.* His poor generalship of his armies.
   ( ) *b.* His lack of as many men as the Federal Union.
   (*) *c.* His lack of communication with his sources of materials and supply.
   ( ) *d.* His lack of ammunition.

In using multiple-choice items, the instructor should realize that less than *four* or *five* choices turns the multiple-choice item almost into a true-false question, or one where the choice is so limited that "guessing at the answer" is encouraged, instead of reasoning.

4. *For mastery at pupil's own speed.* This is a sound type, and should be used more extensively to help pupils to master problems in a normal learning situation. The question which is asked assumes that each pupil reads and therefore masters material and facts at his own reading and working speed; it also recognizes that pupils can learn "on their own." Therefore, most questions of this kind call for the "open-book" or "take-home" quiz. Reverting to the Civil War again, these three questions illustrate well the main variations:

1. Your author of your text states that a variety of causes, rather than any single cause, brought on the Civil War. By quoting from various places in your text, prove or disprove this statement.
2. Was John Brown's raid a "cause" of the Civil War, or an "effect" of the bitter struggle for power when men's minds were heated and clouded? Give evidence from your text to prove your point of view.
3. Do you believe that your text presents the great American struggle, the Civil War, fairly, or not? Give evidence from the text to support your ideas.

5. *For improving study habits and skill in use of reference materials.* The "open-book" type of question, which has just been discussed, can be used successfully for this purpose also. Another device has become established firmly for this; it is called the "study sheet," or "study" questions. Each pupil is given a copy of these study questions; answers to them would contain most of the basic

information and knowledge that the teacher considers important in this unit or block of work. On the high school level, some teachers go so far as to indicate that the questions for the final examination will be taken from the 40 or 50 "study" questions on the work of the course.

Still a third method for developing pupil skills in the use of reference materials involves exercises based entirely upon references. The teacher may (1) give a pupil a grade upon the *completeness* of the pupil's bibliography upon Robert E. Lee or (2) give a pupil a grade upon his *summary or synthesis* of the accounts of various source writers concerning Robert E. Lee as a general. Some teachers also stress the "annotation" of bibliographical references and grade high school pupils upon how well they can summarize a bibliographical item.

One should not leave this section on the development of study habits without mention of "scanning," or reading for one specific purpose. Too many students read to take in *everything* that they are reading; few, even among the bright ones, learn to save time by scanning, or looking in their reading for one specific item of information or opinion. Let us use a student's assignment to develop a study of "Robert E. Lee as a Great General: Pros and Cons" (eleventh-grade project). The pupil will find many references, many writers who refer to Lee as a great military man; much has been written about Lee as a general. The task is (1) to read a lot of material, (2) to pick from it that part which deals *only* with Lee as a general, (3) to gather that together, and (4) to arrange it in the two categories, one favorable to Lee's generalship and one unfavorable. It takes practice to do good "scanning," but students can learn to do it well.

6. *For leisure and free-time reading.* One of the most important tasks of the school is to teach students to like to read, to want to read whether in or out of school. Now this liking does not come without the attainment of some competence in reading. How can the teacher measure this liking and competency from time to time? There are several successful ways for evaluation of this aspect, all of them of the *creative* type; only creative devices will work successfully here.

One way is to ask the individual pupil to report orally on "his most interesting story" or on "his book this week." Another device involves writing a brief character sketch of the most interesting new person the pupil encountered in his reading; or a description of the most exciting, or frightening episode of the week. Another well-known way is for the pupil to construct or paint a scene to represent the book or its title.

A newer device is the posting of a list of books suitable for the pupil and his age, vocabulary, and interest level. One pupil reads what he wants; another reads what he wants; and so on. At the end of the week or of a period of time, these "readers on their own" get together in a period set aside for them and exchange and share their reading experiences. Another method is the building of the individual pupil's own library over a period of years, with help from both the teacher and librarian. Still another method is the encouragement of reading of the original play, drama, or story upon which a well-known motion picture or radio or television program is based.

In all methods of evaluation of leisure and free-time reading, each pupil is an individual case by himself, giving evidence of growth and new interests; therefore, each pupil's progress can be measured only in terms of *his own* increase in amount of material read and interest acquired over a period of time.

3. Making the final evaluation of pupil outcomes and growth. Checking these against the purposes that were determined, this third and final step in the evaluation of pupil progress always has to be carried out in terms of the purposes and point of departure or beginning that were established. Did the pupil accomplish the aims of the work? How well did he acquire the facts and information involved in the block or unit of work? How well did he develop skills and use study habits? Did his attitudes improve? How? Questions of these kinds are important for this third evaluative step which has to be taken by the teacher in the case of each individual pupil.

Many teachers are being trained now to use the teacher-pupil cumulative folder for this final evaluation. This personal folder is built up on each pupil during the year, and contains a large number of both formal and informal records for each student. Gwynn has described well how this works:

The Teacher-Pupil Individual Folder for Evaluation [2]

The teacher will have to revise his system of grading and marking pupils in the light of recent tendencies and movements in evaluation. If he is really interested in his own growth and in the maximum growth of his pupils, he will gradually develop a system of informal records which might be described as the "teacher-pupil personal folder." The teacher should file within this folder everything which the student has contributed in written form, and the impersonal comments and observations which he has made from time to time throughout the work about the student and his progress. For example, in this folder will be found the pretests and the teacher's notation of the stage of achievement at which the pupil started; the pupil's written contributions and reports in the course from time to time, with careful judgments by the teacher of the progress made, impartial comments as to growth or lack of it, and suggestions on how growth can be secured; the pupil's midterm, monthly, or unit tests, with the written notations of the teacher; and the student's opinion of the course, the work in it, ways in which it could be improved, and other suggestions.

Such a cumulative record gives the teacher evidence of the progress of the pupil from the time that he entered the course until he finished it. The record should be equally available to the teacher and to the pupil at all times, but it should be filed in a place where other students do not have access to it. The student should be urged, and, if necessary, required to read the cumulative record of his progress from time to time as it develops; he should confer frequently with the teacher upon matters to which the teacher has called his attention, or on various ways in which he needs to grow and improve his work.

When the time comes for handing in the final grades, the teacher is able to gauge that pupil's performance on the basis of how far he has progressed from the point at which he started; he does not grade him only on the basis of his comparative standing with the rest of the group, or with the average. If this procedure is followed, the student awakens to a realization of the fact that marks as such do not control absolutely his success or failure in school, because he has before him the actual record of what he has done and how he has grown or has not developed. He begins to pay less attention to artificial awards, and more attention to the rewards and satisfaction which come from the growth which has been stimulated and which is actually shown in the form of

[2] J. Minor Gwynn, *Curriculum Principles and Social Trends*, 3rd ed. (New York: The Macmillan Company, 1960), pp. 466-467. Used with permission of The Macmillan Company.

his record. This system of record keeping will inspire in the pupil the desire to improve himself; it develops in the teacher the realization that individual and group growth spring from the individual's development, rather than from his performance in relation to the average perform-ance or the superior achievements of others.

Teacher-made objective and essay tests. It is not the purpose of this chapter to discuss these types of tests and their construction. There are two good reasons for this omission. First, the teacher-edu-cation institutions do a rather good job of training the teacher-can-didate in regard to teacher-made tests of all sorts in subject-matter areas. Secondly, books on tests and measurements are available which present clear and detailed information.[3] Both supervisors and teachers should consult these basic resources on the finer points of test construction. In doing so, one should bear in mind that objec-tive tests on subject matter should not be used to the exclusion of other types just because they are easier to score.

In his final evaluation of outcomes, therefore, the teacher may use many or most of the instruments and devices which have al-ready been described; he may also use group tests of achievement and individual reports, oral and written. He may assess voluntary contributions, co-operative work and activities with small groups or with the class, and other performances of a miscellaneous nature. In this final evaluation, one must remember that he can aid the teacher most by insistence that the individual pupil's progress should be measured in terms of his growth and improvement from the point at which he was when he started in a room, a course, or a block of work.

Promotion Policies and School Promotion Systems as Factors in Evaluation

A cold and impersonal examination of this subject leads one to the flat conclusion: "Few school systems have well-established pro-motion policies." On the other hand, most schools have loosely-de-fined understandings about the promotion of pupils. Why is this true? There are several reasons. In the first place, custom has operated for years in most places to promote children who "pass" or meet certain scholastic achievement standards, and to retain or

[3] A bibliography at the end of this chapter includes basic references in the area.

retard pupils who "fail" or who do not meet those standards. Note that the major emphasis here is upon *one* standard, namely, scholarship; growth in habits, skills, attitudes, and adjustment are seldom considered in this type of promotion.

Secondly, from time immemorial wise school administrators in general have left the matter of the promotion of an individual pupil (1) to the individual teacher on the elementary school level, and (2) to the principal's ruling according to *number of subjects passed* on the high school level. This custom has established two distinct systems or policies of promotion as between the elementary and the secondary school.

In the third place, the formation of a system-wide policy of pupil promotion requires much hard work over a long period of time, quite a bit of "give and take" between teachers and administrators and parents, a compromise on some fundamental differences as to bases of grading and marking. As a result, few school systems are willing to spend the amount of time and labor that is necessary for working out a consistent promotion policy for a school.[4]

Finally, it takes time to tell a couple of parents why their individual child is failing. It is easier administratively, and more economical of time for the teacher to use a system of comparison for pupil's grades than it is to tell each parent why an individual pupil is failing. It is also easier to do this because the parent was graded by that method when he was in school and understands it better than a new method that he may be unfamiliar with. This factor alone, that of the parent and his understandings about promotion, can operate to make a new school promotion policy unsuccessful unless the parent is taken along with the overall planning.

SOCIAL PROMOTION

There has been a rapid growth of the concept of "social promotion" within the last quarter of a century. Social promotion sends a pupil on to the next grade with other pupils of his own age and grade level, on the grounds that (1) the pupil will get more from his age associates than he will from repeating the grade, and (2) retardation dubs the child a failure, and therefore discourages him.

---

[4] *Cf. Reporting Is Communicating*, Association for Supervision and Curriculum Development (Washington, D. C.: National Education Association, 1956). This bulletin illustrates the difficulties involved.

This theory of social promotion has been practiced much more widely on the elementary school level than in the high school. As a matter of fact, promotion in most secondary schools rests primarily upon the *number of subject courses passed,* not on passage of a grade level as in the elementary school.

The controversy over social promotion in the public schools probably will continue for some time if recent findings are considered carefully. For example, James J. Jones made a study of recent research in promotional theory and practice. These significant trends in promotion and nonpromotion in the elementary schools are summarized from his report.[5]

1. Of the elementary school enrollment, 10 per cent are repeaters.
2. In a school system, there is usually four times as much retention or retardation as there is acceleration.
3. Preponderant evidence exists which shows that a pupil should continue to progress with his own age group and that he will learn more from promotion than from retention.
4. Most of those who believe in nonpromotion are in favor of retardation only under unusual or extreme circumstances.
5. Most of the evidence is in favor of promotion over retention.
6. Acceleration of brighter children has been beneficial. But enrichment of the child's program is preferred to acceleration. There is more enrichment in the schools now and a decline in the number of pupils who have been allowed to "skip a grade."
7. Special administrative provisions are slowly, but effectively, overcoming one of the liabilities of acceleration, namely, gaps in a child's knowledge and work of the grade that he skipped. One of these provisions is the special progress class. Another is the grouping of all primary grades (1-3) into a *primary level* or *block*, with promotion of the child when he has completed the entire level, not at the end of each school year; there is grouping also of grades 4-6 into the *elementary level* or *block*. The pupil is promoted from the *primary block*, for example, when he is ready for the work of the *elementary block*, whether it takes him two years, the normal time of three years, or longer.
8. The so-called benefits of retention are not realized in practice.
9. Studies of early school leavers indicate that failure of a grade or subject was symptomatic of later withdrawal.

[5] James J. Jones, "Recent Trends in Promotional Theory," *Progressive Education,* vol. XXXIII (January, 1956), pp. 5-6, 15.

With information from these findings, the supervisor is ready to tackle more successfully those promotional problems which trouble both school personnel and parents. He has these principles to guide him, regardless of the promotional policy of the system in which he works:

1. If the promotion of a pupil is in doubt, all factors should be considered before a final decision is made, including his age, his social experiences and maturity, his mental maturity, his achievement in subject-matter areas, and his attitude and wishes. In addition, the parents and all school personnel involved with the pupil should cooperate in making the final decision.

2. Social promotion in practice operates more frequently in cases of marginal pupils or failures, or in cases under the most extreme circumstances.

3. If a school uses a policy of social promotion, it is an inescapable responsibility of the school itself to adapt the program and teaching procedures in each grade to the individual needs and state of achievement of the pupils. Continuous promotion of pupils who are below the standards of a grade places in each grade each year from four to eight pupils who are working at a lower grade standard. Consequently, the teacher must start these pupils at a different point and use different methods to carry them on from there.

4. On the high school level, the general policy of promoting by total number of subjects passed acts at times as a form of social promotion, with provision for individual needs. For example, the freshman in high school becomes a sophomore if he passes only three of his four subjects; provision is made for him to repeat the subject or course that he failed while he continues right on in the subject areas which he passed.

Record Keeping and Reporting

PURPOSES OF REPORTING SYSTEMS

One prime purpose is to report to parents, pupils, and others about the quantity and quality of work being done by pupils; this purpose would naturally include also pupil promotion and failure. Another purpose is to inform students more accurately of the reasons for their being in school. A third purpose is to help to define for teachers the goals of the school. Still another purpose is to help parents and pupils to know what they may in reason expect from the teachers.

EVALUATION OF PROGRESS OF

GROWTH is indicated as our best estimate of your child's achievement in terms of his individual ability and effort.

ACHIEVEMENT is indicated in terms of our expectations of children in his grade.

I. ACADEMIC AREAS

First Report: Marked / Moderate / Little — Above Average / Average / Below Average
Second Report: Marked / Moderate / Little — Above Average / Average / Below Average

Academic Areas
READING
ORAL LANGUAGE
WRITTEN LANGUAGE
SPELLING
HANDWRITING
MATHEMATICS
SCIENCE
SOCIAL STUDIES

II. SPECIAL AREAS

ART – HEALTH – HOME ECONOMICS – INDUSTRIAL ARTS – LIBRARY – MUSIC – PHYSICAL EDUCATION – SPEECH

These areas are essential parts of your child's school program and his classroom work. They provide many useful situations for learning and using academic knowledges and skills. In addition they make unique contributions to the over-all development of children. Your child's progress in these areas can best be reported through conferences with teachers.

III. ATTITUDES AND WORK SKILLS

First Report: Consistently / Usually / Seldom
Second Report: Consistently / Usually / Seldom

Attitudes and Work Skills
Is courteous
Listens effectively
Follows directions
Plans and organizes well
Uses initiative and is resourceful
Cooperates in group activities
Fulfills responsibilities
Uses property and materials carefully

Figure 8. Elementary School Report Card

This is the "Progress Report" used in grades 3-6 of the Great Neck (New York) public schools. (No report cards are issued for the primary grades.) The report card is sent home in December and May and a parent-teacher conference is arranged before each card date. The report attempts to evaluate the child's school life in three ways: first, by indicating his achievement in terms of his individual ability and effort; second, by appraising his achievement in terms of the school's expectations of children in his grade; and third, by assessing factors which contribute to his social and academic development. Emphasis is also given to special areas.

Reproduced by permission of the Superintendent of Schools, Great Neck, New York.

Much time and effort have been devoted in recent years to study of school reporting systems. Out of these studies have come many good ideas for fundamental improvement of the system. One fact should be kept in mind, however, concerning revisions of school reporting systems. Where the supervisor and the administrator have carried out a co-operative study with teachers, pupils, and parents, the revision usually has been accepted and has been successful; where there were study and change without this type of co-operative effort, the revision has eventually been only partially successful, or violently unsuccessful.

CHANGES IN ELEMENTARY SCHOOL REPORTING

In the elementary school two fundamental changes usually have accompanied the revision of the report card: (1) the elimination of the *numerical* (1 to 100) or *letter* (A, B, C, D, F) grade and (2) a more definite statement of progress in terms of the pupil's abilities, attitudes, knowledge, and skills or habits to be acquired. These changes and the trend toward the teacher-parent conference about pupil progress are well illustrated in the Great Neck (New York) report card in Figure 8.

This latest type of report card for the elementary school is becoming familiar to parents now in many sections of the country. It has been especially well received for reporting in the primary grades but perhaps has been less favored by parents in grades 4-8 unless they have been particularly well educated to it as it was developed. If a system operates with a junior high school, the supervisor has a special responsibility in regard to acquainting parents thoroughly with a type of pupil report card usually quite different from the new type in the elementary grades.

PRESENT-DAY REPORT FORMS FOR THE HIGH SCHOOL

In general the latest type of report card for the high school tries to give evaluations in terms of two factors: (1) a definite grade or mark in a subject and (2) evaluation of skills and/or attitudes related to the subject. The report card reproduced in Fig. 9 illustrates some of the main features of today's high school report form. It is in effect a compromise between the advocates of the old type who believed in a report form for subject-matter grades only and those who believed in the new type which would evaluate skills and attitudes more adequately. It is not unusual to find this type in use in a school and to discover that one teacher gives on it only a subject grade while another adds information about the intangibles as well as giving a subject-matter grade.

WESTOVER HIGH SCHOOL REPORT

NAME William M. White   REPORT PERIOD V   YEAR FRESHMAN

SUBJECT	GRADE	COMMENTS BY TEACHER IN REGARD TO THE GRADE
MatH I (Algebra) Hawkins	B	Bill is good in computation, and accurate in it—but he is having some difficulty right now in learning how to state problems for solution. He is working at it, and improving. W.H.
Latin I Williams	C+	Bill is much more interested in the history of Rome than in cases and declensions. Quick to learn, he does not yet spend time enough studying to master his grammar. He translates pretty well. A.W.
English I Cole	A	It is a pleasure to have Bill this year. He likes English, and is doing some good creative writing now. a.C.
Science I Ward	A	I hope that Bill continues to take more science courses. He won't accept things without proof to back them up. M.W.
Civics Holt	B	Bill can do better.
COMMENTS ON STUDENT ACTIVITIES		Bill is taking part in football, the student council, and the glee club this year. He is interested in each of these and seems to carry them all well along with his school work.

W. W. White _____ STUDENT   WW White _____ PARENT

DATE ____ 4/21/60 ____

Figure 9. **High School Report Form**

Reproduced by permission from the records of J. Minor Gwynn.

In the use of these up-to-date report cards, both administrators and supervisors should make provision for a "report-card day" in the high school. This is necessary if each pupil is to get a rating from each of four or five individual teachers on his attainment of skills in each subject-matter area. From experience the writer knows that one teacher needs all of the time in a one-hour period in order to write in for 30 pupils both a subject grade for each subject and an estimate of student skills related to each subject. The time can well be scheduled for this particular purpose, rather than for teaching; thus, the pupil has the opportunity to talk to the teacher individually about his progress or lack of it.

TEACHER-PARENT CONFERENCES

Most schools agree in philosophy that the teacher-parent interview is a most valuable way of improving parent-school relations and teacher-pupil understanding. Schools vary in the treatment of teacher-parent interviews. Some schools use these conferences primarily for getting acquainted or for obtaining information on the background of the pupil and the parents. In growing number, however, schools are using these interviews for carefully planned, face-to-face conferences as a means of evaluating a child's progress in school or of supplementing the written report card. The number of parent-teacher interviews may vary from one to four during a school year. In some schools, the pupils do not report to school on the days on which these conferences are held; in others, substitute teachers take over while the regular teacher has her interviews. In any case, definite planning in advance for the conference is essential if it is to be profitable.

The teacher new to a policy of parent-teacher interviews for evaluation or the beginning teacher could be terrified at the idea of a parent interview. This fear could be reduced greatly if the supervisor helped the teacher to prepare for the interview. The teacher should be enlightened as to when to discuss a student with a parent and when *not* to! The supervisor could be instrumental in establishing a school policy that interviews should be *scheduled in advance,* thus giving a teacher time to prepare for the interview. The teacher should be thoroughly familiar with the philosophy of the school in regard to curriculum offerings, marks and grading, promotion policy, and the like; these matters the supervisor could explain.

These are ways by which the teacher could prepare himself thoroughly for interveiws: [6]

1. The teacher should make a careful study of all records available on the student—his case history; his marks, especially the ones for the previous year; and his scores on standard tests. He should have at his fingertips the facts on the matters which *could or should be discussed.* (His class rollbook is a convenient place for recording some of these for quick reference.)
2. The child's present grades should be available, with ample illustrations of his tests and daily work. These could be kept in an individual folder in the classroom, thus providing means of self-evaluation for the pupil as well as examples of progress for the teacher and parent.
3. The child should understand clearly all of his grades, through conferences with the teacher(s).
4. The teacher should be ready with an explanation of the relative weight of grades on various aspects, for example, mastery of subject matter or of a skill. He should also have at hand the scope and sequence of the work for his grade or class.
5. The teacher should be reminded to let the parents do most of the talking, especially if they are irate, or at least until he has learned their questions and problems.
6. If the teacher has the unpleasant task of discussing a slow child with parents who are unwilling to acknowledge that the child is slow, he can say all the nice things he knows about the child and slip in the sad facts with a "but": for example, "Johnny gets along beautifully with the group, *but* he is quite weak in his arithmetic fundamentals."
7. The teacher should realize that the parents are having the interview in order to help their child and it is his job to help the child; therefore, there is a common bond between the teacher and the parents.
8. The teacher can learn much from the parents to give him deeper insight into the child's personality, background, and experiences.
9. Though the parents may seem formidable, the teacher has been trained in his field to be a teacher just as they have been trained in their businesses. He should face them with tasteful humility and a sense of self-security.

[6] Some systems give valuable help to new teachers by preparing data and information in regard to parent-teacher conferences. A good sample is *The Handbook for Parent-Teacher Conferences,* mimeographed (Long Beach, California: Long Beach Public Schools).

10. The teacher should write an impersonal account of the interview within 24 hours after it is over and keep it on file.

How Evaluation Can Improve a Teacher's Teaching

As a matter of fact, evaluation can be one of the most important ways by which a teacher can improve his teaching technique, if he is willing to use it. Let us look at this more closely:

1. Good evaluation helps a teacher to improve his instruments of measurement. For example, the employment of different types of tests, each for a different purpose, enables a teacher to identify those items that he should use in an instrument.
2. Good evaluation assists a teacher in clearer recognition of the different kinds of growth to be measured. An illustration of this occurred in the case of the teacher who had been trying to measure the intangible aspect of attitude in a student. She said, "I can give Jim White an open-book type of test now and watch his reactions, how he works, and get a much more accurate idea of his attitude toward his work."
3. Good evaluation helps a teacher to use a total set of measuring instruments for total evaluation of a pupil's growth, rather than depending upon one or two instruments for this total assessment. This procedure results in a procedure fairer to the pupil. Good evaluation makes the teacher recognize that there is *no one all-purpose test* in appraisal of a student's progress.
4. Good evaluation makes a teacher realize that he has to make his goals very clear to the pupil if he is to expect the pupil to attain them. Hazy goals which are set for pupils invite hazy responses.
5. Good evaluative procedures on the teacher's part make the pupil realize the fairness of a battery of instruments for appraisal of his work, as compared with the use of one instrument.
6. Adequate evaluative procedures make students look forward to, rather than fear tests; they know the purposes of the tests and expect them as a normal part of their work.
7. Sound evaluative procedures force a teacher to assess the items in a test in terms of (a) the purposes which were established, and (b) the way the block of work developed. Any items which were included that were not based on these two foundations would have to be discarded, or little weight given to them. In other words, a test on subject matter must be based upon the work or the unit as it developed, not upon it as preconceived by the teacher.
8. Good evaluation takes into account the grading or assessing of an in-

dividual's success (1) in individual work, drill, or problem solving; (2) in small-group work of a co-operative nature; and (3) in large-group work, with the whole class. For each of these situations the teacher has to develop definite instruments or techniques for appraisal.

9. Good evaluative techniques make more extensive use of methods for appraisal of *individual growth* up to the preadolescent age, and more extensive use of methods for *group competition and co-operation* in adolescence. Thus the teacher makes use of natural motivations, growth, and rewards in learning and teaching at each age range and grade level.

Problems for Individual Study and Class Discussion

1. Are evaluation and testing the same, or different? Explain.
2. Is the old percentage system an effective grading instrument for appraising progress in the modern school? Why or why not?
3. What do teachers mean when they say that they grade pupils "on the curve"? Identify what they mean exactly by "the curve."
4. Why has the elementary school made more progress than the high school in definite statement of knowledges, skills, and attitudes that the teacher must appraise?
5. Your principal gets the bright idea that his elementary school should revise its type of report card; he turns his idea over to you, his supervisor, for implementation. How would you proceed to get all people concerned together to work on this revision?
6. Do you consider yourself a good supervisor? By what standards do you make this evaluation? How often do you evaluate your performance? How objectively?
7. In *your* opinion, what would be the most satisfactory method of reporting to parents on a pupil's school progress if the element of time were not involved? Would you recommend that time be taken during school hours to allow the teacher to report to parents personally? Or not? Explain.
8. Make a study of parent-teacher interviews for the evaluation of a pupil's progress in school.
9. Do teachers tend to be influenced by the "halo" effect in grading a pupil, that is, because the child makes an A in reading and social studies, he hesitates to mark him very low in arithmetic, even though he is poor in it. Why or why not?
10. Is an objective type of achievement test, in social studies, for example, any better than a good, clear, well-constructed essay-type of test in the same subject? Support your position.
11. Why do teachers tend to grade pupils in comparison with the best and the poorest, rather than individually? Explain.

12. How can you train your teachers in wise use of the "take-home type" or "open-book" type of test?
13. As a supervisor, write out your philosophy of grading and marking children. Should this philosophy be imparted to your teachers? Why or why not?

Additional Selected References for Problem or Unit Study

Adams, G. S., and Torgerson, T. L., *Measurement and Evaluation for the Secondary School Teacher* (New York: The Dryden Press, 1956), *passim*.

Ahmann, J. S., and Glock, M. D., *Evaluating Pupil Growth* (Boston: Allyn and Bacon, 1958), *passim*.

Association for Childhood Education International, *Reporting on the Growth of Children*, revised periodically (Washington, D. C.), *passim*.

Association for Supervision and Curriculum Development, National Education Association, *A Look at Continuity in the School Program*, 1958 Yearbook, ch. XIII, and *Human Variability and Learning*, 1961, *passim*.

Bean, K. L., *Construction of Educational and Personnel Tests* (New York: McGraw-Hill Book Company, Inc., 1953), *passim*.

Buros, O. K., ed., *The Fifth Mental Measurements Yearbook* (Highland Park, N. J.: Gryphon Press, 1959). A comprehensive list and evaluative reviews of standard tests of all kinds.

Burton, W. H., and Brueckner, L. J., *Supervision: A Social Process* (New York: Appleton-Century-Crofts, Inc., 1955), ch. IX.

California Journal of Secondary Education has a good symposium on "The Place of Testing and Evaluation in Learning" (city, county, state, and national programs), vol. XXXV (January, 1960), pp. 40-65.

Cramer, R. V., and Domian, O. E., *Administration and Supervision in the Elementary School* (New York: Harper and Brothers, 1959), ch. X.

Downie, N. M., *Fundamentals of Measurement: Techniques and Practices* (New York: Oxford University Press, 1958), *passim*.

Educational Leadership from time to time has entire issues devoted to aspects of evaluation.

Elsbree, W. S., *Pupil Progress in the Elementary School* (New York: Teachers College, Columbia University, 1953), *passim*.

Furst, E. J., *Constructing Evaluation Instruments* (New York: Longmans, Green and Company, 1958), *passim*.

Gerberich, J. R., *Specimen Objective Test Items: A Guide to Achievement Test Construction* (New York: Longmans, Green and Company, 1956), *passim*.

Greene, H. A., Jorgensen, A. N., and Gerberich, J. R., *Measurement and Evaluation in the Elementary School* (New York: Longmans, Green and Company, 1953), chs. VI-VII.

———, ———, ———, *Measurement and Evaluation in the Secondary School* (New York: Longmans, Green and Company, 1954), chs. I, VI, VII.

Hicks, H. J., *Educational Supervision in Principle and Practice* (New York: The Ronald Press Company, 1960), ch. VI.

Langdon, G., and Stout, I. W., *Helping Parents Understand Their Child's School* (Englewood Cliffs: Prentice-Hall, 1957), chs. XVII-XIX.

———, ———, *Teacher-Parent Interviews* (Englewood Cliffs, N. J.: Prentice-Hall, Inc., 1954), *passim.*

NEA Journal in 1959-1960 had three special features on evaluation: "Has Testing Gone Too Far?" vol. XLVIII (November, 1959), pp. 15-31; "Reporting," vol. XLVIII (December, 1959), pp. 15-28; and "Promotion," vol. XLIX (April, 1960), pp. 15-23.

Osborne, E., *The Parent-Teacher Partnership* (New York: Teachers College, Columbia University, 1960), *passim.*

Rothney, J. W. M., *Evaluating and Reporting Pupil Progress*, No. 7, "What Research Says to the Teacher," Department of Classroom Teachers and American Educational Research Association (March, 1955).

Sarason, S. B., *et al.*, *Anxiety in Elementary School Children: A Report of Research* (New York: John Wiley and Sons, 1960), *passim.*

Schwartz, A., and Tiedeman, S. C., *Evaluating Student Progress* (New York: Longmans, Green and Company, 1957), chs. I-XII, XV-XIX.

Shane, H. G., and McSwain, E. T., *Evaluation and the Elementary Curriculum*, revised edition (New York: Henry Holt and Company, 1958), *passim.*

Thomas, R. M., *Judging Student Progress* (New York: Longmans, Green and Company, 1960), Parts II and III.

Torgerson, T. L., and Adams, G. S., *Measurement and Evaluation for the Elementary School Teacher, with Implications for Corrective Procedures* (New York: The Dryden Press, 1954), ch. X.

Wellington, C. B. and J. W., *Teaching for Critical Thinking* (New York: McGraw-Hill Book Company, Inc., 1961), *passim.*

Wiles, K., *Supervision for Better Schools*, 2nd ed. (Englewood Cliffs, N. J.: Prentice-Hall, Inc., 1955), ch. XIII.

Part IV

SPECIAL PROBLEM AREAS

IN SUPERVISION

CHAPTER 10

Aid to the Beginning Teacher

THE BEGINNING TEACHER is a contradictory character, fully understandable only to those who have been beginning teachers and have remembered those early professional experiences. As a beginner he is full of confidence in his ability to improve the teaching profession; yet he lacks confidence in himself, in his ability to be successful in this new venture. He tends to "know all the answers" in his special subject areas of teaching for which he has been trained; yet he is just ready to begin to discover all of the answers. He feels that he can remake and reform poor school practices; yet he carries into the schoolroom some poor teaching practices which he has acquired along the way.

He thinks that he knows what is good for the children he is teaching, no matter what age range or grade level he teaches; on the other hand, he is woefully ignorant of the fact that he frequently does not know what is good for himself. He plans to live his own life, to speak his mind; and he urges his pupils to "speak up," to act naturally in the schoolroom. Yet he does not let pupils live their own lives, frequently inhibits their speaking their own minds because of the regimentation that he establishes in the classroom. He is enthusiastic to try out a new method of teaching, or a new textbook; yet he insists that his pupils follow rather closely his methods of teaching and learning. He usually is interested in many activities and takes part in many; but he insists frequently upon limiting the activities of his pupils on the grounds that they cannot do too many things well at one time.

He wants to be both respected and liked as a teacher; yet he has not yet made the distinction which a pupil makes early in school, namely, that the *best-liked* teacher is not always the *best* teacher. He is secure in his ambitions, but either socially or financially insecure. He is professional in his outlook, but tends to be on the defensive in his attitude toward school administrators and supervisors. He believes in helping each child to grow and develop normally as an individual; but he teaches primarily subject matter, for he has no sure subject matter which has been taught to him in this business called child growth and development. Finally, he knows well his subject areas; yet because of this fact, he tends to teach subject matter primarily, instead of children—until he learns more by experience of how to teach children. He thinks that he is making points clear to students; yet he frequently uses a vocabulary that is "over their heads." He tends to take the attitude that he is "open minded"; on the other hand, more often than not he "jumps to his own defense" if any suggestion is made that his teaching is not being effective.

All in all, the beginning teacher is a strange mixture of self-confidence and insecurity, a promising person who needs all of the sympathetic and intelligent aid that a wise supervisor can give him. The supervisor cannot help him with all of his problems; but he can give some suggestions in certain areas, some "I saw this happen" ideas, or "How would this work?" comments, or "How would you like to do this?"

The Beginning Teacher's Development of Self-Confidence

Self-confidence usually develops in several well-defined ways. The teacher acquires one form of confidence in himself by mastering his teaching area or subject area so well that he feels that he cannot often be "stumped" in it by pupils, parents, or administrators. In like manner, if a beginner is successful in his first task, in his first day of teaching, his self-confidence develops fast. Another way of developing self-confidence is to become so well acquainted with his students and the homes from which they come that the teacher has a sense of "belonging" in this situation; similar to this is the growth of the teacher in understanding and knowing well the community in which he teaches. A salary large enough to live on comfortably and to set something aside in savings operates powerfully to give teachers a sense of security and self-confidence. Acceptance by a circle of friends who have like tastes and interests is another powerful factor in developing confidence; praise for a task well done is still another factor, as is public recognition of service which is rendered beyond the usual run of duty. The acquisition of outstanding skill in some activity or hobby is another important way of developing self-confidence. Being liked or being respected by the opposite sex is another confidence builder. Recognition by pupils as a good or effective teacher operates powerfully and positively on the ego. A sense of security in regard to his spiritual and religious life is another factor, as is confidence in his perfect physical health. Even such a small thing as the locality in which he lives can improve or decrease a teacher's self-confidence.

For example, a young beginning teacher might find himself a member of a faculty composed primarily of older and experienced teachers. His association with these older teachers could take several directions—he could be ill-at-ease with them, find them tedious, dull, and boring, and be lonely for his own age group. Or, he might become friendly with them, earn their respect and improve his own teaching by listening to and profiting from their experiences and suggestions. Pleasant relations with older and "master" teachers will give a beginner a sense of security which could be a big step toward his developing a sense of security in other matters.

Supervisory Help for the Beginning Teacher in Specific Problem Areas

A part of the supervisor's job is to help teachers of varying age groups to adjust and work together for the best that they can give to the children whom they teach. It is of great importance to the teaching profession that capable people be attracted to it and wish to remain in it. Therefore, one of the supervisor's tasks is to help a beginning teacher develop confidence and self-satisfaction from a job well done, to help him like, even love his work.

It is obvious that the beginning teacher will have to develop his own self-confidence; but there are many ways to help him to acquire it. Discussion will be centered around the supervisor's responsibilities to the beginning teacher in these five areas: (1) Aid in meeting problems of the new situation; (2) Aid in the planning of work; (3) Aid with problems involving pupil management and control; (4) Aid in problems of record keeping and reporting; and (5) Helping with problems of community responsibilities and contacts.

AID IN MEETING PROBLEMS OF THE NEW SITUATION

A family's moving into a new community presents a situation comparable to a teacher's moving into a new community. Each has to put down new roots, make adjustments to new social, economic, and spiritual situations, make new friendships, and gain acceptance in the new community. Analysis of the problem shows that the new teacher has to get acquainted with a new family which includes pupils, co-workers among the school personnel, parents, and people in the community.

Pupils' reactions to a new teacher are somewhat predictable. They want to see what he looks like; they want to "try him out" to see how he reacts, to test him. The supervisor should show the new teacher by his own example that "how you look" is very important; young men teachers should "look like a million dollars," and young women beginners should dress to "knock your eye out"—all because these first impressions are lasting upon young pupils, and can influence them favorably or unfavorably without a word's being spoken. A teacher can possess a limited wardrobe and yet constantly impress his students with his neatness, his alternation of color in ties or hose, his well-laundered linen, and his clean-shaven appearance.

Another valuable service to the newcomer will be the introduction of his pupils to him. The ideal way to do this is for the beginner to visit in the school the preceding spring so that he can become acquainted with classes or pupils that he will teach later. Lacking this ideal situation the supervisor can:

1. Arrange for him to come during the summer and examine the building, the classrooms, and the records of the pupils whom he is to teach.
2. Furnish him with the names of those of his prospective pupils who are skilled in handling individual and group responsibilities.
3. Help him to prepare in advance pupil name-tags or a class seating chart for the first day, so that both teacher and pupils can get well acquainted quickly.
4. Acquaint him with the philosophy, attitudes, and general practices of the pupils in the school. If there is a student handbook, indicate

points of value. If there is a student council, explain its point of view and practices.

5. Assist in planning an attractive homeroom display and arrangement for the opening day of school.
6. Aid him in planning an interesting program for the first day of school, such as suggested definite activities, and a learning situation.
7. By exhibiting patience, help the beginner to realize that patience with learners is of paramount importance in teaching.

We have developed more methods of acquainting new teachers in advance with their colleagues than we have with their future pupils. Schools with an effective administrative and supervisory organization use one or more of these means:

1. Individual conferences with his superintendent, principal, and supervisor.
2. Meeting with the "Big Brother" or "Big Sister," the older teacher in the system who will help to introduce the newcomer to the system during the first weeks or month or two. Perhaps a better term for this person is "helping" teacher.
3. Providing the beginner with the local newspaper that features a story on staff and newcomers to the faculty.
4. Work conferences or teacher workshops, of from two days to a week or more in length just prior to the opening of school, where the beginner is introduced to others working in his area or on his grade level and has a good opportunity to establish preliminary social and professional contacts with colleagues.
5. Library, lunchroom and other special conferences, at which these specialists acquaint the new arrival with these services.
6. Party or reception or picnic by the school board, P.T.A., or the administration for teachers new to the system.
7. Guided tour of school buildings, facilities, and resources.
8. Introduction to the professional library of the school, to the curriculum laboratory, the audio-visual division, or the materials center.
9. School handbook and calendar, hours and customs in regard to ground duty, promotion and grading policies, assignments of teachers, extracurricular responsibilities or duties, and the like.
10. Acquainting the new teacher with the philosophy of the school in regard to joining professional organizations; attending professional meetings; receiving gifts, such as Christmas presents, from the students; attending school functions other than on his own teaching level; and with the reasons behind this philosophy.

The promising movement in recent years of involving intelligently the adults of a community in co-operative planning for better schools has contributed some good ideas and practices that help the beginning teacher to understand the parents and the community better. Among these are:

1. The tour of the community, to show new teachers the community resources for teaching and the types of population.
2. Providing services that would locate the teacher in a good place to live, such as a list of desirable rooming facilities or apartments or guide services in looking for a place to stay; meeting new teachers as they finally arrive before school and having the apartment or house open and attractive; and furnishing a meal to the married people who are moving furniture in and getting settled.
3. Furnishing a directory of local churches and church services.
4. Party or social gathering for teachers new to the system, preferably at a place used primarily for recreation, such as the country club, the park, or the recreation center.
5. Preparing and presenting an introductory packet of materials and data on the town and its facilities, including guest tickets to a couple of local shows or functions.
6. A special note and perhaps a flower or some suitable token on each beginner's desk on the first day of school.
7. Appointing a sponsor for each new teacher. This may be another teacher in the same school building, or it may be a member of the P.T.A. The idea is that this sponsor can help the teacher to get answers to his questions about the community more rapidly.

Finally, the smart beginner can help himself if he will make intelligent use of the many facilities at the command of the supervisor. For example, he can secure in advance the names of most of the parents of the pupils that he is going to teach, and can look over the school records in regard to the size of families, types of employment, and other background data. He can become acquainted with the informal knowledge that the minister of his church has about the people and community. He can make brief notes of interesting people and facts as each pupil talks to him. He can become thoroughly familiar with supplementary teaching materials. And he can show a real interest in people by learning to listen more than he talks when out of school.

AID IN THE PLANNING OF WORK

It is in the planning of work that the teacher education institutions are perhaps doing their best work as they prepare teachers. At the same time the trend toward requiring full-time practice teaching in a school system for a period in a regular teaching situation has intensified the emphasis on careful planning.

For the supervisor, the key to successful work with the beginning teacher in his planning is the ability to help him or her to make progress *from the point at* which he is when he starts. For example, if the beginning first-grade teacher did his practice teaching in April and May, he is likely familiar with grouping for reading, with how to teach pupils to do simple number work, and with how to plan a central activity with the grade over a period of time. But he may have had little or no actual teaching experience with readiness materials for children, which are used extensively at the beginning of grade 1. So the main task of the supervisor at the year's start might be to assist him for a week or so with *how* to employ these readiness materials to best advantage, or how to work out satisfactory plans for the first day, or first few days of school.

Another illustration may be given on the high school level. The social studies teacher may have had good training and successful practice-teaching experience in the planning of subject-matter blocks of work and subject-matter units in American history, teacher-planned, in advance. He may wish now to begin to do more planning with his students on teaching units which bring together not only American history, but also the customs, the writings and authors, and the economic growth of the nation. In this case, the supervisor might have to give major attention to this teacher's needs and plans for a week or longer; and he should give this help.

The beginning teacher or new teacher is given frequently those subjects, sections, classes, duties or responsibilities which either were left open in the schedule or no one else wanted. Even though the teacher is certified, he might not be or feel qualified for one of these tasks. The supervisor could and should help him by means of techniques which are applicable to the situation, such as furnishing new texts, suggesting effective audio-visual materials, or training him "on the job" for sponsorship of a student activity unfamiliar to him.

Other ways to aid the new teacher are well known. They include help on such problems as:

1. How can I make the most effective use of the library in my work?
2. What audio-visual materials are available for this part of my teaching? How can I work them into my planning?
3. What are the possibilities for field trips to supplement my teaching? For bringing in resource persons to my class?
4. How can I plan to meet better the individual differences among my pupils? Their special interests? Their creative urges?
5. How can I make full use of the work and planning of other teachers who are teaching the same grade or subject that I am teaching? Is there a possibility of seeing them teach? Of some resource planning with them?
6. How can I learn to use textbooks more effectively? What, if any, is the place of the workbook in my teaching?
7. What provisions does the school make for remedial work for individual pupils who need it, such as in arithmetic or reading? What is my responsibility in these problem areas? How can I meet it?
8. How should my planning of my work fit into the scope and sequence of the curriculum for the primary grades? For the grammar grades? For the whole school?
9. How can I evaluate my planning of my classwork? How can the supervisor help me to do this more effectively?

In helping the teacher to plan his work, the supervisor might keep constantly in mind two controls: (1) When helping a new teacher in planning, there is no time limit for me—I must give him all of the help that he needs, *now,* over a period of time; if he needs a major part of my time for three days, for two weeks, for a month, I must arrange to give it to him; doing so may save him to the teaching profession, may mean the difference between success and failure, between a fast-growing and a slow-growing teacher. After all, the teacher was hired on the basis of his capabilities and potentialities, his qualifications and promise. If the teacher fails to make good, then have *I,* the supervisor, also failed? (2) I should always remember, and help the teacher to remember that he cannot always take for granted that his pupils know certain facts and have certain skills just because they have been promoted to this grade level or class; he has to discover for himself their degree of mastery of knowledge and skills, and has to plan his work to "hook up with" their degree of advancement and their level of vocabulary mastery.

AID WITH PROBLEMS INVOLVING PUPIL
MANAGEMENT AND CONTROL

The few studies which have been made of the main problems of beginning teachers indicate that the new teachers identify that of pupil control and discipline as one of the most crucial.[1]

"To try out the new teacher" is the ancient and honorable prerogative of the pupils; this has been true ever since children began to be taught in groups instead of individually. This testing of the new teacher is characteristic of all group activity; for it is the same as the testing of new leadership in any group. Until the new leader, the teacher, establishes his leadership, he cannot be fully effective. *But he can be partially effective and can become more effective as he develops leadership competencies and qualifications* "on the job." Therefore the supervisor's task here is to help the beginner (1) to analyze his leadership competencies or lack of these competencies, (2) analyze his group and the potential or actual leaders in it, and (3) improve his qualities and skills of leadership.[2]

Turning briefly to a consideration of the student's point of view, he expects the teacher to assume leadership of the group in the classroom. The pupil also wants normally an atmosphere in his classroom conducive to study, concentration, and learning; the typical pupil does not want to go to school each day in a room in bedlam. The student also wants an opportunity to assume himself some responsibility for learning and for activities in his classroom; and he appreciates the opportunity from time to time to plan his work co-operatively with his teacher. The pupil also wants his teacher to be consistent in his rules and regulations, in his assignment of outside study or "homework," in his marking and grading, and in the types of punishment which he imposes. The normal student wants to be busy, to have something to do, and he likes to look up to his teacher as a person who is serious and who provides worthwhile things for him to do. Finally, the pupil likes to behave nor-

---

[1] "These Are Our Concerns: Beginning Teachers Statements," *Educational Leadership*, vol. V (December, 1947), pp. 145-54. In comparison with other aspects of supervision, the author has found little research on the special problems of beginning teachers. The references which form the basis for this presentation are gathered together in one place at the end of this chapter.

[2] For a fuller treatment of these three aspects, turn to the discussion of leadership qualities and characteristics in chapter 17 on group processes.

mally in the classroom, to laugh when something funny happens, to applaud when something outstanding occurs, to cry or gripe when disappointed, to visit around a little occasionally without being accused of disobedience, to lead as normal a life as is possible in a classroom, and to vary his work and activities throughout the day.

In the final analysis, no individual can teach a teacher how to handle problems of pupil management and discipline; the teacher has to learn how himself. But supervision can be of help at one time or another if the teacher remembers these important principles:

1. Keep pupils busy on activities which have meaning and which they have had a part in planning. Busy people tend to have little time to "raise the devil." The surest way to keep pupils busy is by careful planning and preplanning of classwork.

2. Provide for variety in learning activities and situations. The "concentration span" of the typical pupil seldom exceeds 30 minutes in length with profit upon any one phase of study.

3. The positive approach to the control of a room full of pupils is vital, even if the teacher has to start out with a control that is almost military in nature, such as marching in and out of the classroom in line. "Control first, teaching can follow" is an important principle for the beginning teacher to grasp. Be the master of the classroom from the beginning.

4. Place pupils in positions of leadership and responsibility, or in situations where they will work on their own only as they exhibit qualities of leadership and willingness to take the responsibility that goes with more freedom.

5. Be sure that the punishment for misbehavior or an infraction of of rules "fits the crime." For example, to make a pupil "stay in after school" for stealing is not a punishment that fits this social and moral misbehavior; but it would fit the breaking of the rule of being tardy to school without reasonable excuse.

6. Avoid personality conflicts with pupils, even if you "lean over backwards" sometimes to do so. Remember that in the case of most personality conflicts the pupil is so like the teacher in a certain respect that they have difficulty getting along together. Also remember that the pupils in most of these cases are "on the side of" the pupil.

7. Do *not* punish a whole room full of pupils for infraction of some rule unless the whole room is guilty. For example, two boys throw erasers at each other; the teacher cannot get anyone to tell who threw them; so he keeps the whole room in after school in punish-

ment, while 28 out of 30 pupils are innocent and boiling mad at the injustice.

8. Make set rules of conduct only when matters of safety, health, or protection are involved, and get your pupils to help to set up these few, necessary regulations. The fewer rules you have, the fewer rules pupils will be tempted to break and try to get away with it.

9. Accept the responsibility that the law places in your hands, namely, that pupil discipline and control are your job, not the task and responsibility of pupils to administer to each other.

10. Look for *causes* of misbehavior. For example, the "show-off" can often be handled successfully if he receives feelings of satisfaction from achievement. Therefore, help him plan work that he can do successfully. Give him attention enough so that he will feel wanted and useful.

Helping the beginner to recognize classroom climate. A beginning teacher may have trouble in recognizing and developing a "climate" in his classroom which is conducive to learning and good living. How strict should he be? How much freedom should the children have? Is his class too loud? Never a sound is heard from the children next door! *Where is—what is* the "happy medium"? This, in part, is an aspect of discipline. For most beginning teachers, one cannot emphasize too strongly that this is a competency which new teachers must acquire quickly, or fail.

Often the novice knows what he should be teaching but does not know *how* to do it, that is, the techniques and methods to use to put his subject matter across. There are teachers who are doing an acceptable or even a good job but who feel insecure and do not realize that their work is producing good results. What can the supervisor do to help these people?

One of the most valuable means of helping these teachers is to let them observe other teachers. All of them have had opportunity to observe in classrooms during their college preparation for teaching; but most would agree that, if only they had an opportunity to observe now that they have their own classes, it would be far more meaningful to them. Arrange for the teacher who is disturbed over the climate in his classroom to visit a class with a desirable climate —help him to analyze the factors which contributed to create this climate. Let the teacher in a new field observe an experienced teacher in the same field. If a teacher feels he is getting "stale," let him observe someone to pick up new ideas. This observation, properly carried out, could be one of the most valuable types of in-service training.

Finally, the beginning teacher might keep this old saying in mind, from his first day of teaching, concerning the control of pupils: "It is easier to lighten up than it is to tighten up."

AID IN PROBLEMS OF RECORD KEEPING AND REPORTING

Problems of reporting and appraisal of pupil progress were considered at some length in Chapter 9. The suggestions which were given there are as pertinent for the beginning teacher as for all teachers, and they will not be repeated here. However, there are certain problems relating to the keeping of records and reports upon which the supervisor can furnish help.

In the first place, the supervisor can sit down with the teacher and show him that a minimum number of records and reports are necessary, and that the teacher is the only one who can keep some of these records and reports accurately, such as attendance, grades or marks given to pupils, and reports to parents. Most teachers cease to rebel against keeping necessary records when they *know the reasons* for having to keep them.

In the second place, supervisors can help teachers to learn *how* to keep records and make reports. For example, many beginning teachers do not understand the difference between "membership" and "enrollment" on the attendance forms. Another example involves the giving of a grade, such as A, B, C, and the like, with written, additional comments. The new teacher needs samples of the kinds of written comments that are made on the reports; he also needs much help in expressing his comments without personal bias; and he has to learn how to describe a child's actions impersonally in a situation as an example of growth or lack of growth. Still another illustration might deal with help that the beginner needs in keeping and making reports on free or rented books. A further example might involve an explanation of the yearly "inventory" required of all teachers. Again, the supervisor might suggest to the teacher ways of keeping the pupils occupied as he completes certain reports or records.

In the third place, the supervisor can aid the new teacher by showing him the types of records and reports for which he is not responsible, but which could not be made by the supervisor or principal without the teachers' help and teachers' reports that are turned in. Reports of this sort include usually the pupil's cumulative (permanent) record, the principal's or supervisor's annual and preliminary reports, the school bus (transportation) reports, reports to state and regional accrediting agencies, transcripts for colleges and business concerns, and equipment and supply records.

HELPING WITH PROBLEMS OF
COMMUNITY RESPONSIBILITIES AND CONTACTS

Stress has been placed by teacher education institutions upon the teacher's responsibility in the community. The teacher-candidate is told time and time again that he ought to become a part of his community, identify himself with it, and take part in community activities. What is the responsibility of the supervisor to the beginning teacher in this kind of activity?

Perhaps one of the first decisions that the new teacher faces, other than where to live and where to eat, is that of what groups he will affiliate himself with. What church shall he attend? Should he join the Lions Club, or Kiwanis, or Rotary? Should he become a member of the Country Club? The Community Club? The American Legion or V.F.W.? Or should she join the Woman's Club? The D.A.R.? A Book Club? As the teacher is faced with one or more of these decisions, the supervisor can help by furnishing him with a list of the community's churches, service clubs, veteran's organizations, social groups of an organized nature, restricted and unrestricted, and other community groups.

Another decision that the beginner has to make is an important one for him, for it is related to his teaching load; that is, "How many community responsibilities and jobs can I take on and still do my work well?" Here again the supervisor can help. Most administrators agree that there is a limit beyond which teachers find themselves handicapped in their work; but that limit has to be set by each teacher, since some can "get around" more than others. In general, people who get along well with both adults and children can carry successfully two major outside activities without any observable adverse effect on their teaching. A few carry three community activities; the writer knew of a man who was Scoutmaster, teacher of a Sunday school class, and president of the Country

Club. Again, the teacher must consider whether he can take on an additional responsibility, or whether he should drop one that he already has in order to assume another. The work and time involved should help the new teacher to make his decision.

There are a few facts that a new teacher should know without having to discuss them with the supervisor. However, so many cases arise from either ignorance or carelessness concerning these, that it seems necessary to mention them here.

Certainly a beginning teacher should be wise enough *not* to date high school students! It is also somewhat unwise for the teacher to date young people who, though not in school, are part of the "high school crowd" and of about the same age While it is certainly not the responsibility of this author, the school personnel, or citizens to dictate a person's social life, it is the smart newcomer to a community who is careful to select friends who fit into the social strata to which he likes to belong. In general, the well-balanced school teacher usually forms more of his close friendships among people who live in the community and are not connected with the school.

Along this same vein, the beginning teacher or newcomer to a community should know the public places in and around the community which are approved by the citizens. In other words, the teacher should know where he should and should not be seen.

It is well known that cliques exist in every school. The wise person does not join a clique; he is friendly to all, listens, and watches; but he keeps himself removed from petty grievances and cliques. By doing so, he gains respect and subsequent security.

Teachers sometimes forget that they belong to the "example" group in society. They are teachers of children, molders of character and habits, and community leaders. Such details as poor table manners, lack of *savoir-faire* in the social graces, and inappropriate dress can cause a teacher to lose his hard earned status, or prevent him from ever gaining it. If the teacher is lacking in these respects, then he can certainly study, observe, and learn!

Finally, the new teacher might profit from the sage remark of a successful superintendent old at the game; he said, "I find it most profitable to walk to school and back home again at least twice a week. That way, people get a chance to talk to me, to let off steam, and I seldom have a parent come to school to complain about a teacher or a school situation." The beginning teacher might find it of value to forget his automobile twice a week, in like fashion, and learn to make his community contacts at first hand.

Problems for Individual Study and Class Discussion

1. Every new teacher has to start teaching somewhere. Should a teacher who was reared in the country begin his teaching in a rural or city school? Or does it matter? Give reasons for your stand.
2. Can a supervisor give a new teacher a sense of security? Or does the beginner have to acquire it himself? Explain.
3. Should a supervisor talk with the beginner about whether to accept gifts from children or their parents? Support your position on this question.
4. What could the supervisor do to help the beginning teacher who is assigned to a mixed grade in the elementary school? Or to a course that no one else wants in the high school?
5. Write a handbook for the beginning teachers in your school.
6. How would you as a supervisor handle the problem of a new teacher who is aggressive? Homesick? Or who has poor taste in dress or manners?
7. Would it be a good policy to schedule regular periods for new teachers to come in and discuss their problems with the supervisor? Take a stand pro or con, and defend it.
8. The young mother, supplementing the family income, is coming to be an important part of the teaching staff in every school system. List the advantages of having such women on the staff, the special problems their presence brings, and draw implications for the young unmarried teachers with whom they work.
9. Do you believe that the supervisor should be consulted in the hiring of new teachers? Give your reasons for your belief.
10. You have the problem of a transferred teacher, with long experience, whose common complaint is, "We didn't do it this way where I used to teach." What steps could you take to help this teacher to a better adjustment in your school?

Additional Source References for Problem or Unit Study

Allen, W. C., and Lassoie, J. P., "Follow-Up of Beginning Teachers—A Team Responsibility," *Educational Leadership*, vol. XI (November, 1953), pp. 78-81.

Bartky, J. A., *Supervision as Human Relations* (Boston: D. C. Heath and Company, 1953), ch. XI.

Christopher, L. M., "The Assignment and Induction of New Teachers," *The Bulletin of the National Association of Secondary-School Principals*, vol. XL (May, 1956), pp. 98-103.

Cramer, R. V., and Domian, O. E., *Administration and Supervision in the Elementary School* (New York: Harper and Brothers, 1960), ch. XII.

Elsbree, W. S., and Reutter, E. E., Jr., *Staff Personnel in the Public Schools* (Englewood Cliffs, N. J.: Prentice-Hall, Inc., 1954), chs. IV-V.

Eye, G. G., and Lane, W. R., *The New Teacher Comes to School* (New York: Harper and Brothers, 1956), *passim.*

Ferguson, M. E., and Rouse, H. R., "Principal and Supervisor Help the New Teacher," *Educational Leadership,* vol. XIII (October, 1955), pp. 11-13.

"First-year Teachers in 1954-55," *National Education Association Research Bulletin,* vol. XXXIV (February, 1956), chs. I-III, V, VII.

Helping the New Teacher (Washington, D. C.: Association for Supervision and Curriculum Development, National Education Association, 1956), *passim.*

Hicks, H. J., *Educational Supervision in Principle and Practice* (New York: The Ronald Press Company, 1960), chs. XI and XIII, *passim.*

Hicks, W. V., and Jameson, M. C., *The Elementary School Principal at Work* (Englewood Cliffs, N. J.: Prentice-Hall, Inc., 1957), ch. IV.

Jantzen, J. M., and Stone, J. C., "More Effective Supervision of Beginning Teachers," *The Journal of Teacher Education,* vol. X (June, 1959), pp. 246-248.

Jersild, A. T., *When Teachers Face Themselves* (New York: Teachers' College, Columbia University, 1955), *passim.*

Kearney, N. C., *A Teacher's Professional Guide,* (Englewood Cliffs, N. J.: Prentice-Hall, Inc., 1958), chs. I-VIII, XIV, XVI-XVIII.

Lambert, S. M., "The Teacher's First Year," *NEA Journal,* vol. XLV (March, 1956), pp. 152-153.

Langdon, G., and Stout, I. W., *Teacher-Parent Interviews* (Englewood Cliffs, N. J.: Prentice-Hall, Inc., 1954), *passim.*

Lewis, C., and Winsor, C. B., "Supervising the Beginning Teacher," *Educational Leadership,* vol. XVII (December, 1959), pp. 137-141.

Mitchell, K. A., "Orientation of the Newly Appointed Teacher," *The Bulletin of the National Association of Secondary-School Principals,* vol. XXXIX (May, 1955), pp. 80-88.

Muldoon, M., *Learning to Teach* (New York: Harper and Brothers, 1958), *passim.*

Richey, R. W., *Planning for Teaching,* 2nd ed. (New York: McGraw-Hill Book Company, Inc., 1958), parts V and VI.

Rodes, F. G., and Peckhaw, D. R., "Evaluation of Beginning Teachers," *The Journal of Teacher Education,* vol. XI (March, 1960), p. 55.

Stinnett, T. M., *The Teacher and Professional Organizations,* 3rd ed. (Washington, D. C.: National Education Association, 1956), sections I and II.

Stoops, E., "Administrator's Responsibility for 'Helping the Beginning Teacher,'" *The Nation's Schools,* vol. LVII (April, 1956), pp. 72-74.

Teacher Orientation: Off to a Good Start (Washington, D. C.: American Association of School Administrators, 1956), *passim.*

Weber, C. A., *Personnel Problems of School Administrators* (New York: McGraw-Hill Book Company, Inc., 1955), chs. III-IV.

Werner, LaV. E., "Know Where You're Going from the Very First Day of School," *NEA Journal,* vol. XLIV (September, 1955), pp. 335-336.

Wiles, K., *Supervision for Better Schools,* 2nd ed. (Englewood Cliffs, N. J.: Prentice-Hall, Inc., 1955), ch. XI.

Yauch, W. A., Bartels, M. H., and Morris, E., *The Beginning Teacher* (New York: Henry Holt and Company, Inc., 1955), part III, and especially appendix.

Yeager, W. A., *Administration and the Teacher* (New York, Harper and Brothers, 1954), ch. VIII.

CHAPTER 11

The Supervisor's Special Problems

on the High School Level

SUPERVISION IN THE HIGH SCHOOL has not been developed and carried out as effectively as in the elementary school. J. A. Bartky indicates that secondary school supervision is still bogged down in school management and that although there is some planning and direction of the instructional program there are neither extensive training programs for teachers in service nor organized conferences of a face-to-face nature.[1] Harold Spears goes further and says that the high school classroom and the high school teacher have suffered more from neglect of supervision on that level than from misuse of supervisory techniques.[2] As a matter of fact, among the many textbooks on supervision which appeared during the middle of the century, few major publications were devoted exclusively to supervision on the secondary school level.[3]

What are the special problems of the supervisor on the secondary school level? What causes them? The answers to these

[1] J. A. Bartky, *Supervision as Human Relations* (Boston: D. C. Heath and Company, 1953), ch. XIV.

[2] Harold Spears, *Improving the Supervision of Instruction* (Englewood Cliffs, N. J.: Prentice-Hall, Inc., 1953), ch. XIV.

[3] Consult Charles W. Boardman, and others, *Democratic Supervision in Secondary Schools* (Boston: Houghton Mifflin Company, 1953); Robert C. Hammock and Ralph S. Owings, *Supervising Instruction in Secondary Schools* (New York: McGraw-Hill Book Company, Inc., 1955). In addition to those two, another is perhaps focused more on the secondary school than on the elementary level, namely, Thomas H. Briggs and Joseph Justman, *Improving Instruction Through Supervision* (New York: The Macmillan Company, 1952).

224

two questions center around departmentalization and the teacher as a specialist in high school work.

Types of Supervisory Problems in the High School

In the secondary school each teacher is a specialist or thinks he is; in this situation he feels, and rightly so, that only another specialist in his subject area can know enough and be skilled enough in it to check up on his work, his materials, his methods, and his success.

Another difficulty for both the supervisor and the teacher who is being supervised arises from the time and class schedule which has been established for departmentalized work in the secondary school. Few schools have a period for one subject-matter class longer than an hour; most periods will not average 55 minutes in length in the clear after pupils have changed classes and become settled. A class period of this length offers to both the teacher and supervisor just about enough time to see the teacher "take hold" or get started; the visitation must be continued at the same period the next day, and the next, until the supervisor gets at least the equivalent of a complete day's time with a teacher and a particular class. In comparison, a supervisor can spend a whole day in an elementary school classroom with the same teacher and begin to get a well-balanced concept of what the teacher is trying to accomplish with his pupils.

The vested interests of the principal and of the teachers also operate to block effective supervision. The principal inherited a type of high school program, a schedule, departmentalization, and specialists; he tends to perpetuate these forms of organization and curriculum, not so much from lack of desire for improvement as from lack of knowledge of how to go about improving the high school program for his students. In like manner, the subject-matter teacher inherits his vested interests; and he naturally tends to promote and protect those interests, such as the requirement of four years of English for graduation based primarily each year upon time allocated respectively to grammar, composition, and literature. The specialist also tends to perpetuate the existing or accepted methods of teaching in his field, such as the analytical or grammatical method of teaching modern foreign languages, even though the oral-aural (the direct) method has proved much more effective and interesting to pupils in attaining a "talking" and reading mastery of the language.

Student or extracurricular activities in the secondary school are just as likely to be carried on separately as they are likely to form a part of the regular classroom work. For example, a supervisor who wishes to become familiar with a beginning English teacher's work may have to visit his classroom, visit after school the dramatics club of which the English teacher is the sponsor, and observe the activities of the homeroom over which the English teacher has supervision. In contrast, most student activities in the elementary school are carried on as a regular part of the day's work and experiences and as part of the school day, not "apart" from the school day.

The fact that the supervisor really lacks training for secondary school supervision operates at times to make supervision a more involved process. Some excellent elementary school supervisors have failed in high school supervision, and vice versa. A minimum requisite for success in high school supervision is successful experience in teaching on the secondary school level. Most authorities also indicate that one other qualification should be included, namely, that the supervisor should have had training in at least two subject-matter teaching areas.

Finally, the different types of curricular programs on the high school level, each established for a particular purpose to meet different interests and needs of students, operate to make supervision a more difficult task. As an illustration, the vocational programs in agriculture or in business education usually require specialized teaching and related or part-time "work experiences" outside of the school walls; in comparison, all of the curricular activities and courses for the college preparatory program can be taken in the school building. How can the supervisor help to improve these special programs? Or should he depend on experts from the state department of education or from outside to help him with these vocational areas?

Special Competencies and Knowledges
Needed by the High School Supervisor

Some of the special information and skills needed by the secondary school supervisor have already been discussed in detail.[4] Attention here, therefore, will be devoted (1) to those problem areas which admittedly cause the supervisor most trouble in carrying on a supervisory program and (2) to a list of references helpful to high school teachers in various teaching fields.

UNDERSTANDING THE VARIOUS CONCEPTS
OF GENERAL EDUCATION

Differing concepts of general education are a major cause of disagreement among high school personnel. Where different teachers hold conflicting concepts, supervision suffers in effectiveness unless the supervisor understands all of the concepts and can work with each teacher within the bounds of his philosophy and his concept.[5]

Some high school teachers and principals believe that *general education is and should be centered around information, facts, and knowledge* that everyone should gain about our heritage, our life, our customs and beliefs, our society and its agencies, our history and our progress, our inventions and discoveries. In order to teach these basic facts to students, the materials in each subject-matter area are organized into "general" and "specialized" courses. Of these, the "general" or "survey" courses are those courses through which pupils achieve the general education that they need; each student takes a minimum number of these general courses; when he has mastered these general courses in different subject-matter areas, he has the general education that he needs. For example, the student is required to take work in general mathematics, general

---

[4] See earlier chs. 3 on texts and text materials, 7 on guidance, 8 on student activities, 9 on evaluation; and 6 on supplementary materials and aids.

[5] Several authors present the different concepts of general education in the curriculum: Harold Alberty, *Reorganizing the High School Curriculum,* rev. ed. (New York: The Macmillan Company, 1953), chs. V-VIII; J. Minor Gwynn, *Curriculum Principles and Social Trends,* 3rd ed. (New York: The Macmillan Company, 1960), chs. IX, XIII; J. Paul Leonard, *Developing the Secondary School Curriculum,* rev. ed. (New York: Rinehart and Company, Inc., 1953), chs. XIII-XIV; Lucile L. Lurry and Elsie G. Alberty, *Developing a High School Core Program* (New York: The Macmillan Company, 1958), chs. I-IV, VII; and Stephen Romine, *Building the High School Curriculum* (New York: The Ronald Press Company, 1954), ch. XII.

science, and civics, history and citizenship in grades 7 and 8 of the junior high school, biology and health in grade 9, world history in grade 10, American history in grade 11, and problems of American democracy in grade 12. At the same time he takes language arts and English through all these grades as a way of acquiring our literary heritage.

In order to help teachers who have this concept of general education, the supervisor has to:

1. Study and become familiar with all courses and texts used in his school as "general" or "survey" courses. The list of these will probably include general mathematics; general science; civics; general language; biology; world history; problems of American democracy; senior mathematics; consumer mathematics, consumer science, and consumer education; sociology; homemaking; shop work and industrial arts; typing, and courses in occupations or vocations.
2. Study and discover, with the help of the English teachers, what work in language arts and English is considered primarily as "general education."
3. Try to *understand* and work with this point of view of general education; try not to change it too fast.

Another concept of general education is that it includes the development also of those skills and competencies, attitudes and patterns of conduct that enable an individual to get along satisfactorily with other human beings and at times happily by himself. This concept of general education puts equal emphasis upon acquiring facts and knowledge on the one hand and attaining skills and competencies through experiences and activities on the other. In addition to taking general or survey courses, pupils learn fundamentals of citizenship by participating in the student council or homeroom organization; by learning typewriting as a tool; by following up biology teaching with the collection of specimens on a field trip or bringing in resource persons like doctors, veterinarians, or nurses; and by participation in intrascholastic or interscholastic competition as a training in teamwork, higher skills, and decision making.

To help the teacher with this concept of general education, the supervisor can:

1. Help to arrange the schedules of the school and of individual students so that participation in both group activities and skill experiences can take place.

2. Aid teachers in planning for a specific activity or experience, such as a field trip, a debate, a panel, or a film.
3. Try to understand and capitalize on this point of view of general education.

There is a *third concept* of general education, still emerging, but now clearly defined. *This concept accepts both the "heritage of the race" idea and the acquisition by the pupils of skills, competencies, attitudes, and patterns of conduct. It differs from the other two concepts primarily in the methods of attaining this general education.* Discarding the idea of general or survey courses as the main means, it uses a natural center of interest as the method in learning and acquiring general education. Around this center of interest the pupil learns in a natural, lifelike situation. For example, units on "Transportation and Communication" and "How to Buy Wisely" are centers of interest in the social studies; "How to Select My Reading Wisely" and "How to Improve My Vocabulary" are centers of interest for work in English; "How Sanitation Protects Health" and "How to Care for Babies" are centers of interest in homemaking. For the center of interest, the teacher and pupils draw materials and information from any subject-matter area when needed and make any trips or use any activities that contribute naturally to the mastery of the center of interest.

When the work in general education for a whole year is planned around large centers of interest in natural sequence, the resulting program is called a "core" or "common learnings" or "basic" program. Such programs are found more frequently in the junior high school grades. One-third to one-half of the pupil's program is devoted to this core and the rest to special subject or special area interests, as algebra in mathematics, dramatic arts in English, physics or chemistry in science, or American history or commercial geography in the social studies.

To help teaching personnel who have this concept of general education, the supervisor has to

1. Become thoroughly familiar with resource units and unit teaching, especially unit teaching focused around centers of interest which take materials from any subject-matter field.[6]
2. Be familiar with rich sources of materials for such teaching, includ-

---

[6] *Cf.* chs. 4 and 5 on the unit method of teaching.

ing texts, workbooks, and seatwork books for drill, supplementary texts and materials, and group activities of many kinds.
3. Learn to understand and capitalize on this point of view of general education.

FAMILIARITY WITH SUBJECT-MATTER AREAS

Teachers tend to feel that they own their subject-matter fields after they have taught for a number of years in them, that they or their colleagues in the same area have most of the answers. This is a natural tendency and builds up in the teacher a feeling of security in his area and in his teaching. On the other hand, this feeling puts pressure upon the supervisor to show the specialist in subject matter that he is familiar enough with the teaching area to give help and suggestions in it.

The supervisor has to take steps like these to make himself more competent in the subject-matter area or to see that a specialist is available to help him and the teacher:

1. He realizes that the areas of learning in subject matter on the high school level, with a few exceptions, are areas that he mastered in his own high school career; in many of those areas, also, he had further training in college. He figures that he had four years of English in high school and at least two further courses in college; that he had at least one and a half years of algebra and a year of plane geometry in high school, followed by some college mathematics; that he had American history and at least one other course in the social studies in high school, and that he had at least two other courses in the social sciences in college; that he had from one to two years of science in high school, and perhaps one to three courses in college; and that he had at least one foreign language in high school, and either a continuation of it for a year or a new foreign language in college. As he looks back on his training and qualifications, he comes to the realization that most high school work, even through grade 12, is of an elementary nature and that he has had enough basic work in each subject area to supervise in that area *provided* he is willing to study the texts that are used in each area, to "freshen up" on his knowledge, and to bring himself up to date. By such study and application, taking one subject-matter area at a time, the supervisor gradually becomes familiar again with subjects in which he was not specially trained later in college. This is really not as big a task as it sounds, since he is presumed to be specially certificated or trained in at least two of these subject fields.

2. He asks the teacher to allow him to "sit in," so that he can bring himself up to date on the subject-matter area as he listens to the teacher and students.
3. He requests the teacher's lists of references, so that he can examine closely any with which he is not familiar.
4. He examines materials and supplementary sources available in the high school library and among the audio-visual aids.
5. He attends departmental meetings to familiarize himself with the special problems of that subject area.
6. He accompanies the teacher and pupils upon field trips and excursions, as opportunity arises.
7. In case he knows nothing about a subject—for example, if he has never had Latin, or studied physics—he makes arrangements for teachers competent in these areas to visit and help his teachers.

ASSISTING HIGH SCHOOL SPECIALISTS

Specialists on the secondary school level furnish another challenge to the supervisor. A specialist might be defined here as a person highly trained in an area, cutting vertically across all school levels. For example, a teacher of home economics is a specialist and would be qualified in some states to teach it on either the elementary or high school level. The same would be true of the industrial arts teacher, or of the agriculture or business education teacher, or of the music or art instructor. These specialists are valuable personnel, prepared as they are to give training to students and teachers in the creative, appreciative, recreational, and vocational sides of life and living.

How can the supervisor aid these specialists? And how can the intensive training of these specialists enrich the school program? To accomplish these purposes the supervisor must:

1. Study the areas of the specialists to see how they can enrich the entire program; for example, discover that the home economics specialist can enrich the seventh-grade program by offering homemaking to both boys and girls three times a week or that the business education teacher can be used to start classes in typing as a tool subject for pupils in the seventh or eighth grade.
2. Look for ways in which these specialists can use their particular knowledge and skill in aiding and training other teachers. For instance, the senior play may need background music for the production, which can be furnished by the co-operation of the school orches-

tra under the direction of the music instructor. Or the piano pupils may be pianists for rhythmics or dancing for the physical education groups. Or the art instructor and her pupils may paint the sets and background props for the presentation of the school play or operetta.

3. Assist the specialists in their areas by getting state department supervisors or specialists from other systems to visit and give suggestions and help. For example, such supervision for federally aided vocational programs is established in each state department.

4. Learn by keen observation during visitation of the main purposes of the special areas. There is no reason why a well-educated supervisor cannot observe and understand most of the materials, texts, class sessions, and individual projects of pupils in home economics, agriculture, industrial arts, and many aspects of vocal music, art, health, physical education, and part-time work and part-time school programs, such as diversified occupations and distributive education.

5. Attend professional meetings of these specialists in order to learn more of their purposes, work, and methods of teaching.

Supervision by the Department Head

The department head might be defined as a director and supervisor of all work which is carried on in his department. The very fact that a department is established in a school and that a head is selected for it implies that the administration delegates some supervisory responsibilities to this department head.

The position of department head came into being early in the development of the secondary school; the present-day emphasis upon it seems to be the result of the rapid consolidation of high schools in the nation. This consolidation, plus the increase in school enrollment, have added to the supervisory burden of the high school principal; now he frequently lacks the time for adequate supervision, as well as the specialized knowledge desirable in a supervisor.

Literature on this subject is meager. Although writers of books on supervision include from a sentence or two to an entire chapter on the activity of the department head, most of these have drawn their conclusions from the same sources. Harlan C. Koch in the 1930's gathered a lot of information upon the duties, responsibilities, and selection of department heads.[7]

---

[7] There was significant interest in the department head as a supervisor in the Depression Decade. For example, read Harlan C. Koch, "Some Aspects of the Department Headship in Secondary Schools" and "Is the Department Headship in Sec-

More recently the Association for Supervision and Curriculum Development of the National Education Association made a study of the department head, with special emphasis upon his role in instructional improvement.[8] These surveys set forth those duties and services commonly found to be provided by the department head, and both revealed that the department head performed in 1950 just about the same activities that he performed in 1930. Of significance here are the supervisory techniques and activities which the 1948 study found to be used most by department heads (see p. 234).

From this report one sees that the department head employs just about the same techniques and devices that the supervisor would employ at one time or another. The main difference between his supervisory task and that of the high school supervisor would be found in the amount of time that he could devote to the task; the department head carries on the average a teaching load of from three to five periods in a six-period day, in addition to looking after his routine reports, materials, and the like. He would thus have much less time to spend on supervision than the principal or the supervisor.

If the department head is to be used as a major supervisory person, the following guiding principles as to selection and allocation of responsibilities are important if he is to be effective:

1. The person chosen for the department head must be well trained and a successful teacher in his subject-matter area.
2. He must be able to "get along with" adults and must possess characteristics of leadership.
3. He must be relieved of enough teaching responsibility to do an effective job of classroom observation and follow-up work.

---

ondary Schools a Professional Myth?" *School Review,* vol. XXXVIII (April and May, 1930), pp. 263-295 and 336-349 respectively; and "Significance of the English Department Head," *English Journal,* vol. XXI (May, 1932), pp. 372-378. However, writers on high school administration and supervision differ sharply now concerning effective use of the department head as a supervisor, as is seen from reading H. R. Douglass, *Modern Administration of Secondary Schools* (Boston: Ginn and Company, 1954), pp. 13-14, 31-33, 114; William M. French, *American Secondary Education* (New York: The Odyssey Press, 1957), pp. 458-459; Robert C. Hammock and Ralph H. Owings, *Supervising Instruction in Secondary Schools* (New York: McGraw-Hill Book Company, 1955), pp. 78-82; and Paul B. Jacobson, *et al., The Effective School Principal* (New York: Prentice-Hall, Inc., 1954), p. 109.

[8] Association for Supervision and Curriculum Development, *The Department Head and Instructional Improvement* (Washington, D. C.: National Education Association, 1948).

Table 5. Supervisory Techniques Used by Department Heads *

	Number of Heads Giving Each Rating		
	Excel-lent	Satis-factory	Unsatis-factory
Informal individual conferences (chats after school or during teachers' free periods)	95	27	2
Group conferences of individuals teaching the same subject	77	32	1
Departmental meetings	63	50	3
Special committees	39	23	4
Research in curriculum	34	43	9
Directed observation and intervisitation	29	24	8
Demonstration teaching	28	29	12
Research in methods	28	41	7
Development of a professional library	27	49	9
Postvisitation conferences	26	31	9
Classroom visitation	25	47	24
Supervisory bulletins	19	42	15
Announcements	15	54	11
Directed professional reading	14	61	13
Previsitation conference	8	28	15
Directed study in:			
Correspondence courses	1	13	11
Extension courses	11	11	10
Summer school courses	11	14	6

* Reprinted with permission from Association for Supervision and Curriculum Development, *The Department Head and Instructional Improvement* (Washington, D. C.: National Education Association, 1948), pp. 13-14. Based on responses from 124 department heads. Compare with these the findings of Fred M. King and James V. Moon, "The Department Head in the Public Secondary School," *The Bulletin of the Association of Secondary-School Principals*, vol. XLIV (March, 1960), pp. 20-24. The only new trend is toward the establishment of a smaller number of division heads.

4. He ought to be given on-the-job training as he prepares to take over his new task.

5. He must realize that he exists primarily to improve instruction and close the gap between the classroom and the principal's office.

6. He should have a complete understanding of and agreement with the principal as to his duties and responsibilities.

7. He should realize that he is a teacher of teachers, and plan and act accordingly.
8. He should keep up to date on new materials, supplies, sources, and methods of teaching.
9. He should realize that the principal must have the final decision on any matter where he differs in opinion from the principal.

In summary, the department head is found usually in the larger schools; smaller schools do not justify the expense of both a department head and a principal. He should be selected because of his knowledge of his subject, his ability to lead adults, and his desire to improve instruction. He is the leader of the teachers in his department, just as the principal is the educational leader of the school. Just as he is a leader and co-ordinator of his teachers, so is he subordinate to the principal, who must supervise the department heads and co-ordinate their work.

The Principal as Supervisor

It is common practice for the high school principal to act as the supervisor as well as principal; this is especially true of high schools which do not exceed more than 300 in enrollment. In this situation, the principal is acting as the special or subject-matter supervisor, in contrast to the general supervisor found more commonly on the elementary school level.

Where the principal is the supervisor of the secondary school, his problems, duties, responsibilities, and techniques for supervision would be similar in most respects to those of the high school supervisor, which were described in the first part of this chapter. There is one important difference, however. No matter how hard he may labor to make them forget it, he still stands as the administrative officer in the eyes of the teachers. As such, he is likely to find teachers more willing to adopt his ideas because he is the recommender for promotion than because he has good ideas.

The California Journal of Secondary Education has presented good analyses of the developing role of the principal and of other special administrative officers for supervision.[9] Half of the high

9 "Symposium,—The Status and Role of Curriculum Assistants and Department Heads in Secondary Schools: How Schools Organize for Instructional Improvement,"

schools in California have a system of department heads; many of the junior and senior high schools have vice-principals, or assistant principals and head counselors. Intelligent use of this newer type of administrative assistant offers good possibilities for the improvement of instruction. Under the direction of the principal, these curriculum assistants work in the following ways:

1. By the formation of small study groups and curriculum committees.
2. By helping to orient substitute teachers and teachers new to the school.
3. By keeping the staff up on new materials, methods, and ideas in the curriculum and in teaching.
4. By planning or arranging field trips and suggesting ways of both preparation and follow-up.
5. By acting as co-ordinating agents between curriculum workers and supervisors in the central office and teachers in the classroom.
6. By planning with resource people, in order to make full use of these specialists in art, audio-visual aids, guidance, music, physical education and health, and the like.
7. By helping to plan better articulation between elementary and junior high school, and between junior and senior high.

Aiding the Substitute Teacher

At all times the substitute teacher has been an instructional problem for the supervisor and the principal. By the very nature of his job the substitute tends to break the continuity and even prog-

---

The California Journal of Secondary Education, vol. XXX (March, 1955), pp. 157-187. Read also Charles M. Long, "Duties of Secondary School Vice-Principals," vol. XLI (February, 1957), pp. 26-32, and "The Principal's Role: Improving the Curriculum," vol. XLIII (February, 1959), pp. 1-119, both in *The Bulletin of the National Association of Secondary School Principals.* The views of administrators are represented by Harl R. Douglass, *Modern Administration of Secondary Schools, op. cit.,* ch. VI; J. B. Edmonson and others, *The Administration of Modern Secondary School,* 4th ed. (New York: The Macmillan Company, 1953), ch. XVIII; Paul B. Jacobson and others, *The Effective School Principal, op. cit.,* chs. V and XXIII; Roland C. Faunce, *Secondary School Administration* (New York: Harper and Brothers, 1955), chs. IV-V; E. L. Prestwood, *The High School Principal and Staff Work Together* (New York: Teachers College, Columbia University, 1957), *passim;* W. L. Cooper and O. D. Miser, "How Can the Principal Achieve Effective Supervision?" *The Bulletin of the National Association of Secondary-School Principals,* vol. XLIV (April, 1960), pp. 233-238; "What Should You Demand of a High School Principal?" *School Management,* vol. IV, no. 9 (September, 1960), pp. 34-38, 84-86, 88; and J. F. Corbally, Jr., *et al., Educational Administration: The Secondary School* (Boston: Allyn and Bacon, 1961), ch. V.

ress of the teaching and learning in a grade or a classroom. The principal and the supervisor should have worked out a list of the approved substitute teachers for each grade or subject, their addresses, and their telephone numbers. They should become thoroughly familiar with the qualifications and experiences of each; and they should try to assign each substitute to the grade level or subject-matter area in which he is best qualified. The supervisor in charge, whether it be the principal, his assistant, a department head, or a special supervisor, can do some advance planning and work with the members of the substitute staff. He can:

1. Have a planning session with them prior to school opening in which the scope and sequence of the various courses are presented in brief form.
2. See that each substitute has in his possession for study the texts used in the classes in which he is to teach.
3. Prepare for the substitute teachers a list of the supplementary texts used in each subject-matter area.
4. Prepare and send to each substitute after school opens a room chart of each floor, with numbers of the various rooms, the library, and the teachers' names.
5. Send to each substitute the schedule of classes, showing hours and room numbers.
6. Supply information to each substitute concerning eating facilities and transportation routes.
7. Keep the list of substitute teachers up-to-date throughout the school year.

Other Problems of the High School Supervisor

The supervisor's responsibility is not so clearly defined in regard to certain other problem areas in the secondary school. These cover a wide range from subject-matter problems to others involving matters of curriculum organization or experimentation. They may be classified roughly into several categories.

PROBLEMS IN SUBJECT-MATTER AREAS

One problem is concerned with several differences of opinion about the teaching of English. Should a high school divide its English instruction into "college preparatory" and "terminal" or "preparation-for-life" groups? Should all teachers be teachers of English? Of reading? Of remedial reading? Where should the main emphasis upon the teaching of grammar come—in the elementary school, in the intermediate grades, or in the high school? Do we try to teach too much grammar of kinds not necessary for competence in writing? [10]

Foreign language teaching poses another problem. Since certain experiments took place in teaching modern foreign language rapidly to military personnel during World War II, other experiments have continued to be made. Issues include where to begin modern foreign language—in elementary, junior high, or senior high school? What methods to employ in teaching? Its place in general education? And its relationship to the modern high school program? To this date the conflict still rages as to the relative difficulty of high school subjects and whether a student can carry successfully two foreign languages at the same time.[11]

Other supervisory problems in high school include how to

[10] Samples of thinking on these problems will be found in: John J. DeBoer, "Grammar in Language Teaching," Elementary English, vol. XXXVI (October, 1959), pp. 413-420; Wilfred Eberhart, "What About Grammar?" The High School Journal, vol. XXXVII (January, 1954), pp. 106-111; "English Aims for Terminal Students," Report of the National Council of Teachers of English Committee on English Terminal Secondary Education, The English Journal, vol. XLIII (December, 1954), pp. 488-492; Maurice L. Pettit, "Should We Give Up on High School English?" The Bulletin of the National Association of Secondary School Principals, vol. XXXIX (November, 1955), pp. 133-137; Robert C. Pooley, "Grammar in the Schools of Today," Elementary English, vol. XXXI (May, 1954), pp. 268-272; and "Teaching Reading for the Gifted in Secondary Schools," and Joseph Mersand, "Individualizing Instruction in English in Large and Small Classes," The Bulletin of the National Association of Secondary School Principals, vol. XXXIX (October, 1955), pp. 1-72, and LXIV (March, 1960), pp. 111-123, respectively.

[11] Recent representative writing on these controversies includes James B. Conant, The American High School Today (New York: McGraw-Hill Book Company, Inc., 1959), pp. 1-64, passim; Manual H. Guerra, "New FLES Adventures and the Villain of Articulation," The Modern Language Journal, vol. XLII (November, 1958), pp. 320-324; G. C. Kettlekamp, "A Comparison of Teaching Objectives in Foreign Language Classes of Western Europe and the United States," The Bulletin of the National Association of Secondary School Principals, vol. XLIV (March, 1960), pp. 105-108; Robert G. Mead, "The Modern Language Association Foreign Language Program," Hispania, vol. XL (December, 1957), pp. 469-477; "Modern Foreign Languages in the Secondary School," The Report of the Committee on Curriculum Planning and Development of the National Association of Secondary School Principals, printed in The Bulletin, vol. XLIII (September, 1959), pp. 1-14; and Jacob Ornstein, "The Crisis in Language Training," The American Scholar, vol. XXIX (Winter, 1959-1960), pp. 75-81. The reader should turn to Chapter 13 of this book for a fuller presentation of the problems of foreign language teaching in the elementary school (now commonly referred to as the FLES program).

teach citizenship education, the place of controversial issues in the schoolroom, and consumer education and education for economic competence through the social studies.[12] Another problem for supervisors is the place of arts and crafts on the secondary school level, and the "what" and "how" of the program in schools of different sizes.[13] The program for the gifted pupil is still another.

PROBLEMS OF ORGANIZATION AND EXPERIMENTATION

There are many kinds. For example, some administrators and supervisors think in terms of freeing the teacher at some time in the day for a reasonable period of relaxation and rest. Others would like to provide time for the teacher to devote to his own study and planning of his work. Provision of time for special experiences for pupils in vocational education or in programs of work experience in high school is another problem. Other problems arise in experimentation for better teaching and methods of teaching; for example, trial has been made of such plans as multiple-period classes, advanced standing for superior students, and the one-subject plan of learning and teaching.[14] Driver education, homemaking and home and family living, industrial arts for girls as well as boys, and the effective development in adolescents of problem-solving skills—

[12] *Cf. Educating for Economic Competence* (Washington: Association for Supervision and Curriculum Development, National Education Association, 1960), *passim;* Jonathon C. McLendon, *Teaching the Social Studies,* No. 20 in the series "What Research Says to the Teacher" (Department of Classroom Teachers and American Educational Research Association, 1960), *passim;* and Franklin Patterson, *High Schools for a Free Society;* Education for Citizenship in American Secondary Schools, prepared by the Tufts University Civic Education Center (Glencoe, The Free Press of Glencoe, 1960), *passim.*

[13] *Cf.* "Symposium on Creative Arts and Crafts in Secondary Education," and G. T. Elmgren, Jr., "Industrial Arts Teachers Place Emphasis on Communication Skills," *California Journal of Secondary Education,* vol. XXVIII (April, 1953), pp. 182-228, and vol. XXXIV (November, 1959), pp. 417-419, respectively.

[14] For samples of views and reports on these aspects, read Marion Cranmore, "Free Time for Teachers," Edward S. Jones and Gloria K. Ortner, "Advanced Standing for Superior Students," *NEA Journal,* vol. XLIII (February, 1954), pp. 85-86 and 107, respectively; Edward A. Krug and others, "Multiple-Period Classes in Wisconsin," *Educational Leadership,* vol. XI (March, 1954), pp. 363-367; Will C. Jumper, "The Gifted Child in the High School," *California Journal of Secondary Education,* vol. XXVI (February, 1951), pp. 76-82; E. H. Lacy, Jr., "The One-Subject Plan in Teaching" and "Advanced Placement Programs in Secondary Schools," Parts I and II, *The Bulletin of the National Association of Secondary School Principals,* vol. XXXIX (November, 1955), pp. 58-60, and vol. XLII (December, 1958), pp. 1-171, respectively; and the special feature in the *NEA Journal* on "Grouping," vol. XLVIII (September, 1959), pp. 17-28.

these are newer subjects or skills calling for emphasis in the high
school curriculum.[15]

Problems for Individual Study and Class Discussion

1. How could you get your staff to study the advantages and disadvantages
   of departmentalization on the secondary school level?
2. Trace the development of general education in the high school. How can
   the supervisor clarify the goals of general education to teachers?
3. Should the department head be trained in general supervision, since he is a
   type of supervisor? Why or why not?
4. Make out an information folder for the substitute teachers, giving necessary
   and pertinent information. Be sure to include such information as to where
   to find: (a) class rolls, seating charts, and register; (b) courses of study;
   (c) textbooks; (d) teaching plans, and the like.
5. If all courses in all subject-matter areas were made elective, would the result
   be better teaching in all areas? Or not? Support your point of view.
6. Identify "multiple-period" classes, and give examples of how such a program
   would operate.
7. The local Chamber of Commerce has proposed that your high school offer
   driver-education training to older boys and girls, and they have furnished
   free the cars with dual controls to be used in the program. The principal
   asks you, the supervisor, to work out a plan for it, including the teacher who
   is to be the instructor. How will you proceed?
8. How would you proceed to gather objective data on whether a pupil can
   carry successfully two foreign languages at the same time? Explain.
9. What opportunities does the secondary school supervisor have for group
   guidance? Identify them.

Special Bibliography for the High School Supervisor

This Special Bibliography includes primarily only *recent, selected* references, easy to procure and still available in print. This selective process forced

---

[15] These selected references point up these difficult problems and offer some
suggestions for solutions: O. L. Davis, Jr., "Children Can Learn Complex Concepts,"
Educational Leadership, vol. XVII (December, 1959), pp. 170-175; "High School
of the Future," a symposium, *California Journal of Secondary Education*, vol. XXXIV
(October, 1959), pp. 363-384; "Is Driver Education a 'Frill'?" *School Management*,
vol. III, no. 9 (September, 1959), pp. 57-58, 62-63; Lucien B. Kinney, "Developing
Problem-Solving Skills in Adolescents," *The High School Journal*, vol. XXXV (January, 1952), pp. 113-119; Frank B. Lindsay, "How Can the Instructional Program in
California High Schools Be Improved?" *California Journal of Secondary Education*,
vol. XXXV (January, 1960), pp. 5-11; and Joseph T. Nerden, "Industrial Education
for Today and Tomorrow," *American Vocational Journal*, vol. XXXIV (April, 1959),
pp. 15-16.

the omission of some of the older classical treatises that are well known in the field of supervision, and of most single periodical references.

NOTE: For brevity the following key to professional organizations and/or publications is used:

AAHPER   American Association for Health, Physical Education, and Recreation
AASA   American Association of School Administrators, National Education Association
ASCD   Association for Supervision and Curriculum Development, National Education Association
Cal. Jour.   *California Journal of Secondary Education*
EPC   Educational Policies Commission, American Association of School Administrators and National Education Association
H.S. Jour.   *The High School Journal*
NASSP   *The Bulletin of the National Association of Secondary School Principals,* National Education Association
NCSE   National Commission on Safety Education, National Education Association
NCSS   National Council for the Social Studies, National Education Association
NCTE   National Council of Teachers of English, Chicago
NEA   National Education Association, 1201 Sixteenth Street, N. W., Washington 6, D. C.
NSSE   National Society for the Study of Education
NSTA   National Science Teachers Association, National Education Association

ART

Conant, H., and Randall, A., *Art in Education* (Peoria: Charles A. Bennett Company, 1959).
Jefferson, B., *Teaching Art to Children* (Boston: Allyn and Bacon, 1959).
Lowenfeld, V., *Creative and Mental Growth,* 3rd ed. (New York: The Macmillan Company, 1957).
————, *Your Child and His Art* (New York: The Macmillan Company, 1954).
Wickiser, R. L., *An Introduction to Art Education* (Yonkers-on-Hudson: World Book Company, 1957).

CURRICULUM

Alberty, H., *Reorganizing the High School Curriculum,* rev. ed. (New York: The Macmillan Company, 1953), parts II-V.
Conant, J. B., *The American High School Today* (New York: McGraw-Hill Book Company, 1959).
————, *The Child, the Parent, and the State* (Cambridge: Harvard University Press, 1959).

Douglass, H. R., ed., *The High School Curriculum*, 2nd ed. (New York: The Ronald Press Company, 1956), chs. VII-VIII, XII, and XXII-XXXII, for trends and the subject-matter and special teaching fields.

Krug, E. A., *Secondary School Curriculum* (New York: Harper and Brothers, 1960), arranged by subject matter and special teaching areas, *passim*.

Leonard, J. P., *Developing the Secondary School Curriculum*, rev. ed. (New York: Rinehart and Company, Inc., 1953).

NASSP, "Human Relations in Secondary Education," vol. XXXIX, no. 209 (March, 1955), pp. 1-109.

Romine, S., *Building the High School Curriculum* (New York: The Ronald Press Company, 1954).

The Secondary School Curriculum, The Year Book of Education, 1958 (Yonkers-on-Hudson, World Book Company), Section III, chs. I-V.

DRIVER EDUCATION

Hyde, M. O., *Driving Today and Tomorrow* (New York: Whittlesey House, 1954).

NCSE, *Policies and Practices for Driver Education* (1954).

ENGLISH

Blair, G. M., *Diagnostic and Remedial Teaching* (New York: The Macmillan Company, 1956).

Burton, D. L., *Literature Study in the High Schools* (New York: Henry Holt and Company, Inc., 1959).

Fay, L. C., *Reading in the High School*, No. 11, "What Research Says to the Teacher," Department of Classroom Teachers and American Educational Research Association, NEA (1956).

Kerber, A. B., and Jett, T. F., Jr., *The Teaching of Creative Poetry* (Indianapolis: The Waldemar Press, 1956).

NASSP, *English Language Arts*, vol. XL, no. 258 (October, 1960), pp. 46-58.

————, *Reading Problems in the Secondary School*, vol. XXXIX, no. 212 (September, 1955), pp. 3-125.

NCTE, Commission on the English Curriculum: *The English Language Arts* (1953).

————, ————: *The English Language Arts in the Secondary School* (1956).

Norvell, G. W., *The Reading Interests of Young People* (Boston: D. C. Heath and Company, 1950).

Pooley, R. C., *Teaching English Grammar* (New York: Appleton-Century-Crofts, Inc., 1957).

Saltzberg, G., *Knowing Your Newspaper* (Yonkers-on-Hudson: World Book Company, 1953).

Sauer, E. H., *English in the Secondary School* (New York: Holt, Rinehart and Winston, Inc., 1961).

Simpson, E. A., *Helping High-School Students Read Better* (Chicago: Science Research Associates, 1954).

Thomas, C. A., *Language Power for Youth* (New York: Appleton-Century-Crofts, Inc., 1954).

Wolfe, D. M., *Creative Ways to Teach English* (New York: The Odyssey Press, 1958).

FOREIGN LANGUAGE

Huebner, T., *How to Teach Foreign Languages Effectively* (New York: New York University Press, 1959).

Stack, E. M., *The Language Laboratory and Modern Language Teaching* (New York: Oxford University Press, 1960).

White, D. S., *The Teaching of Latin* (Chicago: Scott, Foresman and Company, 1941).

GENERAL EDUCATION, COMMON LEARNINGS OR THE CORE, AND UNIT TEACHING

AASA, Thirty-Second Yearbook (1954), *Education for American Citizenship.*

Faunce, R. C., and Bossing, N. L., *Developing the Core Curriculum*, 2nd ed. (Englewood Cliffs, N. J.: Prentice-Hall, Inc., 1958).

Hanna, L. A., Potter, G. L., and Hagaman, N., *Unit Teaching in the Elementary School* (New York: Rinehart and Company, Inc., 1955).

H.S. *Jour.*, "General Education in the Secondary School," vol. XXXVII (1953-1954).

Hock, L. E., and Hill, T. J., *The General Education Class in the Secondary School* (New York: Holt, Rinehart, and Winston, Inc., 1960).

Jewett, A., *Recordings for Teaching Literature and Language in the High School*, including a bibliography of 500 titles, Federal Security Agency, Office of Education, Bulletin 1952, no. 19.

MacConnell, C. M., and others, *New Schools for a New Culture: The Story of the Evanston Township High School Core Program*, rev. ed. (New York: Harper and Brothers, 1953).

NCSS, *Social Understanding Through Literature* (1954).

GUIDANCE

Loughary, J. W., *Counseling in Secondary Schools* (New York: Harper and Brothers, 1960).

McDaniel, H. B., *Guidance in the Modern School* (New York: The Dryden Press, 1956).

Miller, C. H., *Foundations of Guidance* (New York: Harper and Brothers, 1960).

NASSP, *Guidance Practices in Secondary Schools*, vol. XXXVIII, no. 200 (February, 1954), pp. 1-159.

Peters, H. J., and Farwell, G. F., *Guidance, a Developmental Approach* (Chicago: Rand McNally, 1959).

Traxler, A. E., *Techniques of Guidance*, rev. ed. (New York: Harper and Brothers, 1957).

HEALTH AND PHYSICAL EDUCATION

AAHPER, *Physical Education for High School Students* (1955).

AASA, Twentieth Yearbook, rev. ed. (1951), *Health in Schools*.

Atkins, A. J., and Gwynn, J. M., *Teaching Alcohol Education in the Schools* (New York: The Macmillan Company, 1959).

Baruch, D., *New Ways in Sex Education* (New York: McGraw-Hill Book Company, 1959).

Byrd, O. E., compiler, *School Health Sourcebook* (Stanford: Stanford University Press, 1955).

Cal. Jour., "Symposium on Health, Physical Education, and Recreation," vol. XXVII (April, 1952), pp. 189-241.

Cassidy, R. F., *Curriculum Development in Physical Education* (New York: Harper and Brothers, 1954).

Grout, R. E., *Health Teaching in Schools: For Teachers in Elementary and Secondary Schools*, 2nd ed. (Philadelphia: W. B. Saunders Company, 1953).

NASSP, *Administration of the Health, Physical Education and Recreation Program in Secondary Schools*, vol. XXXVII, no. 195 (May, 1953), pp. 1-136.

———, *Fitness for Secondary School Youth*, vol. XL, no. 218 (March, 1956), pp. 1-150.

———, *Outdoor Education for American Youth*, vol. XLI, no. 229 (May, 1957), pp. 1-155.

———, *Health, Physical Education, and Recreation in the Secondary Schools*, vol. XLIV (May, 1960), pp. 1-197.

Wiles, K., Brown, C., and Cassidy, R., *Supervision in Physical Education* (Englewood Cliffs, N. J.: Prentice-Hall, Inc., 1956).

INDUSTRIAL AND PRACTICAL ARTS

Cal. Jour., "Changing Conceptions in the Practical Arts," vol. XXIX (March, 1954), pp. 143-176.

NASSP, *Home Economics in the Secondary School*, vol. XXXVII, no. 196 (October, 1953), pp. 1-124.

MATHEMATICS

Brown, C. H., *The Teaching of Secondary Mathematics* (New York: Harper and Brothers, 1953).

Butler, C. H., and Wren, F. L., *The Teaching of Secondary Mathematics*, 3rd ed. (New York: McGraw-Hill Book Company, Inc., 1960).

Eves, H., *An Introduction to the History of Mathematics* (New York: Rinehart and Company, Inc., 1953).

Fehr, H. F., *Teaching High-School Mathematics*, "What Research Says to the Teacher, No. 9" (Washington, D. C.: Department of Classroom Teachers and American Educational Research Association, NEA, 1955).

Morton, R. L., *Teaching Children Arithmetic* (New York: Silver Burdett Company, 1953).

NASSP, *Mathematics in Secondary Schools Today,* vol. XXXVIII, no. 203 (May, 1954), pp. 1-196.

Reeve, W. D., *Mathematics for the Secondary School* (New York: Henry Holt and Company, Inc., 1954).

MUSIC

Marrel, L., *The Music Consultant at Work* (New York: Teachers College, Columbia University, 1960).

Mathews, P., *You Can Teach Music* (New York: E. P. Dutton and Company, Inc., 1953).

Morgan, H. N., ed., *Music in American Education* (Chicago, 4: Music Educators National Conference, 1955).

Mursell, J. L., *Education for Musical Growth* (Boston: Ginn and Company, 1948).

NASSP, *The Function of Music in the Secondary-School Curriculum,* vol. XXXVI, no. 189 (November, 1952), pp. 1-57, and *Music—A Vital Force in Today's Secondary Schools,* vol. XLIII, no. 245 (March, 1959), pp. 1-115.

Righter, C. B., *Success in Teaching School Orchestras and Bands* (Minneapolis: Paul A. Schmitt Music Company, 1945).

Snyder, K. D., *School Music Administration and Supervision* (Boston: Allyn and Bacon, 1959).

Sur, W. R., *Music Education for Teen-Agers* (New York: Harper and Brothers, 1958).

SCIENCE

Burnett, R. W., *Teaching Science in the Secondary School* (New York: Rinehart and Company, Inc., 1957).

Chase, J. B., Jr., *A Guide to Curriculum Study, Science: Grades 1-12* (Raleigh: State Board of Education, 1959).

H. S. Jour., "New Trends in Science Education," vol. XLIII (March, 1960), pp. 302-342.

Laybourn, K., and Bailey, C. H., *Teaching Science to the Ordinary Pupil* (New York: Philosophical Library, 1958).

Morholt, E., and others, *A Sourcebook for the Biological Sciences* (New York: Harcourt, Brace and Company, 1959).

NASSP, *Science in Secondary Schools Today,* vol. XXXVII, no. 191 (January, 1953), pp. 2-207.

NSTA, *School Facilities for Science Instruction* (1954).

——, *Science Teaching Aids,* II, edited by Abraham Raskin (1955).

Richardson, J. S., *Science Teaching in Secondary Schools* (Englewood Cliffs, N. J.: Prentice-Hall, Inc., 1957).

Roucek, J. S., ed., *Challenge of Science Education* (New York: Philosophical Library, 1959).

Science Education in American Schools, Forty-sixth Yearbook, part I (1947), and *Rethinking Science Education,* Fifty-ninth Yearbook, part I (1960),

National Society for the Study of Education (Chicago: the University of Chicago Press).

Thurber, W. A., and Collette, A. T., *Teaching Science in Today's Secondary Schools* (Boston: Allyn and Bacon, 1959).

SOCIAL SCIENCES

ASCD, *Educating for Economic Competence* (1960).

Cal. Jour., "Symposium: The Social Studies in California's Secondary Schools," vol. XXX (May, 1955), pp. 277-311.

Gross, R. E., and Zeleny, L. D., *Educating Citizens for Democracy* (New York: Oxford University Press, 1958).

H. S. Jour., "New Approaches to Social Studies," vol. XLIII (April, 1960), pp. 346-397.

Horwitz, R., and others, *Civic Education in the United States: A Directory of Organizations*, and *Supplement* (University of Chicago, University College, and Michigan State University, School of Business and Public Service, 1954 and 1958-1959, respectively).

Hunt, M. P., and Metcalf, L. E., *Teaching High School Social Studies: Problems in Reflective Thinking and Social Understanding* (New York: Harper and Brothers, 1955).

Johnson, E. S., *Theory and Practice of the Social Studies* (New York: The Macmillan Company, 1956).

Logasa, H., *Historical Fiction and Other Reading References for Classes in Junior and Senior High Schools*, 5th ed. (Philadelphia: McKinley Publishing Company). Issued periodically.

McLendon, J. C., *Teaching the Social Studies*, no. 20 in the series, "What Research Says to the Teacher" (Washington: Department of Classroom Teachers and American Educational Research Association, National Education Association, 1960).

Moffatt, M. P., *Social Studies Instruction*, 2nd ed. (Englewood Cliffs, N. J.: Prentice-Hall, Inc., 1954).

NCSS, *Social Studies in the Senior High School* (1953).

——, *Skills in Social Studies*, Twenty-fourth Yearbook (1954).

——, *Improving the Social Studies Curriculum*, Twenty-sixth Yearbook (1956).

——, *Citizenship and a Free Society: Education for the Future*, Thirtieth Yearbook (1960).

NSSE, *Social Studies in the Elementary School*, Fifty-Sixth Yearbook (1957), part II.

Patterson, F., *High Schools for a Free Society: Education for Citizenship in American Schools* (Glencoe: The Free Press of Glencoe, Illinois, 1960).

——, and others, *The Adolescent Citizen* (Glencoe: The Free Press of Glencoe, 1960).

Preston, R. C., ed., *Teaching World Understanding* (Englewood Cliffs, N. J.: Prentice-Hall, Inc., 1955).

Tiegs, E. W., and Adams, F. E., *Teaching the Social Studies* (Boston: Ginn and Company, 1959).

Wesley, E. B., and Wronski, S. P., *Teaching Social Studies in High Schools*, 4th ed. (Boston: D. C. Heath and Company, 1958).

SPEECH

Eisenson, J., and Ogilvie, M., *Speech Correction in the Schools* (New York: The Macmillan Company, 1957).

Friederich, W. J., and Wilcox, R. A., *Teaching Speech in High Schools* (New York: The Macmillan Company, 1953).

NASSP, *A Speech Program for Secondary Schools*, vol. XXXVIII, no. 199 (January, 1954), pp. 1-234.

STUDENT AND SCHOOL ACTIVITIES

ASCD, *School Camping: A Frontier of Curriculum Improvement*, by John W. Gilliland (1954).

EPC, NEA, and AASA, *School Athletics* (1954).

Kraus, R., *Recreation Leader's Handbook* (New York: McGraw-Hill Book Company, Inc., 1955).

Lease, R., and Siks, G. B., *Creative Dramatics in Home, School, and Community* (New York: Harper and Brothers, 1952).

Scott, H. A., *Competitive Sports in Schools and Colleges* (New York: Harper and Brothers, 1951, 1954).

MISCELLANEOUS

AASA, *The High School in a Changing World*, Thirty-Sixth Yearbook, 1958.

ASCD, *Leadership for Improving Instruction*, 1960 Yearbook.

———, *What Shall the High School Teach?* (1956).

H.S. Jour., "How Will the New School Library Standards Affect High School Libraries?" by E. E. Ahlers, vol. XLIII (November, 1959), pp. 42-46.

Koerner, J. D., ed., *The Case for Basic Education: A Program of Aims for Public Schools* (Boston: Little, Brown and Company, 1959).

NASSP, *The Effective Secondary-School Library*, vol. XLIII (November, 1959), pp. 1-190.

———, *Public Relations for the American High School*, vol. XLIV, no. 257 (September, 1960), pp. 1-137.

Orchard, N. E., *Study Successfully* (New York: McGraw-Hill Book Company, Inc., 1953). For students and teachers' use with students.

Parrish, L., and Waskin, Y., *Teacher-Pupil Planning for Better Classroom Learning* (New York: Harper and Brothers, 1958).

Smith, D. V., *Communication, The Miracle of Shared Living* (New York: The Macmillan Company, 1955).

Vocational Education for Rural America, 1958-1959 Yearbook, Department of Rural Education, National Education Association.

Zapf, R. M., *Democratic Processes in Secondary Education* (Englewood Cliffs, N. J.: Prentice-Hall, Inc., 1959).

CHAPTER 12

Supervision in the

Junior High School

THERE IS LITTLE ATTENTION GIVEN to supervision on the junior high school level. Most writers seem to take it for granted that elementary school supervision usually takes in the seventh and eighth grades as part of its responsibility, and that high school supervision includes grade nine.

However, the rapid growth of the junior high school as a separate educational level for young adolescents [1] has resulted in a demand for better ways of improving its instruction. This chapter will be devoted to the primary purpose of suggesting steps the supervisor may take to work toward improvement of junior high school teaching, without repeating the techniques of supervision which have been presented in other chapters or duplicating the special problems in supervision found on the secondary and elementary school levels.

Steps in Program Planning for the Junior High School

1. RECOGNIZING THE CHARACTERISTICS OF EARLY ADOLESCENCE

Perhaps the soundest reason for the establishment of the junior high school as a separate educational level is to care for the special problems of early adolescence. With the onset of pubescence, the

---

[1] Cf. W. H. Gaumnitz and committee, *Junior High School Facts—A Graphic Analysis*, Misc. No. 21, November, 1954 (Washington, D. C.: U. S. Department of Health, Education, and Welfare, 1955), *passim*.

248

young adolescent begins the transition from individual to group control; from primarily individual activity to group activity; from dependence upon adult control to independence of adult authority; from boyhood and girlhood to manhood and womanhood; and from family controls to societal controls. During the junior high school years, approximately from twelve to fifteen years of age, the young adolescent exhibits the following characteristics which the teacher and supervisor should capitalize upon and use to advantage in the instructional program: [2]

Showing gradually emerging heterosexual development.

Showing the emerging of a new pattern of religious problems.

Seeking security in regard to his adult status, his own peer group, or "gang," and himself.

Desiring group approval.

Self-conscious and bashful.

Feeling a need for independence from parental authority, manifested at times by defiance toward other forms of adult authority.

Daydreaming and prone to emulate other personalities in the process.

Feeling more intensified emotions than adults, but for shorter periods of time.

Awkward.

Prone to save face.

Widening in his interests.

Self-centered, as evidenced by carelessness and thoughtlessness, resulting primarily from physical and emotional changes.

Tending to be overly aggressive when thwarted.

Highly physically resistant to disease.

Showing off, as evidenced by being faddish and boastful.

After looking carefully at this list of characteristics, supervisors formulate the following rather simple set of working principles as they try to help the teachers of this young adolescent:

(1) the young adolescent is establishing himself as a young adult, desiring to establish his independence from adults, and wishing to be treated as a young adult; (2) in establishing himself as a young adult, the youth is insecure in adult society, does not know exactly how to act,

---

[2] The characteristics set forth here, and the principles concerning their use which follow are quoted or presented in modified form, with permission, from J. Minor Gwynn, *Curriculum Principles and Social Trends,* 3rd ed. (New York: The Macmillan Company, 1960), pp. 432-434.

but decidedly does not want to act as or appear to be still a child; (3) a youth at this age, in the process of becoming an adult, must establish himself in his gang or peer group, among the other boys and girls who are becoming young adults; therefore he must adhere more to the ideas, customs, and rules of the gang than he does to those of adult authority; (4) each boy and girl has an irregular growth pattern at this age, peculiar to himself alone; and each is particularly resistant to physical ills at this time; (5) the normal development of a boy or girl in early adolescence leads eventually to emerging interest in the *opposite*, not primarily in the same sex; (6) since the adolescent is establishing new group standards and values at this age, he is more likely to tell his teacher the truth about himself and his actions than he is to give information or "tell" on the actions or behavior of others; and (7) the punishment by the gang of a youth who has broken the code of the gang is usually much more severe than any punishment that the teacher might give to a student under similar circumstances.

2. DETERMINING STAFF QUALIFICATIONS FOR JUNIOR HIGH SCHOOL WORK

Not many teachers are trained specifically for teaching on the junior high school level. A few states provide for the issuance of a teaching certificate for the junior high school, with prescription of courses that presumably will prepare a candidate adequately.[3] In most states the prevailing practice is (*a*) to allow a teacher with an elementary or grammar grade certificate to teach in the junior high school also, preferably in grades seven and eight and/or (*b*) to permit a high school teacher with a subject-matter certificate to teach either on the senior or junior high school level.

Differing types of preparation. There is general agreement among educational writers that the teacher for the junior high school should have a broad training in general education and that he should have more concentrated training in from two to as many as four of the subject-matter areas commonly taught in the intermediate grades.[4]

---

[3] For example, California, Maine, Maryland, and Wisconsin. *Cf. A Manual on Certification Requirements for School Personnel in the United States,* Office of Education, Circular No. 290, (Washington, D. C.: Federal Security Agency, 1951); and R. C. Woellner and M. A. Wood, *Requirements for Certification of Teachers and Administrators* (Chicago: University of Chicago Press), an annual publication.

[4] *Cf.* J. L. Wattenbarger, "Competencies Needed by Core Teachers," *Educational Research Bulletin,* vol. XXXII (October 14, 1953), pp. 181-185; *Developing Programs for Young Adolescents* and *Preparation for Core Teachers for Secondary*

The more recent recommendations for the preparation of teachers for fused or core work in the junior high school range from 80 to 100 hours in the four general areas of the humanities, the social sciences, the sciences, and the arts.

On the other hand, junior high schools seem to recruit more of their teachers from those trained for high school work. This results usually in more subject-matter specialists in the junior high school; fewer elementary teachers with more general training for the upper elementary grades choose to work in the junior high. In this situation the main task of the supervisor emerges clearly—it is to help these high school specialists through in-service education to broaden their training and outlook in order to meet the special needs of these young adolescents better, in order to see more clearly the interrelationships of the basic subject-matter areas, and in order to eliminate needless duplication of subject matter in the middle grades.

How to identify teaching competencies needed in the junior high school. One method of in-service education is to identify the teaching qualifications and guidance competencies in each member of the staff. After this information has been accumulated, the staff of a school can really begin to know how rich a program it can offer to young adolescents. Table 6 illustrates the large number of teaching areas and interest areas in which a group of 15 people as the theoretical staff of a 350-pupil junior high school were competent to give instruction and guidance.[5]

An analysis of the qualifications and competencies of this staff of fifteen teachers reveals the remarkable fact that they can give both competent instruction and guidance to young adolescents in (1) all regularly recognized subject-matter areas; (2) in introductory vocational work, except vocational agriculture; (3) in music and art, except in instrumental music for band and orchestra; and

---

Schools, Association for Supervision and Curriculum Development (Washington, D. C.: National Education Association, 1954, 1955), Part III and *passim,* respectively; and H. W. Koolen and G. L. Ogden, "Teachers," ch. 4 in "Organizing the Junior High School," *The Bulletin of the National Association of Secondary-School Principals,* vol. XXXV (December, 1951), pp. 45-58.

[5] These 15 teachers in summer school decided to explore their preparation and competencies for junior high school work. After listing their professional and human resources, they placed themselves in an actual new junior high school situation to see what kind of program they could offer. Of course a fictitious name has been given to both the new junior high school and the urban-fringe community which it now serves.

Table 6. Preparation and Competencies of a Junior High School Staff of Fifteen*

ANDERSON: Experience, 2 years in D and S
Social Studies
English
Physical education
Photography
Student government
Coach (B and G)

CORBIN: Experience, 2 years in D and S; O
Science
Mathematics
Physical education
Industrial arts
Coach

WARD: Experience, none; Y and D
English
Social studies
Typing
School publications
Spanish

SHAW: Experience, 1 year; O and D
Mathematics
Latin
School publications

BUCHANAN: Experience, 4 years in D and S; O
English
Social studies
Journalism and publications
Music appreciation
Poetry

ATKINSON: Experience, 10 years in D and S; Y
Science
Social studies
Librarian
Dramatics

DANIELS: Experience, 2 years in D; O
Social studies (High School)
Grades 7 and 8 (D)
Electronics
Guidance
International affairs

HAMPTON: Experience, 30 years in D and S
Any regular subject
Latin
Spanish
German
Clubs
Dramatics
Grades 7 and 8 (S)
Publications
Handling activities finances
Consumer education
Driver education
Sex education
Homemaking
Coach

HAYS: Experience, 16 years in D and S
Lunchroom and cafeteria
Social studies
7-8-9 (D)
Driver education
Vocational education program and teaching
4-H Clubs
PTA liaison

HUSKINS: Experience, 8 years in D and S
Science
Mathematics
Physical education
Social studies
Guidance
Work with slow groups
Student government
Audio-visual

HUSKINS (*cont.*)
Clubs
City recreation centers

POPE: Experience, 5 years in D; O
English
Social studies
Grades 7 and 8 (S)
Dramatics
Guidance
Debating
Music appreciation

PENDERGRAFT: Experience, 2 years in D and S; O
Vocal music
French
English
Model building
Photography

WOOSLEY: Experience, 3 years in D and S; O
English

WOOSLEY (*cont.*)
Piano
Square and social dancing
Glee club and chorus
Dramatics

HANES: Experience, 2 years in D and S
English
Grade 7 (S)
Art
Debating
Dramatics
Librarian
Creative writing

McDONALD: Experience, 12 years in D and S
Social studies
Health and physical education
Grades 7 and 8 (S)
Audio-visual
Student council
Coach

---

* Key to teaching preferences and experience:
  O = Older children   D = Departmentalized
  Y = Younger children   S = Self-contained
  B and G = Boys and girls

---

(4) in hobbies and exploratory activities of many kinds, as well as in almost any kinds of student or extracurricular activities. This is a good illustration of the opportunities that would be available to adolescents in depth of exploration.

3. FITTING STAFF QUALIFICATIONS AND COMPETENCIES INTO A PROGRAM FOR A PARTICULAR SCHOOL

This third step naturally follows. The first step is to recognize the special characteristics and needs of adolescents; the second step is to discover the subject-matter and special competencies of the staff for meeting those needs. The third step is to use the general and special competencies of the staff to institute a program to meet the young adolescent's special characteristics and needs in a particular community.

Each junior high school will have its own community background into which its program must fit. One community will be primarily rural, and its educational needs will be more rural than otherwise. Another community will be urban, with little or no rural needs and contacts for its children. Still another may include both town and country population and show need for more diversification in its educational program.

Are the qualifications and competencies of this staff of 15 adequate for a rich and satisfactory program for any type of community? Let us place it in a 350-pupil, new junior high school in an urban-fringe community which has three characteristics:

A. *Location and background*

    1. Geographical location: The new Stevenson Junior High School is located in the eastern part of Strong County, in a southeastern state, approximately one mile from the city limits of Caropolis; this city has a population of 150,000; is a manufacturing and industrial center; serves as wholesale distribution center for two states; and has a population of one million within a 30-mile radius.

    2. *School area*: This new junior high school has a 12-mile radius merging into the Caropolis city limits. All students attending this school are from the county school system, with the exception of tuition-paying students from the city system. The majority of the school population is from the fringe area bordering the city.

    3. *Background*: At the present time there are six junior high schools in eastern Strong County. A rapid increase in population and immigration into the area necessitated the construction of a new school to release room for the influx of elementary school children. The new Stevenson Junior High building will accommodate grade levels 7, 8, and 9 from four of the six present junior high schools in the eastern part of Strong County.

B. 1. *Population*: Population is increasing at a rapid rate in this area; according to a recent survey this junior high school might be incorporated into the city school administration in the future.

C. *Economic-sociological factors*:

    1. *Parents*: A great percentage of the parents living in this suburban or fringe area own homes and are employed or have business establishments within the city. The greater majority of the homes have all modern city conveniences. In sociological classification, approximately one-third of the families belong in the upper, one-third in the middle, and one-third in the upper lower-class level. A very small percentage of ethnic elements is present.

2. *Students*: Students promoted from Stevenson Junior High will attend the consolidated senior high school approximately one mile away. Many students in the senior high possess or have the use of automobiles.

   Approximately 20 per cent of the students from the senior high school enroll in college; about 5 per cent engage in dairy or truck farming. The remaining students attend local city business colleges or secure employment within the city.

3. *Teaching Personnel*: The majority of the teachers reside within the city or suburban area. A residence is provided for the principal near the school site.

D. *Transportation*: The school has access to the primary highway system. Buses are provided for all students. Many students have or have access to private automobiles for transportation to and from school.

As the description of the community reveals the situation and its economic, social, and population factors, one becomes increasingly aware of the fact that this relatively young faculty could put into operation as rich a program as this community could desire. Their lack of training in instrumental music and vocational agriculture will be no real handicap, since arrangements can be made for this work with the consolidated senior high school one mile distant.

The first task of the principal as supervisor of the junior high school, or of the junior high school supervisor, is that of getting faculty members to list their academic training, their hobbies and special interests, the age and grade levels on which they want to teach, the subject-matter areas that they want to teach, and the special interests that they want to handle that coincide with pupils' exploratory work and hobbies at this early adolescent age. Once this task is done, the foundation has been laid for the richest type of program.

Curricular Problems Peculiar to the Junior High School

The introduction of departmentalization into the intermediate grades which comprise the junior high school was the starting point for a sharp difference of opinion concerning the kind of curricular program which was desirable. One point at issue was the place of the junior high school in general education; another involved the methods of learning and teaching at this level which are considered soundest according to the findings of the experts in child growth and psychology.

TYPES OF PROGRAMS FOR GENERAL EDUCATION

The three major concepts of general education and the curriculum program that would attain each have already been presented in detail in Chapter 11.[6] In the junior high school, these ways have been advocated for the student to acquire general education:

1. To attain the *heritage of the race concept*, through required subjects, particularly through "general" or "survey" courses in the major subject-matter areas of the language arts and English, mathematics, science, social studies, and health and physical education.[7] Teachers who believe in this concept usually prefer to have departmentalization complete in the junior high school from grade 7 through grade 9, just as the senior high school work is departmentalized. Almost all of the work is required in grades 7 and 8; the ninth-grade work is pointed more toward the first year of a four-year high school than toward general education and exploratory interests.

2. To attain the *knowledges-and-skills concept of general education*, through both (a) general and survey courses and (b) correlation of work in subject-matter courses with activities and learning experiences of a practical nature. An example of how a teacher who believes in this concept accomplishes his purposes can be taken from the field of the social studies. The teacher in grade 8 will take the children to the water plant, the filter station, the local abattoir, and the veterinarian's office to study sanitation and the local government's responsibility for it; at the same time, he will correlate these trips and this study with other aspects of science, such as how water is purified, and why sewage has to be handled properly. This approach still sticks to subject matter as basic areas of learning but makes better use of units, resource materials, and experiences in a natural learning situation.

---

[6] See pp. 227-230.

[7] The supervisor should turn back to ch. 11 for suggestions to assist any teacher who believes in any one of these three concepts of general education.

3. To attain the *"common learnings"* or *"basic" program,* or *"core"* concept of general education, through classwork planned around large centers of interest in natural sequence without regard for subject-matter lines. One-third to one-half of the student's program in the junior high school would be devoted to this "core" for the purposes of general education; the rest of the pupil's time would be given over to exploring special interests or taking work in special subject-matter areas. Authorities differ as to whether correlation and fusion of subject-matters are a type of "core" or "common learning" program.[8] In order to help teachers who have the core concept of general education, the supervisor has to be thoroughly familiar with units of work and unit teaching and with units or centers of interest which take materials and activities from any related subject-matter area.[9] He must also be aware of rich sources of materials for this kind of teaching, including texts, supplementary texts and materials of many sorts, workbooks and seatwork drill books, and group activities of many kinds.

THE EMERGENCE OF THE CORE CURRICULUM

The core curriculum has several characteristics which mark it. Generally it is a course designed to meet the general needs of all pupils; it has a center of interest or a cluster of problems which involve material or information from two or more related subject-matter fields; it involves the same teacher and the same group of pupils for a double period or a block of time longer than one regular period; it is characterized by teacher-pupil planning; and it furnishes many opportunities for guidance for pupils in a lifelike situation.[10]

The educator should have the following facts on the core

[8] *Cf.* Harold Alberty, *Reorganizing the High School Curriculum,* rev. ed. (New York: The Macmillan Company, 1953), ch. VI; Roland C. Faunce and Nelson L. Bossing, *Developing the Core Curriculum,* 2nd ed. (Englewood Cliffs, N. J.: Prentice-Hall, Inc., 1958), chs. II, III, XI-XIII; Gwynn, *op. cit.,* pp. 406-418; J. Paul Leonard, *Developing the Secondary-School Curriculum,* rev. ed. (New York: Rinehart and Company, Inc., 1953), chs. XI, XIII-XIV, XV-XVII; and Louise E. Hock and T. J. Hill, *The General Education Class in the Secondary School* (New York: Holt, Rinehart, and Winston, Inc., 1960), *passim.*

[9] *Cf.* See preceding chs. 4 and 5 on the unit around a center of interest; and Mary Wilcockson, "Why Children Do or Do Not Accept Responsibility," *Social Education,* vol. XXIV (January, 1960), pp. 25-27.

[10] Ralph W. Tyler analyzed the growth of the core over the preceding twenty years in "The Core Curriculum," *NEA Journal,* vol. XLII (December, 1953), pp. 563-65.

curriculum before he attempts to help teachers with it or tries to institute such a program:

1. The core curriculum is found more frequently in junior high schools than in other types of secondary schools.
2. Its use of the center of interest, teacher-pupil planned, is very similar to teacher-pupil planned units or activities on the elementary school level. It also makes use of resource units just as the good elementary teacher does. It is, in effect, an extension upward of the general education of the elementary school through unit or center-of-interest methods of teaching and learning.
3. There is more core work found in the seventh and eighth grades than in the ninth—the higher the grade, the less core work is likely to be found.
4. Social studies and English comprise the core work more frequently than any other subject-matter areas, with science and some other subject area as the second most frequent combination.
5. The core is more likely to be composed of fields of knowledge and activities that have close relationships. The core does not necessarily have to use all fields of knowledge to solve its problems.
6. The core makes provision for learning situations which are similar in both school and life.
7. The core provides for training in a wide variety of skills and competencies. Drill in fundamentals is included, usually in special periods.
8. Most teachers have not had preservice training in core work; they have to be trained on the job.
9. The core program is the nearest approach yet devised on the high school level to a "problem-solving" method of teaching and learning.
10. For the core to work, each teacher must have faith in the other teachers that they will do a good job in combining information from various subject areas to solve the problems involved. Likewise, each supervisor must have faith in each teacher's ability to do this.
11. In general, each teacher must have some experience in correlating materials from at least two subject-matter areas before he can tackle the core curriculum approach successfully.
12. Experience in preparing resource units or centers of interest will be of great value to the teacher prior to his first attempt to teach the core program successfully. These resource units will form the foundation for his planning with students on the center of interest later.

Helpful source materials for core work. Much has been published on the core or common learning program in the last decade. Here is a brief, annotated list of selected publications on the core for the supervisor:

Core Curriculum Development: Problems and Practices, Bulletin 1952, No. 5, *Core-Curriculum in Public High Schools*, Bulletin 1950, No. 5, and *Block-time Classes and the Core Program in the Junior High School*, 1958, by Grace S. Wright, Washington Federal Security Agency, Office of Education. The first two bulletins bring together information on what constitutes core curriculum and how it works in practice as well as information from more than 500 schools through questionnaires, from visits to schools, and from the literature. The third amplifies the situation in the junior high schools at a later date.

Developing the Core Curriculum, 2nd ed., by Roland C. Faunce and Nelson L. Bossing (Englewood Cliffs, N. J.: Prentice-Hall, Inc., 1958). Chapters II, III, VI-VII, X, and XI give definitions, the core class in action, planning and learning how to teach the core program.

Developing a High School Core Program, by Lucille L. Lurry and Elsie J. Alberty (New York: The Macmillan Company, 1957). Shows the relation of the core program to general education, defines core, and shows how to design it. Also makes clear the resources needed for a core program and gives many descriptions of the core curriculum in action.

Developing Programs for Young Adolescents (Washington, D. C.: Association for Supervision and Curriculum Development, National Education Association, 1954). Describes different programs for seventh, eighth, and ninth grades in the South and Middle West.

Education for All American Youth—A Further Look (Washington, D. C.: Educational Policies Commission, 1952). Common learnings program for American City, pp. 219-264.

The General Education Class in the Secondary School, by Louise E. Hock and Thomas J. Hill (New York: Holt, Rinehart and Winston, Inc., 1960). A recent book approaching general education through the core concept. Practical suggestions are given on specific aspects such as problem-solving, unit planning, cooperative teacher-pupil planning, and the development of values and standards.

Guides to a Curriculum for Modern Living, by Florence Stratemeyer, and others (New York: Teachers College, Columbia University, 1952). Mainly paragraphic and pictorial, how to plan a curriculum centered around the persistent life situations faced by children and youth.

The Junior High School Program (Atlanta: The Southern Association of Colleges and Secondary Schools, 1958), ch. IV for instructional program.

The Junior High School—Today and Tomorrow, by Gertrude Noar (Englewood Cliffs, N. J.: Prentice-Hall, Inc., 1953). Parts III and IV are devoted to the content in the core class, the language arts and other curriculum areas in the core class, techniques of teaching, resource unit outlines, and reports of classroom work of pupils.

New Schools for a New Culture: The Story of the Evanston Township High School Core Program, rev. ed. (New York: Harper and Brothers, 1953).

Preparation of Core Teachers for Secondary Schools (Washington, D. C.: Association for Supervision and Curriculum Development, National Education Association, 1955). Preservice education, competencies needed, suggestions for in-service training.

Unit Teaching in the Elementary School, by Lavone A. Hanna and others (New York: Rinehart and Company, Inc., 1955). Unit teaching and problem solving in integrative or basic learnings work.

Work in the Core Program in Burris Laboratory School, by Myrtle Dewey Toops (Muncie: Ball State Teachers College, 1955). Objectives, program planning, place of the core in the total school program, preparation of resources and materials, methods of teaching; co-operative planning, the place of subject matter in the core, and evaluation of the core.

From the Self-Contained Classroom to Departmentalization

The supervisor is confronted from time to time with problems which stem from a teaching situation in the junior high school different from the one the teacher is familiar with or accustomed to. The teacher who comes to the junior high from the upper elementary grades is usually more familiar with the self-contained classroom situation, in which he has almost complete control throughout the day of the subject matter and other activities of about 30 pupils. Specialists in music, art, and physical education may come in to help him from time to time; but he deals with these 30 pupils for four-fifths of the school day, and he can arrange his methods and teaching schedule to suit his own ways of teaching and the pupils' most successful ways of learning.

In contrast to this teacher's experience with the self-contained classroom situation, the teacher who has been trained for high school teaching thinks of himself more as a specialist, more as a teacher of subject matter than as a teacher of children, more as a teacher of 100 or more pupils for a shorter time than as a teacher of 30 pupils for a longer time. Because of his departmentalized training, he tends to think in terms of separate subjects, rather than in terms of teaching problems cutting across subject-matter lines.

The supervisor should recognize frankly that he has these two sharply differing points of view on his staff, that each represents a natural attitude, and that it is not his main task to make either give up or change his point of view. Rather, it is his job to make clear to each teacher that (1) the pupil is the focal point for all staff members; (2) it is generally conceded by all teachers and administrators that the junior high school should offer to its pupils a gradual transition from a self-contained classroom situation on the sixth grade level to almost complete departmentalization in the first year of the senior high school; and (3) that it is easier for the pupil to make this transition if he is made conscious of learning through problem situations which require for solution related information and knowledge from other subject-matter fields.

A good illustration of how pupils make the gradual transition from a classroom schedule that is mostly self-contained to a more departmentalized schedule is shown in Table 7. This transition aids in articulation between both the elementary school and the senior high school. Note that the pupils in the seventh grade have at least 3 different teachers, in the eighth grade at least 4, and in the ninth grade, 6 teachers. For effective work in the junior high school, especially in "core," "block," or "center of interest" programs, a good library and wide and comprehensive use of it are essential. The librarian can and should be most helpful to the supervisor and class teacher—in effect, another kind of "specialist."

In a school with a program of this kind, "block" or double-period work for pupils gradually becomes less in amount; but block or fused work continues in *some* amount even through grade 9. The experienced teacher familiar with the self-contained classroom has to alter his teaching to plan blocks of work that do not duplicate other blocks taught by other teachers, whereas formerly he had to worry only about avoiding duplication in his own teaching. The experienced subject-matter teacher, on the other hand, has to learn to teach subjects interrelated with each other for the purpose of helping the pupil to acquire a general education, as he solves problems or masters centers of interests. The supervisor who can help both of these kinds of experienced teachers to fit into this program (Table 7) successfully is "doing all right."

Table 7. Pupil Programs in Grades 7-9 *

Gr. 7: 6-Period Day	Gr. 8: 6-Period Day	Gr. 9: 7-Period Day
3 *Class Periods of Block Work,* based on centers of interest primarily from language art and social studies under the same teacher, who will guide the class and plan with them.	2 *Class Periods of Block Work,* based on centers of interest taken from subject areas of English and social studies (history, geography, civics), under the same teacher.	2 *Class Periods of Block Work,* fused around subject areas of social studies and science, a required block of work, under same teacher.
2 *Class Periods of Block Work,* based on centers of interest drawn from subject areas of math, science, and health, under the same teacher, who will present materials on basis of achievement, needs, interests, and abilities of the class.	2 *Class Periods of Block Work,* based on centers of interest taken from subject areas of science, math, and health, under the same teacher, who will consider the interests, advancement, and abilities of the class for purposes of enriching the program.	2 *Class Periods of Block Work,* student may choose either English and a foreign language, or a block of English and some other elective; these courses may or may not be fused; the block of time is under the same teacher.
Single Class Periods, 3 times each week, of exploratory activities of an individual and group nature, from homemaking, music, handicrafts, exploratory foreign language (Spanish, French, Latin), typing, and/or other hobbies. 2 times a week of physical education, a broad program of indoor games and sports.	*"Split"* 2-*Class Period Block of Work,* 3 double periods a week of exploratory activities of an individual and group nature, from homemaking and home economics, industrial arts, handicrafts, publications, music, hobbies, exploratory foreign language (French, Spanish, Latin), typing. 2 double periods a week of phys. ed. and social development. This split period under different teachers.	*Single Class Period* of math required, either general math or algebra, under a different teacher.
		Single Class Period. Elective chosen from home econ, typing, consumer education, occupations, general business, music appreciation, piano, band, chorus or vocal music, or other activity.
		Single Class Period. 3 times a week of physical education and health, and 2 times a week of guidance and clubs under the homeroom type of organization, under 2 different teachers.

* Credit is given to Martha Garris Atkinson and Warren G. Anderson, graduate students at the University of North Carolina, who summarized this school schedule from the pupil's point of view.

Other Problems of Supervision in the Junior High School

In general, the activities connected with both the subject-matter teaching of the intermediate grades and with pupil interests tend to be somewhat more like those of the elementary school than the senior high school. They are more of an extension upward of the practices and activities of the elementary school; more of these pupil activities are carried on as a regular part of the classroom work than separately from the classroom as "extracurricular" activities. There are some exceptions to this trend, however, and these exceptions give rise upon occasion to other problems.

THE LIBRARY

Use of the library in the junior high school involves certain training and skills not necessarily mastered earlier in school. For example, pupils begin here to be taught how to use the library as a major source of references and resource materials, how to trace down the writings on a certain topic or problem, how to study, how to read or scan books for a particular item of information or for a particular purpose, and how to identify a real biography of a famous person in contrast to a fictional account which does not follow the history and the facts of the era under consideration. The supervisor can aid the teacher in making provisions for these types of training, both through enlisting the librarian's help and by helping the teacher to become more expert in the use of the library himself.

STUDENT ACTIVITIES

Some controversy has arisen over activities of an interscholastic nature in the junior high school. As has already been indicated,[11] the trend in the junior high school is toward more voluntary informal recreation, organized physical education and intramural activities for all boys and girls, and more play days and some informal contests.

[11] See ch. 8. Cf. also *Desirable Athletic Competition for Children, Joint Committee Report* (Washington, D. C.: American Association for Health, Physical Education, and Recreation, National Education Association, 1952), and *School Athletics: Problems and Policies* (Washington, D. C.: Educational Policies Commission, National Education Association, 1954).

At the same time interscholastic competition in organized sports is apparently on the increase in junior high schools in some sections. In a preliminary report on his study of junior high schools, James B. Conant told school administrators meeting in Atlantic City, New Jersey in February, 1960:[12]

I am sorry to report that in many localities the local interest in football and basketball has been almost a determining factor in regard to the junior high school. I wonder if community leaders and the education profession have done enough to strengthen the hands of superintendents, who in some localities are fighting an almost vicious overemphasis on athletics.

It is a fact that interscholastic competition in organized sports is nonexistent in many junior high schools or strictly curtailed and limited to a few contests in others.

The trend in some other interscholastic activities has not developed clearly yet. For example, in journalism, many junior high schools send their representatives to the national contests sponsored by the Columbia Scholastic Press Association. In some states, their student council representatives and delegates go to the State Student Council meetings, or their glee clubs and bands compete in the state music contests. In other school systems, junior high school pupils are not allowed to complete in any of these contests.

The supervisor will have to learn as much as he can about all activities and contests of an interscholastic nature and be guided in general to give aid in line with the trends indicated at the end of Chapter 8.

GUIDANCE AND ARTICULATION

These have been rather well covered.[13] In many junior high schools three devices are widely used to guide and counsel students: (1) placement tests for grouping for subject-matter classes, (2) the homeroom for individual and group counseling, and (3) interest inventories or preference tests to discover emerging interests.

---

[12] Reported in The Gist, vol. XXVIII, no. 3 (February 16, 1960), p. 1. Cf. also his address before the National Association of Secondary School Principals, "Some Problems of the Junior High School," reported in The Bulletin, vol. XLIV (April, 1960), pp. 310-321.
[13] See ch. 7.

Summary

The principal should select a faculty broadly trained for the work in the junior high school. He or the supervisor should help these teachers to continue their education, especially in regard to mastery of centers of interest and problems particularly appealing to the youngster who is beginning adolescence. Such training will involve learning how to prepare resource units co-operatively with other teachers, how to plan with students for teaching units or centers of interest, how to continue the general education of these pupils, and how to help them to explore new areas and interests. Finally, the supervisor will have to trust each of his teachers to do a good job of general education in his teaching, each by his own methods, since seldom do the teaching methods of two different teachers agree.

Problems for Individual Study and Class Discussion

1. Can you write down the kind of curricular program that you would like for your boy to have in junior high school? Your girl?
2. Are students at the early adolescent age capable of taking as much responsibility as at senior high school age? Why or why not?
3. A teacher comes to your junior high school trained and certified only in English. How would you train him so that he would feel qualified in a second teaching field also, for example, in social studies?
4. Miss A is competent in music, and Miss B in art. A teaches social studies in grade 8 and B mathematics and science in grade 9. How can you arrange it so that the children in both eighth and ninth grades can get both music and art?
5. Make out a check-list sheet which you can use to obtain information on the special competencies and hobbies of your junior high school teachers.
6. Is one form of organization of the junior high school any more efficient for teaching than another, for example, the 6-3-3, or 6-6, or the 6-2-4? Give reasons for your opinion.
7. If a parent came to you as the supervisor and asked you what the "core" program in the junior high school meant, how would you go about answering her?
8. Is there any need for workbooks in the subject fields on the junior high school level? Why? Or why not?
9. How can the supervisor get the teacher with the "subject-matter" point of view and the teacher with the "common-learnings" point of view to see that they have some common ground and agreement between them?

10. Would you limit the types of student activities in the junior high school? Extend them? Give reasons for your answer.

Additional Selected References for Problem or Unit Study

The Bulletin of the National Association of Secondary School Principals, "Organizing the Junior High School," vol. XXXV (December, 1951), chs. II-VII, pp. 20-98; and "The Daily Schedule in 1250 Junior High Schools," vol. XL (May, 1956), preprint, pp. 1-12; "The Junior High School Today and Tomorrow," vol. XLIV (November, 1960), pp. 1-132; and "Quality Science for Secondary Schools," vol. XLIV (December, 1960), pp. 7-76.

Butterweck, J. S., and Spessard, K. H., *The Unified Curriculum: A Case Study, Grades 7-8* (New York: Holt, Rinehart, and Winston, 1960), *passim.*

California Journal of Secondary Education, "The Challenge of the Junior High School," a symposium, vol. XXIX (May, 1954), pp. 243-244 and 263-301; and "The Junior High School Today," vol. XXXI (May, 1956), pp. 285-307.

Conant, J. B., *A Memorandum to School Boards: Recommendations for Education in the Junior High School Years* (Princeton: Educational Testing Service, 1960), *passim.*

Corbally, J. E., Jr., *et al., Educational Administration: The Secondary School* (Boston: Allyn and Bacon, 1961), ch. X.

A Design for Early Secondary Education (Albany, New York: State Department of Education, 1954), *passim.*

Educational Leadership, "Junior High School: Issues and Prospects," a symposium, vol. XVIII (December, 1960), pp. 138-167, 189.

Evaluative Instruments for the Junior High Schools. Among several evaluative instruments that have been developed, these two seem to include the various features:
Criteria for Evaluating Junior High Schools, 1959 ed. (Austin: The University of Texas, The Texas Study of Secondary Education); and *Junior High School.*
Evaluative Criteria (Salt Lake City: State of Utah, Department of Public Instruction, 1960).

Ferguson, W. J., "Opening a New Junior High School," *California Journal of Secondary Education,* vol. XXXV (April, 1960), pp. 219-227.

Gesell, A., and others, *Youth: The Years from Ten to Sixteen* (New York: Harper and Brothers, 1956), chs. 4-8.

Gruhn, W. T., and Douglass, H. R., *The Modern Junior High School,* 2nd ed. (New York: The Ronald Press Company, 1956), chs. V-X, XIII, XVI-XVII.

Hanna, L. A., and others, *Unit Teaching in the Elementary School* (New York: Rinehart and Company, Inc., 1955), part II.

Herriott, M. E., "The Master Schedule of Classes in Junior High School," *California Journal of Secondary Education,* vol. XXXIV (November, 1959), pp. 403-407.

The High School Journal, vol. XL (December, 1956), is devoted to "Looking at the Junior High School," pp. 82-141.

Johnson, M. J., et al., *Junior High School Guidance* (New York: Harper and Brothers, 1961), *passim.*

Knapp, D. L., "High School Principals Look at the Block-Time Class," *The Bulletin of the National Association of Secondary School Principals,* vol. XLIV (March, 1960), pp. 53-55.

Koos, L. V., *Junior High School Trends* (New York: Harper and Brothers, 1955), chs. VI-VII.

Krug, E. A., *The Secondary School Curriculum* (New York: Harper and Brothers, 1960), ch. VIII.

Loomis, M. J., *The Preadolescent* (New York: Appleton-Century-Crofts, Inc., 1959), *passim.*

Mooney, Ross L., *Mooney Problem Check List: Junior High School Form* (Columbus, Ohio State University). Instrument to help identify problems of early adolescents.

Mott, K., "Language Arts-Social Studies Fusion in the Junior High School Block Period," *The Bulletin of the National Association of Secondary School Principals,* vol. XLIV (March, 1960), pp. 124-131.

National Society for the Study of Education, *Adapting the Secondary-School Program to the Needs of Youth,* Fifty-second Yearbook, part I (Chicago: The University of Chicago Press, 1953), chs. VII, IX, XI, XIII.

Parrish, L., and Waskin, Y., *Teacher-Pupil Planning for Better Classroom Teaching* (New York: Harper and Brothers, 1958), *passim.*

Perdew, P. W., *The American Secondary School in Action* (Boston: Allyn and Bacon, 1959), ch. V.

Romine, S. A., *Building the High School Curriculum* (New York: The Ronald Press Company, 1954), chs. IX-XII, XIV.

Snyder, E. R. (ed.), *The Self-Contained Classroom* (Washington: Association for Supervision and Curriculum Development, 1960), *passim.*

The Southern Association of Colleges and Secondary Schools, Atlanta 8, published recently (1958) a comprehensive three-year study entitled *The Junior High School Program,* looking at its development, purposes, program, organization, staffing, and evaluation.

Stewart, L. J., and others, *Improving Reading in the Junior High School* (New York: Appleton-Century-Crofts, Inc., 1957), *passim.*

Super, D. E., Overstreet, P. L., and others, *The Vocational Maturity of Ninth-Grade Boys* (New York: Teachers College, Columbia University, 1960), *passim.*

Van Til, W., et al., *Modern Education for the Junior High School Years* (New York: The Bobbs-Merrill Company, Inc., 1961), *passim.*

Wright, G. S., *Block-Time Classes and the Core Program in the Junior High School,* Bulletin 1958, No. 6, and *The Core Program: Abstracts of Unpublished Research,* 1946-1955 (Washington, D. C.: U. S. Department of Health, Education, and Welfare, Office of Education, 1956).

CHAPTER 13

Special Problems of Supervision

in the Elementary School

WHEN THE FIRST CHILD of a proud father and mother enters the first grade, they want him to have the best teacher in the school. They feel that he will learn to read quickly; they want him to be in the fastest section, in the most advanced group; and they want to "show off" his achievement, his knowledge, and his precociousness. If it turns out that he is a slow learner, or not ready to make his social adjustments satisfactorily yet, these parents are much disappointed, their pride is hurt; they are likely to blame the school for his lack of progress.

Fortunately for the overworked and criticized first-grade teacher, most families now have more than one child, each of an age different from the other. By the time the second child in the family has entered grade one and has been there a year, these same parents have come to a realization that their two children differ greatly in many ways, ranging all of the way from aptitudes and intellectual capacity to differences in skills and speeds. They discover that the same teacher under whom the first child learned so slowly seems to be highly successful with the second child. As child number three and child number four follow and go through school, these parents slowly come to the conclusion that the school and the teachers are doing rather successful teaching in the elementary school, all things considered. So, when they attend the Parent-Teacher meetings now, they listen to the younger parents find fault with the school; then they frequently speak up and point out how all of their own children differed sharply, and how the school tried to help each one to develop satisfactorily.

There has always been criticism of the public school since its establishment in America. It is a public institution, not private or sectarian; it is supported and owned by the public and belongs to it; it makes mistakes from time to time; and it can benefit from constructive criticism and being called upon to re-examine its purposes and its methods. On the other hand, there is evidence that criticisms and attacks upon the public schools have been more numerous in the last decade.[1] These criticisms of the elementary school have created some additional problems for school personnel to solve.

The Three R's in Today's Elementary School

There can be little doubt that parents and the public think that pupils should develop today a high type of effectiveness in reading in the public schools, and many expect their children to read better and with more comprehension than they themselves read. Parents also expect their children to write, and want handwriting emphasized, even though typing as an additional tool in writing is becoming more and more of a necessity in the mastery of the immense cultural heritage of our race.

Both parents and educational specialists agree that vast and swiftly moving changes in America and the world demand greater competence in the fundamentals than ever before. Since this is so, what do we know *definitely* about the teaching of the three R's in the elementary schools today? How good is it? How can it be improved? The answers to these questions are important if school personnel are to do a better job.

WHAT THE SPECIALISTS SAY ABOUT
THE TEACHING OF THE THREE R'S

Several reliable research studies answer this question. The authorities agree in general that: [2]

[1] Compare two recent critical anthologies: Henry Ehlers, ed., *Crucial Issues in Education*, rev. ed. (New York: Holt, Rinehart, and Winston, 1959), *passim;* and C. Winfield Scott and others, eds., *The Great Debate: Our Schools in Crisis* (Englewood Cliffs, N. J.: Prentice-Hall, Inc., 1959), *passim.*

[2] These general conclusions are based primarily upon William A. Brownell, "The Revolution in Arithmetic," *The Arithmetic Teacher,* vol. I (February, 1954), pp. 1-5; C. W. Hunnicutt and W. J. Iverson, eds., *Research in the Three R's* (New

1. There is not enough evidence from research to show whether the teaching of reading, writing, and arithmetic is distinctly better than the teaching of these subjects a generation ago, or worse.

2. From what evidence is available, the teaching of the three R's has continued to be as effective with the unselected school population of today as it was with a more selective population of a generation ago.

3. Achievement in silent reading appears equal to and perhaps greater than children's achievement of a generation ago.

4. Average achievement in oral reading is not as high today as formerly, due to change in emphasis from oral to silent reading.

5. It is difficult to compare schools as to achievement in reading, or to compare a school's achievement today with what it was 20 years ago, because of such factors as changes in population and inability to secure well-prepared teachers.

6. Each individual school should appraise frequently the progress and needs of their students in reading.

7. Effectiveness in teaching the fundamentals can be improved if all teachers are trained adequately to use improved methods.

8. Large classes hinder even good teachers, for we know little about how to teach the three R's in large groups.

9. There is need for well-organized research to determine the actual achievement of pupils, to gather objective evidence until we can justify the pupil's level of achievement in reading in each school system.

10. There is improvement in arithmetic instruction, mainly because of more emphasis on reasoning and problem solving and less emphasis upon memoriter drills per se.

READING

Many books have been written since 1940 on reading; most of these books tell the prospective teacher or the teacher in service how to teach reading. Most of them make fundamental use of readiness methods and materials and of the word-recognition approach in teaching reading. However, the parents of many of today's children were taught during the 1920's and 1930's by phonics,

York: Harper and Brothers, 1958), *passim;* Herbert G. Espy, "What Specialists Tell Us About Improving the Teaching of the Three R's," *The Nation's Schools,* vol. LIV (November, 1954), pp. 52-55; Vincent J. Glennon and C. W. Hunnicutt, *What Does Research Say About Arithmetic?* (Washington, D. C.: Association for Supervision and Curriculum Development, National Education Association, rev., 1958), *passim;* and William S. Gray and William J. Iverson, "What Should Be the Profession's Attitude Toward Lay Criticism of the Schools? With Special Reference to Reading," *The Elementary School Journal,* vol. LIII (September, 1952), pp. 1-44.

learning letter by letter and sound by sound. The sequence went from sounding letters to sounding syllables; then from sounding syllables to sounding words, then to sentences. Writing accompanied speech, and sounding the words accompanied the sight of them. The grandparents of the children in today's schools were taught to read and to spell by still another method, the syllabification method, that is, learning to spell by spelling each syllable separately, to pronounce by repeating the syllables and then repeating the whole word correctly, without much regard for its meaning.

Each of these methods of teaching used the best thought and methods of its era. The syllabification method was deemed beyond compare in the primary school days of this writer, when a majority of children learned to read and write but a very large minority did not—and no one cared too much whether they learned or not. The phonic method was the "latest word" from 1920 to the 1930's, based as it was on the latest findings of research into reading and spelling. Since 1940, the word-recognition method has perhaps had more emphasis in use than either of the other two methods. The term *word recognition* as employed here involves the use of several methods. The child already knows a few words by sight, but the term refers to how he comes to recognize and know a new word. In helping him to learn to recognize the new word the teacher may use (1) a picture clue; (2) a context clue; (3) phonics; (4) word analysis, including prefix and suffix, compound words, big or little words; and (5) use of the dictionary. Good teachers make use of *all* these methods from time to time as needed in their work with individual children.

In manner like unto method, the purposes of reading differ in part today from the purposes of 50 years ago. Good oral reading was considered an important part of reading then; today much more emphasis is placed upon efficiency in comprehension in silent reading, mainly because pupils have so much more to learn today in order to get along successfully in the world. During all of these changes in purpose and methods in reading, the parent or the critic of the teaching of reading has more frequently than not been ignorant of *what* the teacher in the modern school is trying to do and *how* he is trying to do it.

The Flesch controversy. Rudolf Flesch brought criticism of the teaching of reading in the schools to a head in 1955 when he attacked the word-recognition, or sight method, and offered *one* method for teaching reading, a phonics method of instruction for parents to use at home.[3] Emmett A. Betts offers perhaps the sanest and most constructive comment on Flesch's criticisms. Betts admits that the teaching of reading to all children is a difficult problem which teachers have been struggling with for many years; that the problem is made up of many smaller problems, such as spelling, pronunciation of words, word recognition, and memorization; that the specialists in reading differ in opinions on the problem; that responsible journalists present the issues in teaching of reading fairly and irresponsible journalists tend to distort facts and oversimplify the complex problem. Betts [4] sets forth what his study shows him are the three fundamentals of reading instruction, namely the development and growth in the child of

1. Permanent interests in reading which are worth while.
2. Skills necessary for the perceiving and recognizing of words, whether phonic or related skills.
3. The capacity to think in the reading situation.

Betts believes that the teacher of reading who keeps these three essentials of a good reading program constantly before him will do a pretty successful job and will use any method in the teaching of reading to the child that is in accord with all *three* of these basic principles.

Problems of reading disabilities. Arthur E. Traxler defines reading disability strikingly when he indicates that a pupil possesses such a disability when he cannot read well enough to be adequate to the demands of his environment.[5] Traxler states also that what

---

[3] Rudolf Flesch, *Why Johnny Can't Read—and What You Can Do About It* (New York: Harper and Brothers, 1955), *passim*. One might compare the method of Flesch's book with that found in Kathleen B. Hester, *Teaching Every Child to Read* (New York: Harper and Brothers, 1955); and with Alvina T. Burrows, "The Conflict over Phonics Is Still Raging," *The Reading Teacher*, vol. VI (May, 1953), pp. 12-17. *Cf.* also Arthur I. Gates, A. *Review of Rudolf Flesch, Why Johnny Can't Read* (New York: The Macmillan Company, 1955), and Edna L. Furness, "Why John Can't Spell," *School and Society*, vol. LXXXII (December 24, 1955), pp. 199-202.

[4] Emmett A. Betts, "What About Phonics?" *Education*, vol. 75 (May, 1955), pp. 547-559; *cf.* also "Is Phonics a Cure-All?", discussed with its implications in *Defense Bulletin*, no. 61 (May, 1955), "The Dr. Cure-Alls and the Public Schools," National Commission for the Defense of Democracy through Education (Washington, D. C.: National Education Association), pp. 1-4.

[5] Arthur E. Traxler, "Measurement and Improvement of Reading," *Baltimore Bulletin of Education*, vol. XXXI (November, 1953), pp. 16-31.

might be a reading disability for one person in one environment might not be a disability in another environment. Therefore, one way of helping reading disability in a child can be by making changes in the environment. For example, pupils can be supplied with books that have been simplified in vocabulary content and in English sentence structure.[6] Another way to remedy the disability would be to provide a corrective reading group with a competent teacher and assign the pupil to it. The teacher, the supervisor, and the administrator will have to decide in the long run what will be best for the individual student.

The enlargement of the three R's through language arts. Modern living and teaching have combined to enlarge the concept of the three R's in the elementary school. For example, one group adds all of the communication skills to reading to form the three R's; these skills are reading, writing, spelling, listening, speaking, and observing.[7] Their emphasis is upon acquiring competencies through practice in a natural setting. The National Council of Teachers of English stresses listening, speaking, reading, and personal and creative writing (including spelling) in the elementary school.[8]

It is a well-known fact that the child's reading vocabulary is larger than his writing vocabulary; furthermore, it is usually larger than his speaking, his thinking, or his listening vocabulary. Supervisors have the special problem of training teachers in service so that they can help the child to build a strong vocabulary. The child can do this by consciously transferring words which he learns in his reading to his thinking and speaking and writing vocabularies. This practice prevents reading from being separated from other skills. In general, most teachers place primary emphasis only on those words which are important in the child's writing, and this method slowly but surely leads to less effective and exact communication of meanings.

[6] *Cf.* ch. 3 for discussion of materials of this nature.

[7] *The Three R's in the Elementary School* and *Research Helps in Teaching the Language Arts,* Association for Supervision and Curriculum Development (Washington, D. C.: National Education Association, 1952 and 1955 respectively), *passim;* and the feature on "Individualized Reading," *NEA Journal,* vol. XLVII (March, 1958), pp. 162-163.

[8] *Language Arts for Today's Children,* prepared by the Commission on the English Curriculum of the National Council of Teachers of English (New York: Appleton-Century-Crofts, Inc., 1954), part II.

In this connection, it is important for the teacher to realize that the dictionary is not the last authority on the meanings and usage of words and that the grammar book is not the supreme authority in regard to language structure and formation. The dictionary and the grammar are *guides* to word meaning and language usage, not authorities to teachers and pupils for awkward, stilted forms of expressions. For example, there are no "right" or "wrong" meanings for words; instead, there are *different connotations in meaning* which permit people to express themselves more or less exactly. There are no right and wrong forms of phrases or clauses; there are different ways in which people express themselves, as more emotionally, concisely, or briefly.[9]

Another special problem in the elementary school is deciding when to start the teaching of English grammar and how much of it to teach. Some authorities in English contend that early exposure to analysis of the intricate structure of our English language is of little if any benefit to youngsters in the elementary school because it does not contribute much to correct use in writing and in speaking and because it has little or no value which is recognized as such by children.[10] The new position in regard to the teaching of grammar in the grades is called the "tool" position, as contrasted with the "subject" position that has been in operation so long. Guiding principles for this approach would:

1. Start the teaching of grammar where it can really begin to be useful to the pupil.
2. Slowly, thoroughly teach a few concepts at one time.
3. Emphasize those parts of grammar which help to improve sentence building, for example, employment and placement of modifiers and phrases, apposition, or the use of clauses to say more in one sentence.

[9] Good suggestions will be found in these references: Lynwood Carranco, "Let's Stop Worshiping the Dictionary," *The Clearing House*, vol. XXIX (October, 1954), pp. 72-76; Dorris Lee and Murray Lee, "Spelling Needs a Teacher," *Elementary English Review*, vol. XXIII (May, 1946), pp. 203-206; and Lillian Gray, "Making It Their Own," *NEA Journal*, vol. XL (September, 1951), pp. 405-406.

[10] *Cf.* Robert C. Pooley, "Grammar in the Schools of Today," *Elementary English*, vol. XXXI (May, 1954), pp. 268-272; Louis Foley, "Defenders of Grammatical Heresy," *The Phi Delta Kappan*, vol. XXXIV (December, 1952), pp. 101-103; Maurice L. Pettit, "Should We Give Up On High School English?" *The Bulletin of the National Association of Secondary School Principals*, vol. XXXIX (November, 1955), pp. 133-137; and Thurston Womack, "Teachers' Attitudes toward Current English Usage," *The English Journal*, vol. XLIII (April, 1959), pp. 186-190.

4. Teach for best usage and expression in a particular sentence or paragraph, as an aid toward better and clearer expression.

By grade 7 boys and girls are perhaps ready for some beginning analysis of English language structure, but emphasis should be upon mastery of a few principles, still slowly and thoroughly. There seems little agreement on what English teachers are trying to do, and therefore there is little agreement on how to teach English grammar and language structure. One wonders why pupils who write well and clearly are not always good grammarians! The pupil has to see some purpose in grammar before he will apply himself willingly.

ARITHMETIC

The big problem in the teaching of arithmetic has been to help the teacher (1) make arithmetic meaningful to each pupil, and (2) avoid needless repetition of arithmetic fundamentals for those pupils who have already mastered them and are ready for advanced work in problem solving and reasoning. To make arithmetic meaningful to the child, the supervisor should furnish many concrete aids to the teacher, such as wooden blocks in a frame; the abacus; linoleum blocks; toothpicks; counting frames; discs; peg boards; flannel board and its felt pieces; paper blocked off in squares of 5's, 10's, and 100's; wooden spools; and dictionary cards for the fundamental processes. For avoiding needless repetition of fundamental processes and drills for pupils who are masters of these, the supervisor needs to supply the teacher with supplementary basic arithmetic texts; with workbooks containing problems of an advanced nature; with modern audio-visual materials like charts, graphs, models, and mock-ups; and with the equally interesting machines of today, such as adding machines, calculators, scales and their calculators, cash registers, and posting machines. These materials help children to approach reality in problem solving, a *must* for creative work in advanced arithmetic.

NEW SUBJECT-MATTER AREAS IN THE THREE R'S

The social studies. The oldest of the additions to the three R's is the "social studies," made up of what was formerly designated as geography and history for the elementary school. The main purposes are to relate geography to American history, government, and economics; to help the pupil understand his environment and his relationships to it, from his local surroundings to the world, past and present, and to help the pupil in his social development in his environment.

Science. More recently science as a subject area has been added to the three R's. Formerly science was seldom found as a separate subject in grade 1 through 6. Instead, the skilled teacher wove the science work into a kind of "fused" center of interest which would comprise also aspects of the social studies, reading, writing, and spelling. Now elementary science develops concepts in physical science—of the child's physical environment, of what man has done to this environment, of the possibilities of this modern scientific world, of the way that the child can develop the scientific attitude and experimental method.

It is undoubtedly true today that modern means of communication, such as radio and television, make young children ready for science experiences much further advanced than some textbooks in science contain for a specific grade level. The modern child's growth in science knowledge has pinpointed two problems: (1) Shall we advance the scope and sequence of the science curriculum for the elementary school grades? If so, how? and (2) Would the use of specialists in science, or "team teaching" in science, make for better teaching? In team teaching, there is a team leader who is primarily responsible for the educational growth of the whole child, but delegates certain duties and teaching to specialists, aids, interns, and clerks.[11] For example, a team for mathematics and science

[11] For more on team teaching read Paul Woodring's *New Directions in Teacher Education* (New York: The Fund for the Advancement of Education, 1957), ch. V, and *A Fourth of a Nation* (New York: McGraw-Hill Book Company, Inc., 1957), ch. V. For discussion of scope and sequence, compare *The Review of Educational Research*, vol. XXVII (October, 1957), ch. I, "Science in the Elementary Grades," pp. 311-328, and ch. II, "Mathematics in the Elementary Grades," pp. 329-342; *Conservation Experiences for Children,* U. S. Department of Health, Education, and Welfare, Bulletin 1957, No. 16; *Science in the Elementary School,* "What Research Says to the Teacher" Series, Bulletin No. 12, Department of Classroom Teachers and American Educational Research Association, National Education Association (1957); *Rethinking Science Education,* Fifty-ninth Yearbook, National Society for the Study of Education, Part I (1960); and Sam S. Blanc, "Guideposts in Science Education; A Report on a Survey of Trends at the Elementary and Secondary Levels," *The Science Teacher,* vol. XXV (March, 1958), pp. 82-83, 109-112. For grouping, enrichment, and acceleration of the talented pupil, read *Education for the Gifted,* Fifty-seventh Yearbook of the National Society for the Study of Education, part II, 1958, chs. VIII-XI, and James J. Gallagher, *The Gifted Child in the Elementary School,* "What Research Says to the Teacher" Series, Bulletin No. 17, *op. cit.* (1959).

might be responsible for teaching these subjects all the way from elementary grades through high school for part of the day, while the child studies other subjects in the regular manner for the rest of the day.

Health. Another subject-matter area is health, to which physical education and safety have been added in the elementary schools of some states. Through this study pupils are supposed to develop a knowledge of public health provisions, diseases, diet, prevention of disease, good rest and work habits, and ways for safe and relaxing recreation and the development of good mental health.

Ample texts and materials of an interesting nature have been prepared in these three newer areas of the three R's, as indicated in Chapter 3.

HELP ON PROBLEMS OF TEACHING IN THE THREE R'S

Supervisors are fortunate in having available in simple form from several sources the results of studies and research in the three R's which can be used to improve teaching:

"Place of Subject Series," Federal Security Agency (now U. S. Department of Health, Education, and Welfare), Office of Education:
Bulletin 1951, No. 7: *How Children Use Arithmetic*, by Effie G. Bathurst
Bulletin 1952, No. 7: *How Children Learn to Read*, by Helen K. Mackintosh
Bulletin 1953, No. 2: *How Children Learn to Write*, by Helen K. Mackintosh and Wilhelmina Hill
"What Research Says to the Teacher" Series: Department of Classroom Teachers and American Educational Research Association, National Education Association (1953-1959):
No. 1: *Teaching Reading*, by Arthur I. Gates
No. 2: *Teaching Arithmetic*, by R. L. Morton
No. 3: *Teaching Spelling*, by Ernest Horn
No. 4: *Teaching Handwriting*, by Frank N. Freeman
No. 5: *Personality Adjustment of Individual Children*, by Ralph H. Ojemann
No. 6: *The Learning Process*, by William C. Trow
No. 7: *Evaluating and Reporting Pupil Progress*, by John W. M. Rothney
No. 8: *Guided Study and Homework*, by Ruth Strang
No. 12: *Science in the Elementary Schools*, by Gerald S. Craig
No. 17: *The Gifted Child in the Elementary School*, by James J. Gallagher
No. 18: *Group Processes in Elementary and Secondary Schools*, by Louis M. Smith
Research in the Three R's, edited by C. W. Hunnicutt and W. J. Iverson (New York: Harper and Brothers, 1958)

Other Controversial Areas in the Elementary School

Not only have marked changes in methods of teaching taken place in the elementary school. Significant changes have taken place in the content of instruction, in methods of evaluation, in the grouping of children for instruction, in experiments in providing for both the superior and the slow-learning pupil, and in less reliance upon a single source of instruction, that is, the textbook. These changes, most of which have already been treated in this volume, have forced the elementary school to deal with some controversial problems which will be analyzed briefly here. The particular task of the supervisor is to know enough about the problem which is being argued to be able to help the teacher to obtain adequate information upon both sides, to furnish enough data for wise decision making.

FOREIGN LANGUAGE TEACHING IN ELEMENTARY SCHOOLS [12]

The first large-scale experiment with teaching foreign languages to elementary school children took place in 1922, when Cleveland started it in the first grade in a number of its public schools.[13] Other experiments took place over a period of years in

[12] Now generally abbreviated FLES.
[13] Cf. Theodore Andersson, The Teaching of Foreign Languages in the Elementary School (Boston: D. C. Heath and Company, 1953), passim, a major informational source on this new development—illustrates the methodology with 15 sample lessons for elementary teachers. Representative references pro and con are: George Borglum, "Revolution in the Teaching of Modern Foreign Languages," and Earl J. McGrath, "Broadening the Base of Language Study in America," School and Society, vol. 79 (May 1, 1954), pp. 129-134, and vol. 77 (February 7, 1953), pp. 81-83, respectively; Ernest E. Ellert and Lois V. Ellert, "Teaching Modern Languages to the Elementary School Child," Educational Research Bulletin, vol. XXXII (January 14, 1953), pp. 1-6, 27; Daniel P. Girard and Herbert F. A. Smith, "Foreign Language in the Elementary School?" NEA Journal, vol. XLIV (May, 1955), pp. 270-271; "Conference of Foreign Language Teachers" (The Washington Conference) in Improving Education in Kentucky, Bulletin of the Bureau of School Service, College of Education, University of Kentucky, Lexington, vol. XXVI (March, 1954), pp. 59-72; Theodore Andersson, "Training Tomorrow's Language Teachers," School and Society, vol. LXXXIV (August 4, 1956), pp. 41-43; and Lillian S. Adams, "Foreign Language in the Grades? Yes," and Frederick E. Bolton, "Not Worth the Cost," NEA Journal, vol. XL (October, 1956), pp. 444-445. For current status and practices, read E. E. Thompson and A. E. Hamalainen, Foreign Language Teaching in Elementary Schools, Association for Supervision and Curriculum Development, National Education Association (1958). Good samples of teachers' guides are San Diego City Schools' Guide to Resource Materials for the First Year of Spanish in the Elementary Grades, Grade IV (1953), and A Guide for the Teaching of Spanish in the Elementary Schools of the Public Schools of the District of Columbia (1952).

Los Angeles, Brooklyn, San Diego, Somerville (N.J.), Washington (D. C.), and in New England. The year 1952 marked the beginning of nation-wide interest, when former U. S. Commissioner of Education Earl J. McGrath made an address to language teachers in St. Louis; he proposed to revolutionize foreign language teaching by placing it in the curriculum of the elementary school.' Following his address, the National Conference on the Role of Foreign Languages in American Schools was held in Washington in January, 1953. McGrath's position essentially was:

1. That America is an international leader.
2. That Americans need to have proficiency in foreign languages for this leadership role.
3. That foreign languages as taught at present give pupils little facility in oral or written expression.
4. That students through foreign language teaching should learn to understand and use, both orally and in written form, the idiomatic speech and the everyday language of other lands with as little accent as possible.

To achieve his goals, McGrath proposed the start of foreign languages much sooner in school than at present; he also indicated that young children learn a new language more readily than older pupils.

The modern language people were immediately divided into two camps by McGrath's proposal. Some favored the idea, called attention to the fact that some schools had had such instruction for years, and observed that the best way really to learn a new language is by learning to speak it, that is, by the aural-oral method. On the other hand, many language teachers opposed the plan. Their main arguments were: (1) We cannot sacrifice time for teaching the fundamentals to teach intensively a subject of such doubtful value; (2) Foreign language should be taught by a thoroughly trained person, not by an amateur, which is what an elementary school teacher would be; (3) The teaching of foreign languages in elementary schools is not a major way by which we

---

For a recent evaluation of the effects of foreign language instruction in the elementary school, read the symposium, "Foreign Languages in the Elementary School," in the *NEA Journal*, vol. XLIX (February, 1960), pp. 33-36. The author is indebted to Walter D. Creech, a former member of the Romance Language Department at the University of North Carolina, for some of the basic research on this aspect.

can gain international understanding and peace; (4) Most children in America have no need for a "second" language (English is the *first* language); and (5) To understand a language, a pupil must know its grammatical structure well, and the limited time for foreign language in the elementary school will not give the student this necessary mastery.

Foreign language teaching in the elementary school definitely has status, and the program is growing. Prevailing practices show that the beginning of instruction may come in the kindergarten, in the first grade, or in the third or fourth grade. In like manner, the instruction may be given from kindergarten through grade 6, or from grade 1 through grade 6 or 8, or from grade 3 or 4 through grade 6 or 8. French and Spanish are the languages given most frequently, though a few schools give German and Latin. The fourth grade is the place selected most frequently for beginning foreign language, which is taught as a special subject; but it is correlated with the other work in the grade whenever the opportunity to do so is present, as, for example, with art, language arts, music, social studies, and reading.

The method which is used most often is aural-oral, with emphasis upon songs, dialogue, games, and activities centered around the life and customs of the people who speak the language. The period of instruction is some 20 minutes in length, three or four times a week, sometimes daily. There seems to be little planning for a continued program from elementary through high school, perhaps a weakness of some of the programs. In most of the schools which reported to the Washington Conference, the program did not cause additional expense, since it had been experimental in many schools and was carried on by teachers already in the system. Some of the programs use the regular classroom teacher, but others use teachers regularly certified in the languages or elementary teachers specially prepared for foreign language teaching in the grades, as in Cleveland. Many supervisors have used workshops for elementary teachers in a foreign language with much success for in-service preparation.

Finally, some schools teach foreign language to all children in a given grade group; other schools permit children or parents to elect foreign language, and still others select pupils for foreign language instruction on the basis of mental ability or reading ability.

SEX EDUCATION IN SCHOOLS

There is another problem of a controversial nature, and one about which the supervisor must have some knowledge of materials and practices. There has been good teaching of sex education in the schools for many years, and most of this instruction has been done by good teachers without mentioning the word "sex" very often. For example, there are series of modern texts in health and physical fitness which explain many aspects of growth and maturing; another series of literature texts for grades 4-6 make child growth and self realization the basis of the read-text series; and there are newer psychology texts and texts on home and family living that offer valuable basic materials for teaching sex education in a natural way along with other subjects in the grades. There are also a few good books for children on sex education.

RELIGIOUS EDUCATION IN PUBLIC SCHOOLS

Like the problem of sex education, this controversial issue is explosive at times. It is not the task of the supervisor to decide upon policy for the school board and administrator—they are the people who decide whether a school should teach sex education or religious education in the school. But it is the supervisor's responsibility to be prepared to assist a teacher who has to teach such a controversial subject as sex education or spiritual values.

There are several basic references which the supervisor might have at hand in regard to religious education, secular education, and moral and spiritual values in the elementary school:

The Function of the Public Schools in Dealing with Religion: Report on the Exploratory Study Made by the Committee on Religion and Education (Washington, D. C.: American Council on Education, 1953). This second report of the Committee attempted to explore the possibility and desirability of studies planned to find what the function of the public schools is in dealing with religion. Opinions of leaders in education and religion were obtained, as well as illustrations of present practice.

Moral Values in Public Education, by Ellis F. Hartford (New York: Harper and Brothers, 1958). The Kentucky Experiment; how public schools are meeting the clamor for more emphasis on the teaching of moral and ethical values.

Public Education and Its Critics, by V. T. Thayer (New York: The Macmillan Company, 1954). This small volume is a fair presentation of issues such as sectarian attacks by religious groups, discussion and teaching of controversial issues, indoctrination of pupils, freedom of teaching, and charges that the public schools are secular.

The *Role of the School in American Society*, by V. T. Thayer (New York: Dodd, Mead and Company, 1960). Part IV presents critical issues in education; Chapters 18-20 are particularly concerned with problems of religion and the public schools.

The *State and Sectarian Education*, NEA Research Bulletin, vol. XXXIV, no. 4 (December, 1956). This bulletin gives the background, constitutional provisions and their implementation, and state supervision of sectarian education.

The *Study of Religion in the Public Schools: An Appraisal*, edited by Nicholas C. Brown (Washington, D. C.: American Council on Education, 1958). Reviews the policies and activities of the Committee on Religion and Education since 1947, surveys the constitutional and legal limits of religious education in public schools, explores religion in American history and ideas, and recommends problems for research in the future.

The teacher is selected for his high standards and his character. In engendering fine spiritual and ethical standards in his students, he is but seeing the reflections of his own fine spiritual and ethical and moral life. The supervisor can help him to keep an even balance in preparing for and carrying out activities for these purposes.

THE COMICS CONTROVERSY

The controversy over the effects of "comic" book reading on the growing child has been revived with such force that its impact again has led the publishers of this type of material to attempt to police their own industry. The writer traced the rise of the comic magazine, analyzed the literature on this aspect to 1950, and supervised careful studies of types of comics and how they could be employed in school libraries and school work to lead children to be interested in classics of adventure, fantasy, family life, war, heroism, history, humor, mystery, and science.[14] He also called attention to those factors outstanding in the comics which influence and control pupils' readiness to read or to start a new interest in reading. His study showed that the first big controversy arose in 1947-1948 over whether comic magazines were harmful to the morals, ideals, habits, growth, and development of children. As a result of this first controversy, the Association of Comics Magazine

[14] J. Minor Gywnn, *Curriculum Principles and Social Trends*, 3rd. ed. (New York: The Macmillan Company, 1960), pp. 98-101, 300-311.

Publishers was formed, with a code of ethics by means of which the Association proposed to screen all magazines and place on each one a seal of approval, showing that it complied with the code.

Somehow, this self-regulation of the comics magazine industry did not work out. The industry grew bigger, and many new types of comics appeared, among them some best-sellers like "romance comics," "crime" and "horror" or "terror" comics, and science-fiction comics depicting destruction and terror. In 1953-1954 Fredric Wertham, a New York psychiatrist, made the public conscious for the second time of the uncontrolled publication of all kinds of comics, whether they were wholesome for youngsters or not.[15] Dr. Wertham made a careful study of the effects that certain kinds of comic books have on the minds and on the behaviors of children. His book is pointed specifically at comic books on crime, horror, terror, and destruction. He makes a good case against these types, giving examples from comics and citing cases of children who were influenced toward cruelty, crime, or delinquency.

Following the publication of Wertham's book, many groups began to investigate the comics; many people and many editors wrote upon the controversy, pro or con; some TV programs were examined for similarity to those stories found in some comics and possible bad effects on children's growth and development. Some groups tried to connect the increase in juvenile delinquency with the reading of the comics and child crime. Some states even passed comics censorship laws; for example, legislation in North Carolina (1955) made county sheriffs censors to determine whether charges are to be preferred against persons possessing for sale any comic books portraying murder, mayhem, or use of narcotics.

During this period of charge and countercharge concerning the comics, the Comics Magazine Association of America was formed late in 1954 for the specific purpose of reviewing and passing upon the contents of comics magazines before they are printed. Again, there is a code to which the contents must conform before the Association gives its approval and awards the seal of approval, which appears prominently on the outside cover of the comic.[16] Since

[15] Fredric Wertham, *Seduction of the Innocent* (New York: Rinehart and Company, Inc., 1953, 1954). Dr. Wertham was a leader in the first questioning of the effects of comic books on young children in the 1947-48 controversy.

[16] The code can be obtained from The Comics Magazine Association, 300 Fourth Avenue, New York 10.

1954 the Association has approved over 5,000 comic books; by 1958, 90 percent of all publishers and distributors of comic magazines had become members of the Association. The code is similar in many respects to that proposed in 1947-1948.

There is another way, perhaps much more effective in the long run, for the supervisor and the teachers to handle the comics problem. This method has been tried out successfully for a number of years in Cincinnati, where The Committee on Evaluation of Comic Books has assessed comic books each year for more than a decade.[17] The "raters" were a group of outstanding citizens of Cincinnati, including experts in sociology, psychology, and child growth and development, persons working with children in the community, and a sampling of other interested people. They worked out standards for the comics, keeping in mind such questions as whether there is anything wrong with comic books; if so, what; and how can comics be fairly evaluated.

In any community, the supervisor can help the individual teacher and his children to establish good standards for comic books, and he can help the parents who want to establish sound standards for comic books. The two sources which have just been described offer suggestions for a starting point for either group, or for the school librarian at a loss to know whether to include any comics in his resources.

Other Types of Elementary School Problems

The elementary supervisor never knows what kind of a problem a new school day will bring to him. Of course, it is impossible in the bounds of one book to include all of the experiences and problems which come to a supervisor for solution; in like manner it is impossible to present or suggest a ready-made solution to each of these problems. The remainder of the discussion in this chapter will therefore be devoted to the identification of other *types* of special problems and ways by which they have been satisfactorily settled.

[17] For more information on the comics and aspects of reading readiness found in them, turn to Gwynn, 3rd ed., *op. cit.*, pp. 297-311.

TEACHER-PUPIL PLANNING

Whether by intention or by accident, much more co-operative planning of schoolwork by teachers with their pupils occurs on the elementary than on the secondary school level. This is one competency in teaching that has to be acquired by practice—no one is born with it or acquires it merely by mastering subject matter. Teacher-pupil planning is also an aspect of teaching that is most important in today's school—by giving the pupil the opportunity to help set up the goals and to know what he is working to master, it furnishes him with natural motivation for learning.

Intelligent teacher-pupil planning includes making provision for children's creative interests and efforts, for working together in class activities, for working together in matters or problems of concern for the whole school, for working on individual problems, and for ways to use "free time" most constructively.[18] The supervisor can help the teacher acquire skill in planning by:

1. Exploring with him all aspects of the proposed activity, so that he is not at a loss for ideas; this would include lists of references and books, pictures, materials of all kinds, resources in the library, and the like.
2. Suggesting that he identify both leaders in the class, those ready and willing to take responsibilities, and those not yet ready to take leadership roles; this identification will lay the basis for group assignments and work later.
3. Providing for him observation of good co-operative planning-in-action, as another competent teacher carries it out with his class.

[18] Historically, the reader can trace teacher-pupil planning through the following references: H. H. Giles, *Teacher-Pupil Planning* (New York: Harper and Brothers, 1941); three Yearbooks of the Association for Supervision and Curriculum Development (Washington, D. C.: National Education Association): 1945 Yearbook, *Group Planning in Education;* 1949 Yearbook, *Toward Better Teaching;* and 1954 Yearbook, *Creating a Good Environment for Learning; The Teacher's Role in Pupil-Teacher Planning,* Horace Mann-Lincoln Institute of School Experimentation (New York: Teachers College, Columbia University, 1947); Federal Security Agency (Now U. S. Department of Health, Education, and Welfare), Office of Education, "Place of Subject Series": *How Children Learn About Human Rights,* by W. Hill and H. K. Mackintosh, Bulletin 1951, No. 9; *How Children and Teacher Work Together,* by E. Schneider, Bulletin, 1952, No. 14; and *How Children Can Be Creative,* by W. Hill, H. K. Mackintosh, and A. Randall, Bulletin, 1954, No. 12; and Alice Miel and Associates, *Co-operative Procedures in Learning* (New York: Teachers College, Columbia University, 1952).

4. Suggesting that he start with a *smaller* activity with his class, rather than a large one; thus making it possible for him to work up to more complex planning situations.
5. Inquiring of him how he would "get out" all opinions of the children, how to record their suggestions, how to set up machinery to arrive at agreement on the goal or aims.
6. Suggesting that he plan for individual projects, as well as for group work; that he provide for construction or audio-visual activities and the use of the special skills of his pupils, as well as for writing and oral participation.
7. Suggesting that sharing, reporting, listening, and summarizing are all a natural part of co-operative evaluation of group planning and work.

THE USE OF SPECIALISTS

The supervisor is faced from time to time with the problem of how to use his specialists most effectively. Specialists usually are employed in art, music, physical education, home economics and homemaking, library work, shop work and industrial arts, or handicrafts. The old method of using these specialists was for each to teach his subject two or three times a week in each classroom; he went in and took over from the regular teacher and taught music or art directly to the children. Each had a full teaching schedule in his area.

The new approach makes use of the specialist as a resource person, a consultant, and a helper to the teacher in his work and teaching activities; at times the specialist helps a group of teachers in some joint project of a larger nature, as with a chorus from several rooms, or in a display of children's art for parents.

Good examples of how a specialist can be used effectively are found in *Music in the Elementary School*.[19] The idea is: What is a good music program for my school? The program should contain general music activities for the school, music for the self-contained classroom, opportunities for creative music, and types of programs for music appreciation. In the primary grades, emphasis through singing, rhythmics, listening, and playing is upon singing freely and easily, upon learning to carry a tune. In the intermediate grades,

---

[19] *Music for the Elementary School*, Music Educator's National Conference (Chicago: printed by the Conference in co-operation with the Department of Elementary School Principals, National Education Association, 1951).

children naturally want to learn to sing in parts; listening to music grows in importance to the pupil, who may even begin to collect his own record albums. Circle games, singing games, acting out what the song says, folk dancing, and free and interpretative dancing are a part of music, of play and physical education, and of reading.

The specialist can enrich the elementary school program if he is used to co-ordinate, to supplement, and at times to act as the curricular program for a day or so. Each supervisor will have to study each of his specialists, learn their individual points of view, how they can be used to best advantage, how far they can go now in helping to correlate their special areas with the total program of a grade. The supervisor will then be ready to plan for educating his specialists "on the job" to help them see the natural interrelationships of their areas with other closely related areas.

OTHER PROBLEMS

From time to time in the elementary school other problems face the supervisor. These are: (1) how to help a teacher to discover what is in the elementary school library and how to use this resource more effectively; (2) the requests by agencies in the community to use the elementary school for the promotion of the activities of their organization, such as promotion for the garden club or the essay contest staged by a patriotic organization, or the distribution of free advertising materials of one sort or another, ranging from stamped pencils and booklets to kits, maps, charts, posters, films, and the like; (3) how to aid a teacher in regard to scope and sequence in his work; (4) how to identify the different teaching approaches for the primary, the grammar grade, and the intermediate grade levels; (5) how to group more satisfactorily for instruction in the intermediate grades; (6) problems concerned with changes in grading, marking, or promotion; and (7) what kind of a schedule the supervisor should follow in any one week or period of time.

Suggestions for solving these and other types of problems have been given in other parts of this book. In the final analysis, each special problem has its own set of surrounding circumstances, its own personalities, its time when a solution is needed. Of course it follows that the supervisor will have to tackle each problem as it arises and work toward a solution in the light of all of its contributing factors.[20]

Problems for Individual Study and Class Discussion

1. Can a supervisor be proficient in helping teachers equally well at all grade levels? Would assistance to primary teachers differ from that given to teachers of higher grades? In what ways?
2. Do the seventh and eighth grades belong under the supervisory leadership of the elementary school or of the secondary school? State reasons for your belief.
3. Would you urge your teachers to make special preparations for visitors? Why or why not?
4. Can you suggest ways by which a supervisor might encourage larger participation in P.T.A. activities by men and nonparents?
5. Your superintendent asks you to set up machinery by which he and the school board can obtain accurate information on how well the schools in the system are teaching the three R's. What steps will you take to project such a study?
6. Compare the older methods of using specialists in the elementary school with the newer methods. How did this change come about in the elementary school?
7. Can the supervisor prevent bright pupils from becoming bored by having to repeat subjects and skills on the seventh- and eighth-grade levels that they have already mastered? How?
8. How does well-planned scope and sequence aid the teacher in her work in the elementary grades? Should this planning be co-ordinated with that of other grades? What is the implication here for the supervisor?
9. What responsibility, if any, does the supervisor have for visiting in the homes of elementary school children? Give reasons for your stand.

Special Resource Bibliography on Teaching in the Elementary School

NOTE: This bibliography has been restricted mostly to recent materials which are available and easily secured. Articles from the educational journals are so numerous that the reader is referred to the *Readers' Guide to Periodical Literature* and the *Education Index* for them.

[20] The reader will gain a good insight into some very recent controversial problems of the elementary school by referring to *Educational Leadership,* vol. XVIII (November, 1960), "Elementary Education: Issues and Prospects," pp. 74-100.

ARITHMETIC

Clark, J. R., and Eads, L. K., *Guiding Arithmetic Learning* (Yonkers-on-Hudson: World Book Company, 1954).

Grossnickle, F. E., and Breuckner, L. J., *Discovering Meanings in Arithmetic* (Philadelphia: The John C. Winston Company, 1959).

The Growth of Mathematical Ideas, Grades K-12 (Washington, D. C.: National Council of Mathematics, 1959).

Hollister, G. E., and Gunderson, A. G., *Teaching Arithmetic in Grades I and II* (Boston: D. C. Heath and Company, 1954).

Marks, J. L., Purdy, C. R., and Kinney, Lucien B., *Teaching Arithmetic for Understanding* (New York: McGraw-Hill Book Company, Inc., 1958).

Mueller, F. J., *Arithmetic: Its Structure and Concepts* (Englewood Cliffs, N. J.: Prentice-Hall, Inc., 1956).

Spitzer, H. F., *The Teaching of Arithmetic*, 2nd ed. (Boston: Houghton Mifflin Company, 1954).

Swain, R. L., *Understanding Arithmetic* (New York: Rinehart and Company, Inc., 1957).

Wheat, H. G., *How to Teach Arithmetic* (Evanston: Row, Peterson and Company, Inc., 1957).

ARTS AND CRAFTS

Barkan, M., *Through Art to Creativity: Art in the Elementary School Program* (Boston: Allyn and Bacon, 1960).

Benson, K. R., *Creative Crafts for Children* (Englewood Cliffs, N. J.: Prentice-Hall, Inc., 1958).

Conant, H., *Art in Education* (Peoria: Charles A. Bennett, 1959).

Erdt, M., *Teaching Art in the Elementary School* (New York: Rinehart and Company, Inc., 1954).

Gaitskell, C. D., *Children and Their Art* (New York: Harcourt, Brace and Company, Inc., 1958).

Gerbracht, C., *Industrials Arts for Grades K-6* (Milwaukee: Bruce Publishing Company, 1959).

Jefferson, B., *Teaching Art to Children* (Boston: Allyn and Bacon, 1959).

Logan, F. M., *Growth of Art in American Schools* (New York: Harper and Brothers, 1955).

Lowenfeld, V., *Your Child and His Art* (New York: The Macmillan Company, 1954).

Moore, F. C., Hamburger, C. H., and Kingzett, A. L., *Handcrafts for Elementary Schools: A Handbook of Practical Suggestions for Teachers* (Boston: D. C. Heath and Company, 1953).

Siks, G. B., *Creative Dramatics: An Art for Children* (New York: Harper and Brothers, 1958).

Wickiser, R. L., *An Introduction to Art Education* (Yonkers-on-Hudson: World Book Company, 1957).

CURRICULUM

Beck, R., and others, *Curriculum in the Modern Elementary School*, 2nd ed. (Englewood Cliffs, N. J.: Prentice-Hall, Inc., 1960).

Dutton, W. H., and Hockett, J. A., *The Modern Elementary School* (New York: American Book Company, 1960).

Lee, J. M., and D. M., *The Child and His Curriculum*, 3rd ed. (New York: Appleton-Century-Crofts, 1960).

Ragan, W. B., *Modern Elementary Curriculum*, rev. ed. (New York: Henry Holt and Company, 1960).

HEALTH AND PHYSICAL EDUCATION

Atkins, A. J., and Gwynn, J. M., *Teaching Alcohol Education in the Schools* (New York: The Macmillan Company, 1959).

Baruch, D., *New Ways in Sex Education* (New York: McGraw-Hill Book Company, 1959).

Bucher, C. A., and Reade, E. M., *Physical Education in the Modern Elementary School* (New York: The Macmillan Company, 1958).

Byrd, O. E., compiler, *School Health Sourcebook* (Stanford: Stanford University Press, 1955).

Cassidy, R., *Curriculum Development in Physical Education* (New York: Harper and Brothers, 1954).

Children in Focus: Their Health and Activity, 1954 Yearbook, American Association for Health, Physical Education, and Recreation (Washington, D. C.: National Education Association).

Farina, A. M., *Growth Through Play* (Englewood Cliffs: Prentice-Hall, 1959).

Godshall, F. R., *Nutrition in the Elementary School* (New York: Harper and Brothers, 1958).

Grout, R. E., *Health Teaching in Schools*, 3rd ed. (Philadelphia: W. B. Saunders Company, 1958).

Humphrey, J. H., *Elementary School Physical Education* (New York: Harper and Brothers, 1958).

Jones, E., and others, *Methods and Materials in Elementary Physical Education*, new ed. (Yonkers-on-Hudson: World Book Company, 1957).

Kraus, R., *Play Activity for Boys and Girls* (New York: McGraw-Hill Book Company, Inc., 1957).

Nielson, N. P., and Van Hagan, W., *Physical Education for Elementary Schools* (New York: A. S. Barnes and Company, 1954).

Roberts, N. H., and others, *Physical Education Handbook for Elementary Teaching* (San Antonio: The Naylor Company, 1957).

Shepard, N. M., *Foundations and Principles of Physical Education* (New York: The Ronald Press, 1960).

Smith, H. N., and Wolverton, M. E., *Health Education in the Elementary School* (New York: The Ronald Press Company, 1959).

Walker, H., *Health in the Elementary School* (New York: The Ronald Press Company, 1955).

Wescott, H. E., *A Guide to Teaching Materials in Elementary Health Education* (San Francisco: H. Chandler, 1959).

LANGUAGE ARTS

Anderson, T., *The Teaching of Foreign Languages in the Elementary School* (Boston: D. C. Heath and Company, 1953).

Dawson, M. A., *Guiding Language Learning* (Yonkers-on-Hudson: World Book Company, 1957).

Greene, H. A., and Petty, E. T., *Developing Language Skills in the Elementary Schools* (Boston: Allyn and Bacon, 1959).

Hatchett, E. L., and Hughes, D. H., *Teaching Language Arts in Elementary Schools* (New York: The Ronald Press Company, 1956).

Herrick, V. E., and Jacobs, L. B., eds., *Children and the Language Arts* (Englewood Cliffs, N. J.: Prentice-Hall, Inc., 1955).

Hildreth, G., *Teaching Spelling* (New York, Henry Holt and Company, Inc., 1955).

Huebner, T., *How to Teach Foreign Languages Effectively* (New York: New York University Press, 1959).

Language Arts for Today's Children, prepared by the Commission on the English Curriculum of the National Council of Teachers of English (New York: Appleton-Century-Crofts, Inc., 1954).

MacRae, M. W., *Teaching Spanish in the Grades* (Boston: Houghton Mifflin Company, 1957).

Mass Media and Education, Fifty-third Yearbook, Part II, National Society for the Study of Education (Chicago: University of Chicago Press, 1954).

Strickland, R. G., *The Language Arts in the Elementary School,* 2nd ed. (Boston: D. C. Heath and Company, 1957).

Tidyman, W. F., and Butterfield, M., *Teaching the Language Arts,* 2nd ed. (New York: McGraw-Hill Book Company, Inc., 1959).

MUSIC

McMillan, L. E., *Guiding Children's Growth Through Music* (New York: Ginn and Company, 1959).

Marvel, L., *The Music Consultant at Work* (New York: Bureau of Publications, Teachers College, Columbia University, 1960).

Mathews, P., *You Can Teach Music* (New York: E. P. Dutton and Company, Inc., 1953).

Morgan, H. N., ed., *Music in American Education* (Chicago, 4: Music Educators National Conference, 1955).

Myers, L. K., *Teaching Children Music in the Elementary School,* 2nd ed. (Englewood Cliffs, N. J.: Prentice-Hall, Inc., 1956).

Nye, R. E., and Bergethon, B., *Basic Music for Classroom Teachers* (Englewood Cliffs, N. J.: Prentice-Hall, Inc., 1954).

Pierce, A. E., *Teaching Music in the Elementary School* (New York: Henry Holt and Company, Inc., 1960).

Sheehy, E. D., *Children Discover Music and Dance* (New York: Henry Holt and Company, 1959).

Snyder, K. B., *School Music Administration and Supervision* (Boston: Allyn and Bacon, 1959).

Sur, W. R., and Schuller, C. F., *Music Education for Teen-agers*, (New York: Harper and Brothers, 1958).

READING

Artley, A. S., *Your Child Learns to Read* (Chicago: Scott, Foresman and Company, 1955).

Betts, E. A., *Foundation of Reading Instruction*, rev. ed. (New York: American Book Company, 1957).

Brogan, P., and Fox, L. K., *Helping Children Read* (Yonkers-on-Hudson: World Book Company, 1955).

Burton, W. H., *Reading in Child Development* (Indianapolis: The Bobbs-Merrill Company, 1956).

Dawson, M. A., and Bamman, H. A., *Fundamentals of Basic Reading Instruction* (New York: Longmans, Green and Company, 1959).

Development in and Through Reading, Sixtieth Yearbook, Part I, National Society for the Study of Education (Chicago: University of Chicago Press, 1961).

Dolch, E. W., *Teaching Primary Reading*, rev. ed. (Champaign: Garrard Press, 1960).

Gray, L., *Teaching Children to Read*, 2nd ed. (New York: The Ronald Press Company, 1957).

Gray, W. S., *On Their Own in Reading*, rev. ed. (Chicago: Scott, Foresman and Company, 1960).

Harris, A. J., *How to Increase Reading Ability*, 3rd ed. (New York: Longmans, Green and Company, 1956).

Heilman, A. W., *Principles and Practices of Teaching Reading* (Columbus: Charles E. Merrill Books, Inc., 1961).

Hester, K. B., *Teaching Every Child to Read* (New York: Harper and Brothers, 1955).

Hildreth, G., *Readiness for School Beginners* (Yonkers-on-Hudson, World Book Company, 1950).

Hunt, J. T., "Easy and Interesting Fiction for the Handicapped Reader," *The High School Journal*, vol. XXXIX (April, 1956), pp. 378-385.

McKim, M., *Guiding Growth in Reading in the Modern Elementary School* (New York: The Macmillan Company, 1955).

McNamee, M. B., *Reading for Understanding*, rev. ed. (New York: Rinehart and Company, Inc., 1958).

Newton, J. R., *Reading in Your School* (New York: McGraw-Hill Book Company, Inc., 1960).

Strang, R., and others, *Problems in the Improvement of Reading*, 2nd ed. (New York: McGraw-Hill Book Company, Inc., 1955), chs. I-VI, XVII-XVIII.

Tooze, R., *Your Children Want to Read: A Guide for Parents and Teachers* (Englewood Cliffs, N. J.: Prentice-Hall, Inc., 1957).

Veatch, J., *Individualizing Your Reading Program: Self-Selection in Action* (New York: G. P. Putnam Sons, 1959).

Witty, P., *How to Improve Your Reading* (Chicago: Science Research Associates, 1956).

Woolf, M. D., and J. A., *Remedial Reading: Teaching and Treatment* (New York: McGraw-Hill Book Company, Inc., 1957).

Yoakam, G. A., *Basal Reading Instruction* (New York: McGraw-Hill Book Company, Inc., 1955).

SCIENCE

Blough, G. O., and Campbell, M. H., *Making and Using Classroom Science Materials in the Elementary School* (New York: The Dryden Press, 1954).

———, and others, *Elementary School Science and How to Teach It*, rev. ed. (New York: The Dryden Press, 1958).

Brandwein, P. F., *The Gifted Student as Future Scientist* (New York: Harcourt, Brace and Company, Inc., 1955).

Burnett, R. W., *Teaching Science in the Elementary School* (New York: Rinehart and Company, Inc., 1953).

Chase, J. B., Jr., *A Guide to Curriculum Study: Science*, Grades 1-12 (Raleigh: State Board of Education, 1959).

Craig, G. S., *Science for the Elementary School Teacher*, 2nd ed. (Boston: Ginn and Company, 1958).

Freeman, K., and others, *Helping Children Understand Science*, rev. ed. (Philadelphia: The John C. Winston Company, 1959).

Hubler, C., *Working with Children in Science* (Boston: Houghton Mifflin Company, 1957).

Rethinking Science Education, Fifty-Ninth Yearbook, National Society for the Study of Education, Part I (Chicago: University of Chicago Press, 1960).

Science for Today's Children, Thirty-second Yearbook, Department of Elementary School Principals (Washington, D. C.: National Education Association, 1953).

Tannenbaum, H. E., and Stillman, N., *Science Education for Elementary School Teachers* (Boston: Allyn and Bacon, 1960).

Vergara, W. C., *Science in Everyday Things* (New York: Harper and Brothers, 1958).

SOCIAL STUDIES

Hill, W., *Social Studies in the Elementary School Program* (Washington: U. S. Office of Education, Bulletin 1960, No. 5).

Jarolimek, J., *Social Studies in Elementary Education* (New York: The Macmillan Company, 1959).

Michaelis, J. W., *Social Studies for Children in a Democracy*, 2nd ed. (Englewood Cliffs, N. J.: Prentice-Hall, Inc., 1956).

Moffatt, M. P., and Howell, H. W., *Elementary Social Studies Instruction* (New York: Longmans, Green and Company, 1952).

Otto, H. J., *Social Education in Elementary Schools* (New York: Rinehart and Company, Inc., 1956).

Preston, R. C., *Teaching Social Studies in the Elementary School* (New York: Rinehart and Company, Inc., 1958).

Skills in Social Studies, Twenty-fourth Yearbook, National Council for the Social Studies (Washington, D. C.: National Education Association, 1954).

Social Studies for Older Children: Programs for Grades Four, Five, and Six, Curriculum Series No. 5, 1954, and *Social Education of Young Children: Kindergarten-Primary,* Curriculum Series No. 4, 1956 edition, National Council for the Social Studies, National Education Association.

Social Studies in the Elementary School, Forty-sixth Yearbook, Part II, National Society for the Study of Education (Chicago: University of Chicago Press, 1957).

Thralls, Z. A., *The Teaching of Geography* (New York: Appleton-Century-Crofts, Inc., 1958).

Tiegs, E. W., and Adams, F., *Teaching the Social Studies: A Guide to Better Citizenship* (Boston: Ginn and Company, 1959).

Tooze, R., and Krone, B. P., *Literature and Music as Resources for Social Studies* (Englewood Cliffs, N. J.: Prentice-Hall, Inc., 1955).

SPEECH

Anderson, V. A., *Improving the Child's Speech* (New York: Oxford University Press, 1953).

Ogilvie, M., *Speech in the Elementary School* (New York: McGraw-Hill Book Company, Inc., 1954).

Van Riper, C., and Butler, K. C., *Speech in the Elementary Classroom* (New York: Harper and Brothers, 1955).

SPELLING

Hildreth, G., *Teaching Spelling: A Guide to Basic Principles and Practices* (New York: Henry Holt and Company, Inc., 1955).

Russell, K. V., and others, *Developing Spelling Power* (Yonkers-on-Hudson: World Book Company, 1957).

MISCELLANEOUS

Arbuthnot, M. H., *Children and Books* (Chicago: Scott, Foresman and Company, 1957).

Banning, E. I., "Social Influences on Children and Youth," *Review of Educational Research,* vol. XXV (February, 1955), ch. IV, pp. 36-47.

Berson, M. P., *Kindergarten: Your Child's Big Steps* (New York: E. P. Dutton & Company, 1959).

Brogan, P., and Fox, L. K., *Helping Children Learn* (Yonkers-on-Hudson: World Book Company, 1955).

Creating a Good Environment for Learning, 1954 Yearbook, Association for Supervision and Curriculum Development (Washington, D. C.: National Education Association).

Dutton, W. H., and Hockett, J. A., *The Modern Elementary School: Curriculum and Methods* (New York: Rinehart and Company, Inc., 1959).

Foster and Headley's Education in the Kindergarten, rev. by Keith E. Headley, 3rd ed. (New York: American Book Company, 1959).

Goodlad, J., *The Nongraded Elementary School* (New York: Harcourt, Brace and Company, 1959).

Hanna, G. R., *Books, Young People, and Reading Guidance* (New York: Harper and Brothers, 1960).

Hanna, L., Potter, G. L., and Hagaman, N. C., *Unit Teaching in the Elementary School* (New York: Rinehart and Company, Inc., 1955).

Heffernan, H., ed., *Guiding the Young Child: Kindergarten to Grade Three,* 2nd ed. (Boston: D. C. Heath and Company, 1959).

Johnson, E., and others, eds., *Anthology of Children's Literature* (Boston: Houghton Mifflin Company, 1959).

Klausmeier, H. J., and others, *Teaching in the Elementary School* (New York: Harper and Brothers, 1956).

Lee, J. M. and D. M., *The Child and His Curriculum,* 3rd ed. (New York: Appleton-Century-Crofts, Inc., 1960).

Logan, L. M., *Teaching the Young Child: Methods of Preschool and Primary Education* (Boston: Houghton Mifflin Company, 1960).

McKim, M. G., and others, *Learning to Teach in the Elementary School* (New York: The Macmillan Company, 1959).

Miel, A., and associates, *Co-operative Procedures in Learning* (New York: Teachers College, Columbia University, 1952).

Nesbitt, M., *A Public School for Tomorrow: A Description of the Matthew F. Maury School, Richmond, Virginia* (New York: Harper and Brothers, 1953).

Thomas, R. M., *Ways of Teaching in Elementary School* (New York: Longmans, Green and Company, 1955).

Wilt, M. E., *Creativity in the Elementary School* (New York: Appleton-Century-Crofts, 1959).

CHAPTER 14

Helping the Teacher with
His Personal Problems

PERSONAL PROBLEMS OF TEACHERS do not stem only from the class-room—they arise from other pressures and influences. Usually one can trace these personal problems to a social, emotional, economic, or community situation in which the teacher finds himself. The supervisor can help at times in the solution of some of these problems, provided that (1) he is well balanced himself, and usually capable of solving his own personal problems and (2) he does *not* profess to "know all the answers" to other people's problems. It is important for the supervisor to be aware that such problems exist and that they may complicate supervisor-teacher relationships, or the teacher's teaching, whether or not the supervisor actually ever plays a part in the solutions.

The purpose of this chapter, therefore, is to help the supervisor to identify the main types of personal problems and to illustrate situations in which the teacher may need help. The reader should note that some of the "case histories" show clearly the potential dangers if a supervisor tries to interfere too quickly or freely in the personal affairs of teachers.

Sources of Problems

The teacher's personal problem may come from one source, or from a combination of two or more sources. Some problems originate from his state of health. A teacher may not be sleeping as well as usual, and he may begin to worry over staying awake at night; the more he thinks about it, the more he is conscious of it, the more emphasis he puts upon getting enough sleep, and the more he worries because he cannot sleep the whole night through. Another teacher may worry because of the state of health of a loved one. For example, he may be worried because his father's recovery from an automobile accident is very slow, or because his mother has developed heart trouble and has had to curtail her activities.

A second source of anxiety for the teacher is the economic situation in which he operates. It is well known that if a person is assured of financial security, he is more likely to feel self-confident and secure in his work and other contacts. Examples of problems in this area are inability of the teacher to live on his salary without going into debt, emergency hospitalization of wife or husband, extra expenses upon the arrival of a new member of the family, lack of funds to join a service club or social organization such as the country club, and financial inability to buy a car or as good clothes as some other teacher. Pressure for more money to meet any of these situations might cause the teacher to take on an additional job, outside, which might not hurt his effectiveness as a teacher.

A teacher's social life and contacts furnish another source of problems. Teaching is a "status" job in all cultures, whether it pays well financially or not. The public gives status, primarily social status, to the teacher; he is given it as long as he behaves reasonably well; he does not have to fight for it. However, some teachers cause themselves endless worry by feeling that they have to fight for this social status, and these are usually designated by the term "social climbers." Other types of problems are the feeling of "being left out" or not being invited, the insecure feeling of not knowing whether he "belongs," and the problem of "keeping up with the Joneses."

A teacher's emotions, psychology of life, and spiritual experiences are other sources of his personal problems. A person quickly aroused and quick to speak will tend to "say too much" that he will be sorry for later. Some serious problems, on the other hand, stem from a damning up of emotions without opportunity to "talk" troubles out and thus release oneself from tension. For example, the belief that excessive drinking is a sin instead of an illness can create a problem for a teacher at times most troublesome to him. The teacher is just "looking for trouble" and will certainly have plenty of it if he believes in always "speaking what he thinks" and acts accordingly. In the realm of religion and the spirit, problems arise concerning the amount of control which the church should exert over the teacher's life and acts, over the amount and extent of church attendance, and over the teacher's concept of interracial and intercultural contacts or customs.

Finally, in some cases two or more complicating factors operate to create a big problem. For instance, a teacher learns that his younger brother has just had a nervous breakdown and has entered a hospital for treatment. Here three factors may operate to upset the teacher. First, psychiatric treatment is very expensive, and where is sufficient money for treatment to come from? Secondly, will his brother really recover, or will he become permanently institutionalized? And thirdly, why did this terrible thing have to happen in his family, to him? What has he done to deserve it? Thus economic, health, and emotional factors operate to upset the teacher.

Women may vary more than men in the sources of their personal problems. Some young teachers are just out of college, accustomed to many dates—or no dates; they may come into a situation which is the reverse of this. Are they frustrated? Or a teacher may be a mother with sick children. Another may have a husband in college, and be supporting the family and putting him through school.

Problem Indicators

There are several symptoms which may foretell the development of a personal problem in a teacher. In summary form, here is a list of typical warning signals, not in order of importance:

1. When a teacher cannot sit down and talk quietly and at length, but has to stand up, and perhaps walks about while talking with the supervisor or another colleague.
2. When a teacher who has normally been rather talkative becomes suddenly and unexplainably more silent than talkative. And the reverse of this, when a teacher who is normally prone to be rather silent changes radically into a very talkative person.

3. When a teacher's classes have a much larger number of "personality conflicts" than usual between teacher and pupils.
4. When a teacher who has been consistently pleasant and mild in attitude becomes "snappy" and fault-finding with his pupils.
5. When a teacher who has a record of promptness gets into the habit of not being able to complete tasks or responsibilities on time.
6. When a teacher develops suddenly a tic or nervous mannerism which he did not have before.
7. When little things or irrelevant matters irritate a teacher easily and assume an importance that is not warranted.
8. When a teacher begins to tell the same story, the same episode over and over again to the same person with the same details, not realizing that he is doing it.
9. When a teacher who is normally rather calm and of moderate voice tone changes and each day starts on a high key, with his voice getting louder and higher, until all children are keyed up and talking excitedly too.
10. When a teacher begins to lose or gain weight steadily and noticeably when not on a diet under a physician's care.
11. When a teacher consistently cannot wait for you or another person to get through before he interrupts.
12. When a teacher begins to blame someone else or some thing for his own failure to perform a task well or to carry out a responsibility.
13. When a teacher who is well known for his liking and love for children changes his attitude to one of constant criticism of pupils.
14. When a teacher who is a temperate person begins to drink more or less steadily.
15. When a teacher who likes social life and contacts begins to withdraw more and more into privacy and solitude.
16. When a teacher who formerly seemed to love and enjoy his work dreads to go to school in the morning, no longer finds joy or satisfaction in his work, and thinks only of dismissal on Friday.

Illustrations of Typical Problems

It is a well-known fact that the supervisor cannot and does not become acquainted with all of the personal problems of his staff. It is also equally well known that teachers solve the majority of their personal problems themselves. The typical problem referred to here is one that is persistent and worries the teacher to the extent that worry is noticeable or has an adverse effect upon teaching efficiency.

The brief cases which are described here happened in real life; they came to the attention of the supervisor or administrator who was acting in a supervisory capacity. They were cases in which the supervisor noted some difficulty and approached the teacher or the teacher came to the supervisor with his or her problem, or they were cases which were settled without direct action on the part of the supervisor.

CASE 1

The principal and his physical education man, who was also his coach, boarded at the same place. The principal noted in November that the coach was missing breakfast rather often; yet he was at school promptly and at work. After another two weeks of the same kind of "breakfast missing," he spoke to the man casually, saying "Where are you eating breakfast when you don't come to Mrs. Black's? Can't you take her food?" The reply was open and frank: "I don't have much appetite any more for breakfast—not too much for any meal, in fact." The principal continued, "Always been that way?" "No," said the physical ed. man, "just since last August." "Why not check with Dr. Bellows and see what he says?"

The coach agreed, and went to the doctor's office that afternoon. After a series of tests, it was shown from the X-rays that he had peptic ulcers, apparently in the beginning stage. Treatment and diet followed, he recovered completely, and his problem was solved.

CASE 2

Miss Green was a striking, red-headed girl, not pretty, but vivacious, witty, and as keen as she could be. She was the seventh-grade teacher, and she roomed in one of the best homes in town with the fifth-grade teacher, Miss White, a pretty brunette of the soft-voiced, dependent variety. Both were teachers new to the system this year. The supervisor was a woman, who supervised the elementary grades. In January there occurred a sharp increase in the number of disciplinary cases that Miss Green sent to the principal. When this continued until February, the principal and the supervisor agreed that something ought to be done to discover why Miss Green's control of her room was breaking down. Making an analysis with the principal of the types of misbehavior of the children sent by Miss Green to the office, the supervisor discovered that they involved primarily the aggressive pupils in her room. With this to go on, the supervisor double-checked to see whether the grades of the children in these disciplinary cases showed any fluctuation—they did, sharply downward. With these facts at her disposal, the supervisor requested Miss Green to meet her on Tuesday afternoon at her last period, when Miss Green was free because her pupils finished the rest of the day in free-choice activities under other teachers. When faced with the facts which the supervisor had gathered, Miss Green admitted them, broke down, and revealed the real source of her mounting difficulties—she could never get away from her roommate, Miss White, in hours after school, even for a little while. Miss White clung to her like a leech, relied on her for advice, insisted upon accompanying her on all occasions, even once or twice attempted to go on her "dates" with her; she spoiled her, but wanted to direct and control her out-of-school activities. In short, Miss Green was in an impossible situation, did not see any way out of it without hurting or humiliating a fine woman and a good teacher, and as a result became more irritable each day, unconsciously "taking out her frustration" on students who were aggressive, just as she was being bothered by an aggressive woman. The supervisor knew that Miss Green's mother was an invalid, who lived in a town some twenty miles away; she also knew that Miss Green owned her own car. She asked Miss Green if her mother's poor health might not demand that she live at home and commute to work for the rest of the year; she offered to help Miss White find another roommate or another place to stay if Miss Green had to do this. Miss Green accepted the suggestion enthusiastically; and for the next year she secured a nice one-room apartment by herself. With the help of the supervisor Miss White obtained another roommate who was congenial. Miss Green's teaching effectiveness returned to normal, even improved.

CASE 3

One Monday morning Mr. B, principal of a small-town high school, received an early-morning call from Mr. Hightower, president of the local bank and a member of the school board, too. He wanted a conference, and so B took himself off down town at his first free period, 10:00 a.m. It developed that Mr. Pierson, able social studies teacher and a successful member of the faculty for many years, had recently overdrawn his account at the bank; and further investigation disclosed that his charge accounts at the stores were running far behind what they usually did as he made periodic payments on them. The investigation also revealed that this "straining of his credit" had developed rapidly in the last six months. Should the principal do anything about it? It was a difficult situation, for there was no evidence that Pierson was spending any more money than he usually received from his salary and other sources. In this case the principal took the frontal approach, since he had known Pierson for many years both professionally and personally. He picked Pierson up as usual after school to give him a lift home and said: "John, Hightower phoned me this morning and asked if I would find out whether you needed a temporary loan for an emergency—your account was heavily overdrawn for the second time in a month." Pierson sat still a minute, then turned a tortured face to his friend: "B," he said, "My youngest brother is in a private sanitarium with a nervous breakdown; the family doesn't want our friends to learn about it; and I'm trying to carry most of the financial load and going crazy doing it! What can I do?" Once the problem was identified, the banker, the principal, the local and state hospital authorities, and Pierson worked out a plan that eventually both restored this brother to health and work and John Pierson to normal life and teaching again.

CASE 4

Miss Brandywine, the elementary school supervisor, was sitting in her office on a beautiful Friday afternoon, late in May, trying to get up enough energy to start sorting her materials and data for her annual report to the principal and superintendent. It had been a good year, except for one teacher, a twenty-four-old third-grade teacher who had been with them for four years. But this year she had become snappy and irritable with her children, late in turning in her reports, and had developed a tendency to keep more to herself with less contact with other teachers. "I wonder what is bothering her," she was musing, when the door opened and the teacher, Mary Exom, appeared in person. Mary came in, sat down, and said, "I've got to talk to someone, and you're at hand."

Then the girl told her problem. She was a daughter of a Protestant minister and had fallen in love with a young man whose religion was different and whose beliefs in regard to authority, home, family and children differed radically from hers. The young fellow was a successful engineer with an electric company, and resources were ample for them to marry and live comfortably. They had discussed the problem of the differing beliefs and customs many times; theoretically, she felt that they could settle it satisfactorily; practically, she wondered in her heart whether she could accept wholeheartedly the beliefs and controls of his religion. And he was not willing to change his and accept hers.

The situation at present was this. After knowing him well for one year, he wanted her to marry him. He was in love with her, and she with him. He had visited in her home, and she in his. Each felt the same way about the other's family—"If we could live our lives without them, and their opinions, we could marry and be happy." She wanted a home and family, but she was unsure about this particular situation's ever developing into a happy home and marriage. She was unhappy, she said, frustrated, and doing poor teaching on account of it, and she knew it. What should she do?

Miss Brandywine felt most inadequate in this situation. But she felt that the girl would not have confided in her unless she trusted her. She asked Mary if she had taken her problem to anyone else; Mary had not. She ascertained that Mary's faith in God and in her religion were as strong as ever, that Mary knew little of the faith to which her fiancé belonged, that she had not read widely about it or studied it. She also discovered that Mary had dated often since she was sixteen but that this was her first serious love affair. She asked Mary if her tastes, likes, and interests were the same, or different from those of this young man who wanted to marry her. And whether they were much alike in temperament or markedly different. She also asked Mary whether a year far away from this young man, teaching in a different situation and community, would help her to make up her mind more definitely as to whether she wanted to marry him.

These simple questions, asked for information, acted as points of departure for Mary Exom to study her problem and to work on it more intelligently. Of her own accord she studied her problem within the framework of these questions, eventually going to another distant teaching position and staying a year. There she met another fine young man of like tastes and interests, and of the same faith; the acquaintance grew into courting, and eventually into a happy marriage.

Cases 5 and 6

Mr. Woodson, the supervising principal of Deep Glen, had two interesting and profitable experiences in his professional work during this first year of supervision. From them he learned certain techniques that stood him in good stead as he steadily climbed the ladder to administrative success in schoolwork.

The first case involved Virginia Dale, a young lady of twenty who came as a beginning teacher to his school. She was pretty, intelligent, well trained, of a fine family, enthusiastic, ambitious, and an endless worker. Her pupils in grade 6 loved her, respected her, and bragged about her. In February Woodson's wife asked him how Virginia was doing; he told her that in the last two weeks she seemed to have had a little disciplinary trouble. His wife then told him that she understood that Virginia was dating a high school senior regularly, that high school pupils were talking about it, and that even Miss Dale's pupils were teasing her about it. Nonplussed, the principal did not know what to do, asked his wife's advice. She suggested that he do nothing yet, since the boy was a fine fellow and was, after all, not in Virginia's grade, and not being taught by her.

However, a school board member telephoned Woodson the next day, and talked with him about the case, said that the spectacle of teacher courting pupil, and vice versa, was both upsetting school morale and destroying the role of the teacher, namely, that of being "in loco parentis" to pupils. Worried, Woodson thought the matter over again and again decided to take no action yet. A week later, the boy who was being dated by Virginia came to see him, wanted his advice; the youngster said that he was genuinely in love with the teacher, but too much in love with her to hurt her effectiveness in teaching and her standing in the community. The principal asked him if he would take the matter up with the teacher, telling her what he had just told him. The boy did so; they decided to date no more until after school was out in the spring, and the problem solved itself.

The second experience which Woodson recalled involved another problem of dating which concerned one of his experienced teachers. Miss Tolliver had taught the first grade for ten years at Deep Glen, was perhaps the best teacher on his staff, and was liked and respected. She lived with the Baptist minister and his wife, in a nice room; they had a house full of children, five to be exact, ranging in ages from five to fifteen.

Mr. Brower, a hardware merchant of thirty-five, and a member of the school board, had become much interested in Miss Tolliver about a year ago, and they had begun "going steady" since last August. There was a fine courtship going on, apparently approved by everybody, until one day in early November a prominent lady in town, member of the Baptist Church, paid Woodson a visit, the purpose, to see whether he knew that Brower and Miss Tolliver dated practically every night, that most of their time was spent parking in a local Lovers Lane, and that she seldom got home before 1:00 to 3:00 a.m.

Woodson asked the defender of public mores and morals if anything were going on that was not proper and honorable, and she admitted that there was no breath of scandal attached to the two; she also admitted that she had not heard of any change in Miss Tolliver's teaching efficiency or lack of responsibility for her duties.

After talking with his wife about this case also, Woodson sat tight. His wife told him that there was quite a bit of talk about the manner of courting, but that there was no scandal, no rumor of misbehavior; and that Miss Tolliver had practically no access to the parlor of the parsonage for her dates, since the minister's children kept it in constant use.

He figured that Miss Tolliver was perhaps doing as well as she could do under the circumstances. He dropped by to see the lady who had reported the matter to him, told her of the results of his investigations, and hinted tactfully of the fact that it might be wise not to spread rumors about a couple who were likely to strike back forcefully if there came to their ears any attack upon their characters.

The course of action "paid off." Two weeks later Miss Tolliver came in and told Woodson that she and Brower planned to be married in the summer. He and his wife invited them to use their home for dating until the marriage. And a problem that arose unknown to the teacher was settled unknown to the teacher.

Case 7

Miss Casey, a teacher of four years' experience in the system, came in to see the supervisor, Mrs. Hardison, one afternoon. Miss Casey was a high school English teacher, a good one, who also handled dramatics, the high school publications, and school radio programs on the local radio station. She told Mrs. Hardison that she had been asked to head up the annual community Red Cross drive. Upon inquiry, Mrs. Hardison found that she already had these community activities: Girl Scout-leader, teacher of a Sunday School class, and secretary of the History Club. She asked Miss Casey if she had time to take on an additional major community responsibility; the answer was no. She then asked her which three she wanted or which one she could give up if she took on the Red Cross work. Miss Casey left, pondering. Within two weeks another Scoutleader had been found for the girls, and Miss Casey took over the chairmanship of the Red Cross.

Case 8

Miss Karpenfeld, a high school English teacher, was having trouble with her discipline, as usually happened in the review and study period before exams, and during the last two months of the year. Miss Karpenfeld was 48, inclined to be fat and somewhat careless about her dress. She was an inspiring teacher of poetry and drama, an uninteresting drill master in grammar, and a creator of drudgery for children in composition and writing. She had been teaching in Bixby High for seven years, well liked by many of the people in the community, and never believed anything really bad about anyone. Having trust in others herself, she trusted her students and found it difficult to believe that any one of them could ever be a young "hellion" or an impertinent adolescent.

As the years had gone by, Miss Karpenfeld had not tended to improve all of her teaching practices. Able to read poetry aloud so that it could hold her audience enthralled, she was likewise a past master at drilling for and staging dramatic performances; in this area of competency she had continued to grow over the years. On the other hand, her daily assignments of written work piled up on her desk to be tackled on the week-end; eventually, she got around to returning to each student only about one-half of what he had handed in. At the end of each school year, the janitor would collect the desk full of papers left uncorrected and burn them. Her students hated grammar, and many failed that part of her course each year and had to take the grammar work over again the next year.

When Mr. Blanton came in as principal last year, he was told about her and her weaknesses in teaching. The superintendent also told him that she was a first cousin of the chairman of the school board and that firing her was not the solution to this problem. But he hoped that Blanton could help her to solve some of her problems and improve her teaching.

During the first year, he suggested that she attend the state meeting of English teachers for new ideas. She did. But her teaching remained the same. He suggested a summer school term, with major work in English at a metropolitan university famed for its work in improvement of methods of teaching. She was enthusiastic, went, and came back raving over the people she met and the new methods that she saw used successfully—but none of the new methods had "rubbed off" on her teaching this year.

During this year he had arranged for her to visit and observe two very good grammar and composition teachers, both in other school systems. She enjoyed the intervisitation and the demonstrations, but did not adapt any of the successful methods to her own teaching.

In desperation near the end of his second year, Blanton asked for and got an appointment with Mr. Jones, the superintendent, to report and talk about Miss Karpenfeld. The superintendent listened sympathetically to his report and his recommendation that Miss Karpenfeld not be re-elected. Then Jones asked: "Is Miss Karpenfeld a poor or bad character influence on the pupils?" The answer was "No." "Is she on the job, apparently working at her teaching the best that she can?" The principal had to admit that she was. "Does she get along all right with teachers and parents?" Blanton said that she did.

Jones then asked Blanton what real grounds he had for recommending that she not be retained. Blanton replied, "Incompetency." Jones responded: "That is the hardest charge to sustain and prove; the board will want more proof than you have given me. Why not wait a while? She may resign, or want to move to another job, or leave to take a job nearer home." It was left at that. Three years later Miss Karpenfeld moved to another position in her home town, so she could live at home and take care of her mother. Though not solved immediately, this problem worked itself out for that principal over a period of years.

Characteristics of Well-Balanced Teachers

In considering the different kinds of personal problems of teachers, the supervisor might keep in mind the qualities that are characteristic of well-balanced and well-rounded teachers. One characteristic is that such a teacher can take part in an increased number of activities of a community nature and usually do them as well or better than others. Another is that a variety of experiences are necessary to make an all-around person of a teacher, including some social, some mental or intellectual, some emotional, some strictly recreational, and some of a spiritual and creative nature. In the third place, the well-adjusted teacher is usually companionable, interested in a tremendous number of activities and aspects of life, and gregarious. In the fourth place, an even-tempered and adjusted teacher is able to be happy in an individual hobby or in an activity that he can do alone, as well as in an activity that demands the presence of other people. Finally, the well-balanced person can laugh at himself as well as at others, is sympathetic, realizes his own limitations and is happy in that situation, has a true respect for the problems of others, and possesses a sound set of ethical standards of his own.

The supervisor to whom teachers turn naturally for help in the solution of their personal problems is not only a well-balanced person. He is also an excellent listener, a person who never betrays a confidence, a tolerant person, a keen student of human nature and behavior, and a truly modest person looking for no credit of his own from the trials and troubles of others. He keeps in mind that any personal problem of a teacher can be solved only in terms of the individual teacher's own good taste, standards, and satisfaction. Teachers have individual differences, too; and the supervisor has to study them.

TEACHERS' IDENTIFICATION OF THEIR OWN PROBLEMS

The writer has found few studies comprehensive enough to give a true picture of the personal problems which teachers identify as having a major effect upon their teaching.[1] The research that has been done shows that teachers on a scale of frequency ranked financial problems, problems of health, and problems concerned with living and working conditions first. Personal problems of a family nature and concerned with colleagues ranked second. Rather interesting is the fact that problems arising because of community demands or restrictions ranked relatively low in frequency among teachers.

There is a need for more basic research in the area of the teacher's personal problems and the teacher's functions in the social structure of the community. It would also be most valuable for school authorities to learn how much impression the teacher exerts as a model or example upon his pupils.[2]

Problems for Individual Study and Class Discussion

1. Many educational authorities believe that teachers have more freedom from narrow, social mores today than they had 30 years ago. List a few ways in which the modern teacher has been freed from the stereotype of earlier days.
2. Is a social club for teachers a good idea? Or should they plan to associate more with people other than teachers in their off-duty hours? Support your position.
3. Would you advise teachers to take definite stands on controversial issues in the community? Or not? Why?
4. What is meant by the expression, "Don't be a 12 o'clock girl in a 9 o'clock town"?
5. If every teacher were started at a salary of $3,600 a year and could eventually make up to $10,000 a year with experience and additional training, would that make each teacher feel financially secure and thus result in more effective teaching? Explain.
6. Do "personality conflicts" occur between supervisor and teachers? What causes such conflicts? How can the supervisor reduce such conflicts to a minimum?

[1] Cf. "Teachers as Individuals," *Educational Leadership*, vol. XVI (March, 1946), pp. 251-281; and *Review of Educational Research*, "Teacher Personnel," vols. XIX (June, 1949) and XXII (June, 1952), *passim*.

[2] Brookover, W. B., "Teachers and the Stratification of American Society," *The Harvard Educational Review*, vol. XXIII (Fall, 1953), pp. 257-267.

7. Are you a well-balanced supervisor? How do you know that you are or are not?

Additional Source References for Problem or Unit Study

Association for Supervision and Curriculum Development, National Education Association, Washington, D. C.: 1950 Yearbook: *Fostering Mental Health in Our Schools,* chs. I, IX. 1951 Yearbook: *Action for Curriculum Improvement,* ch. I. 1954 Yearbook: *Creating a Good Environment for Learning,* ch. VII.

Bartky, J. A., *Supervision as Human Relations* (Boston: D. C. Heath and Company, 1953), chs. X-XII.

Bent, R. K., and Kronenberg, H. H., *Principles of Secondary Education,* 3rd ed. (New York: McGraw-Hill Book Company, Inc., 1955), ch. XVII.

Bossing, N. L., *Teaching in Secondary Schools,* 3rd ed. (Boston: Houghton Mifflin Company, 1952), ch. XXI.

Brookover, W. B., and others, *A Sociology of Education* (New York: American Book Company, 1955), chs. IX-X.

Davis, R. A., and others, "The Teaching Problems of 1,075 Public School Teachers," *Journal of Experimental Education,* vol. IX (September, 1940), pp. 41-60.

Dutton, W. H., and Hockett, J. A., *The Modern Elementary School* (New York: Rinehart and Company, 1959), ch. I.

Edwards, Newton, "Legal Status of the Teacher," in *The Teacher's Role in American Society,* Lindley J. Stiles (ed.), Harper and Brothers, 1957, pp. 264-275.

Garrison, N. L., *The Improvement of Teaching* (New York: The Dryden Press, 1955), chs. IX-XV.

Gould, G., and Yoakam, G. A., *The Teacher and His Work,* 2nd ed. (New York: The Ronald Press Company, 1954), II, III, and XV.

Gruhn, W. T., *Student Teaching in the Secondary School* (New York: The Ronald Press Company, 1954), ch. XIII.

Hicks, H. J., *Educational Supervision in Principle and Practice* (New York: The Ronald Press Company, 1960), ch. 10.

Huggett, A. J., and Stinnett, T. M., *Professional Problems of Teachers* (New York: The Macmillan Company, 1956), chs. I, X-XI, XIII.

Jersild, A. T., *When Teachers Face Themselves* (New York: Teachers College, Columbia University, 1955), *passim.*

Kearney, N. C., *A Teacher's Professional Guide* (Englewood Cliffs, N. J.: Prentice-Hall, Inc., 1958), II-IV, XIV, XVI-XVII.

Lehner, G. F. J., and Kube, E., *The Dynamics of Personal Adjustment* (Englewood Cliffs, N. J.: Prentice-Hall, Inc., 1955), chs. II-V, IX-XIII, XV-XVI.

Mental Health in Modern Education, Fifty-fourth Yearbook, National Society for the Study of Education, Part II (Chicago: University of Chicago Press, 1955), chs. XIII-XV.

Packard, V. O., *The Status Seekers* (New York: David McKay Company, 1959), *passim*.

"Problems of the Teaching Personnel," a symposium, *California Journal of Secondary Education,* vol. XXXI (October, 1956), pp. 351-376.

Quillen, I. J., "The Education of Teachers: Quest for Quality," *The Education of Teachers, Curriculum Programs,* Official Report of the Kansas Conference, National Commission on Teacher Education and Professional Standards (National Education Association, 1959), pp. 31-40.

Redl, F., and Wattenberg, W. W., *Mental Hygiene in Teaching,* 2nd ed. (New York: Harcourt, Brace and Company, Inc., 1959), ch. XVI.

Rugg, H., *The Teacher of Teachers* (New York: Harper and Brothers, 1952), ch. VII.

"The Status of the American Public-School Teacher," *Research Bulletin,* vol. XXXV, no. 1 (February, 1957), chs. I, III, VI, VIII-X.

Stiles, L. J., and others, *Teacher Education in the United States* (New York: The Ronald Press Company, 1960), chs. I-III.

Stuart, Jesse, *The Thread That Runs So True* (New York: Charles Scribner's Sons, 1949).

Taylor, L. O., *et al., The American Secondary School* (New York: Appleton-Century-Crofts, Inc., 1960), ch. V.

Wiles, K., *Supervision for Better Schools,* 2nd ed. (Englewood Cliffs, N. J.: Prentice-Hall, Inc., 1955), ch. IV.

Yauch, W. A., *Helping Teachers Understand Principals* (New York: Appleton-Century-Crofts, Inc., 1958), *passim*.

Yeager, W. A., *Administration and the Teacher* (New York: Harper and Brothers, 1954), chs. XV-XVIII.

Part V

TECHNIQUES AND METHODS

FOR THE IMPROVEMENT

OF TEACHERS IN SERVICE

CHAPTER 15

Organizational Arrangements
Employed in Supervisory Programs

Developing Trends in Forms of Supervisory Organizations

SUPERVISORS ARE EXPENDABLE! This is a fact from the history of supervision for the second quarter of the twentieth century.[1] Robert Hanes' study applies primarily to supervision on the high school level; yet the findings of his investigation parallel the evidence from the literature in regard to the elementary school. He found that in periods of economic prosperity the supervisory program in the schools picks up momentum and is enlarged in scope. On the other hand, supervision is one of the first services of the school program to be reduced or eliminated in times of economic depression, or of personnel shortages and unusual increases in school enrollment. The rise and decline of the state-wide program in supervision in North Carolina from 1925 to 1956 illustrates Hanes' findings. Supervision developed rapidly until 1931; the program was practically eliminated in the early 1930's; it took on new life and was expanded largely from 1946 to 1954; it was reduced slightly in scope and personnel in 1955-1956 due to an anticipated decline in tax revenue for school purposes and the need for more money for teaching personnel to handle sharply increased school enrollments.

[1] Cf. Robert C. Hanes, A Study of Trends and Changes in Secondary School Supervision from 1925 to Mid-Century, unpublished master's thesis, University of North Carolina, 1954, chapter VII.

Though supervisors are expendable, there has been a trend in larger school systems toward the employment of highly trained personnel for supervision and curriculum co-ordination. This trend has been identified on both the state and local levels, especially since there have been sharp increases in school enrollment, increases which will continue for at least another decade or so. School boards have found it necessary to relieve school administrators of much of their supervisory responsibility so that they can attend to the other tasks occasioned by the tremendous increase in enrollment. It is therefore becoming common today to find a director or co-ordinator of instruction, or a curriculum co-ordinator, in school systems of even moderate size. He or she is usually a highly trained individual, with at least a master's degree in the areas of supervision and curriculum; frequently he has a doctor's degree. His main responsibility is for the success of the instructional program of the system and for the improvement of the staff in service. More and more he is coming to be the person to whom principals and all types of supervisory and service personnel turn in regard to the supervision and improvement of instruction.

A NEW TYPE OF SUPERVISOR AND A NEW TYPE OF SUPERVISION

This new development in supervision in effect *centralizes* authority for instructional improvement in an administrative and supervisory official who is not the superintendent (Fig. 10). Such a development also tends administratively to perpetuate the dualistic type of supervisory organization. On the other hand, this new office, if properly handled, tends to decentralize supervision by placing major responsibility for the improvement of the teaching-learning situation on each individual school unit, its principal and its faculty; they work together as a unit and also individually to improve the program in their particular school. The responsibility is the school's, as it should be, and the school personnel use all kinds of supervisory personnel to help them in their task. The supervisor, whether general or special, becomes in this situation a stimulator, a resource person, an encourager, a person with leadership qualities who wisely plays many different roles to get the principal and his staff to work at their job. The supervisor helps the principal to develop leadership competencies, the teachers to work co-

operatively in groups and individually on a special teaching problem—he is in effect both a leader and a teacher of teachers.

State departments of public instruction saw the need for this
type of supervisory leadership some time ago. They changed their
method from a type of inspectional supervision of six schools in

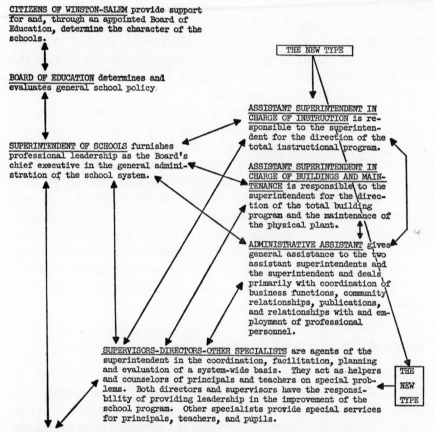

CITIZENS OF WINSTON-SALEM provide support
for and, through an appointed Board of
Education, determine the character of the
schools.

THE NEW TYPE

BOARD OF EDUCATION determines and
evaluates general school policy.

ASSISTANT SUPERINTENDENT IN
CHARGE OF INSTRUCTION is responsible to the superintendent for the direction of the
total instructional program.

SUPERINTENDENT OF SCHOOLS furnishes
professional leadership as the Board's
chief executive in the general administration of the school system.

ASSISTANT SUPERINTENDENT IN
CHARGE OF BUILDINGS AND MAIN-
TENANCE is responsible to the
superintendent for the direction of the total building
program and the maintenance of
the physical plant.

ADMINISTRATIVE ASSISTANT gives
general assistance to the two
assistant superintendents and
the superintendent and deals
primarily with coordination of
business functions, community
relationships, publications,
and relationships with and employment of professional
personnel.

SUPERVISORS-DIRECTORS-OTHER SPECIALISTS are agents of the
superintendent in the coordination, facilitation, planning
and evaluation of a system-wide basis. They act as helpers
and counselors of principals and teachers on special problems. Both directors and supervisors have the responsibility of providing leadership in the improvement of the
school program. Other specialists provide special services
for principals, teachers, and pupils.

THE
NEW
TYPE

PRINCIPALS are the executive heads of the schools and furnish instructional and
community leadership for the educational program.

TEACHING AND NON-TEACHING PERSONNEL provide stimulating experiences and health-
ful and wholesome surroundings for pupils.

CHILDREN AND ADULTS OF WINSTON-SALEM are provided rich educational experiences
resulting in responsible citizenship.

*Figure 10. The New Type of Supervisor and of Supervision, Winston-Salem
(North Carolina) City Schools*

Reproduced by permission of the Winston-Salem City Schools.

one county in one day, for example, to a type which involved the presence of the state official in that one county for a period of three days to a week. During that time, the state supervisor acted as stimulator and resource person to help in the programs which the county had projected, to train the county supervisor and the building principals for better supervision. In turn, the county supervisor spends his school year of 36 or more weeks in acting in the same sort of capacity for the 10 to 15 principals and their individual schools in this county, going when called upon, staying in an individual situation as long as needed, reporting at the end of the year his activities and accomplishments, leaving to the principal to report those of his school and staff.

This is in effect a new type of organization for supervision, requiring a high type of leadership from dual supervisors, from the principal as the school unit leader and from the supervisor as resource person and teacher of the principal and the staff in service. The principal continues as the administrative and supervisory head of his school, with full authority over all instructional personnel and organizational details. The supervisor's task is not administrative, but that of a stimulative trainer of school personnel for better instruction for children. To the extent that modern supervision results in a better teaching-learning situation for children will administrators and school boards retain supervision among valuable school services.

Types of Organizations for Supervision

Some type of supervisory organization, actual or projected, already exists in most school systems. The larger the system, the more complicated is the form of supervisory organization. Conversely, the smaller the school system, the simpler the organization tends to be. The supervisor or director of instruction has to operate and plan within the framework for supervision that has already been established for his system, rather than attempt to overturn the existing organization.

A second important conditioning factor is concerned with the *success* which a certain kind of supervisory organization has had in a particular system. For example, if a dual system of administration and supervision has worked well in a metropolitan school network, those in charge will hesitate to make changes in the form of supervisory organization. On the other hand, if another large city school system has used their supervisors primarily as staff personnel for 25 years and has found that this kind of line-and-staff organization is entirely satisfactory to them, the officials will probably continue with this type of organization.

The two foregoing factors operate constantly to influence each supervisory situation. No two supervisory situations are exactly alike, just as no two school communities are exactly alike. Therefore, there is no supervisory formula, no particular type of supervisory organization which can be adapted successfully to every school system. Rather, there are many types of organization for supervision which have proved adequate in one school system or another. It is the purpose here, then, to illustrate representative types of organizational arrangements which are being employed successfully in school systems of different sizes in the nation.[2]

Seven organizational charts in all are reproduced in this chapter. The second one shows the organization for supervision in a state, North Carolina (Fig. 11). Correspondence and personal interviews reveal that the personnel in the division of instruction act as staff members, furnishing primarily consultant services to county and city administrative units.

A city system with ten elementary and three high schools is represented in Fig. 12. The chart shows that the organization in Grosse Pointe, Michigan, provides for supervision mainly as a staff service for school principals and through them to teachers and other personnel.

The organization of a large county school system is given in Fig. 13. San Diego County's supervisory organization is similar to that of Grosse Pointe in regard (1) to establishment of the office of director of instruction or curriculum, (2) to emphasis upon supervision as a staff service, and (3) to emphasis upon in-service training and growth of the instructional staff through supervision. The

[2] The student who wishes to trace historically the development of types of supervisory programs might start with the Eighth Yearbook of the Department of Superintendence, now known as the American Association of School Administrators, *The Superintendent Surveys Supervision* (Washington, D. C.: National Education Association, 1930), and then follow the growth by reading the statements of various other authorities from that date to now. A representative, selected list of these references is found in the bibliography at the end of this chapter.

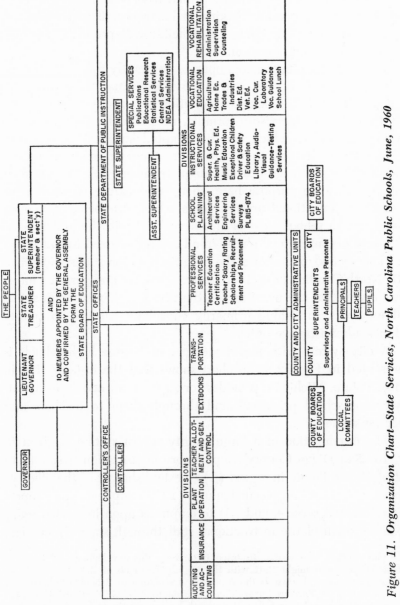

Figure 11. Organization Chart—State Services, North Carolina Public Schools, June, 1960
Reproduced by permission of the State Superintendent of Public Instruction.

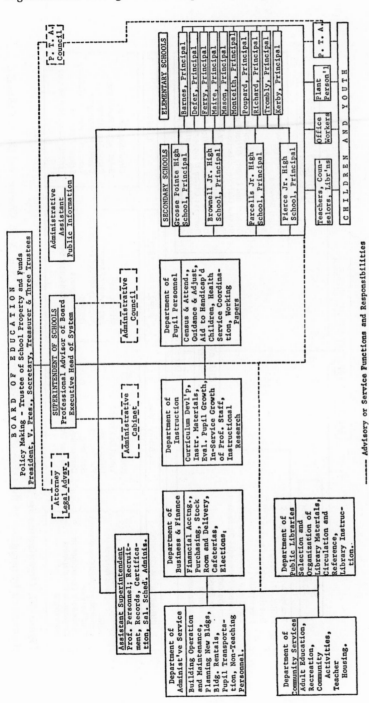

Figure 12. Organization at Grosse Pointe, Michigan

Reproduced by permission of the Superintendent of the Grosse Pointe Public School System.

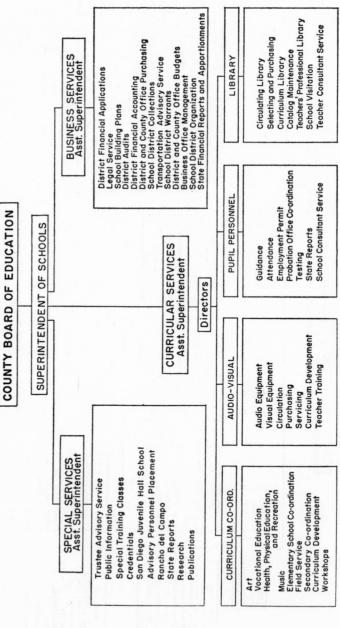

IT HAS A BIG RESPONSIBILITY The many types of services maintained by the County Office for the benefit of school districts and the lines of organizational responsibilities are indicated on the chart below.

COUNTY BOARD OF EDUCATION

SUPERINTENDENT OF SCHOOLS

SPECIAL SERVICES Asst. Superintendent

Trustee Advisory Service
Public Information
Special Training Classes
Credentials
San Diego Juvenile Hall School
Advisory Personnel Placement
Rancho del Campo
State Reports
Research
Publications

CURRICULAR SERVICES Asst. Superintendent

Directors

CURRICULUM CO-ORD.

Art
Vocational Education
Health, Physical Education, and Recreation
Music
Elementary School Co-ordination
Field Service
Secondary Co-ordination
Curriculum Development
Workshops

AUDIO-VISUAL

Audio Equipment
Visual Equipment
Circulation
Purchasing
Servicing
Curriculum Development
Teacher Training

PUPIL PERSONNEL

Guidance
Attendance
Employment Permit
Probation Office Co-ordination
Testing
State Reports
School Consultant Service

LIBRARY

Circulating Library
Selecting and Purchasing
Curriculum Library
Catalog Maintenance
Teachers Professional Library
School Visitation
Teacher Consultant Service

BUSINESS SERVICES Asst. Superintendent

District Financial Applications
Legal Service
School Building Plans
District Audits
District Financial Accounting
District and County Office Purchasing
School District Collections
Transportation Advisory Service
School District Warrants
District and County Office Budgets
Business Office Management
School District Organization
State Financial Reports and Apportionments

Figure 13. Organization in San Diego County, California

main difference between the two is that the director of instruction at Grosse Pointe has close relations with the department of pupil personnel and other service staffs, whereas in San Diego County the three directors of audio-visual services, pupil personnel, and libraries are independent of and co-ordinate with the director of curriculum co-ordination.

How a small, rural county with full-time teaching principals can organize its supervision is well illustrated in Fig. 14. The chart is almost self-explanatory and shows how careful planning and organization in a limited situation can be productive of much assist-

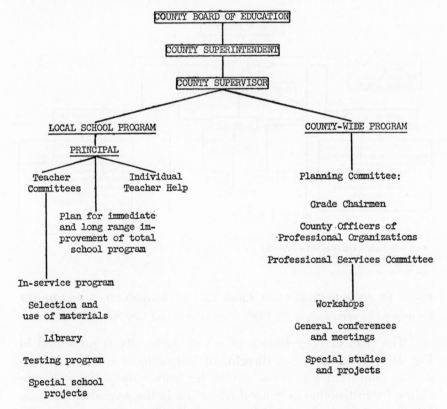

Figure 14. Supervisory Organization for a County System Having One Supervisor for Grades 1-12

(Seven of the nine principals in this county teach full time.)

Chart prepared by Dorothy Y. Zimmerman and reproduced by permission of the Caswell County (North Carolina) Schools.

ance. Note that in this county supervision is a "one-woman show" and that it will succeed only as the leadership and resources of the supervisor bring help and services to *both* principals and teachers. The supervisor is the only resource person available to all principals and teachers.

The Chula Vista, California, chart (Fig. 15) illustrates how curricular and supervisory services are administered in an elementary school organization by staff personnel through principals to teachers. It shows clearly also the newer concept of the important help and resources that the curriculum director can and should furnish to the superintendent too.

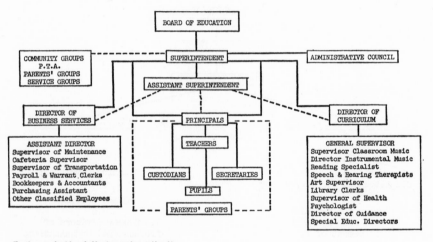

Chart organization indicates major authority or line relationships. Heavy lines indicate direct relationship; dotted or broken lines are indicative of advisory function.

Figure 15. Organizational Chart, Chula Vista (California) City School District
Reproduced by permission of the Chula Vista (California) City School District.

The plan of organization of a very large city is presented in Fig. 16. Baltimore has a director of instructional services in secondary education who is responsible for leadership of the staff providing for instruction in *general education* in the secondary schools. His supervisors and specialists act as staff officers and resource personnel for the staffs of the high schools. The development of curriculum materials and programs for professional improvement of the school staff are also a particular responsibility of the director of instructional services.

Summary

The types of organization for supervision which have been presented in this chapter show several trends. In the first place, school systems are thinking in terms of the combination of supervision, supervisory services, and curriculum improvement and con-

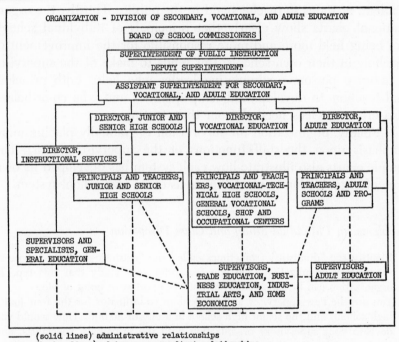

———— (solid lines) administrative relationships

–––– (broken lines) advisory or consultant relationships

Director of Instructional Services in General Secondary Education

Under the direction of the Assistant Superintendent of Secondary, Vocational, and Adult Education, the Director of Instructional Services in General Secondary Education will be responsible for leadership of the staff providing instructional services in general education in the secondary schools. He will direct the work of all the supervisors, specialists, and other staff members assigned to this duty and will work in a co-operative relationship with the instructional staffs attached to the Division of Vocational Education and the Division of Adult Education. In the field of general education he will work with the members of his staff to provide for all the junior and senior high schools the usual supervisory and resource services required to build instructional programs of high quality in the several subject fields. He will give leadership to the preparation of curriculum materials and will work with the respective directors and principals in developing programs for the professional improvement of educational staffs in all secondary schools. Under co-operative arrangements to be developed by the assistant superintent he will make his services and those of his staff members available to the vocational and adult schools. He will be responsible also for such school community activities in the secondary program as are now represented by the Youth City Council, the Civic Experience Program, and similar enterprises.

Figure 16. Supervisory Organization in Baltimore, 1960

Reproduced with permission from the Baltimore Public Schools *Staff Newsletter*.

struction under what used to be called supervision. The supervisor or director of instruction today, therefore, has to be highly trained, experienced, and aware of the many resources and materials that can be used effectively in modern teaching.

In the second place, the supervisor is becoming more and more responsible for the instructional program of the school system; at the same time, he is also responsible *to* principals, *to* the superintendent, at times *to* teachers and *to* the public. Thirdly, the organizational charts show clearly that principals of individual schools are being held more and more responsible for the improvement of teaching in their own schools; this tends to make of the supervisor a resource person, a stimulating leader who helps both principal and teachers to develop leadership qualities and who co-ordinates also other services needed from time to time.

Finally, organization for supervision is gradually placing more emphasis upon the staff functions of the supervisory staff. The sample charts also illustrate how each system has developed its own type of organization to meet the needs of its own school system.

Problems for Individual Study and Class Discussion

1. Identify the "dualistic" (sometimes called the "extrinsic-dualistic") type of supervisory organization. Do you feel from your study that this type of organization can be satisfactory, or not? Support your point of view.
2. You are the new supervisor and curriculum co-ordinator for the four junior high schools and the senior high school in a city of 80,000. How would you develop your supervisory organization with the principals, specialists, and teachers with whom you will have to work?
3. As elementary school supervisor for a small rural county, you are called upon by the superintendent to collect the yearly reports from the ten district principals and make out the superintendent's annual report to the state department. Is this one of your supervisory duties? Give evidence to support your point of view.
4. What is the difference between the "line-and-staff" type of supervisory organization and the "dualistic" system? Is one any better than the other? Why, or why not?
5. Should the school librarian come under the organizational authority of the principal or of the supervisor, or both? Why, or why not?
6. Is the modern trend sound toward combining the duties of the supervisory organization and the curriculum department under one department with a director and staff responsible for both supervision and curriculum improvement? Support your position.

7. Can special staff services, such as the library and audio-visual department, be as effective in aid to teachers as a supervisor who co-ordinates these services when they are needed? Why, or why not?

Additional Source References for Problem or Unit Study

Association for Supervision and Curriculum Development, Thirty-Fifth Yearbook (Washington, D. C.: National Education Association, 1957), ch. X.

Bartky, J. A., *Supervision As Human Relations* (Boston: D. C. Heath and Company, 1953), ch. XV.

Bent, R. K., and McCann, L. E., *Administration of Secondary Schools* (New York: McGraw-Hill Book Company, 1960), ch. IV.

Boardman, C. W., and others, *Democratic Supervision in Secondary Schools* (Boston: Houghton Mifflin Company, 1953), ch. III.

Briggs, T. H., and Justman, J., *Improving Instruction Through Supervision* (New York: The Macmillan Company, 1952), ch. IX.

Burton, W. H., and Brueckner, L. J., *Supervision: A Social Process* (New York: Appleton-Century-Crofts, Inc., 1955), ch. V.

Cramer, R. V., and Domian, O. E., *Administration and Supervision in the Elementary School* (New York: Harper and Brothers, 1960), ch. VI.

Elsbree, W. S., and McNally, H. J., *Elementary School Administration and Supervision*, 2nd ed. (New York: American Book Company, 1959), chs. VIII and IX.

Hanes, R. C., "Do Economic and Educational Conditions Influence Supervision?", *The High School Journal*, vol. XXXVIII (February, 1955), pp. 174-176.

Hicks, H. J., *Educational Supervision in Principle and Practice* (New York: The Ronald Press Company, 1960), ch. XIII.

Savage, W. W., "State Consultative Service in Education," *The Phi Delta Kappan*, vol. XXXVII (April, 1956), pp. 291-294.

Shuster, A. H., and Wetzler, W. F., *Leadership in Elementary School Administration and Supervision* (Boston: Houghton Mifflin Company, 1958), ch. VII.

Spears, H., *Improving the Supervision of Instruction* (New York: Prentice-Hall, Inc., 1953), chs. VII-VIII, IX, XII.

Stiles, Lindley J., and others, *Teacher Education in the United States* (New York: The Ronald Press Company, 1960), ch. 16, pp. 367-390, "Programs for Continuing Professional Development."

Thurston, L. M., and Roe, W. H., *State School Administration* (New York: Harper and Brothers, 1957), ch. V.

CHAPTER 16

Devices Used in Supervision

IN THE BOOKS ON SUPERVISION much space is devoted to methods and devices for supervision. Many of these techniques have been in use for years and are still as sound and valuable as ever; examples of these are classroom visitation, the interview or individual conference, and the group meeting. Other methods are comparatively new, such as the workshop or work conference, co-operative curriculum study, action research, the curriculum laboratory or library, and the field trip for supervisory purposes. In effect, all of these are devices for effective in-service education of teachers at one time or place or another.

To make it possible for these supervisory devices to be identified more effectively, they have been divided traditionally into two general classifications: (1) group devices and (2) individual devices. The reader should keep in mind as he studies these devices that no one device is better for use than another; rather, each of them has been proved to be sound upon occasions when the supervisory situation called for the employment of that particular method. Since the maximum growth and improvement of the teachers in service is the main goal for the supervisor, he must be familiar with all of these devices, and he must be able to recognize the situation in which he may suggest that one device might be more effective than another.

Listed alphabetically, these supervisory devices are:

Group Devices [1]	Individual Devices
1. Committees	1. Classroom observation
2. Course work	2. Classroom experimentation

[1] Starred (*) items will be presented in detail in Chapter 17.

3. Curriculum laboratory
4. Directed reading
5. Demonstration teaching
6. Field trips for staff personnel
7. Institutes and lectures
8. Panel or forum discussions
9. Professional libraries
10. Professional organizations
11. Supervisory bulletins
*12. Teachers' meetings
*13. Workshops or group conferences

3. Conference (the interview)
4. Intervisitation and observation
5. Selection of materials for teaching
6. Self-evaluation

Discussion of these devices will necessarily be limited (1) to identification or definition of the device or technique and (2) to possible constructive uses, with notation at times of the limits of its effectiveness.

Group Devices for Supervision

COMMITTEES

This small-group device is analyzed in some detail under the presentation of group processes and workshop techniques (Chapter 17), where it belongs properly as a constructive method of improving teachers in service. The small committee as a fact-finding device for the larger faculty group is valuable and has its place when further information is needed. On the other hand, the division of the larger staff group entirely into small committees without clear definition of their work and responsibilities is of questionable value; as an administrative device "to make everybody work," it has no place in good supervisory practices.

The writer has seen excellent use made of small committees in a few school systems and in many school building units. These faculties, in effect, carried on most of their routine business and study projects by the "committee" method. There were standing committees, of four or five persons each, for routine matters which demanded attention from time to time, such as committees on Reports to Parents, on the School Calendar with its events and special occasions, on School Assemblies, and on Special Reports.

For their study projects, there were different small committees which accepted certain responsibilities for exhaustive study of one aspect of a project, compiled their findings, and reported them in oral or written form for discussion or action to the larger group. For example, one study project was devoted to audio-visual materials. One committee studied and reported on educational films suitable for science activities, another on films valuable for supplementary use in the language arts, and a third committee worked on a study of pictures and filmstrips helpful for activities and classes in the social studies on the fifth- and sixth-grade levels. Small committee work planned and carried out in this manner can be a valuable device for use at times in a supervisory situation.

COURSE WORK

This refers specifically to work taken by teachers—usually in the form of extension or summer school courses, field courses, correspondence work, late afternoon or evening classes or clinics—at institutions of higher education for credit or training in service. Some of this work is on the graduate level and for graduate credit, some for certificate renewal, and some merely for adult education purposes. Some school systems set salary scales which give increments for a certain amount of course work taken and passed satisfactorily; they thus recognize the principle that improvement in service and in teaching can come from additional college course work. The graduate teaching certificate in some states is based on the same principle, with the master's degree in course work as the minimum requirement for it. Some colleges and school systems have collaborated to bring the work to the systems and their classrooms, making a sort of laboratory for college course work. Disadvantages of this method of in-service training are: (1) Some courses are difficult to adapt to a laboratory situation; (2) Some instructors do not know how to use actual practices in the classroom to illustrate principles; (3) The formal and academic approach of the lecture method is unsuited to the development of new methods; and (4) Some instructors fail to become aware of the everyday problems and needs of the teachers in these courses.

CURRICULUM LABORATORY OR CURRICULUM LIBRARY

This center for instructional materials and literature is a newer departure; it acts both as a source of materials and of encouragement for the professional in-service program. The curriculum laboratory is sometimes called the "Materials Bureau" or "Materials Center." Characteristic of the curriculum "Lab" are its:

1. Professional books and periodicals.
2. Instructional materials of many kinds, such as units of work, pictures, posters, charts, maps, pamphlets, audio-visual helps, supplementary readers and texts, manuals and workbooks, and teaching guides.
3. Work space for study by small groups and individuals.
4. Projection facilities.
5. Files of different kinds of tests, both standard and teacher-made.
6. Facilities for typing or reproducing materials.
7. Qualified person in charge, trained both in library techniques and in audio-visual skills.

If centrally located and well run, there are many advantages to the curriculum laboratory; materials are readily available and can easily be charged in and out. The atmosphere is conducive to work. The supervisor is usually the trained expert who is familiar with all of the resources of the laboratory and who is ready to help individual teachers to learn how to use them effectively.

DIRECTED READING

The new term for this is "guided" or "suggested" reading. It involves professional reading primarily, stimulated by the supervisor. Articles or selections of a shorter nature are suggested which give the teacher a new slant on an old method or an introduction to a new method or new materials. Teachers frequently adopt from the literature ideas which they would not accept from the supervisor. In some ways, this directed reading is similar to the old "reading circle" technique of 30 years ago. Teachers should be encouraged to read along the lines of their needs and special interests and to tackle and improve their areas of weakness or lack of knowledge.

Limitations of directed reading as a method of improving teachers in service are: (1) the slow reading rate and comprehension of some teachers, which in turn involve expenditure of more time than some teachers are willing to spend on it, (2) the desire of some teachers to learn in groups, and (3) the lack at times on the part of the supervisor of definite knowledge of the teaching area of the teacher. Some authorities maintain that directed reading is an individual, rather than a group supervisory device.

DEMONSTRATION TEACHING

This device must be classified as of either the individual or group type. It is a group device if the supervisor takes charge of a room or class with several teachers present to illustrate good teaching, or if a master teacher does the same before a group of visiting teachers. It is an individual supervisory device if the supervisor takes over a class from a teacher upon his request and illustrates good techniques in teaching for *one* teacher with his own class. Good demonstration teaching is not "hit or miss"; it is carefully planned and has a definite goal or goals, furnishing an opportunity for teachers to see new or different methods of teaching. The observing teacher should be aware of the purposes of the demonstration, should take notes carefully on it, and should discuss the performance with the other observers and the demonstrating teacher or supervisor after it is over.

The main drawbacks to demonstration teaching as an in-service device are: (1) the development of teaching around a center of interest or an activity, which requires a longer period of demonstration teaching, (2) the inability of some supervisors to do good demonstration teaching, and (3) the unwillingness of many excellent teachers to "demonstrate," or to help the supervisor in demonstration teaching.

FIELD TRIPS FOR STAFF PERSONNEL

While field trips have been used for many years by teachers with children, the field trip for the in-service education of teachers is a relatively new departure. The principles are the same in each case. Now it is the teachers who talk with the supervisor; who plan a visit to a company or a place in or away from the community in order to learn of further educational values and possibilities; who make the trip, ask questions, take notes; and who evaluate the teaching resources and possibilities upon their return. The field trip has audio-visual possibilities for teachers; it is the most satisfactory way for teachers to learn to use community resources in their schoolwork. Travel to other places in the United States or excursions and tours abroad are other kinds of field trips of an individual or group nature. The field trip for teachers has similar limitations to those concerning the use of the field trip with children; it should be employed when it will furnish a richer and more realistic learning experience than some other way of learning.

INSTITUTES, LECTURES, ADDRESSES

These devices are more of a "sitting" type of in-service education, similar to the old fashioned teachers' meeting where a special speaker was brought in each time or for a number of meetings to talk on current problems, or new methods, or professional topics. However, there is a limit to "sitting absorption" without encountering the law of diminishing returns; even the best and most stimulating speakers seldom are successful in holding the complete attention of a group for much more than 20 to 30 minutes. The teachers' institute has been replaced primarily by the "work institute" or "work conference."

PANEL OR FORUM DISCUSSIONS

This newcomer to the field of teacher education is based on the sound premise that every one wants to make a good impression before his colleagues. He therefore prepares his part in the presentation thoroughly, learning a lot in the process. The recent introduction on radio and TV of programs illustrating the work of schools has stimulated more use of the panel discussion. By employing this device, the supervisor can succeed in encouraging some teachers to work hard because they are desirous of appearing in a a public assembly—teachers who might otherwise resist study and new effort. If this device is used too frequently, the teacher may fail to understand the necessity for continuous *individual work* if he is to improve in service; group participation and activity are not the only ways in which growth takes place.

PROFESSIONAL LIBRARIES

Some schools combine the professional library for teachers with the curriculum library or laboratory. Other school supervisors maintain that each school building should have its own professional library; that its books, periodicals, and materials should be carefully selected for teacher growth and improvement; that it should be a pleasant and relaxing room, with easy chairs, excellent lighting, and good equipment; that it should be growing constantly by the addition of new and pertinent materials; that teachers should have individual keys to it and be free to come and go and take materials as they wish; and that it should be equipped also for the meeting of small groups on common problems. The only limitation to the use of this type of device is that the school building is usually locked from late in the afternoon until the next morning; the supervisor would have to work to change this prevailing custom or furnish keys to each teacher.

PROFESSIONAL ORGANIZATIONS AND MEETINGS

Organized professional groups with like interests and problems are coming to be one of the most powerful influences for in-service training on both the state and national levels. Many strong national organizations have branch groups organized and working effectively on the state level. Examples of these are the local or state branches of such groups as the National Council for the Social Studies, the Association for Supervision and Curriculum Development, the National Council of Teachers of English, the National Association of Secondary School Principals, and the Association for Childhood Education. These state groups meet each year for a work-conference of several days on problems and plans for better teaching and use of materials. The meetings of these groups are a far cry from the old state convention of teachers; they more nearly resemble workshops for large- and small-group work procedures in the solving of common problems. One supervisor described them once as "work-conferences, composed of smaller workshop groups."

These types of professional meetings on state and national levels are excellent in-service training devices. They also have extensive social values for teachers, many of whom thus meet new people and make new friends. Many superintendents and supervisors plan definitely for teachers from their schools to attend and take part in these work-conference meetings; some systems even pay part of the travel expense of these representatives.

On the other hand, the traditional state convention for teachers or the national meeting of the "prominent speaker and sitting" type is still in operation. The one who attends gets some inspiration from speeches and some practical ideas from swapping experiences with friends. But the values derived are relatively small compared to the real stimulation and growth that come from the workshop or work conference type of meeting.

In connection with national and state meetings of a professional nature, there is a good opportunity to stimulate teachers to report on them in writing for the benefit of others. Of course, the writing and publication of an article for a professional magazine may also be a by-product of attendance and work at these meetings.

SUPERVISORY BULLETINS, HANDBOOKS, AND GUIDES

The supervisory bulletin is a valuable group device for a large school system or for one very large school building housing in the thousands. Its purposes are to acquaint all personnel more exactly with new plans and projects, new methods and materials; to prepare for specific studies or reports; to initiate new interests; and to let the rest of the staff know what interesting practices are being carried on in their midst.

On pages 334-335 is a short sample of a proposed supervisory bulletin for a school in a rural county. The school term starts near the end of July, and then the entire school takes a six-week recess in the fall so that the children can help to harvest the crops. The topics in the bulletin show rather clearly how the contents can be used to improve the instructional program.[2]

In the small school system of 30 teachers or less there may be little need for an elaborate supervisory bulletin, since all teachers see each other every day. At times, the supervisory bulletin may take the form of a handbook or guide. For example, the problem of substitute teaching might require several supervisory bulletins or forms which are usually made out by the administrator and the supervisor. One form should be made out as a principal's guide in securing and training substitute teachers. Another simple form should be provided on which the substitute teacher reports what he and the students did while he was there. Still a third form would be a list which had been prepared for all teachers concerning supplementary materials and audio-visual materials in the schools. Another would be a supervisory bulletin or handbook containing a list of those things about which the supervisor should inform the sub-

---

[2] The author is indebted to both his graduate students and to supervisors in the field for many of the suggestions for this bulletin and for the ones that follow on substitute teachers.

stitute teacher at the beginning of the year or at the first meeting of substitute teachers. This bulletin would probably contain the following information, forms, and provisions:

1. *A welcome to the school,* such as:

TODAY YOU ARE A TEACHER

This is a welcome to you as an important member of the Silton Schools teaching faculty, for on the days that you teach you are a teacher

---

WACO SCHOOL SUPERVISORY BULLETIN

TEACHERS' MEETING PRIOR TO SCHOOL OPENING

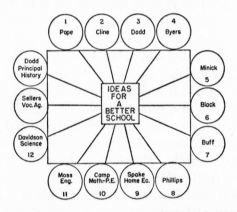

HAPPY NEW YEAR!

Although it isn't the kind of new year associated with January 1st, the principal wishes to take this opportunity to wish you in advance a happy new school year. Let's resolve to make this the best school year we have ever had. This bulletin was prepared for the purpose of helping you with instructions and materials throughout the year. Should you find need for assistance, please feel free to call upon your supervisors or principal at any time.

CALENDAR OF EVENTS

July 21 -- Preschool teachers' meeting.

July 23 -- School opening 8:30 A.M. - 3:00 P.M.

Aug. 26 -- County-wide teachers' meeting.

Nov. 24-25 -- Thanksgiving holidays.

Dec. 24 through Jan. 1 -- Christmas.

March 30 and April 2 -- Easter.

(Dates subject to change, and other events to be announced at later date.)

SCHOOL TO OPEN JULY 23

The Waco School teachers are asked to meet at the school on July 21 at 9:00 A.M. in preparation for the opening of school on the 23rd. Books will be issued to teachers for distribution to the students so that no time will be lost in beginning classes on opening day. Other important items relative to the opening of school will be discussed. Please be on time, and be prepared to offer suggestions which you think will help us in having a successful year.

PROFESSIONAL GROWTH PROGRAMS

Several in-service programs are being planned to meet requests for help in subject areas. These will be kept to a minimum with regard to number of meetings and the time involved. For maximum benefits, regular attendance and wholehearted participation in the workshop are required. Time and dates will be announced later.

County Workshops -- To provide opportunities for teacher growth and enriched experiences workshops are being planned in art, science, reading, mathematics, and elementary physical education. Watch for further announcements.

alongside the regular faculty members. Like the other teachers in Silton, you have one of the most noble tasks of all—*helping young people grow.*

Your service is doubly important because you become a Silton teacher often on only a few minutes notice. This means that your regular plans for the day have to be changed or canceled abruptly and that you have but little time for preparation for teaching. Your service is important too for the fact that you are willing to come to the cause of education of children when help is urgently needed because of the absence of a regular teacher.

Local In-Service Programs -- Local programs of professional study are encouraged by the state department, and some worthwhile studies have been undertaken in the various schools. Some topics that have been chosen for this year include public relations, discipline, attendance, pupil dropouts, and accreditation. It is also requested that teachers examine several books of a professional nature. Several copies of current volumes are now available in the supervisor's office and may be checked out upon request.

KEEPING ABREAST OF THE TIMES

With changing patterns of living, modern scientific discoveries, and new knowledge about child growth and development, it is necessary that our tools of working be kept up to date. New books which are constantly being introduced in our schools help us in equipping our children to live in today's world.

Supplementary Readers -- An ever-increasing and more varied supply of supplementary readers is being found each year in our elementary school classrooms. These books help teachers provide for individual differences, as well as furnish attractive and interesting reading material. Samples of all books on the State-approved list are available in the offices of the supervisors.

Library Books -- A limited amount of money for library books is available each year from state funds. In order to secure as many first-choice books as possible, it is advisable that orders for library books be made early in the year.

Textbooks -- The following are recently adopted free elementary school textbooks which are being placed in the schools as fast as they are allotted to the county by the North Carolina Division of Textbooks:

Growth in Arithmetic Series (World Book Company) will be used in Grades 3-8.

Health and Personal Development Series (Scott, Foresman and Company) will be used in Grades 4-8.

Language for Meaning Series (Houghton, Mifflin Company) will be used in Grades 3-8.

Word Mastery Spellers (Charles E. Merrill Company) will be used in Grades 2-8.

Exploring the New World (Follett Company) will be used in Grade 5.

During the past few years new adoptions have been made in most or all high school subjects. New titles are being introduced in the schools as fast as finances will permit.

TESTING PROGRAM

The regular program of diagnostic testing will be continued in all Cleveland County Schools in Grades 1-8. Information and testing materials will be distributed through the testing chairman appointed in each school. New forms of the same tests will be employed this year with one exception. The fourth-grade teachers will administer the California Achievement Test, Primary Battery, instead of the Elementary Battery.

Testing dates are: August 15, 16, 17.

Class summary sheets are to be turned in to the County office: September 2.

AUDIO-VISUAL MATERIALS

Educational Sound Films -- 132 sound films are owned by the County. (See separate listing.)

Human Torso -- This is a plastic model of the human body with vital organs removable. It is suitable for use in upper grade and high school health classes.

Elementary Microscopes -- Two sets of six microscopes each are available for use in the elementary grades.

NOTE: All instructional supplies are requested through principals. Audio-visual materials are requested through the Visual-Aid Chairman in each school.

This bulletin along with the materials provided with it is designed to assist you in the important service of substitute teaching. From time to time, please reacquaint yourself with the information so that you can give of your best to our Silton boys and girls.

You can be of the most efficient service if you can carry on as smoothly as possible with the regular learning activities and work of the class. This will help the regular teacher to be "caught up" when she returns from her absence. Do not be concerned unduly with the possible necessity of some "repetitious" reteaching after the regular teacher returns. Receiving two different adult viewpoints and approaches is a valuable contribution to the growth of children.

2. *The school handbook:* This describes the purposes and philosophy of the school system, gives the schedules and calendar for the school year, and includes also any special school rules. If it is not in the *Handbook,* the substitute teacher should be handed information on the rate of remuneration for both actual teaching and in-service training, procedures for filing application for appointment as a substitute, professional information concerning educational organizations which might help him, and information concerning the ethical practices of the school.

3. *Pertinent information concerning the school, the school district, and the community:* (1) A map of the school district showing the location(s) of the school(s), and a floor plan of the particular school that he is to teach in, showing the assignment of teachers and classes; (2) plans for guided tours of the school system and of the community early in the school year; (3) A list of both the regular teachers and the other substitute teachers and their telephone numbers; (4) A list of materials in the professional library, such as curriculum guides, manuals, resource materials for teachers, and administrative and supervisory newsletters and bulletins; (5) information concerning the audio-visual services, school library, counselors, and other special service personnel.

4. *Provision at the first meeting of the year for the principal to introduce regular and substitute teachers,* to begin organization of committees for co-ordination of regular and substitute staff members' co-operative work on improving instruction, to provide opportunities for substitute teachers to observe the work of outstanding regular teachers, and to organize methods of evaluating the work and practices of the substitute teacher.

5. *Information about the preparation expected of the regular teacher for the arrival of the substitute teacher.* The regular teacher should give advance notice of absence, if possible. In so doing she should leave for the substitute teacher textbooks and lesson plans, seating arrangements, information about individual pupils and groups, names of pupil assistants, the advance preparation expected of students, and an expression of appreciation.

6. *Information concerning the responsibility of the principal and supervisor to the substitute teacher upon his arrival at the school.* The principal and supervisor should designate as special helper and adviser to each substitute, some regular staff member who will introduce the substitute teacher to the students and will see that the substitute teacher receives any other aid or information necessary.

7. *Sample daily progress report form for substitute teacher:*

ELEMENTARY

...................Your Name ....Your Address

.... Date ....Dates Taught .... Telephone Number

.... Grade ....Extra Duties

Report of What We Did:

Special Comments and Problems:

8. *Sample daily progress report form for substitute teacher:*

HIGH SCHOOL

...................Your Name ....Your Address

.... Date ....Dates Taught .... Telephone Number

.... Grade ....Extra Duties

Report of What We Did:

First Period:

Second Period:

Third Period: *(continued on next page)*

Fourth Period:

Fifth Period:

Sixth Period:

Special Comments and Problems:

In a similar manner the wide-awake principal and supervisor and their teachers will from time to time prepare bulletins on other pertinent problems or tasks, such as on reports to parents, proposed changes in the school day, system-wide testing programs, field day, the book fair, the science fair, or a new teachers' guide or curriculum bulletin.

Another use of the supervisory bulletin is entirely different; it is to keep the community and the public informed of the work, the plans, and the progress of the school and the pupils. As such, it is closely akin to the superintendent's or principal's news bulletin and is not really a supervisory bulletin for the teaching personnel.

TEACHERS' MEETING OR STAFF MEETINGS

Those aspects of this device that have not already been discussed in this chapter under "institutes and lectures" and "professional organizations" will be analyzed further in Chapter 17 in connection with the workshop and use of group processes.

WORKSHOP OR GROUP CONFERENCE

This newer device is also treated at length in Chapter 17.

Individual Devices in Supervision

CLASSROOM OBSERVATION

This device is one which has been in operation for years for the improvement of teaching; it is still the one most frequently employed today, followed by the individual conference or interview. The visitation can be either announced or unannounced, depending upon the custom in use in the school system in which the supervisor works. There is no "rule of thumb" concerning the classroom visit. It is more congenial to both, perhaps, for the teacher to invite the supervisor to visit him; on the other hand, if not invited, it is the responsibility eventually of the supervisor to visit his teachers—especially is this true in the case of teachers new to the system. In observing teachers in action in their classrooms, several sound principles should be followed by the visitor. He should:

1. Know where the teacher is in his work and what he is doing; look over and study his texts and materials in advance of the visit.
2. Go prepared to study modern teaching focused on a unit or involving a center of interest; this might require all-day visits from two to five days for the supervisor to understand thoroughly what the teacher is trying to do, what the pupils are doing, and how well teaching and learning are taking place.
3. Make all visits "planned-in-advance" visits, whether invited by the teacher or scheduled by the supervisor. Indicate the purposes of the observation.
4. Take notes of the observations—recording exactly, impersonally, what the pupils and what the teacher did. Encourage the teacher to take a tape or wire recording of his teaching, and analyze it.
5. Follow each series of visits with an interview or conference with the teacher and with a co-operative analysis of the teaching in the light of the purposes of the observation.
6. Reserve suggestions for improving the teaching until the analysis of the observation data pushes the teacher to ask for them.

If the supervisor has developed good rapport with the teacher, there usually are no weaknesses in the use of classroom observation.

CLASSROOM EXPERIMENTATION

Through experimentation the teacher develops new techniques, new approaches, new materials for his teaching. This device can also help in evaluation of both the work of the pupils and the effectiveness of the teacher. Each teacher will desire to experiment at his own pace and on what he deems more important or pressing at the time; he should be allowed this choice and be encouraged and given a free hand in his experimentation. The following cautions are important, however:

1. The new method that is tried out should be judged to be as good and as effective as the old method and should not harm the pupil or hinder his learning.
2. Both children and parent should be made aware of the experimenta-

tion and the reasons for it, and their co-operation should be secured in carrying it out.

3. The teacher should not be blamed if the experiment is not as successful as was hoped. Not all experiments succeed.

THE CONFERENCE OR INTERVIEW

The conference has been used for many years successfully in supervisory work. It is perhaps the most direct approach to the individual teacher, with the probable exception of visitation and observation. Certainly the supervisor should always follow up a visitation to a teacher. There are several reasons for this practice. In the first place, a teacher is curious to know what the visitor saw and thought about him and his class. In the second place, the teacher usually expects a conference with the supervisor after being observed—sometimes looks forward to it. In the third place, if no postvisitation interview takes place, the teacher may be uneasy, more unsure of himself. For example, he may wonder what he did that was poor, what the supervisor is thinking, or whether his performance was so bad that the supervisor could find no good points about it. Finally, the postobservation conference is the positive approach to the improvement of instruction, and the positive approach should always be used if possible.

One must remember that a warm human approach to the teacher-supervisor relationship is always important. Teachers need the assurance that someone is concerned about their problems and is willing to do something about them. Teachers cannot be drawn into their rightful places in the school system unless there is praise and concern for the contribution of all, no matter how small or how great the contribution. As a part of his teacher relationship the supervisor can: [3]

1. Have friendly and sincere concern for all teachers as professional people and as individuals.
2. Focus attention primarily on the needs of the pupils in the classroom, not on the teacher and her techniques.
3. Overlook faulty methods as much as possible until confidence can be established and constructive help is requested by the teacher.

[3] Enlarged from Association for Supervision and Curriculum Development, *Group Processes in Supervision* (Washington, D. C.: National Education Association, 1948).

4. Give teachers the opportunity for many rich experiences without requirements or pressure for further professional training.
5. Establish situations as frequently as possible which will allow supervisors and teachers to know each other socially.
6. Praise and encourage good attitudes and procedures, permitting desired participation and sharing to come with the release of fear and strain.

The individual conference is really a part of the problem-solving technique. Every supervisor has almost unlimited opportunities for problem solving. He may find that one of his teachers has created a problem or that he has a problem to bring to him several times a day. He will have his own problems, too, and may use the occasion of a meeting with a teacher to develop and solve his own problem. J. A. Bartky believes that a supervisory act is a problem-solving act and that as such it must involve typical problem-solving techniques. The supervisor will have an interview with the teacher who has hit a problem or presented a problem for solution. Bartky has analyzed the interview as a problem-solving device for individual problems; he feels that the interview will divide itself into five episodes: [4]

1. *The rapport-making episode*—usually controlled by the supervisor, who indicates his attitude toward the teacher. He has an opportunity to be friendly, or stern, or formal, or informal, or to act in whatever manner the situation demands. He tries to "get through to" the teacher's attitude, his state of mind and emotions.
2. *The problem-setting episode*—the teacher may state his problem, or the supervisor may lead him on to it. Often the problem will be obvious and of such a nature that the emotional state of the teacher will constitute a problem.
3. *The catharsis episode*—"talking out" a problem is very important. It hinges upon keen judgment on the supervisor's part; he must be able to spot the point at which the catharsis or "talking out" is complete. Only when catharisis is complete can the problem be attacked.
4. *The treatment episode*—the type of problem will determine the type of treatment. The supervisor cannot solve the problem; the teacher has to do so. This is one of the really big tests of a supervisor in the area of group processes. He should not feel discouraged at every failure, however, for some problems may not lend themselves to solution readily.

[4] Summarized from J. A. Bartky, *Supervision as Human Relations* (Boston: D. C. Heath and Company, 1953), pp. 161-175.

5. *The concluding episode*—bringing the interview to a termination point should be accomplished immediately following the treatment episode. Sometimes the teacher will conclude the interview; when he does not, the supervisor should do it as gracefully as possible, trying to eliminate the creation of a new problem out of one which should now be concluded.

In general there are two types of interview, the one initiated by the supervisor and the one initiated by the teacher. Either type presents certain problems within itself, but whatever the type there are questions which the supervisor considers as he tries to help the teacher in solving the problem: [5]

1. What is the problem?
2. What are my purposes? The purposes of the teacher?
3. Have I made the teacher feel significant in my contact with him?
4. Does the teacher feel secure? How can I bring this about?
5. Have I given the teacher confidence in my leadership ability?

To give the teacher that feeling of security, confidence, and significance, the supervisor uses caution in the approach he makes to him and his problem. He never rushes the interview or stops the teacher before he has finished stating his problem. He is always courteous and considerate of him, and expresses genuine interest in his problem. While he never flatters, he does give praise where it is due, and he makes the teacher feel that he is pleased that he brought his problem to him.

These suggestions and principles do not imply that there is a stereotyped method for handling all individual and group problems. The supervisor must be creative in his leadership to help others solve their problems. Each problem will be new to him, even though he has helped to solve many similar problems. These suggestions merely provide a framework of alternative approaches upon which the supervisor may draw in problem solving.

INTERVISITATION AND OBSERVATION

This can be valuable for the teacher in several ways—to see new methods or materials in use, to observe the use of new equipment, to see a "master teacher" in action who is successful in those ways in which a particular teacher is weak or ineffective. Like

[5] *Ibid.*, pp. 168-169.

demonstration teaching and observation, the purpose of the inter-visitation should be very clear; notes should be kept on the inter-visitation and the teaching; and the visit should be followed up by a conference and discussion of the practices and outcomes in the light of the purposes.

SELECTION OF MATERIALS FOR TEACHING

Teachers tend to grow when they help to select their own texts and materials for teaching. But the supervisor has here a major re-sponsibility—especially in the case of the new or inexperienced teacher—helping the teacher to establish sound standards for the se-lection of materials of instruction. In-service growth in the teacher takes place rapidly if he can use the materials suited best for his technique and style of teaching. Chapter 3 offered many pointers on the selection of teaching materials.

SELF-EVALUATION

One of the teacher's most difficult tasks is that of assessing the effectiveness of his own teaching. Some authorities maintain that it is impossible for human beings to do this fairly or effectively; others say that one can do a good job of it by developing good instruments for self-evaluation. The types of instruments or scales which have been used with some effectiveness are:

1. Opinionnaire forms for students to evaluate the work of a unit or activity, with open-end questions, and no name of any pupil to be placed on the answer sheet. A student committee gathers all of the opinionnaires, compiles a summary, and then turns the findings of the summary in to the teacher. The teacher never sees the individual opinionnaire sheets and cannot know how any individual pupil replies.
2. Analysis of tests on a unit of work in the light of the purposes estab-lished for the unit at its begininng.
3. A written record of the activity of pupils in their work on a unit or block of work—individual, small group, and large group participation.
4. A "log" of each day's work and activities by the teacher, and analysis of the methods used.
5. A recording or stenographic record of the class activities on given days or on the whole of a unit of work; analysis of the recording and constructive criticism of the methods and the responses obtained.

Summary

The supervisor will make use at one time or another of various supervisory devices and techniques that have been developed. These devices include the old, the new, those of a group, and those of an individual nature. No one device can be used to solve all supervisory problems; neither can the same device always be used successfully in a situation that looks the same as another. In the final analysis, the supervisor and the teacher are most successful in solving a problem if they use the device that promises most for solution, never hesitating to turn to another device if the first one failed to work.

Problems for Individual Study and Class Discussion

1. What are the advantages of the letter from the supervisor to his teachers before school opens? The disadvantages? When should it be used?
2. Your superintendent believes that the school should have a stated promotion policy. As his supervisor, you are asked to work with the staff cooperatively and to bring in a suggested statement. How will you proceed to do this?
3. As you enter a new position, should you attempt to locate "trouble spots" among your staff, or should you proceed with an open mind and allow "trouble spots" to appear later? Support your position.
4. Can you help a teacher more effectively if you know his background, training, and experience? Why or why not?
5. A uniformly successful superintendent once said: "Never call a teachers' meeting unless you need it." Evaluate this statement.
6. The modern trend is toward the teacher's inviting the supervisor to visit her. What steps would you take toward observing a teacher who by December 15th had not invited you to visit?
7. How can a supervisor train a group of teachers in effective methods of panel discussion? Of self-evaluation?
8. Collect samples of supervisory bulletins. Then analyze them and summarize their strong and weak points.
9. Two of your teachers want to visit in a neighboring town and observe two teachers in the same grades as theirs. There is a school ruling that no substitute can be paid except when the teacher is sick. What will you do in this situation?
10. Under what circumstances is demonstration teaching a valuable type of in-service training? Explain.

Additional Selected References for Problem or Unit Study

Adams, H. P., and Dickey, F. G., *Basic Principles of Supervision* (New York: American Book Company, 1953), chs. VI-VIII, X-XI.

American Association of School Administrations, *Staff Relations in School Administration*, Thirty-third Yearbook, 1955 (Washington, D. C.: National Education Association), chs. III-V, and Thirty-fifth Yearbook, 1957, *The Superior Superintendent as Instructional Leader*, ch. III.

Association for Supervision and Curriculum Development, *Leadership for Improving Instruction*, 1960 Yearbook (Washington, D. C.: National Education Association), chs. IV and VI.

Ayer, F. G., *Fundamentals of Instructional Supervision* (New York: Harper and Brothers, 1954), chs. III-V.

Bartky, J. A., *Supervision as Human Relations* (Boston: D. C. Heath and Company, 1953), chs. VI-IX, XVI.

Boardman, C. W., Douglass, H. R., and Bent, R. K., *Democratic Supervision in Secondary Schools* (Boston: Houghton-Mifflin Company, 1953), chs. VI-XIII, XV-XVII.

Burton, W. H., and Bruecker, L. J., *Supervision: A Social Process* (New York: Appleton-Century-Crofts, Inc., 1955), chs. VI-VII, XI-XIII, XVII.

Cramer, R. V., and Domian, O. E., *Administration and Supervision in the Elementary School* (New York: Harper and Brothers, 1960), ch. XII.

Crosby, M., *Supervision as Co-operative Action* (New York: Appleton-Century-Crofts, Inc., 1957), chs. VI-VIII, X.

Elsbree, W. S., and McNally, H. J., *Elementary School Administration and Supervision*, 2nd ed. (New York: American Book Company, 1959), chs. IX-X.

Elsbree, W. S., and Reutter, E. E., *Staff Personnel in the Public Schools* (New York: Prentice-Hall, Inc., 1954), chs. IX, XIV.

Griffiths, D. E., *Human Relations in School Administration* (New York: Appleton-Century-Crofts, Inc., 1956), chs. XII-XIII, XVI.

Hammock, R. C., and Owings, R. S,, *Supervising Instruction in Secondary Schools* (New York: McGraw-Hill Book Company, Inc., 1955), chs. IV-IX.

Hicks, H. J., *Educational Supervision in Principle and Practice* (New York: The Ronald Press Company, 1960), Parts II and III, *passim.*

MacVittie, R. W., *Handbook for Substitute Teachers* (Minneapolis: Burgess Publishing Company, 1956).

Moore, H. E., and Walters, N. B., *Personnel Administration in Education* (New York: Harper and Brothers, 1955), ch. XII.

National Society for the Study of Education, *In-Service Education for Teachers, Supervisors, and Administrators*, Part I, 1957 Yearbook (Chicago: University of Chicago Press), *passim.*

Reeder, E. H., *Supervision in the Elementary School* (Boston: Houghton Mifflin Company, 1955), chs. XI-XVIII, XXI.

Shane, H. G., and Yauch, W. A., *Creative School Administration* (New York: Henry Holt and Company, Inc., 1954), chs. X-XIII.

Shuster, A. H., and Wetzler, W. F., *Leadership in Elementary School Administration and Supervision* (Boston: Houghton Mifflin Company, 1958), chs. VI-X.

Spears, H., *Improving the Supervision of Instruction* (Englewood Cliffs, N. J.: Prentice-Hall, Inc., 1953), chs. XIII, XVI-XVIII.

Wiles, K., *Supervision for Better Schools,* 2nd ed. (Englewood Cliffs, N. J.: Prentice-Hall, Inc., 1955), chs. VIII-XII.

Yeager, W. A., *Administration and the Teacher* (New York: Harper and Brothers, 1954), parts IV and VI.

CHAPTER 17

Using the Workshop, Group Processes,
and Action Research
in Problem Solving

ONE OF THE CHIEF VALUES of the group process is that it can save much time. The supervisor can just as easily illustrate a point or help to bring about a solution to a common problem for a group of 20 teachers as he can on 20 visits to separate classrooms. Although he will spend extra time in developing skills in group procedures and in the organization of groups, he will benefit greatly in the long run. He must be very careful, however, to avoid those situations which are a waste of time. It is not necessary to call a group together to meet every trivial problem, to handle a situation that might have been taken care of by a supervisory bulletin, or to give attention to problems not important to members of the group.

This chapter has two main purposes: (1) to present the purposes, techniques, and practices in group processes with which the supervisor should be familiar and (2) to explain how the workshop can be used by groups in solving problems.

The Supervisor's Need for Competency in Group Processes

Along with other skills, every supervisor needs to know how to release the power of a group,[1] how to make staff meetings effective,

---

[1] Cf. Kimball Wiles, *Supervision for Better Schools*, 2nd ed. (Englewood Cliffs, N. J.: Prentice-Hall, Inc., 1955), pp. 161-238, *passim*.

and how to co-ordinate the work of the group. Unless he is competent in these respects, he loses a large part of his effectiveness. His ability to do these things depends not alone on academic training or experience in group participation, but on his knowing the techniques and procedures to be used from the time a problem worthy of group action is recognized until it is successfully met and solved.

POSSIBLE APPROACHES TO A STUDY OF GROUP DYNAMICS

There are a variety of ways in which this study might be undertaken. One of the simplest approaches might be the tracing of the group dynamics movement from its known beginning to the present. Many general and specific writings are available on this topic. While such an approach would list much valuable information, it would not result in the establishment of a pattern for the development of skills in group processes.

Another approach to the subject is the involvement of group processes in relation to the supervisor as a leader, the teachers, other staff personnel, and persons other than staff personnel. This approach comes close to the heart of the matter but does not give answers to all the problems with which the supervisor finds himself faced.

Kimball Wiles' concentration upon five areas—leadership, human relations, group processes, personnel administration, and evaluation—is a type of approach worthy of study.[2] We are more concerned here, however, with a solid approach to one of the areas— group processes in problem solving—than with a more comprehensive study of all of the areas.

The approach which has been selected is that which deals with the interactions between the supervisor and his staff and between members of the staff in getting group processes to work. This approach necessitates, also, the pointing out of the limitations of group processes and the weaknesses and strong points of group discussions.

Man cannot long exist apart from group life. He is gregarious by nature, a lonely being when set off from others of his kind. Even more important, however, is the fact that many of man's problems can be met successfully only by groups of individuals

[2] *Ibid., passim.*

working together. Certainly it is true that our present society has become so complex that each man is dependent upon his neighbors, including those close at hand and those whom he has never seen.[3]

It is paradoxical, then, that man, virtually unable to live alone, finds difficulties in living with others. Our group life is frequently unsuccessful. It is reasonable to assume that this singular lack of success in community living is at least partially caused by lack of understanding of group organization, group production, and group processes. Every person who comes in contact with others can profit greatly from the development of that understanding.

Group dynamics has been studied seriously by many elements of our society in recent years. Business and industry were quick to recognize its possibilities and to incorporate many of the group practices into their systems. Labor, too, has learned rapidly how successful group processes can be in bargaining with industry. Sociologists, politicians, and public administrative personnel also have found that a knowledge of group dynamics is necessary for success in their areas. Education now is aware of the vast potentials for improvement which are presented by this relatively newly-recognized area of human relations. It is with this thought in mind that the remainder of this section is devoted to a study of groups and group processes.

Groups and Group Processes

DEFINITIONS AND FEATURES OF GROUPS

Groups are made up of two or more individuals, associated with each other, who come together to solve some problem which is common to all and which cannot be solved by the individuals alone. In addition to solving the problem the group has the task of building, strengthening, and regulating itself as a group.[4] There are certain productive practices to be followed in performing these functions, the lack of which will cause the group to wither away and die. If the group uses the proper techniques in problem solving and self-perpetuation it will become a mature body, capable of self-

---

[3] K. D. Benne, L. P. Bradford, and R. Lippitt, *Group Dynamics and Social Action*, Freedom Pamphlets (New York: Anti-defamation League of B'nai B'rith, 1950), pp. 4-5.

[4] *Cf.* D. M. Hall, *The Dynamics of Group Discussion; A Handbook for Discussion Leaders* (Danville, Ill.: Interstate Printers and Publishers, 1950), pp. 2-3.

direction and self-control. The individual members will recognize their responsibilities for developing and executing the group's plans, and the group will be characterized by those distinguishing features which indicate an effective body of individuals. There will be a "belongingness" in which all members will share, in which all members will trust each other; there will be an acceptance of social control by the group, and individual members will be well acquainted with the modes of thinking, habits of action, and needed satisfactions of other members of the group.[5]

When a group does not exhibit these distinguishing features, when it becomes impotent and dies, there will be a reason behind its failure. It may be that the group was faulty for its purposes. The organization of the group may have been such that the purpose was made ineffective. Discussion groups must be kept small if there is to be interaction among the individual members. In education, as in other areas, the effectiveness of the group is either greatly hampered or nullified by an organization so cumbersome that there can be no interacting of minds leading to the co-operative and creative thinking necessary for action and growth.

Another factor which can cause group failure is the actual composition of the group. People tend to like those who agree with them; but a group composed only of those who agree cannot make progress, for progress is dependent upon differences. On the other hand, there should not be too great cleavage between members of the group. We can expect, in any normal group, that cleavages will exist between people who take diverse points of view. The primary task here is to find ways by which those cleavages can be eliminated or skills developed for handling them in such a manner that their tremendous psychological waste is avoided.[6]

LEADERSHIP OF THE GROUP

One of the surest ways to destroy the effectiveness of a group is to create an atmosphere which is not permissive—one in which members do not feel free to comment, to question, to compare, and

[5] Cf. Bernice Baxter and Rosalind Cassidy, Group Experience: The Democratic Way (New York: Harper and Brothers, 1943), pp. 20-21; and J. Minor Gwynn, Curriculum Principles and Social Trends, 3rd ed. (New York: The Macmillan Company, 1960), pp. 662-665. Gwynn traces also the earlier developments in group dynamics.

[6] Helen Hall Jennings and others, Sociometry in Group Relations, A Work Guide for Teachers, Intergroup Education in Cooperating Schools (Washington, D. C.: American Council on Education, 1949), ch. IV.

to express a differing point of view. The leadership employed by any group leader usually determines what the atmosphere will be. For our purposes, one should avoid a discussion of the distant-leadership type of supervisor and concentrate upon the direct-leadership type. Leland P. Bradford and Ronald Lippitt look at four kinds of supervisory leadership and at the characteristics of groups working under each kind in the field of management: [7]

1. The Hardboiled Autocrat

Characteristics. The leader gives the orders, the employees are supposed to carry them out. He maintains a constant check on everyone to see that his orders are being followed. He insists upon rigid discipline, limits his praise of members, and is conscious of his authority.

Group characteristics. Members refuse to accept responsibilities. There is a lag in production during the supervisor's absence. There is a lack of unity, and members tend to "pass the buck" and knife others in the back.

2. The Benevolent Autocrat

Characteristics. He is interested in making the members happy. He encourages them to bring problems to him. He is quick to praise, making himself the source of all standards of judgment. When his standards are not met, he is hurt and takes the attitude that there is disloyalty to him personally.

Group characteristics. No member is likely to use his own initiative without finding out what the leader thinks of it. Members retrogress toward dependency, submission, and unwillingness to accept responsibility. The group finally reaches a stage where it can exist only under the first type, namely, autocratic supervision.

3. Laissez Faire

Characteristics. This leader tends to drift and to allow conditions to drift in any direction. He thrusts too much responsibility upon the members. He sets no goals, makes no decisions, and does not help the group to make decisions.

Group characteristics. Without leadership there can be no group. There is no goal, no production, and no sense of personal achievement. The outlook of future lack of direction causes frustration, failure, and

---

[7] Summarized from Leland P. Bradford and Ronald Lippitt, "Building a Democratic Work Group," *Personnel*, XXII (November, 1945), pp. 142-148, reprinted in Kenneth D. Benne and Bozidor Muntyan, *Human Relations in Curriculum Change* (New York: The Dryden Press, 1951), pp. 118-125.

insecurity. A group under this type of leadership is worse off than groups under the other three types.

4. DEMOCRATIC

Characteristics. The supervisor makes every effort to allow the group to share in work planning and scheduling. He explains his reasons to the group when he must make a decision alone. He wants every member to understand his work and to enjoy success in it. Praise on the one hand and criticism on the other are given in terms of the results of work, not in terms of the supervisor's personal likes or dislikes.

Group characteristics. Every member has a sense of belonging to this group. Each member has enthusiasm for his work. Teamwork is evident, and members grow into positions of greater responsibility. There are fewer personal problems, and the supervisor has more time to devote to planning and constructive leadership.

ROLE-PLAYING AS A FACTOR IN GROUP INTERACTION

Role-playing is a factor which, with all other aspects favorable, can make the group highly successful or can make its work fruitless. This is true because all of us play roles naturally, but chiefly we play either the dominating or the submissive role, rather than a role in between these, because these are the ones which come usually within the framework of our experiences. The leader must be instrumental in helping the group to recognize the various roles to be played and in shaping members to play the roles. As soon as the members become familiar with the process and can go about it democratically, the leader can relinquish his power over the playing of the roles. D. M. Hall has identified 15 different roles which probably will be played by the members if the group is to function properly; since his analysis includes practically all roles which are mentioned by other writers, a summary of them is given here: [8]

The Initiator, who offers new ideas and issues, and outlines purposes of the new problems; he helps to change the atmosphere of a group by changing the kind of leadership; he knows the value concepts of the group, and how to suggest objectives based on them.

[8] Compare D. M. Hall, *op. cit.,* pp. 12-16 with Benne and Muntyan, *op. cit.,* pp. 216-247; with Association for Supervision and Curriculum Development, *Group Planning in Education, passim* and *Group Processes in Supervision,* 1945 Yearbook, pp. 20-63; with Gordon N. MacKenzie and Stephen M. Corey, and others, *Instructional Leadership* (New York: Teachers College, Columbia University, 1954), chs. I-III; and with "Human Relations in Education," *The Review of Educational Research,* vol. XXIX (October, 1959), chs. I-IV.

The Orientor, also at times identified as *The Leader* and *The Director,* who helps the group to establish its purposes and to direct its statements to its established aims; he calls for and identifies facts or evidence, and may even ask the group if it has "gotten off of" its subject.

The Facilitator, or *The Promptor,* who endeavors to keep communication open from one member of the group to others, by requesting a definition, a restatement, an analysis, or something of the kind; he assesses the experiences and abilities of members of the group and their possible contributions, not his.

The Encourager, or *The Stimulator,* who encourages and invites participation and approves or recognizes the roles and parts played by others.

The Harmonizer, who insists on presentation of all points of view; recognizes that differences are desirable and necessary for progress; holds the group together by identifying different points of view or relaxing tension by relating humorous episodes.

The Summarizer or *The Synthesizer,* who says "Where are we now? Are we at this point? . . ."; or "How would this idea work out in the classroom?"

The Fact Seeker or *The Information Hound,* who asks for data, information, or examples of a concept or principle, in order to clarify the problem and thinking on it.

The Compromiser, who attempts to resolve a conflict in the group by yielding ground or status without forfeiting his point of view; who suggests that there is some common ground for divergent points of view.

The Fact Giver, or *Fact Man,* or *The Resource Person,* or *The Consultant,* who is an expert in an area; he supplies facts or examples or experiences, or he quotes an authority.

The Expeditor or *The Detail Man,* or *The Arranger,* who looks after provision of facilities for meeting, materials, and such tension relievers as "coffee" or "coke" breaks.

The Spokesman, who speaks for the group in promotion of its progress, and in speaking of its actions, defends them from people or pressures from outside.

The Recorder, sometimes called *The Secretary,* who keeps a record of purposes, problems, issues, ideas, facts, and decisions as they are made by the group and reports these to the group from time to time; he prepares reports and resolutions with other appointed members of the group; he attends intergroup sharing-committee meetings, if any; and he clears the final group report to the proper authority.

The Evaluator, who makes comparisons of facts or activities, assesses the progress made by the group to this point, and helps to set next standards of achievement. Some writers use this term interchangeably with *The Summarizer*. Others think that these duties come under those of *The Analyzer* or *The Observer*.

The Observer, or *The Analyzer*, who analyzes and reports to the group on its own processes, how well it is or is not doing, its use or non-use of resources, the amount of participation, and the like.

The Status Role, the person, usually well known and respected for his accomplishments and attitude, who is accepted both by persons in and outside of the group, and who therefore lends status to the group.

It is the responsibility of the group leader to encourage the members of the group to play these roles, and also at times to play one or another of them himself as the occasion suggests. It is important that as many members as can, learn to play as many roles as possible. Skillful leaders will provide opportunities for individuals to be cast in different roles. The Analyzer in particular will be aware of the possibilities of having others play his role. He and The Evaluator are in positions to know when members are ready for new roles and with The Encourager they will improve the group by improving the individual role-playing. Self-perpetuation of the group depends upon getting skillful leaders, and leaders can be developed from those who can learn to play the roles which strengthen and regulate the group.

GROUP LEADERSHIP ROLES

No group can be effective unless there are skillful leaders to carry out certain indispensable functions. It is essential that these persons know what they are doing and that they have the ability to exercise their skills in an unobtrusive manner. In the field of education, the Association for Supervision and Curriculum Development pioneered in the development and use of group processes in its meetings, as did the Association for Childhood Education. Records of the programs and meetings of the former reveal that they have employed successfully five major leadership roles in group work:

1. *The Leader*, or *Chairman*. He helps the group to become acquainted, to establish "ground rules"; he knows particular contributions that different persons can make; he is familiar with the steps used in

problem solving, knows how to proceed in situations where many, one, or no hypothesis has been formed; he helps to provide situations which fulfill the demands that groups make of themselves—for planning, education, execution, spokesman, status symbols, harmony, enjoyment; he is a master of parliamentary procedure, is able to use his position to draw out the shy person and to keep the dominant individual from monopolizing; he can recognize value in differences; and he is able to keep the group moving forward by providing time for thinking together, keeping the members informed on the method of work being used, allowing for changes in procedure, starting where the group is, and seeing that a group problem is attacked first.

2. *The Recorder.* He keeps a record of and summarizes actions taken, presents a report of actions to the members and to outside groups, classifies comments or arguments in order of importance, and knows and uses the "buzz card" technique in reaching decisions. His role has already been described.

3. *The Observer* or *Analyzer.* His role also has been described; he should also note the roles played by various members of the group and determine what effect each role has within the group.

4. *The Resource Person, Consultant,* or *Fact-Giver.* The role of this leader is also important, and has been described.

5. *The Evaluator,* a role sometimes combined with that of *The Observer,* already presented. He will know how to employ the end-of-the-meeting evaluation sheet and will use it for collecting data; as the group matures, he will allow and persuade other members to criticize processes in the group.

HOW GOOD LEADERSHIP FUNCTIONS

The functions of good leadership in relation to the group are worthy of a great amount of consideration. One of the primary functions of leadership is to see that all members of the group are made as comfortable as physical conditions permit. The leader should see to it that members are well enough acquainted that they can proceed in a cordial, informal way. He has responsibility for seeing that the problem is clearly stated and defined so that it is understood by everyone. He should try to keep members on the topic at hand and headed in the right direction. He should recognize each role as it is played by a member, and he should protect the security and status of each role. Each member should be given a chance to make his contributions and should receive credit where credit is due. The wise leader, too, sees to it that the group has a feeling of accomplishment as it makes progress.[9]

Educational authorities today generally identify two kinds of leaders who furnish leadership in the modern school. Rodney Tillman described [10] these in terms of these characteristics:

Status Leaders	Functional Leaders
Have legal responsibilities.	Are perceptive people of insights and skills.
Have certain recognition.	
Certain things are expected of them by people and by society.	Have freedom of expression and security.
Have certain other responsibilities.	Are motivated to "want to do," to try to move the group forward.

Can status leaders become functional leaders? Yes, one usually thinks of one as he considers the other. The modern, effective educational leader is a co-ordinator, as well as a consultant and resource person.

Principles for Successful Group Work

Whenever a situation does warrant the use of the group process, certain principles and practices are sound. Harold Spears has stated most of them in his list, which is the source of the following summary: [11]

1. Good leadership and practice will lead to a development of that basic capacity for accomplishment which every group possesses.
2. The supervisor may be a force from outside or a worker from within to bring about group action. The worker from within, called the co-operative approach, has been more successful.
3. Co-operation with the group does not deprive the supervisor of his leadership. He still has the responsibility for establishing the group atmosphere and protecting the group situation, even though the responsibility may be shared.

---

[9] American Association of School Administrators, *Staff Relations in School Administration,* Thirty-third Yearbook (Washington, D. C.: National Education Association, 1955), ch. IV.

[10] Summarized from an address during the annual School Week program at the University of North Carolina, June 18, 1956. He was executive secretary of the Association for Supervision and Curriculum Development at the time.

[11] Harold Spears, *Improving the Supervision of Instruction* (Englewood Cliffs, N. J.: Prentice-Hall, Inc., 1953), pp. 104-106.

4. The supervisor has to be ready, when the proper time comes, to trust the capacities of the group.
5. Groups work well together only when they understand what brought them together. Without understanding and early leadership the group will waste time and accomplish little.
6. Under the resourceful supervisor, individual leadership will give way in time to group leadership.
7. Groups must meet frequently to make progress. Reports, questionnaires, check lists, and bulletins cannot take the place of group participation.
8. The supervisor will need to exercise patience while bringing the group to the level of his own understanding and progress.
9. Groups work most effectively when individual members have the feeling that their ideas are important, when these ideas are recorded and considered in the original wording of the participant.
10. The supervisor has the responsibility of seeing to it that no one individual or faction assumes the power of speaking for the entire group. This action may be called also protecting the group from itself.
11. Developing good leadership within the group will call for constant attention to the actions which provide for that development.

An understanding of these principles and procedures will enable the supervisor to make his group meetings effective. He will organize his meetings around problems that seem important to the group, even when he feels that the problems are insignificant. When members learn that irritating small problems can be resolved in group meetings they will be ready and able to proceed to the more important problems. The group should have a definite plan, listing the items which are considered important, and the plan should be made available to members before the time of meeting. A faculty planning committee may be responsible for the establishment of the plan, but all members should have a chance to suggest revisions and rearrangement of items of business. [12]

There has been considerable debate regarding the time when a group such as a school faculty should hold its meetings. Before school, after school, during the school day, and on Saturdays are times which have been suggested and tried. It seems the best practice, however, to allow the group itself to work out the time

[12] An excellent description of how to plan staff meetings and co-ordinate the work of the group is found in Wiles, *op. cit.*, chs. IX-X.

for its meetings and to exercise judgment concerning the length of time for them.

It is good policy to have a "break" during group meetings and to provide time for relaxation and refreshment. Informal seating arrangements and the use of furniture which permits the breaking up of the larger group into smaller working groups also add to the over-all effectiveness.

With large faculties the work of co-ordinating staff activities will present a major problem. This co-ordination can best be done, not by one or two persons in authority, but by a faculty-planned organization which is built around the study of recurrent problems and is flexible enough to be changed as the major problems change. Faculty members should be allowed to work with the phases of the problem which hold the greatest interest for them, and all final decisions should be made by the entire faculty. There should be provisions for committee work, but committee responsibilities should be spread. It is wiser to carry on work through existing committees rather than establish many new ones. The functions of each committee should be well defined. Policies established by the faculty should be implemented and channels for revision of policy kept open. There should be group agreement on regulations for group meetings; and all members, including the leader, should abide by group decisions.

Problem Solving

When a group has been properly organized, is composed of the right combination of persons, has a permissive atmosphere, and when its members are becoming skilled in respective role-playing, it is ready to put into practice the mechanics of problem solving. Although an undercurrent of problem solving runs throughout the discussion which has just been given of principles for successful group work, some space should be devoted to the actual "how" of it.

Authorities generally agree that there are six steps through which a group must carry a problem before a satisfactory solution can be reached. The steps do not have to come in order, but the entire cycle has to be completed in order to solve the problem and reap the benefits from its solution. The six steps in the cycle are as follows: [13]

1. Statement of the problems or objectives.
2. Definition of the problem or the most important problems; their placement in order of priority if there is more than one.
3. Exploration of the problem and formulation of a possible solution or solutions to the problem. The basic process here is group discussion, which
   a. Examines, collects, and classifies available facts and pertinent data.
   b. Appraises critically each proposed solution.
   c. Decides upon the goals, the approach and plan of attack.
4. Co-ordination of the activities of individuals and tapping the resources of agencies capable of working upon the solution.
5. Evaluation and testing out of the results of the group's activities.
6. Extension of the benefits of the study to all persons concerned with it.

The "Curriculum Projects" chart (Figure 17) illustrates agencies and individuals involved in the solution of curriculum problems by a group.

The Workshop as a Study Group

The modern educational workshop may be defined as a group of school personnel working on common problems primarily through group and individual conferences; it is usually flexible in organization, also allowing individuals to work separately on their problems with the help of resource persons and consultants. The workshop and workshop techniques have developed rapidly in the last quarter of a century. The Parker School District of Greenville, South Carolina, was an example of a school system that for many years conducted its own summer or preschool study program for school personnel in advance preparation for the work of the coming school year. The Eight-Year Study of the Progressive Education Association in 1936 organized its first workshop at Ohio State University in the summer to meet the needs of teachers of the schools which were

---

[13] These six steps are refined primarily from the ideas of three writers who have set forth the results of their study; the steps presented by each author differ only in small degree from the others. The sources are: William H. Burton and Leo J. Brueckner, *Supervision: A Social Process*, 3rd ed. (New York: Appleton-Century-Crofts, Inc., 1955), pp. 180-187; John A. Bartky, *Supervision as Human Relations* (Boston: D. C. Heath and Company, 1953), p. 161; and Hall, *op. cit.*, pp. 23-29.

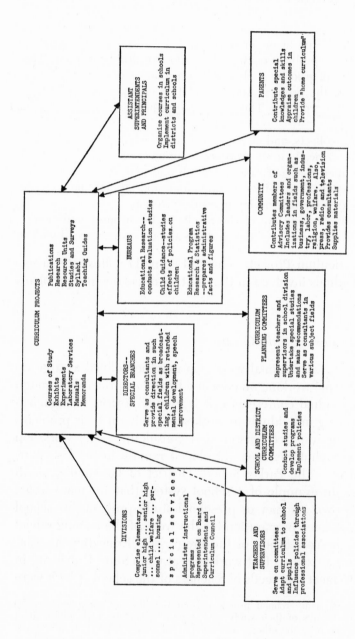

Figure 17. Chart Illustrating Who Shapes the Curriculum and the Process of Curriculum Development

This chart illustrates group processes in handling and solving curriculum problems. It is part of a larger curriculum organization chart of the New York City public schools.

Reproduced with the permission of the Bureau of Curriculum Research, Board of Education of the City of New York.

engaged in this experimental study. The Association designated this as a "summer workshop," and for some years the main use of the workshop was confined to group meetings of school personnel in the summer for periods ranging from three to six weeks in length.[14]

The fact that the workshop can be designed to meet a particular situation or problem and can be planned to fit teachers' needs caused a steady extension of the concept of the workshop. Now workshops differ according to the group which sponsors them or the problems to be tackled and solved. For example, workshops for teachers are carried on by school systems, or units in a larger system during the school year; by colleges in the summer for periods ranging from a week to five weeks; by national organizations independently or in co-operation with schools or colleges, such as the human relations workshops of the National Conference of Christians and Jews or the economic education workshops of the Joint Council on Economic Education.

When one analyzes the educational workshop as to types, he immediately discovers that in one form or another it is rapidly replacing the old-fashioned faculty meeting as a means of professional growth of teachers in service. Harold Spears identifies as many as seven different types of workshops: (1) the faculty workshop, (2) the institute workshop, (3) the graduate workshop, (4) the conference workshop, (5) the summer workshop, (6) the preschool workshop, and (7) the school and community workshop.[15] Of these seven, those emerging slowly as the more effective are:

The faculty workshop, either throughout the school year or for preschool planning under the general direction of the supervisor or the principal. Teachers usually receive regular pay for this, nothing extra.

The "work conference" or conference workshop, (*a*) set up to meet a specific need or situation in school or community, and running from one to five days or (*b*) set up as part of the program of a local or state teachers' organization at its monthly or regular meetings. There is usually no extra pay for this.

The summer workshop, either (*a*) at an institution of higher learning in a particular field or area of interest, or (*b*) in the local school system at a camp or some place away from the school grounds. Many schools pay part or all expenses of teachers to these, or obtain scholarships for teachers to them from sponsoring organizations or colleges.

14 *Cf.* Gwynn, *op. cit.,* pp. 347-348 and 530-534.
15 Spears, *op. cit.,* pp. 364-372.

CHARACTERISTICS OF GOOD WORKSHOPS

The supervisor will have to deal with the faculty workshop or some form of work conference in the in-service education of teachers. He should know and be able to provide for these characteristics of good workshops:

A. Attendance and participation should be voluntary on the part of each teacher; the workshop is open to the teacher, but attendance is not required.
B. The individual problems of the participating teachers should emerge voluntarily, with no pressure or direction from the supervisor.
C. Teachers in the workshop work only on problems that they want to work on. They themselves plan the activities and the schedule.
D. The program of the workshop grows out of the problems which teachers voluntarily suggest that they want to work on. There are no prearranged program, agenda, or arbitrary schedule. This does not mean that there is no preplanning; a good workshop always has sound preplanning, involving at least these steps:
   1. Obtaining from each participating teacher in writing the problem or problems that he desires to work on and have help on during the workshop.
   2. Distribution of a list of these problems to all who are to participate asking from each:
      a. Preference (1st and 2nd choices) of problem areas that he wants to work on individually.
      b. Preference (1st and 2nd choices) of problem or problem area which he would like to have probed in a meeting of all members of the workshop.
   3. After these choices of individual participants have been tabulated, arrangement of small work groups on problems of their choice, convenient meeting room or place, and provision of resources—both of materials and, at times, of resource people or consultants.
   4. Arrangement of opening meeting of workshop with:
      a. Registration and social hour.
      b. A "kick-off" or opening general meeting with keynote talk by proper person concerning the problem picked by the participants for the workshop.
   5. Provision for rest breaks between sessions of a general nature and those of the special study groups.
   6. Suggested social schedule or activities.
   7. Provision for copying, mimeographing, and reporting, and of special lists or materials.
   8. Arrangement of dates for the workshop.
   9. Arrangement for use of any community resources during the workshop.
E. For effective work, the small or "special study" groups will accomplish more if they run in size from 10 to 20, rather than from 20 to 30.

F. "Clinic sessions"—where teachers recount experiences or methods which proved successful in a given situation—are valuable if not used too often and when scheduled so anyone is free to attend them.
G. Group processes and problem solving are a basic part of any ongoing workshop.
H. A well-balanced program in a workshop would have some meetings of all of the participants, perhaps more meetings of the small or special study groups; opportunities for members to have personal interviews with staff members or resource people; and a reasonable opportunity for social and recreational activities.
I. If the workshop is to be held for a longer period at some place away from the school where members will "live together" for the duration of the workshop, the supervisor as director or planner will have these additional duties:
   1. Selection and securing of resource people, consultants, and staff for the workshop, usually on the basis of one staff member to about 15 participants.
   2. Selection of staff primarily for purpose of being guides or consultants, not as "teachers" of the teachers involved.
   3. Reservation of place of meeting and living facilities; notices to participants concerning what bedding or types of clothing or other things to bring with them; how to get there; reception committee, etc.
   4. Planning of an adequate social and recreational program, including facilities and equipment.
   5. Arrangement for permission to visit or use community resources during the workshop.
   6. Knowledge of and familiarity with the "buzz" session or "buzz" group technique, in which a larger group, perhaps of 30, is divided into smaller groups of five or six each, which proceed to discuss the same problem for some 10 to 20 minutes; then each "buzz" group reports its thinking or suggested action back to the larger group.
J. Provision for evaluation of the workshop—its effectiveness or noneffectiveness, "high spots" in the workshop, "low spots," suggestions for improvement if another one is to be held. The supervisor should always hold the "workshoppers" back from trying to evaluate individual members; rather, they should try to evaluate the workshop and the processes which the group used to solve its problem. (Chapter 19 presents a sample opinionnaire by one school staff for the evaluation of its workshop.)

WEAKNESSES OF GROUP PROCESSES

The supervisor should not expect the use of the workshop technique and of group processes to solve every problem. In the first place, it is not possible to solve every problem. In the second place, some teachers do not seem to "catch on" to group processes and group interaction, even if they have been exposed to much experience in group work. Some of these know of no other ways of proceeding than "being told" or "telling"; others are aggressive, tend to dominate, and thereby cause constant personality clashes in the group. In the third place, some teachers seek consistently to use the group situation to seek recognition for themselves, or to do special pleading for their ideas, subject-matter areas, or students. Fourthly, some people always seek help, they do not know how to give help to others; "clinic" sessions occasionally help this kind of person to become a productive participator in the group. In the fifth place, the group situation itself puts an unintentional pressure upon some teachers; one may be influenced to state one opinion to the group and another privately; another may oppose the problem-solving and group processes because he simply resents the group situation. Finally, the supervisor does have to make certain decisions on his own responsibility in the long run; and there are some who figure that he might as well make the decision for the group in the beginning, without discussion by the group or advice from the group.

On the other other hand, group process is in essence the fundamental way in which groups work in a democracy. On a problem involving the improvement of the curriculum or of instruction, the proper use of group dynamics amounts to a group of informed people pooling their knowledge, skill, and experience to solve the problem. Such pooling will not solve all problems satisfactorily, but it will solve many; and it will make all personnel more aware of and familiar with the problems of the school and of each other.

Group Dynamics and Action Research

Are group processes and co-operative action research the same? Or not? Do they try to accomplish the same purposes? Examination of the literature produces an interesting comparison of the procedures involved (Table 8).

As the reader examines this comparative table, he notes that there is some confusion among the authorities over procedures employed in action research as compared to traditional research in supervision. However, he also sees clearly that one fact is evident —*practically all agree that group processes in problem solving are the major factors in carrying out action or co-operative research.*

Practically all writers agree, too, that the educational workshop makes use of group dynamics and interaction for its success.

Accounts of action research began to appear regularly in reports of research findings after 1950.[16] Research in group dynamics is frequently coupled with reports on action research, as are reports on research in human relations. Other names given to action research are "co-operative research" and "co-operative curriculum research," "operational research," "co-operative field experimentation," "research action," "evaluative research" and "evaluative process," and "service research."

As one surveys this relatively new development of the study of human relations and group action and interaction, he might hold tightly to several sensible principles:

1. Good group handling can be a major force for success in supervision.
2. Learning how to handle a group is not easy; one has to work at the job. If one does, then instructional and supervisory leadership develops rapidly and richly.
3. Successful workshops depend upon careful planning and good group handling; no workshop is successful without the adroit use of group processes in problem solving.
4. Research in supervision—whether traditional or action research—can be successful only when it is made objective, namely when it is based upon facts, opinions, or hypotheses; when all relative data are included, whether facts or opinions; and when conclusions are drawn based upon the evidence and in the light of the purpose or hypothesis.
5. Action research might more appropriately be called "social engineering," since it is centered upon human beings and their actions, behavior, and interactions. When impartially carried on, it is an effective and fairly fast method of translating the results of research into practical action.
6. Problem solving takes place in action research, in the workshop procedures, and in group processes involving two persons in an interview or a dozen persons in a group. It is both a process and an instrument with which the supervisor should be very familiar.
7. The study group provides naturally a situation in which action research can take place; it encourages both the individual and the group to experiment. It is the task of the supervisor to help the in-

(continued on p. 368)

16 *Cf. Encyclopedia of Educational Research*, 3rd ed. (New York, The Macmillan Company, 1960), pp. 107-108, 362, 610-611, 1164, 1288-1289; and *Review of Educational Research*, vol. XXII, no. 3 (June, 1953), ch. V and vol. XXIX, no. 4 (October, 1959), chs. I-V.

*Table 8. Comparative Definitions of Research Procedures, Action Research Procedures, and Group Processes in Problem Solving ***

Procedures in Traditional Research	Procedures or Process in Action Research	Group Processes in Problem Solving
AYER (1954)	AYER (1954)	According to BARTKY (1953), BURTON and BRUECKNER (1955), and HALL (1950)
1. Selection and refining of problems	1. A situation demanding action	
2. Survey of related studies	2. A factual investigation	
3. Hypothesis formulation and testing out	3. Goals are set up	1. Statement of problem or objectives
4. Selection and elaboration of research methods to be used	4. A program carried out to attain these goals	2. Definition of the problem, or problems in order of priority
5. Analysis of data	5. Recurrent factual surveys check success or failure of program— revision of program, if necessary	3. Exploration of the problem, and formulation of possible solution(s)
6. Conclusions and generalizations		
7. Reporting the results		a. Examination, collection and classification of facts and data
BOARDMAN, DOUGLASS, and BENT (1953)	6. All concerned get the results, and changes in school program occur more rapidly	
1. Formulating the problem	COREY (1953)	b. Critical appraisal of each proposed solution
2. Planning the investigation	1. Identification of problem area needing individual or group action	c. Decision upon the goals, the approach and plan of attack
3. Collecting the data		
4. Organizing and analyzing the data	2. Selection of one problem; hypothesis formulation implying a	4. Co-ordination of the activities of individ-
5. Interpreting the results		

* The writers in supervision upon which this composite table is based are: Fred C. Ayer, *Fundamentals of Instructional Supervision* (New York: Harper and Brothers, 1954), chs. XIX-XX; J. A. Bartky, *Supervision as Human Relations* (Boston: D. C. Heath and Company, 1953), chs. VIII-IX; Charles W. Boardman, Harl R. Douglass, and Rudyard K. Bent, *Democratic Supervision in Secondary Schools* (Boston: Houghton Mifflin Company, 1953), ch. XI; William H. Burton and Leo J. Brueckner, *Supervision: A Social Process*, 3rd ed. (New York: Appleton-Century-Crofts, Inc., 1955), chs. VI-VII; Stephen M. Corey, *Action Research to Improve School Practices* (New York: Teachers College, Columbia University, 1953), chs. I and II; D. M. Hall, *The Dynamics of Group Discussion: A Handbook for Discussion Leaders* (Danville, Ill.: Interstate Printers and Publishers, 1950), pp. 16-39; J. Minor Gwynn, *Curriculum Principles and Social Trends*, 3rd ed. (New York: The Macmillan Company, 1960), ch. XXI; Early C. Kelley, *The Workshop Way of Learning* (New York: Harper and Brothers, 1951), preface, pp. xi-xiii, and Ronald Lippitt and Marian Radke, "What Is Action Research?", Section XIII in Part III of *Human Relations and Curriculum Change*, edited by Kenneth D. Benne and Bozidar Muntyan (New York: Dryden Press, 1951), pp. 216-222.

Procedures in Traditional Research	Procedures or Process in Action Research	Group Processes in Problem Solving
GWYNN (1960)	goal and way of reaching it	uals and tapping the resources of agencies capable of working upon the solution
1. Selecting, defining, and limiting the problem	3. Record of actions taken—evidence as to attainment of goal, or solution of problem	upon the solution
2. Finding and reporting previous investigations related in part or whole to this problem	4. Generalizations, based on record of actions taken in relation to desired goal	5. Evaluation and testing out of results of the group's activities 6. Extension of the benefits of the study to all persons concerned with it
3. Selecting methods or devising instruments to gather the data	5. Regular retesting of generalizations in action situations	with it
4. Collecting and organizing the data		
5. Analysis and interpretation of data in comparison with the purposes originally set up	KELLEY (1951) *Workshop Way of Learning*—Essentially Action Research	
6. Reporting the findings and comparing them with results of other studies	LIPPITT and RADKE (1946)	
	1. A group need arises	
	2. Group decides "What We Need to Know"	
	3. Research instruments are devised	
	4. How to sample and use these research instruments wisely	
	5. Objective data collected	
	6. Check on changes in attitude	
	7. Co-operative action of specialists in compiling and interpreting facts and data	
	8. What changes in values or attitude took place?	
	9. Spreading the facts to other groups by oral and written reports	

dividual and the group so that its experimentation will be at least as effective as the methods formerly employed.

8. The writing up, or the reporting of co-operative research and experimentation, is not a major task for the supervisor or the group, if a good recorder learns to do his job well.

9. Both group dynamics and action research involve mostly the same procedures.

Group dynamics has gained for itself a respected place in industry, education, and in other elements of our society. Most authorities agree that skill in group processes is essential for successful leadership in all fields of human activity. Supervisors in education are among those who constantly deal with people on both the individual and the group levels. The sincere supervisor, recognizing the value of group processes, will learn those skills which are necessary for effective group relations and will help others to improve as group members or leaders. He will know when it is necessary to use the group process and when his duties go beyond that technique. When it is possible to solve problems more efficiently through group action, he will see to it that the methods which will best provide answers for the problems at hand are used.

Problems for Individual Study and Class Discussion

1. Is the teacher who attends professional work conferences outside his community thereby better fitted for service to his community's schools? Why or why not?

2. How can a supervisor help the teacher to transfer the knowledge and skills derived from a workshop to his classroom?

3. What are the weaknesses of a group discussion where the leader allows 100 per cent permissiveness?

4. What values to a school system can be derived from a program or problem in action research?

5. Is the typical teacher well enough trained to carry on research in the classroom? Could you as his supervisor train him for this, or would you have to call in a research expert to do this in a workshop or conference? Support your position.

6. What influence do teachers' vested interests, that is, their special interest in their subject or in a particular grade, have on group procedures in tackling a particular problem?

7. As the supervisor you are supposed to be the Leader or Chairman of the group. How can you surrender this role to another member of the group? When, and how often, should you do this? Why?

8. Should the problem of the time for the lunch hour be settled by group discussion? The problem of the grouping of children for instruction? The problem of a new kind of report card for parents? Why or why not?
9. Trace the development and use of the "clinic session" in supervision.
10. Think of the most effective speaker that you ever heard. Does your memory of the occasion stem from (1) The subject of his speech? (2) The thought that he stimulated in you? (3) The emotion that he aroused within you? What are the implications here for democratic leadership?
11. What are the differences, if any, between action research and traditional research in supervision?

Additional Selected References for Problem or Unit Study

NOTE: Extensive references on newer development in action research, group dynamics, and the workshop are given in the body of this chapter. This bibliography is restricted to viewpoints and aspects other than these.

Adams, H. P., and Dickey, F. G., *Basic Principles of Supervision* (New York: American Book Company, 1953), chs. III, VIII.

Anderson, V., and Davies, D. R., *Patterns of Educational Leadership* (Englewood Cliffs, N. J.: Prentice-Hall, Inc., 1956), *passim*.

Association for Supervision and Curriculum Development, *Toward Better Teaching*, 1949 Yearbook, chs. I, III, VII; *Research for Curriculum Improvement*, 1957 Yearbook, *passim*; and *Leadership for Improving Instruction*, 1960 Yearbook, *passim* (Washington, D. C.: National Education Association).

Barnes, J. B., *Educational Research for Classroom Teachers* (New York: G. P. Putnam Sons, 1960), *passim*.

The Bulletin of the National Association of Secondary School Principals, vol. XXIX (March, 1955), is centered around "Human Relations in Secondary Education," pp. 1-109.

Campbell, R. F., and Ramseyer, J. A., *The Dynamics of School-Community Relations* (New York: Allyn and Bacon, 1954), *passim*.

Crosby, M., *Supervision as Co-operative Action* (New York: Appleton-Century-Crofts, Inc., 1957), *passim*.

Cunningham, R., and associates, *Understanding Group Behavior of Boys and Girls* (New York: Teachers College, Columbia University, 1951), *passim*.

Educational Leadership has "Group Study Procedures," vol. VII (January, 1950), pp. 214-269, 271; "Research in Action," vol. XI (May, 1954), pp. 463-509; "Human Relations," vol. X (February, 1953), pp. 274-308; and "Role of Research and Evaluation," vol. XIII (April, 1956), pp. 398-443.

Elsbree, W. S., and McNally, H. J., *Elementary School Administration and Supervision*, 2nd ed. (New York: American Book Company, 1959), chs. IX-X.

Giles, H. H., *Human Dynamics and Human Relations Education* (New York: New York University Press, 1954), *passim*.

Grambs, J. D., *Understanding Intergroup Relations* (Washington: Department of Classroom Teachers, American Educational Research Association of the National Education Association, 1960), No. 21 of "What Research Says to the Teacher."

Griffiths, D. E., *Human Relations in School Administration* (New York: Appleton-Century-Crofts, Inc., 1956), chs. I-XII.

Gulley, H. E., *Discussion, Conference, and Group Process* (New York: Henry Holt and Company, 1960), *passim.*

Hammock, R. C., and Owings, R. S., *Supervising Instruction in Secondary Schools* (New York: McGraw-Hill Book Company, Inc., 1955), chs. III-IV, VI-VII.

Hicks, H. J., *Educational Supervision in Principle and Practice* (New York: The Ronald Press Company, 1960), chs. IV, VII, and IX.

Hock, L. E., *Using Committees in the Classroom* (New York: Holt, Rinehart and Winston, Inc., 1958), *passim.*

Krug, E. A., *Curriculum Planning*, rev. ed. (New York: Harper and Brothers, 1957), chs. I-II, IX-XI.

——, and others, *Administering Curriculum Planning* (New York: Harper and Brothers, 1956), chs. VI-IX.

Lindgren, H. C., *Effective Leadership in Human Relations* (New York: Hermitage House, 1954), *passim.*

MacKenzie, G. N., Corey, J. M., and associates, *Instructional Leadership* (New York: Teachers College, Columbia University, 1954), *passim.*

Miel, A., and associates, *Co-operative Procedures in Learning* (New York: Teachers College, Columbia University, 1952), *passim.*

Miles, M. B., *Learning to Work in Groups: A Program Guide for Educational Leaders* (New York: Teachers College, Columbia University, 1959), *passim.*

National Society for the Study of Education, *In-Service Education of Teachers,* Fifty-sixth Yearbook, Part I; and *Dynamics of Instructional Groups,* Fifty-ninth Yearbook, Part II (Chicago: University of Chicago Press, 1957 and 1960, respectively).

O'Rourke, M. A., and Burton, W. H., *Workshops for Teachers* (New York: Appleton-Century-Crofts, Inc., 1957), *passim.*

Reeder, E. H., *Supervision in the Elementary School* (Boston: Houghton Mifflin Company, 1953), chs. IV, VIII-XV.

Shane, H. G., and Yauch, W. A., *Creative School Administration in Elementary and Junior High Schools* (New York: Henry Holt and Company, Inc., 1954), Part I.

Smith, L. M., *Group Processes in Elementary and Secondary Schools,* No. 19 in "What Research Says to the Teacher" (Washington: Department of Classroom Teachers and Educational Research Association, National Education Association, 1959), *passim.*

Thibaut, J. W., and Kelley, H. H., *The Social Psychology of Groups* (New York: John Wiley and Sons, Inc., 1959), *passim.*

CHAPTER 18

How to Organize and Implement

a Supervisory Program

JUST AS IT IS TRUE that no two supervisory situations are exactly alike, so it is true that the supervisor has to plan and to operate within the organizational framework for supervision that has already been established in a school system. Another factor that operates consistently to influence each supervisory situation is the set of human relations involved. In other words, a supervisory program is built on human relations, is centered around individuals and groups of people; therefore, the type of organization cannot be determined exactly in advance. Since these factors operate constantly to condition each supervisory situation, no attempt is made here to advocate any particular type of supervisory organization. [1] On the other hand, emphasis will be placed in this chapter upon the principles and techniques which a beginning supervisor can employ successfully as he starts his work. The "new" supervisor referred to here is not the "director of instruction" for the whole system, with perhaps this title or the title of "assistant superintendent," but the new supervisor who has to work personally with teachers. In the long run, these same principles and methods will be used by any successful supervisor as he enters a position or system new to him.

[1] The reader should refer to ch. 1 for a historical account of the development of types of organization for supervision and to ch. 15 for examples of organizational arrangements in use in modern schools.

371

*How the Beginning Supervisor Goes About His
New Task in His First Year*

Although there is no set formula for establishing a successful supervisory program, this statement does not mean that there is no planning for the supervisor to do *in advance*. There are many steps that the supervisor can take both in his advance planning and in his first year.

PLANNING PRIOR TO SCHOOL OPENING

Most supervisors are engaged for their new work before the end of the current school year, or at least by the middle of the summer. Under these conditions, the new supervisor has ample time to investigate and plan in a preliminary way before school starts in the fall. In the first place, he will, if possible, have additional conferences of some length with the superintendent and the principal(s), with the primary purposes of obtaining a deeper understanding of their point of view about supervision, their philosophy of education and the purposes of their schools, and their concepts of his tasks and responsibilities as supervisor.

In the second place, he can obtain the names of all teachers in the system or in the schools under his direction. This information should certainly include their addresses, home and local; the grades or subject areas that they teach; and their homeroom numbers. The supervisor will pay particular attention to the *new* teachers, their backgrounds, their certification areas and teaching competencies, their experience, and their special interests.

Another part of his work to which the supervisor will devote major attention will be the instructional materials in the schools. He will obtain and examine the regular or basal textbooks for children used in the grades for which he is responsible. Before school opens, he will become familiar with these as well as with the teacher's manuals and the workbooks or aids that are written to accompany them. He will locate the bookroom(s) of the schools, and he will identify the kinds of supplementary texts and reference books which are available for teachers to use in their work. He will note particularly good materials which the teachers might use effectively to help the slow learner or to stimulate the faster pupil.

The libraries of the school buildings in which he is to work are another instructional source to be examined carefully. He will note their resources and enrichment possibilities and the availability of current materials and information. He will inquire particularly as to how fully available these resources are, for example, whether with the help of a full- or part-time librarian, or only through the teacher(s). He will also attempt to meet and talk with as many librarians as possible before school opens. He would not overlook the community as a source of instructional materials and would take preliminary steps both to study the community and to discover how teachers and school personnel employ its resources in their school work and activities.

Another chore which will make the new supervisor much better prepared for the opening of school is learning about the grouping and promotion of pupils. What system is used for the grouping of pupils for instruction? How effectively do the teachers feel that it is operating? What is the administration's or the school system's policy concerning the promotion of children, concerning the grading or marking system? And how are reports to be made to parents about the progress of their children in school?

His first step to become acquainted with the teachers and school personnel with whom he is to work will be taken by the supervisor before school begins. He might formulate and send out to each teacher a *personal* letter, brief, human, yet so interestingly phrased and written that the teacher will want to meet this person who wrote that remarkable letter. The letter might be centered around

1. A request for their co-operation in his new work, and their help to him in order that he might aid them later.
2. Any subject area or problem on which they might desire help soon.
3. Any new ideas or methods that they are experimenting with.
4. Any new materials that they need before school opens.

The supervisor might take his second step to get to know the staff better at the preschool work-conference or workshop. If the main purpose is to introduce the supervisor to the personnel and their problems, a one-day work-conference will perhaps be long enough. If the workshop technique has already become a well established feature for co-operative planning in the system, then the new supervisor can profit greatly by taking part in the preplanning of this preschool workshop.[2]

From his total study of the situation and the system during the summer, the new supervisor will write down for future study those big problems or problem areas that seem to need attention in this school, whether they are mentioned by school personnel or materialize as he studies, confers, examines, listens.

PLANNING DURING THE FIRST THREE MONTHS
OF THE SCHOOL YEAR

With the start of the school year, the planning of the beginning supervisor will take a somewhat different slant. With these facts, figures, information, and opinions "under his belt," the supervisor's main attention turns to exploration of the problems and to attempts to help in the plans of the individuals with whom he is to work. It should be noted here that though the new supervisor is still getting oriented, still learning about his job and the tasks and responsibilities that are his in this new situation, yet he is anxious to visit the teachers, to help the new teachers especially to "get along" on the job. Though past the first stage of preplanning in his program, he is still involved with exploration of the problems which he may be called upon to help in solving, such as:

1. Working to identify and help individual teachers to identify their problems.
2. Continuing to listen and become familiar with the over-all program of the principal(s), the teachers, and the specialists, like those in music, health and physical education, and art. In this way, he acquires a clear view of the scope and sequence of the curriculum and its activities. He will also help in planning if requested to do so.
3. Paying particular attention to new teachers, both those who are beginners and those who are new to the system or school. There are likely to be more potential "trouble spots," as well as more immediate problems needing solution or "quick" help among these newcomers. He will ask whether he can help them and will take advantage of every invitation to visit their classrooms and of every opportunity to get them to talk about their work. If not finally invited to visit in their classes, he may ask what day or days will suit them for him to come. He will prepare so thoroughly for the visit by

2 Ch. 17 gives detailed suggestions for preplanning a workshop.

mastering their textbooks that he will be somewhat at home when he visits.

4. Undertaking, with the co-operation of the principal(s), and all teachers, a study of all retarded children in the school; of the provisions, if any, made to help them and to restore them to normal progress; and of materials that are and can be provided to help in their instruction. This is information that the supervisor must obtain eventually. More important in his beginning duties, it takes him automatically into most classrooms—to observe the retarded or problem children.

5. Co-operating with "the old guard," the established teachers who have been in the system for years, and whose influence is powerful to help or hurt. By listening to them, discovering what they are doing, being "on call" for them, and using some of their suggestions, the supervisor reassures them, makes them feel that he did not come to change their system or to make them change their ways.

6. Attending as many group meetings of teachers as possible, whether grade-teacher meetings, subject-matter teacher meetings, principals' meetings, grade-mother-teacher meetings, or committee meetings. If not invited to some of these, he can ask to be allowed to come so that he can learn more about school problems and teachers' problems. When the supervisor does attend these, he should remember that he is primarily a listener and a learner, not a member of the group. But this role does not preclude his taking part in the discussion if asked to do so; in this case his approach would be more "Have you tried this?" or "Had you thought of this?"

PLANNING FOR THE REMAINDER OF THE FIRST YEAR

By December of his first year, the supervisor will have a rather solid foundation for the supervisory program, but his preliminary work and planning will not yet be complete. It will take the remainder of the school year to accumulate the information and to establish the rapport that he needs for his co-operative supervisory program which will really begin at the fall workshop or work-conference before he starts his second year. The following steps are necessary before the school year ends in June:

1. Studying carefully the methods of teaching employed by the different teachers under his supervision. This requires at times visits of two to five days at a time in the same classroom, especially if the teacher is doing unit teaching around a center of interest.

2. Studying continuously the principal(s) with whom he works, their

actions "on the job," their requirements as to reports and details, their attitudes toward the teachers, how they can give special aid.

3. Examining the public relations of the school, the principal, and the teachers. What are the channels for understanding of the school and its program? The present status of its public relations? The needs in this important area?

4. Analyzing the types of group activities of pupils, how they are organized and carried on, their value to the program, how they are financed and supervised.

5. Making a study of the provisions for guidance for pupils—of the allocation of responsibilities, of the instruments that are used, and of the materials that are needed.

6. Becoming more familiar with the audio-visual materials and aids available in the school(s), the extent and effectiveness of their use, how they are obtained and scheduled, and how they can be made more effective.

7. Studying the home backgrounds of the pupils in the school(s), becoming better acquainted with parents as he meets more and more of them, trying to discover what parents and public want of their schools, carrying further the preliminary survey of the community—its resources for teaching and its services and job opportunities for youth.

8. Analyzing the testing program(s), if any, that have been administered in the school(s), the uses that have been made of the results of the testing program, and the purposes and plans for additional tests.

9. Finally, securing from each teacher (1) his list of needs, whether pertaining to materials and resources or to methods, so that he can do better teaching next year, and (2) his ideas as to problems common to the school faculty upon which the group should work during the next school year. These ideas of the teachers furnish data for preplanning of the "before-school" workshop conference for the following fall.

Planning the Program for the Second Year

As the supervisor goes into his second year of work in this school system, his plan of organization changes slowly into an "action program" to replace the informational, "listening," and observational type that he pursued during the first year. This action program will be built upon (1) the common problem area selected by all teachers the previous spring for concentrated study during the year, (2) the individual problems which individual teachers indicated that they wanted to work on in connection with this common problem area, (3) a careful, analytical study of the methods used by individual teachers in their teaching, and (4) the application with teachers of resources and help that they asked for.

For example, the staff in one school system of medium size with which the writer is familiar decided at the end of the supervisor's first year to make a careful study of their system of reporting to parents on the progress of children in school. Accordingly, the supervisor with a faculty committee representative of all the staff made preliminary plans before school closed in the spring for a three-day, preschool workshop prior to the opening of school in the fall. The main theme of the workshop was "Can We Improve Our Reporting System?" The workshop made provisions for the whole staff to discuss and arrive at decisions concerning a system-wide policy in regard to promotion and concerning variations that might be made in reporting on various grade and age levels. Provision was also made for grade-level groups, such as the primary grade group or the junior high group, to meet in smaller bodies to discuss their problems. Finally, each individual teacher who was interested in *how to grade* or *how to evaluate* in his particular grade or subject area was given an opportunity to work on this individual problem with the help of well-qualified consultants who were experts in those areas.

Following the preschool workshop, the staff continued with the aid of outside consultants to tackle the common problem of reporting, and possible solutions to it, with various committees working on their own assignments. In like manner, individuals continued to work on their individual problems of how to grade; for example, one teacher worked on "What standards should I use to report progress on such intangibles as growth in attitudes or patterns of conduct?" In the meantime, the supervisor and the teachers set up a schedule of individual visitation and conferences, primarily for a careful analysis of each teacher's methods of teaching—his purpose, how he taught to carry out this purpose, and how he could evaluate the results of his teaching most adequately and fairly. During this extended period of observation and visitation, the supervisor brought more and more into focus those helpful materials and resources that the teachers had requested during his first year as the supervisor.

In addition, some teachers elected to go, were sent, or were allowed to go to state, regional, or national conferences which were devoting major attention to policies of promotion and appraisal of pupils' progress. Consultants were furnished to help individuals or groups or *ad interim* committees, as needed throughout the year; and the supervisor requested through the superintendent that enough money be set aside by the school board to care for the expenses of these consultants. Individual teachers were encouraged to report on his most outstanding teaching unit or his most successful project of the year; these reports were made available for all staff members to read in the school bulletin or in special mimeographed reports.

From this illustration one can identify the main objectives and methods to which the supervisor gave more weight in his second year in this particular situation.

TIME FOR PLANNING

While he is proceeding busily with his program in his second year, the supervisor must still remember that few programs succeed unless time is set aside for careful thought and planning. At least an hour every other day should be spent in such long-range planning; during this time the supervisor may work on ideas as diverse as a "Blueprint for better public relations" and "How does retardation affect a child's mental attitude?" At one time he may reread his "log" of what has happened to him and the school since he joined the staff and thus figure what is or might be a next major task. At another time he might spend the time in completing a new list of supplementary readers that are badly needed. In regard to this allocation of the time for planning, *what is important is that the supervisor set aside time for it,* it is unimportant as to when that period for planning comes. It can fit naturally into a short schedule on Tuesday and Thursday; or it might not fit at all into a long session of observation on two successive days.

PUBLIC RELATIONS

During his second year, the supervisor will probably spend much of his time on public relations contacts and in work with the public. Now that he is well acquainted with the philosophy, the work, the progress, and the needs of the school, he should be available to talk to meetings of all sorts of groups that are interested in public education in the town. He also has to be in touch with the local papers and should help the superintendent, principals, and teachers to keep the public better informed about the school and its work. A part of this public relations task involves attendance at quite a few professional education meetings, such as the state teachers' meetings or those of the principals, classroom teachers, and supervisors. In this year, then, the supervisor continues to increase his *useability* by acquiring more and more accurate information on school matters and on his own particular school and community. An *informed* supervisor can talk most effectively with a school board member or a local legislator about school plant and staff needs.

Summary

When a supervisory program is being planned, it is planned to fit and to work in a given situation, not in all situations. The supervisor, realizing this, will lay a solid foundation by long-range planning which involves, for the first year, emphasis upon (1) the acquisition of a full understanding of the school situation, (2) a developing acquaintance and understanding of the school personnel and their problems, (3) mastery of the texts and other teaching materials used in the school, and (4) gaining a good working knowledge of the community, its people, and its resources for teaching.

In beginning his supervisory program, the supervisor will learn, listen, watch, confer, and work with those who ask for help during his first year in this new situation. He will pay particular attention to the teachers new to the system, and he and they as newcomers will work together to "learn the ropes" and identify the problems. Toward the end of his first year, the staff as a group will decide upon the big instructional problem that they want to concentrate on during his second year. Individually, the staff at the same time will indicate the problem that each one wants to try to solve in the following year.

The preschool work conference at the beginning of the second year will set the stage and identify the problems in the main area of study; this work conference will also suggest ways of working at solving the problems during the year and will furnish help and consultants to the individual faculty member as he works on a problem interesting only to him.

Other devices used to achieve the purposes of the second year of the supervisory program are attendance at state, regional, and national conferences on the problem under consideration and study, the employment and use of consultants during the year, the writing up and publishing of interesting experiments and findings, the improvement and use of public relations techniques, and the definite setting aside of time for continued advance planning by the supervisor.

Finally, the supervisor at the end of his second year might well ask himself these questions: How do teachers and administrators look at me? What makes it hard for some systems to keep a good supervisor?

The Co-operative Program in Educational Administration [3] which was fostered by the Kellogg Foundation in the 1950's turned up a host of facts about school administration, administrators, and the competencies needed by successful administrators. Boiled down, their research indicates these significant findings concerning leadership in supervision:

1. To be an effective leader, one must be a rather consistent problem solver. To help to solve a problem, the effective supervisor looks at any one problem in various ways.
2. The group or setting or situation in which one works, the conditions under which he operates are a part of leadership. In other words, what a leader does, he does in conjunction with others.
3. Communication between the leader and those whom he seeks to lead is basic. For example, a reader, a writer, or a listener seldom gets a complete message across; it may mean one thing to one person in this official position, and an entirely different thing to this person who is a parent.
4. The attitudes and values which people hold are more important factors in deciding questions and issues than technical skills or accumulated knowledge.
5. It seems that, within certain limits, intelligence is not a critical factor in leadership. Individuals with only normal intelligence make just as effective leaders, at times more so, than do persons of superior intellectual endowment.

[3] Turn to Chapter 21 for a fuller account of the CPEA.

Problems for Individual Study and Class Discussion

1. What parts of your complete supervisory program cannot be planned in advance? Why? Give evidence for your point of view.
2. How can the supervisor make an effective study of the home backgrounds of the pupils of the school? What methods will he employ? For example, shall he use a questionnaire, visit any in the homes, obtain the data from the teachers?
3. Why does one supervisor succeed in one school situation but fail when he transfers to another?
4. Write out a warm, personal-yet-professional letter of welcome to a new member of the teaching staff whom you will supervise this coming year.
5. Make out a check list or questionnaire that you could use as the new supervisor to obtain more information about the community and its resources that might be used in teaching.
6. How would you go about helping a teacher who did not know that she needed to improve her teaching? Explain.
7. What types of consultants would you need for a preschool workshop centered around a study of drop-outs? For a workshop during the year concentrating on the improvement of supplementary materials in the school?
8. Write out the speech which you as supervisor have been asked to deliver to the Rotary Club on "Promotion policies of our school."

Additional Selected References for Problem or Unit Study

American Association of School Administrators, *Educational Administration in a Changing Community,* Thirty-seventh Yearbook, chs. VI-VIII, and *The Superintendent as Instructional Leader,* Thirty-fifth Yearbook, ch. IX (Washington, D. C.: National Education Association, 1959 and 1957, respectively).

Association for Supervision and Curriculum Improvement, *Action for Curriculum Improvement,* 1951 Yearbook, *passim; A Look at Continuity in the School Program,* 1958 Yearbook, parts I-II; and *Leadership for Improving Instruction,* 1960 Yearbook, chs. I-II, IV (Washington, D. C.: National Education Association).

Boardman, C. W., and others, *Democratic Supervision in Secondary Schools* (Boston: Houghton Mifflin Company, 1953), chs. III-V.

Burton, W. H., and Brueckner, L. J., *Supervision: A Social Process,* 3rd ed. (New York: Appleton-Century-Crofts, Inc., 1955), chs. IV-VI.

California Journal of Secondary Education, "Symposium—The Status and Role of Curriculum Assistants and Department Heads in Secondary Schools: How Schools Organize for Curriculum Improvement," vol. XXX (March, 1955), pp. 157-187.

Crosby, M., *Supervision is Co-operative Action* (New York: Appleton-Century-Crofts, Inc., 1957), section III.

Educational Leadership presents symposia on "Guidance in a Modern Program," vol. X (March, 1953), pp. 338-380; "Supervision Says and Supervision Does," vol. X (November, 1952), pp. 74-117; "Supervision Today," vol. VII (April, 1950), pp. 438-492, 495; "Creativity and the School," vol. XIV (October, 1956), pp. 2-42; and "Organizing for Effective Learning," vol. XVII (April, 1960), pp. 402-438.

Elsbree, W. S., and McNally, H. J., *Elementary School Administration and Supervision,* 2nd ed. (New York: American Book Company, 1959), ch. XI.

Everett, J. B., and others, *Case Studies in School Supervision* (New York: Holt, Rinehart, and Winston, Inc., 1960), *passim.*

Franseth, J., *Supervision in Rural Schools,* Bulletin 1955, no. 11 (Washington, D. C.: U. S. Department of Health, Education, and Welfare), I-II.

Hammock, R. C., and Owings, R. S., *Supervising Instruction in Secondary Schools* (New York: McGraw-Hill Book Company, Inc., 1955), chs. III, V, XI.

Hicks, H. J., *Educational Supervision in Principle and Practice* (New York: The Ronald Press Company, 1960), chs. VII-VIII.

Lawler, M., *Curriculum Consultants at Work* (New York: Teachers College, Columbia University, 1958), *passim.*

McNally, H. J., Passow, A. H., and associates, *Improving the Quality of Public School Programs* (New York: Teachers College, Columbia University, 1960), *passim.*

National Society for the Study of Education, *In-Service Education for Teachers, Supervisors, and Administrators,* Fifty-sixth Yearbook, Part I (Chicago: University of Chicago Press, 1957), chs. V-VIII.

Shane, H. G., and Yauch, W. A., *Creative School Administration in Elementary and Junior High Schools* (New York: Henry Holt and Company, Inc., 1954), ch. IV.

Shuster, A. H., and Wetzler, W. F., *Leadership in Elementary School Administration and Supervision* (Boston: Houghton Mifflin Company, 1958), chs. VII-X.

Stiles, L. J., and others, *Teacher Education in the United States* (New York: The Ronald Press, 1960), ch. XVI.

Spears, H., *Curriculum Planning Through In-Service Programs* (Englewood Cliffs, N. J.: Prentice-Hall, Inc., 1957), *passim.*

Wiles, K., *Supervision for Better Schools,* 2nd ed. (Englewood Cliffs, N. J.: Prentice-Hall, Inc., 1955), chs. III-VII.

Part VI

EVALUATION OF THE

EFFECTIVENESS OF INSTRUCTION

AND THE FUTURE OF SUPERVISION

CHAPTER 19

How to Evaluate

a Supervisory Program

THE GREAT VALUE of supervision to a school system can be recognized readily only when the supervisory program is carefully evaluated. This evaluation has to be carried out not only at the end of each major project and each year but during each project or each year. Evaluation can be done accurately only by those who are affected by supervision, namely, the teachers, the administrative staff, other school personnel concerned, and the supervisor himself. There are several well-known ways of evaluating the effectiveness of the program, but all of them have to be used in the light of one principle, namely, "What are the purposes of the supervisory program for this year?"

Evaluation takes place in terms of purposes, not people. When one studies how to evaluate supervision fairly and effectively, he should keep constantly in mind that it is *the program* that is being evaluated, *not the supervisor.* For example, answers should be sought to such pertinent questions as these: "How well is the program accomplishing the purposes that were set up for this year?" Or, "In what respects has the program failed to carry out the purposes that were set up, and why?" Or, "What parts of this year's program were impossible of accomplishment in one year and should be carried over into another year?" Or "How can we evaluate our work conference?"

How a School Staff Evaluated Its Program

An illustration is presented here of the way a supervisor and a group of teachers proposed to evaluate their supervisory program in terms of its purposes.

OBJECTIVES OF THE SUPERVISORY PROGRAM

The *first step* was to identify and agree upon the objectives of the supervisory program. A committee of the school staff, of which the supervisor was a member, worked out the statement of objectives; these were submitted to the entire faculty, were discussed and modified, and then were restated. Although there were patently more purposes than could be accomplished in *one* year, the list as finally agreed upon was follows: [1]

Objectives of Our Supervisory Program for the Year

1. To develop a continuing program for a better understanding of the growth and development of students.
2. To develop desirable attitudes and appreciations in both students and teachers.
3. To develop an increasing awareness of the varying needs and abilities of individual students.
4. To aid teachers and students in the selection and use of instructional materials.
5. To help teachers in devising and using methods of evaluating the results of their teaching.
6. To develop an increased desire on the part of the teacher for self-improvement, leading to a freer use of supervisory assistance.
7. To effect a closer working relationship between teachers and between teachers and supervisor.
8. To develop a desire for a continuing search by faculty, administration, and supervisor for better and more efficient methods of classroom instruction.

Once these objectives were established, the staff spent some time in discussion of how they could find out how successful they had been in attaining these purposes during the school year. Out

---

[1] The writer is indebted to graduate students in his classes for several years for refinements which were made in these instruments and report forms.

of these extended group discussions grew the *second step* in the evaluation; there was consensus that the value judgments of the supervisory program by members of the staff were necessary, certainly at the close of the school year and perhaps during the year as a major project was completed. Accordingly, another staff meeting was devoted to discussion of how these value judgments were to be obtained. Some teachers proposed that each one should write out at the end of the year her estimate of the supervisory program; most of this group thought that such personal opinionnaires of the "open-end" type, unsigned, allowed each one full leeway to call attention to both strengths and weaknesses in the program. Other staff members agreed that each member of the school staff should participate, without signing his name to the estimate, but they contended that not all personnel had the same point of view. For example, they believed that the principal or the music specialist might have a concept of in-service education different from the seventh-grade teacher or the English teacher; therefore they suggested that a different form for evaluation be made out for the classroom teacher, for the principal, and for the specialist, three forms in all.

INSTRUMENTS DEVELOPED FOR EVALUATION

The staff finally agreed upon different forms for different types of personnel to use in the evaluation, and four different forms were to be worked out in detail by small committee groups. This *third step* in their evaluation resulted in four instruments, one for use by teachers, one for use by principals and other administrative personnel, one for use by specialists, and one for use by the supervisor. In actuality, only three forms for recording evaluations were worked out for the first year; the specialists decided to use parts of those designed for use by teachers and administrative personnel and to try to formulate their own during the following year. The following evaluation instrument was constructed for use by the teachers.

EVALUATION FORM TO BE COMPLETED BY
TEACHERS AT THE END OF THE YEAR

(To be submitted unsigned)

EVALUATION KEY: 1—The condition exists to a maximum degree.
2—The condition exists to a high degree.
3—The condition exists to some degree.
4—The condition exists but could be much improved.
5—The condition does not exist.
0—The condition does not apply.

Professional Growth

1. Supervision has increased my awareness of the many types of professional literature available. ....

2. The program, with the help of the staff, has resulted in a sufficient number of stimulating and helpful professional conferences. ....

3. The supervisory program has acquainted me with the writings and materials of available authorities in my field and the aid that they can give. ....

4. Supervision has inspired me to continue my formal training with the goal of improved instruction for my students. ....

5. I have felt free at all times to bring any instructional problem to my supervisor. ....

6. Our program has utilized the process of group attack on the problems which were common to all the teachers in my school. ....

7. I belong to the professional organizations—state, local, and national—which pertain to my area of teaching. ....

8. I participate actively in the professional organizations to which I belong. ....

9. Through supervision I have come to a more complete realization of the services offered by the professional organizations to which I belong. ....

Use of Physical Facilities

1. Supervision has helped me become more fully aware of the many services of the school plant, such as the library, gymnasium, professional library, or curriculum laboratory. ....

2. I know where to find and how to use effectively all the instructional materials provided by my school, such as maps, globes, duplicators, games, puzzles, and playground equipment. ....

3. I know where to find supplementary books of many kinds and can recognize the different reading levels of each kind. ....

4. Supervisory services have furnished me ready access to instructional supplies such as paper, paste, pencils, crayons, and workbooks. ....

5. I know where to locate and how to use the audio-visual equipment supplied by my school. ....

6. I feel perfectly free to request any type of materials that I may need for instructional purposes, even though money may not be available now to purchase this material. ....

Use of Community Resources

1. Through the efforts of my supervisor I have become better acquainted with my community as to economic structure, cultural level, and social strata. ....

2. The supervisory program has given every help needed in arranging for field trips to points of interest in the community. ....

3. Supervisory planning has supplied me with a list of desirable people in the community who possess special skills or interests which can be used in the classroom for instructional purposes. ....

4. I have become acquainted with the use of community resources in teaching through our supervisory program. ....

Improvement of Classroom Instruction

1. My supervisor has visited with me in my classroom at least once during the year. ....

2. When she came, my supervisor stayed in my classroom long enough to get an adequate picture of what I was trying to accomplish. ....

3. My supervisor has made this a pleasant year by providing the help that I requested, by listening to my problems and by being patient. ....

4. My supervisor has helped me in attempting to meet the needs of each individual child in my classroom. ....

5. My supervisor has helped me by offering suggestions where she thought they were needed but has always allowed me to use the methods that worked best for me. ....

Improvement of Total Program of Education

1. All the faculty and administration have been brought together with the supervisor at least once during the year for the purpose of defining specific goals for our students. ....

2. My supervisor has worked with my grade (or subject area) as a group for the purpose of setting up specific grade (or subject-area) goals. ....

3. My supervisor has helped me to carry out a systematic testing program in order that we may study the growth of my students. ....

For the use of the principals and administrative staff, a different kind of instrument was devised. This evaluation guide takes the positive approach, in which the administrator has to give examples or describe situations in which good supervision operated.

EVALUATION GUIDE FOR THE PRINCIPAL
AND ADMINISTRATIVE PERSONNEL

NOTE: The standards for this evaluation should be the objectives set up at the beginning of the year.

1. Give one specific illustration of help given to a teacher in promoting better understanding of the growth and development of students in each of the following areas:
   - a. Primary grades
   - b. Middle elementary grades
   - c. Upper elementary grades
2. Give an example of attitude changes which have taken place among students in one classroom in this building.
3. Give three illustrations of how the selection and use of instructional materials have been improved this year in this school.
4. Illustrate how a particular teacher's testing techniques have changed.
5. Cite a specific improvement in one area of instruction this year on the following grade levels:

1-2

3-4

5-6

6. List four ways in which community resources have been used to enrich the instructional program through teacher-pupil planned activities.
7. Have you observed that there is better rapport among your teachers this year? _____. If answer is "Yes," give a specific instance.
8. Do all the teachers in this building feel perfectly free to seek assistance from the supervisor? Yes_____ No_____ If "No," can you give a reason, or reasons?

The evaluation form suggested for use by the supervisors differed markedly in several ways from the instruments that the teachers and administrative staff were to use. It was emphasized that this report form was only a type of guide for recording supervisory activities of an individual and group nature.

In addition to this report form, the staff suggested that the supervisor also record throughout the year definite information on the following if they took place:

1. The fieldwork or extension courses that were offered by colleges, the name of the institution offering them, the purposes, the number attending these from various school units, and an assessment of the value of each course.

FORM FOR SUPERVISOR'S REPORT

Name _____ County or City _____ No. of Teachers
Elem. _____
Jr. H. _____
Sr. H. _____

Certificate Held _____ No. of Schools
Elem. _____
Jr. H. _____
Sr. H. _____

I. Visitation to Individual Teachers

School	Grade and/or Subject Area	Teacher's Name	Experience	Purpose	Comments	Follow-up, If Any

II. Group Conferences or Study Groups at School

School	Group (that is, Primary Teachers, English Teachers, Grade Mothers)	Purpose	Comments	Follow-up, If Any

2. The individual conferences which were requested by teachers, the purposes of these, the number which were held, and the time devoted to each.
3. The amount of demonstration teaching that the supervisor did or arranged for, the dates, the school in which each took place, the purpose, a list of those attending it, and the grade level or subject-matter area that was involved.
4. A list of the supervisory bulletins that were issued during the year, showing the purpose of each and to whom distributed. A copy of each bulletin should be attached to this report.
5. A description of the workshops or work conferences that were held during the year, the purpose of each, what decisions were reached, and the evaluation of the workshop by the participating teachers. A copy of each workshop program should be attached to this report.
6. An account of the measures taken by the supervisor for his own professional improvement throughout the year. This should include a record of professional meetings attended—state, regional, and national; membership and offices held in these organizations; and a description of any surveys, research, and publications.
7. A brief progress report in outline form of the long-range supervisory program, with indication of what parts of it were accomplished during this year.
8. The keeping of the supervisor's "log," a periodic recording of the supervisor's activities from time to time.

Most of the methods that have just been listed are familiar to supervisory personnel. Two of them, however, have developed remarkable possibilities for fairer evaluation of the supervisory program, namely, the supervisor's "log" and staff evaluation of the workshop or work conference. More extensive examples of the use of these two techniques will therefore be given here.

THE SUPERVISOR'S "LOG"

This running account of the supervisor's activities started in the early days of supervision when the supervisor was required to make a daily report on his visitations to different teachers. Just as the teacher had to have a daily lesson outline on his desk as evidence of his labors, so the supervisor had to record his visits and his comments as evidence of his effective work.

In the modern school the supervisor's log serves far different purposes. The supervisor uses it as an impartial record of what he saw happen, what he heard, and what he said at particular times. The written account can jog his memory about the first visit to this particular teacher or about the last visit. It will show what suggestions have already been made, or what joint decisions took place between teacher and supervisor. It will impersonally record more clearly than any other instrument the improvement or lack of improvement of an individual teacher. The samples that follow were taken with permission from the log of an elementary school supervisor in a small town. Other than changes in actual names of teachers, schools, and towns, the account is exactly as she wrote it.

Monday 10/5

Up early and at King St. [school] by 8:00. Watched the children gather; quite a bit of playing on grounds before school. [Mrs.] King and [Miss] White on duty early. Bell at 8:30; went in with children, who talked and buzzed happily. King had asked me to come over to watch her geography work in 7 [7th Grade]—she had been talking to me about learning something about unit teaching; didn't know how to start.

After children got settled, they exchanged news and experiences with K and each other for 10 min. Then Geo. class; were studying Central America. Big outline map on board; each pupil went up and wrote in a town or river or mt., and told something about it. K added info. at times. Assignment for next day, each of 30 pupils was given a slip of paper with name of a Central Amn. or So. Amn. leader on it, and book to look him up in; were to be ready to report on it tomorrow.

Talked briefly with K at end of period; I'd enjoyed the map work, & told her so. She wanted to see me Wed. after school, & I arranged to meet her here.

At 10:15 went by T's [the principal's] office—he wanted to see about ordering more supple. readers for grades 4-8. Spent 1½ hrs. with him, checked both state lists and library lists. He asked me to complete the order.

Lunch at 12:00 in the sch. cafeteria. Well behaved bunch of pupils. Teachers had separate room to eat in. 2 on duty each week in supervising children at lunch. Ate with K and W, who are close friends; they say that they went to same college & have taught in same school since then. W asked me to come by and spend the p.m. with her 5th G. Took her up—had a good time. She had a reading aloud period after lunch—she was reading a dog story to them. Then they had arithmetic drill period, with workbooks, and pupils at different places in the workbook, working alone, or with help from the teacher. Then they had free time period, could read or draw, or listen to the record player. Talked to some of the children—they were interested, knew what they were doing. After school, to office, taped this.

Wed. Oct. 7

Today I went with the high brass [Supt.] and a committee of sch. board on a tour of all the elementary schools. The bd. is looking at future bldg. needs, and wanted first-hand info. on conditions now. Went first to L [Lockwood], which has a principal, 12 teachers, a librarian, and a lunchroom and playroom combined. We went into every room and they talked with every teacher. We're crowded now, & next year there will have to be some double shifts until new building is built. They asked each teacher how she felt about the double shift, whether she would prefer to teach it or not, and what grades it would be wiser to have the double shifts in.

Was most interesting day; we covered all 3 schools and all teachers (in Emerywood School and Central, as well as Lockwood). I was surprised! More than ½ of them did not object to teaching on a double shift! Those who did, gave good reasons for wanting the longer day, such as home responsibilities, individual methods of teaching, distance they lived away from school. I was struck by K's answer—said she was just starting to improve her methods of teaching—*i.e., the unit,* and needed full time for herself to make the improvement, as well as full time for her pupils to master it with her!

Conference with K in p.m. after school. She had an outline of references for her first unit on "Natural Resources of Central America." It was good—she is on her way & I told her so. I suggested a few more, & we went to library to check exact chap. and p. refs. I learned from her to let her go at her own pace.

As the supervisor analyzes these two log accounts later in the year, he notes immediately that Mrs. King got started in improving her methods of teaching and worked at it consistently. He also sees the use that has to be made of supplementary materials in both descriptions. Two cautions have to be observed in the employment of the log or diary in evaluation: (1) the account must be impersonal and objective, and it must describe only what happened, what the persons actually said or did, not what the supervisor thinks motivated them to do or say something and (2) different supervisors follow different habits in keeping their logs. Some write one twice a week, some once a week, and a few write one for each day.

Staff Evaluation of the Workshop

Educators have made much progress in recent years in working co-operatively to solve common problems through group processes. The workshop or work conference is usually the medium for this kind of co-operative action. Evaluation of the workshop is one part of the evaluation of the supervisory program. Teachers make evaluative statements after the workshop is completed, or as a follow-up of the values of the workshop several months later. Reproduced here are: (1) a set of evaluative questions which workshop participants made out and answered about their workshop in 1958 and (2) a follow-up questionnaire for use later in the year 1958-1959 with the same participants.

EVALUATIVE QUESTIONS FOR WORKSHOP PARTICIPANTS

In the questions below circle the letter or letters which indicate the answer or answers most nearly correct for you.

1. Why did you participate in this workshop?
   a. required to, *b.* wanted to solve personal problems related to teaching, *c.* others were participating, so you did too, *d.* wanted to see how one worked.
2. Do you feel that the size of the group was:
   a. too large? *b.* just right? *c.* too small?
3. Throughout the workshop were the principles of organization:
   a. democratic, *b.* autocratic, *c.* other? (explain) _____
4. Was the workshop problem-centered?
   a. yes, *b.* no. If answer is "no," why? _____
5. Were the problems stated by your group clearly defined?
   a. yes, *b.* subject to varied interpretations, *c.* no one knew what the problems were.
6. Did you help set up the problems and goals of your group?
   a. yes, *b.* no. If answer is "no," why? _____
7. How interested were you in the problems and goals of your group?
   a. very much, *b.* somewhat, *c.* not much, *d.* not at all.
8. Did you find that a problem you considered only yours was common to others?
   a. yes, *b.* no.
9. In group meetings or activities did you feel that:
   a. one person monopolized the time, *b.* everybody participated, *c.* a few never participated, *d.* a few persons did it all, *e.* everyone hesitated to take part?

10. How often did you speak out in small group meetings?
    a. often, *b.* sometimes, *c.* seldom, *d.* never.

11. How did you think individual differences in your group affected the exchange of ideas—were group members:
    a. too different, *b.* different enough to promote interesting discussion, *c.* too similar?

12. In dealing with problems did your group stick to the point?
    a. always, *b.* usually, but allowed digressions when of general interest, *c.* sometimes, but often got lost in too many digressions, *d.* never.

13. Were general group meetings as valuable to you as small group meetings?
    a. as valuable, *b.* more valuable, *c.* less valuable, *d.* waste of time.

14. Did you have a planning committee to relate whole group work to the problems of small groups?
    a. yes, *b.* no.

15. In the whole or general group meetings were the problems discussed related to those of the small groups?
    a. closely related, *b.* loosely related, *c.* not at all related.

16. Did you feel that speakers and other general programs were of vital interest to:
    a. all members, *b.* many, *c.* few, *d.* none?

17. Were there opportunities for recreation and relaxation?
    a. often, a balance between work and play, *b.* too often, *c.* occasionally, *d.* never.

18. How many new friends did you make during the workshop?
    a. many, *b.* few, *c.* one.

19. Did you feel that the physical environment was:
    a. comfortable and attractive, *b.* uncomfortable, *c.* unattractive, *d.* crowded, *e.* too large?

20. Was the time allotted for the whole workshop:
    a. adequate for solving the problems, *b.* too short, *c.* too long, with much time wasted?

21. Was the time allotted for the small group meetings:
    a. adequate for solving the problems, *b.* too short, *c.* too long, with time wasted?

22. Was there a workshop library?
    a. yes, *b.* no. If answer is "yes," was it adequate? _____

23. Was the supply of informative material (books, pamphlets, periodicals):
    a. excellent, *b.* fair, *c.* limited, *d.* inadequate?

24. Did you feel that the materials for experimentation (construction materials, art media, etc.) were:
    a. excellent, *b.* fair, *c.* limited in quantity, *d.* inadequate?

25. How did you feel about experimenting with new materials and ideas?
    a. unrestrained, *b.* timid, *c.* inhibited.

26. Did you do free reading pertinent to the problems studied?
    a. often, *b.* sometimes, *c.* never.

27. Were staff members, specialists, and resource people available when you needed them?

    a. usually, *b.* sometimes, *c.* never.

28. Do you feel that your group reached the objectives and solved the problems you set up?

    a. as well as you had hoped, *b.* as well as possible, *c.* incompletely, *d.* not at all.

29. How often did you consider your own progress in attaining group and personal goals?

    a. daily, *b.* weekly, *c.* only at the end, *d.* never.

30. How often did your group evaluate its progress?

    a. daily, *b.* weekly, *c.* only at the end, *d.* never.

31. Has the workshop experience changed your attitudes about teaching methods?

    a. about several, *b.* about a few, *c.* about one, *d.* about none.

32. How many new methods or techniques did you learn that you are eager to try?

    a. some, *b.* few, *c.* none.

33. How do you feel about your own problems in teaching since this experience?

    a. much better, *b.* a little better, *c.* no different, *d.* worse.

34. After this experience how do you feel about working with groups—do you feel

    a. that you can always get more done individually, *b.* that people usu-ally profit by an exchange of ideas, *c.* that group work is usually a waste of time, *d.* that a balance between group work and individual work is best in most situations?

35. On the whole, how do you feel about having participated in this workshop?

    a. very glad you did, *b.* too tired to enjoy it, *c.* not very enthusiastic, *d.* could have spent the time to better advantage elsewhere.

36. Describe briefly one thing you learned that was new to you or that was a better way of doing something.

37. Make any remarks you care to about the workshop and what it meant to you, or how it could have been improved.

FOLLOW-UP QUESTIONNAIRE FOR WORKSHOP PARTICIPANTS

The true value of a workshop lies not so much in the enthusiastic plans made during the meeting as in the subsequent effect it will have upon the participant's attitude and teaching during the following school terms. The check list below is designed to be used three to six months later in an attempt to determine the "carry-over" value of the workshop.

To the teacher: In the following questions circle the letter which most accurately fits your case.

1. Have you put into practice new techniques discussed during the workshop?
     a. several, b. one, c. none.
2. To what extent have you found these techniques effective?
     a. very effective, b. somewhat effective, c. not effective.
3. To what extent has your classroom instruction been enriched?
     a. greatly, b. somewhat, c. none.
4. Has the enthusiasm created by your participation in the workshop:
     a. increased, b. survived, c. died?
5. To what extent have you been active in implementing the new ideas and suggestions into your school program?
     a. very active, b. moderately active, c. inactive.
6. Do you feel that you have grown professionally as a result of your experience?
     a. definitely, b. somewhat, c. a little.
7. In what areas have you found the workshop most beneficial? Underscore all areas in which you have benefited; underscore *twice* those in which you benefited most.
     a. Use and acquisition of professional library and materials
     b. Leadership in work conferences
     c. Methods and techniques
     d. Social and professional contacts
     e. Classroom management
     f. Creativity and initiation of new activities
     g. Planning and organizing materials and activities
     h. Understanding of pupils
     i. Security in trying out new ideas
8. Has the administration become more aware of your competences and made use of them?
     a. noticeable increase, b. slight increase, c. none.
9. Describe briefly one new idea that you have tried that was a direct outgrowth of the workshop: _____

These questions for workshop participants cover such a wide range for voluntary reply without necessity for signature that the supervisor and the staff are likely to get a much clearer picture of what teachers are doing and thinking all over the school system. It is agreed generally that each work group should make out its own forms for evaluation, not use forms made out by others. There is also general agreement that the questions should be aimed at evaluation of the workshop and its effects and not aimed at participants in the workshop. It is good practice, too, after the second workshop is held to compare its results with those of the first, and so on.

Evaluation's Enlarging Scope

Modern supervision has to continue to produce results to justify its retention in the organizational structure of the school. How can it do this most effectively? How can it "earn its keep?" Be evaluated? One way it can be evaluated is by discovering the position that the supervisor and his services occupy in the eyes of the school personnel. Good supervision in a school system makes every superintendent, every principal, every teacher, every specialist feel that supervision is too valuable a service to do without, that it helps each one of these school personnel to do a better job. One can identify the various ways by which good supervisors have helped each of these groups to do a better job of instruction, ways which promise much for the future.

CONTINUED HELP FOR TEACHERS

The kind of education supervision can provide for teachers has proved sound. It should take a place of prominence in the future, because it has been effective (1) in training temporary or emergency teachers and substitutes, (2) in helping beginning teachers to orient themselves and to continue their education, and (3) in stimulating regular staff members to improve themselves. Types of the more effective methods for in-service education have been the workshop and the work conference; the co-operative arrangements between school systems and higher institutions for the training of teachers in service; the preschool work conference for the school staff; the co-operative development by a school staff of scope and sequence in the curriculum program; system-wide curriculum study, or study of its program by the staff of an individual school; the growth in understanding and use of group processes; and the meetings and work sessions of professional educational groups concerned with school problems on both the state and national levels.

SERVICES FOR SCHOOL ADMINISTRATORS

For years superintendents and principals have been administering large-scale testing programs in their schools, have been filing the test results carefully in each pupil's permanent record folder, and have been doing little or nothing about using these test results effectively to help the individual pupil to make better progress in

school. During the last decade, supervisors have been the group responsible primarily for helping administrators to utilize these test
results for more effective teaching. For example, elementary principals learn from the supervisor how groupings within the classroom
can be made from the results of reading or arithmetic readiness
tests; how slow readers can be identified and aided on aspects which
need remedying; how retarded readers may be identified, and how
they can be aided by newer textbooks with simplified vocabularies;
and how pupils of promise who learn faster can be challenged by
the use of supplementary or advanced materials to master.

The superintendent discovers that the supervisor is invaluable to him as a resource person, too, in addition to acting as a
liaison agent with the rest of the staff. He now has definite information on the progress of instruction in each school unit, thanks to
the new type of report form made out by the supervisor and the
principals, and which each principal has to make at the end of
each school year. He also realizes how valuable are (1) the list and
summary of the new texts and materials which the supervisor prepares for him and the staff each year and (2) the lists of the new
teaching aids and equipment that the supervisor recommends as
necessary for effective teaching. He is most appreciative of the
total picture of the school which the supervisor's annual report
gives him, showing plans at the beginning of the year, what has
been accomplished, and the unsolved or new problems facing them
for the next year.

HELP FOR SCHOOL SPECIALISTS

Supervision in the future should continue to serve this group
of school personnel most effectively. The wise supervisor for some
time now has been operating to give these specialists both status
and a sense of security as well as of usefulness. One example is
found in guidance on the secondary school level, where the supervisor helps the principal and teachers to realize how rich is the store
of information which the guidance officer has accumulated on each
pupil and how other school personnel can make maximum use of
this in counseling pupils. Another illustration comes from the area
of music, in which the music specialist and the supervisor co-operate
closely to make all teachers conscious of every child's love of music

and how it is related to most other subject areas in one way or another. The library and the librarian furnish still another example of the value of the supervisor to the specialist. Real librarians want the library to be used; and they welcome ways to improve its usefulness. When the supervisor helps to make the teachers in a school "library-conscious," the librarian in turn sings the praises of the supervisor; co-operation breeds co-operation and gratitude.

The writer found little written material in regard to student or pupil opinion of the supervisory program. Pupils have so little continued contact with the supervisor that their opinions concerning the services that are rendered would seem to be of doubtful value.

High morale is found among a staff when they work consciously to improve their teaching practices and tools. In like manner, a supervisor's morale remains high only when he works constantly to improve his methods and services. Evaluation of his program is a necessary step in this improvement.

Problems for Individual Study and Class Discussion

1. Can the supervisor make out by himself a statement of purposes for his supervisory program that would be satisfactory? Or must he have the aid of the teachers to do this? Support your point of view.
2. What steps would you take with the help of the school librarian to make out a series of questions that would reveal how valuable the library had been in the supervisory program for the year?
3. Is it better for a school staff to concentrate on two or three big objectives for the year, or should there be a large number of purposes smaller in scope? Explain.
4. Would you replace the faculty meeting in the supervisory program with the group or work conference? What evidence do you have to make a comparative evaluation of the two?
5. Should the supervisor and the staff members who use the unit method of teaching construct an instrument for evaluating the success of unit teaching? Why or why not?
6. Would you give equal weight to each individual staff member's evaluation of the supervisory program, or not? Why or why not?
7. What kind of evidence for evaluating the program would the supervisor get from the list of individual conferences requested by teachers during the year?
8. Write out an impersonal account or log of your last visit to another teacher. How factual was your description? How impartial?

9. Can you establish a set of principles that will guide you in taking from your log accounts the facts and information that should go into your yearly supervisory report to the superintendent? Explain.

Additional Selected References for Problem or Unit Study

Adams, H. P., and Dickey, F. G., *Basic Principles of Supervision* (New York: American Book Company, 1953), ch. XII and appendixes A and B.

American Association of School Administrators, *The Superintendent as Instructional Leader,* Thirty-Fifth Yearbook (Washington: American Association of School Administrators, 1957), ch. XI.

Association for Supervision and Curriculum Development, *Creating a Good Environment for Learning,* 1954 Yearbook, ch. X, and *Leadership for Improving Instruction,* 1960 Yearbook, ch. VI (Washington, D. C.: National Education Association).

Ayer, F. C., *Fundamentals of Instructional Supervision* (New York: Harper and Brothers, 1954), ch. XXII.

Boardman, C. W., and others, *Democratic Supervision in Secondary Schools* (Boston: Houghton Mifflin Company, 1953), ch. XXI.

Burton, W. H., and Brueckner, L. J., *Supervision: A Social Process* (New York: Appleton-Century-Crofts, Inc., 1955), ch. XVIII.

Cramer, R. V., and Domian, O. E., *Administration and Supervision in the Elementary School* (New York: Harper and Brothers, 1960), ch. XV.

Crosby, M., *Supervision Is Co-operative Action* (New York: Appleton-Century-Crofts, Inc., 1957), ch. XVIII.

Elsbree, W. S., and McNally, H. J., *Elementary School Administration and Supervision,* 2nd ed. (New York: American Book Company, 1959), ch. X.

Franseth, J., *Supervision in Rural Schools,* Bulletin 1955, No. 11 (Washington, D. C.: U. S. Department of Health, Education, and Welfare), III-IV.

Hammock, R. C., and Owings, R. S., *Supervising Instruction in Secondary Schools* (New York: McGraw-Hill Book Company, Inc., 1955), ch. X.

Hicks, H. J., *Educational Supervision in Principle and Practice* (New York: The Ronald Press Company, 1960), ch. XV.

Huggett, A. J., and Stinnett, T. M., *Professional Problems of Teachers* (New York: The Macmillan Company, 1956), ch. XII.

Mackenzie, G. N., Corey, S. M., and associates, *Instructional Leadership* (New York: Teachers College, Columbia University, 1954), ch. VIII and appendix.

O'Rourke, M. A., and Burton, W. H., *Workshops for Teachers* (New York: Appleton-Century-Crofts, Inc., 1957), ch. V.

Shane, H. G., and Yauch, W. A., *Creative School Administration* (New York: Henry Holt and Company, Inc., 1954), ch. V.

Shuster, A. H., and Wetzler, W. F., *Leadership in Elementary School Administration and Supervision* (Boston: Houghton Mifflin Company, 1958), ch. XIII.

Spears, H., *Improving the Supervision of Instruction* (Englewood Cliffs, N. J.: Prentice-Hall, Inc., 1953), chs. X, XX-XXI.

Wiles, K., *Supervision for Better Schools,* 2nd ed. (Englewood Cliffs, N. J.: Prentice-Hall, Inc., 1955), chs. XIII-XIV and appendixes B, C, D, and E.

Wiles, K., Brown, C., and Cassidy, R., *Supervision in Physical Education* (Englewood Cliffs, N. J.: Prentice-Hall, Inc., 1956), ch. XIII.

CHAPTER 20

Teacher and Merit Rating

in Supervision

SYSTEMATIC EVALUATION of instruction in public schools is necessary. Such a process is of value both to the teacher and the school system. Evidence of the need to appraise teaching is found in the results of recent research. The pilot studies of the Co-operative Program in Educational Administration and the co-operative action research on the group dynamics approach of the Association for Supervision and Curriculum Development have both supported this premise.

On the other hand, the situation that prevailed in the 1920's still exists—no clear distinction has been drawn between teacher evaluation and the appraisal of instruction, between rating a teacher for salary purposes and judging instructional strengths and weaknesses for purposes of promoting improvement or identifying appropriate assignments. Opposition by teachers to any form of merit rating on the one hand is pitted against strong support for differentiated salaries and assignments from school boards members on the other; this situation has provoked a nation-wide controversy that must be studied by those engaged in supervision.

Merit Rating in American Culture

The United States Civil Service Commission, the military forces, industry, and the civil service commissions of state, county, and city governments support functioning merit systems. Certain officers, usually administrative or supervisory personnel, are charged with the duty and responsibility of judging the caliber of work being performed by a subordinate. Almost all of the systems for rating employees utilize an instrument that serves the dual purpose of standardizing the evaluation process and of making the ratings a semipermanent record. These instruments have varying titles such as "Rating Report," "Effectiveness Record," "Efficiency Report," or "Performance Report." The type of instrument most frequently used is a kind of graphic scale which provides the rater with a varied list of characteristics of either the job or the person. Each trait is usually defined; and space is provided to indicate several levels of performance, which are also defined. The rater has only to observe critically and estimate the performance level impartially, either on the basis of a spot-check or over a prolonged period of observation. Common concerns of all agencies using a merit system are the validity, reliability, applicability, simplicity, and flexibility of the instrument in use.

Simply defined, merit rating is the systematic evaluation of an individual's "job performance." Job performance is usually rated in the light of the description of the job—job analysis—and those knowledges, skills, and characteristics which one must possess in order to do the job.

The rating of employees appears to be standard procedure for almost all agencies of government. More specifically, these procedures are applied to the majority of employees, with the exception of elected and appointed officers. The United States Civil Service efficiency report is undoubtedly used to judge more persons than any other instrument. Despite its general use, those familiar with it still feel that it can be improved. This instrument consists primarily of a graphic rating scale which lists 31 items and provides for evaluation on three levels of performance. The Commission has provided an excellent handbook to guide the raters. The Hoover Commission was evidently not impressed with this system; it recommended that these records be used primarily for employee improvement, and not for salary increases, lay-off, or dismissal; it also suggested that the rating scale be replaced by a system of annual written evaluations.

At the state and local levels of government, including school systems, there is little standardization of rating procedures. Each civil service commission is an agency of the unit which established it. Most of these commissions have set up a single effectiveness report in the form of a graphic scale; annual or semiannual ratings have to be made on this scale. The California Civil Service Commission has done an outstanding job in developing some 45 scales for different job fields. Certain other municipal, county, and state agencies employ multiple instruments, but their use is not general.

The fields of recreation and social work have met with little success in developing merit systems adapted particularly to their types of work. For the most part, they are controlled and rated within the system provided by the civil service commission of the level of government of which they are a part.

Industrial merit rating plans are a responsibility of the individual company or corporation. Rating systems are employed widely and seem to be gaining in use. This popularity is accounted for by three factors: (1) Industry has money to support extensive personnel departments; (2) Labor organizations demand proof of incompetency before an employee is reduced in rank, laid off, or fired; and (3) A greater concern for the worker has been found to be good for business. Through their trained personnel departments, industry has encouraged experimentation with merit rating systems. The types of instruments in use are the chart, the graphic scale, the order of merit scale, the forced-choice type, and the man-to-man and paired comparison systems.

The military forces require annual rating of every person in uniform, and a separate rating when association with the immediate commanding officer is severed. These ratings are important considerations in promotion and reassignment. The standard instrument is a graphic rating scale listing a few personality traits and personal abilities to be graded on five levels of performance. Enlisted personnel are rated from superior to unsatisfactory on character and job performance ability only. In 1955 the Air Force extended the graphic scale system to include the higher ranks of enlisted personnel.

Toward the close of World War II the Army began using a forced-choice system of selecting reserve officers for retention in the service; this form was developed by the Personnel Research Section of the Adjutant General's office and will be illustrated later.

There is general agreement in those sections of our government which use merit rating systems that systematic rating should take place. Employees are necessarily evaluated, and it is only fair that the method used be as unprejudiced, objective, valid, and uniform as possible. Only a small amount of criticism of rating, if much exists, finds its way into the professional literature. There are, however, several trends that are apparent.[1]

1. The person is being rated rather than the job. In general, the traits listed on the rating scale emphasize co-operation, special knowledge, leadership ability, reliability, and physical and emotional condition.
2. Ratings are becoming more evaluative in nature. Three level scales—outstanding, satisfactory, and unsatisfactory—are becoming more prevalent. This eliminates the feature of comparing employees with one another.
3. Mechanical scoring systems and scales are being replaced by written reports supported by anecdotal evidence.
4. Summary ratings are being eliminated, and a conference with the employee is directed toward encouraging self-improvement in specific areas.

The Status of Teacher Rating in Supervision

Supervisors entered the educational hierarchy as administrative assistants. This administrative heritage, their confidence in their ability to recognize good teaching, their daily contact with the classroom teachers and teaching, and the inspectional philosophy of supervision which existed in the earlier days made them a logical choice for the duty of rating teachers. During this same period, educational scientists and theorists were developing promising instruments to measure teaching efficiency. The adage that "what exists, exists in some quantity and can be measured" was considered to be equally as applicable to teacher efficiency as to building adequacy or pupil achievement. Needless to say, administrators wel-

---

[1] This introductory section is based, in large part, upon the presentations given in the following books and periodicals: William E. Mosher, J. Donald Kingsley, and Q. Glen Stahl, *Public Personnel Administration*, 3rd ed. (New York: Harper and Brothers, 1950); *Proceedings of the Annual Conference on Public Personnel Administration* (Chicago: Civil Service Assembly); *Public Personnel Review;* George D. Butler, *Playgrounds: Their Administration and Operation*, rev. ed. (New York: A. S. Barnes and Company, 1950); *Recreation;* Joseph Tiffin, *Industrial Psychology*, 3rd ed. (Englewood Cliffs, N. J.: Prentice-Hall, Inc., 1952); and Dale Yoder, *Personnel Management and Industrial Relations* (Englewood Cliffs, N. J.: Prentice-Hall, Inc., 1942).

comed this new promised objectivity in the appraisal of teaching, as well as the personnel to implement it.

Earlier changes. In 1920 Fannie Dunn reported that a distinction between the duties and functions of supervisors and those of administrators was needed.[2] Every function was somewhere performed both by the superintendent and the supervisor, but certain functions were more frequently performed by each. Those more frequently performed by the supervisor dealt with supervising instruction and with the in-service improvement of the teachers. This statement summarizes her description of instructional supervision at that time:

> The primary function of supervision is to discover teacher potentialities and develop them; to improve the quality of instruction by promoting professional growth; secondarily, to correct teacher deficiencies by in-service training. Observation and rating are for the purpose of diagnosis. Diagnosis is to allow for co-operative planning for improvement.

The typical approach to rating in the 1920's and 1930's emphasized the process of rating and rating instruments as resources of supervision; the stress was on the co-operative use of these tools by both teacher and supervisor, on the in-service training value of analyzing and using existing rating scales for teacher self-analysis, and on the co-operative construction of a scale for local use. This concept was reflected in textbooks from 1922 to 1938.[3]

[2] Fannie Dunn, "What Is Instructional Supervision?" *Addresses and Proceedings of the Sixty-First Annual Meeting* (Washington, D. C.: National Education Association, 1923), vol. 61, pp. 758-764.

[3] William H. Burton, *Supervision and the Improvement of Teaching* (New York: D. Appleton and Company, 1923); A. S. Barr and William H. Burton, *The Supervision of Instruction* (New York: D. Appleton and Company, 1926); Fred C. Ayer and A. S. Barr, *The Organization of Supervision* (New York: D. Appleton and Company, 1928); George C. Kyte, *How to Supervise* (Boston: Houghton Mifflin Company, 1930); John R. Clement and James H. Clement, *Co-operative Supervision* (New York: The Century Company, 1930); Arthur A. Gist, *The Administration of Supervision* (New York: Charles Scribner's Sons, 1934); Harl R. Douglass and Charles W. Boardman, *Supervision in Secondary Schools* (Boston: Houghton Mifflin Company, 1934); Thomas H. Briggs, *Improving Instruction* (New York: The Macmillan Company, 1938); Samuel Smith and Robert K. Speer, *Supervision in the Elementary School* (New York: The Cordon Company, 1938); and A. S. Barr, William H. Burton, and Leo J. Brueckner, *Supervision* (New York: D. Appleton-Century Company, 1938). For a detailed treatment of the distinction between administrative and supervisory rating, the reader is referred to Barr and Burton, *The Supervision of Instruction, op. cit.*

THE CONTINUING CONTROVERSY OVER MERIT RATING

Except in its earliest days, merit rating has never received wholehearted approval and acceptance by teachers, supervisors, or administrators. The controversy over whether teachers and teaching can be evaluated fairly by a rating system continues. For example, articles such as C. Currien Smith's "Why Teachers Dislike Merit Rating"[4] and the American Federation of Teachers' statement "Dangerous Mirage or Master Plan?"[5] and editorial appeals on the theme "Injustice of Teacher Pay: Good Bad and Indifferent"[6] appear almost monthly. A recent book by the dean of a leading School of Education opposes merit salary schedules.[7]

The Research Division of the National Education Association reported that at the beginning of the 1960's a slight trend had developed toward providing increased salary for quality of service, with one in six urban school districts making such recognition to teachers.[8] At the same time, its conclusions were that the practice of merit pay is questioned by teachers and that the issue is being sidestepped by administrators. Both the National Educational Association and the powerful American Association of School Administrators have considered whether to support plans to provide higher pay for excellence in teaching. As yet neither has done so; but both have authorized the continued study of the issue.[9]

The controversy that has always surrounded merit rating now appears to focus around three rather clearly defined propositions: (1) Systematic evaluation, (merit rating) is necessary and valuable to the teacher and to the school program; this statement implies

[4] C. Currien Smith, "Why Teachers Dislike Merit Rating," *Overview,* vol. 1 (February, 1960), pp. 41-44.

[5] American Federation of Teachers, Research Department, "Dangerous Mirage or Master Plan?" *The Education Digest,* vol. 24 (February, 1959), pp. 6-9.

[6] Editorial in *The Evening News,* Harrisburg, Pa. (February 22, 1960).

[7] Virgil M. Rogers, *Do We Want Merit Salary Schedules?* (Syracuse: University of Syracuse Press, 1960).

[8] National Education Association, "Salary Provisions for Quality Service," *Research Bulletin,* vol. 37 (December, 1959), pp. 106-110.

[9] For extensive treatment of merit rating, the reader should consult: David V. Tiedeman, ed., *Teacher Competence and Its Relation to Salary* (Cambridge, Mass.: The New England School Development Council, 1956); Paul J. Misner, "The Merit Rating Issue," *Seven Studies* (Evanston, Ill.: National School Board Association, Inc., 1958), pp. 42-55. Two older, yet definitive, studies are William C. Reavis and Dan H. Cooper, *Evaluation of Teacher Merit in City School Systems* (Chicago: University of Chicago Press, 1945), and Dwight E. Beecher, *The Evaluation of Teaching* (Syracuse: Syracuse University Press, 1949).

that any qualified professional personnel should be utilized in the process; (2) Merit rating is a function of school administration, and the performance of this duty by supervisory personnel seriously interferes with the human relationships necessary to proper functioning of the total supervisory program; and (3) Merit rating is incompatible with the emerging democratic philosophy of school administration; it should be replaced by democratic co-operative evaluation. Analysis of the literature reveals sound arguments for each position.

1. *Systematic evaluation is necessary.* State or municipal law, school board regulations, public demand, administrative fiat, and tradition would seem to cover all of the situations which demand the operation of a merit system. Those who favor some sort of systematic merit rating call attention to the fact that school administrators and supervisors should establish and test out the best instruments available before states or cities force them to do so by law. An example of such a state law is that of New York (1947), which based salary supplements in part on merit rating; there was strong opposition to this statute.[10] The decision to require systematic evaluation in each case is based on the purported values to be derived from measuring teacher efficiency. There appears to be general unanimity among proponents of merit rating as to what these values are, as this list indicates. In summary, the situations which require systematic teacher appraisal are the following:

1. Decisions to grant, or to remove from tenure.
2. Determination of salary.
3. Determining advancement not only for promotion in the administrative hierarchy, but also in the selection of individual teachers for special projects.
4. Stimulation of teacher growth.
5. Protection of the teacher against injustice, caprice, ill-formed judgments, and antagonistic minority pressures.
6. Administrative reports to higher officers and the public.
7. Protection of the pupil against the hazards of poor teaching.
8. Identification of better teaching.

Since World War II, there has been an increase in the number of articles in the periodical literature which deal with merit rating.[11]

[10] " 'Superior Merit' Rating," *American Teacher*, vol. 32 (October, 1947), p. 34.
[11] Robert C. Hanes, *A Study of Trends and Changes in Secondary School Supervision from 1925 to Mid-Century.* Unpublished master's thesis, Chapel Hill, University of North Carolina, 1954, p. 72.

This probably reflects an increasing incidence of merit rating systems, mentioned by Roma Gans.[12] Chief among the added values recently claimed for merit rating is the mobility of the teaching population, which necessitates records to provide a basis for administrative recommendations or to aid the administrator in helping a new staff member or beginning teacher. Tompkins and Armstrong,[13] reviewing the literature on teacher rating over a 22-year period (1929–1951) found that probationary and experienced teachers are frequently treated differently. The probationer is being appraised for ability and signs of growth prior to permanent appointment; on the other hand, the emphasis in the case of the experienced teacher is primarily on stimulating him toward greater effectiveness.

2. *Merit rating is a function of school administration, not of supervision.* Ever since merit rating was introduced, there has been much written in the literature about the fact that the effective supervisor has to be divorced from the administrative responsibilities of "hiring and firing" teaching personnel. If a teacher's promotion, for example, is to be based upon the supervisor's ratings over a period of a year, then the supervisor tends to become an administrative official rather than a person whose prime responsibility is to help the teacher to improve in service. A well-established theory now is that if the supervisor and teacher make use co-operatively of rating devices, it should be for the purpose of the teacher's individual improvement in one respect or another.

3. *Merit rating is incompatible with the emerging democratic philosophy of school administration.* This latest concept is illustrated well by the position taken in 1950 by the Association for Supervision and Curriculum Development of the National Education Association. Here is the Association's definition of "rating" and of "merit rating": [14]

Rating: A subjective, qualitative judgment of a teacher given by a rater (principal, supervisor, superintendent, or board of education) without the participation of the rated person. It may or may not determine

[12] Roma Gans, "How Evaluate Teachers?" *Educational Leadership,* vol. VIII (November, 1950), pp. 77-81.

[13] Ellsworth Tompkins and W. Earl Armstrong, "Teacher Rating: Persistent Dilemma," *Bulletin of the National Association of Secondary School Principals,* vol. XXV (May, 1951), p. 28.

[14] Used with permission from Association for Supervision and Curriculum Development, Commission on Teacher Evaluation, *Better Than Rating* (Washington, D. C.: National Education Association, 1950), pp. 8-9.

salary. It can be one of several types, from ranking of teachers in sequential order to an elaborate check list. Even when the check list has been democratically developed, it is *rating* if it involves a one-way judgment.

Merit rating: A subjective, qualitative judgment made by a rater without the participation and with or without the knowledge of the person rated for purposes of determining salary, promotion or reward. The only difference betwen rating and merit rating is that "merit rating" is tied to the question of salary. Both these terms imply something done *to* a teacher *by* someone else in a superior-rating-inferior relationship.

In 1948, the annual meeting of the Association for Supervision and Curriculum Development voted to adopt the following resolution, which admits that teaching competence must be identified by some form of evaluation:

We deeply appreciate the increased financial support the public is giving to assure better teaching services to the children and youth of America. Recognizing the importance of evaluating educational services we do, however, oppose the use of administrative ratings of teaching personnel at either local or state level because such practices are undemocratic, ineffective, and destructive of good human relations. We, therefore, propose that ASCD establish a commission to seek and develop procedures by which the teaching profession can democratically further and recognize teaching competence.[15]

The Association for Supervision and Curriculum Development has not yet, however, presented definite procedures to be used for the appraisal of teacher worth; the Association has contented itself with presenting several principles around which such a plan could be developed. It is to be hoped that this organization will do further work on identification of both teacher competence and instruments for systematic evaluation of teaching, similar to the study of teacher competence being conducted jointly by the American Association of School Administrators, the N.E.A. Department of Classroom Teachers, and the National School Boards Association.

CRITICISM OF MERIT RATING

Writers in supervision differ widely in regard to their attitudes toward merit rating, just as teachers, supervisors, and administrators

[15] *Ibid.*, p. 6. Used with permission of Association for Supervision and Curriculum Development.

do.[16] Some reject rating as unsatisfactory on all counts, and indicate that it is an administrative device that is a hindrance to the improvement of instruction. Kimball Wiles is a writer who illustrates this position; he interprets supervision as instructional leadership and indicates that the most satisfactory instrument for improving instruction is the effective use of group processes and research. E. H. Reeder also rejects merit rating because of its destructive reaction upon a satisfactory supervisor-teacher relationship.

On the other hand, some authors recognize distinct diagnostic advantages and values in the employment of rating instruments. William H. Burton, Harl Douglass, and Charles W. Boardman take this point of view. As a group, authors of books on supervision recognize, without positive approval or disapproval, that teacher rating is being done by both administrative and supervisory personnel. Since this is so, an analysis of the types of criticisms of merit rating and teacher rating is pertinent here.

Criticisms of merit rating conveniently arrange themselves into three categories: criticism of the theory, of the rating or evaluating instrument, and of the rater or evaluator. The professional literature since the early 1920's abounds in specific attacks against ratings based on both empirical reasoning and research findings. Without any attempt to be exhaustive or scientific, those criticisms which seem to occur most frequently are listed here in summary form:

Criticisms of the Theory:

1. Rating is undemocratic, that is, it is done to the teacher, emphasizing individual, rather than group accomplishment.
2. Rating is psychologically unsound, that is, it poses a threat to the security and mental health of the teacher, thus disrupting interstaff relationships.
3. Rating is unnecessary, that is, it is not necessary because adequate evidence of proficiency can be secured by other means.
4. Rating is technically unsound, that is, it does not measure the teacher's worth; it measures the process of teaching, not the product. Furthermore, it tends to standardize the process of teaching.

[16] The bibliography at the end of this chapter lists specific references from recent authors on supervision in regard to merit rating and systematic evaluation of teaching.

Criticisms of the Instrument:

1. The scales or instruments do not eliminate subjectivity; they merely convert subjective judgments into a quantitative score.
2. Items listed on the scales are not necessarily measurements of teaching effectiveness and vary greatly in significance.
3. Scales are not conducive to continuous evaluation.
4. Uniform interpretation of the scale items is impossible.

Criticisms of the Rater or Evaluator:

1. Raters are subject to the universal error of personal bias, that is, toward either leniency or severity.
2. Evaluators are subject to the error of "central tendency," that is, hesitancy to use the extreme ends of the scales.
3. Raters are subject to "logical error"; that is, the evaluator presupposes a general ability level because of inability to isolate and identify individual traits.
4. Raters are subject to the error of the "halo" effect; that is, high or low rating in a specific trait is reflected in the judgment of all traits.

Principles That Should Be Employed in Any Rating System

Evidence has already been introduced to show that the appraisal of teaching is necessary, that rating and merit rating in education are very controversial, and that rating is being used by both administrators and supervisors. In the light of these facts, the probability is that many supervisors will continue to be associated with some sort of a rating system regardless of their personal preference. Therefore, they should endeavor to see that the system conforms to those sound principles which have been developed, namely: (1) Teachers should either be made well acquainted with or assist in the development of the evaluating criteria; (2) Teachers should also participate in the rating process so that improvement becomes a personal challenge; (3) As many ratings as practical, made by more than one person, should compose the final evaluation; (4) A conference in which the individual's strengths and weaknesses are discussed should follow each rating; and (5) The rating system should be tailored to accomplish specific purposes; the degree of distinction in the ratings made should be only so fine as necessary to fulfill the purposes of the rating.

Finally, the teacher should be encouraged to construct and use a self-rating scale. The professional literature has no record of opposition to the idea that teacher self-improvement can be one successful result of self-analysis. Almost all of the scales developed for supervisory and administrative use claim self-diagnosis as one of the basic values to be derived from using the instrument. As in-service training devices, these instruments undoubtedly focus attention on the traits, qualities, and practices considered important to effective teaching per se. In the use of scales, whether ready-built or "homemade," precautions should be taken to prevent the two objections to self-evaluation made by V. T. Thayer in 1926,[17] namely, (1) self-evaluation with a rating scale focuses attention on only the most obvious factors in the teacher or teaching situation and (2) the attention of the teacher is distributed over a multitude of items, whereas improvement requires concentration in one or two significant problem areas.

With some knowledge of the characteristics of scales, and possibly using one or two as a model, the teacher should find little difficulty in developing an instrument. It is the function of the supervisor to encourage and help the *interested* teacher to make a rating scale as part of the job of stimulating teacher growth. Special attention should be given (1) to aiding the teacher in identifying the particular areas that need immediate improvement most and (2) to holding down the size of the instrument so that it will not be filled with unimportant minutiae; its use should not become a chore. A good length would seem to be of approximately 10 or 12 items.

The self-made scale can be as detailed and applicable to the teacher's particular problem area as the insight of the teacher allows. For example, an area selected for improvement—such as "providing for individual differences"—could be broken down into such items as "Do I provide supplementary readers for the interests and reading level of each pupil?" and "Did every pupil get a chance to be successful today?"

Self-constructed scales promise more for self-improvement than either published scales or co-operatively developed instruments because they make the teacher, and the teacher alone, responsible for progress; they cease to be an administrative device and become a

17 V. T. Thayer, "Teacher Rating in the Secondary Schools," *Educational Administration and Supervision,* vol. XII (September, 1926), pp. 376-377.

personal tool. The fact that the scale becomes a personal responsibility of the teacher, however, does not in any way relieve the supervisor of his responsibility for assistance in both the construction and effective use of the instrument.

Types of Rating Instruments

Any instrument used in rating must be constructed on the basis of the job requirements and the eventual use of the ratings. For example, the specific knowledges, skills, and qualities most desirable in a primary teacher could be different from those most desirable in the teacher of a junior high school core program or in the senior high school mathematics teacher. The rating scale should reflect these differences. Similarly, a rating instrument to discover prevalent teacher weaknesses that can form the basis for an in-service training program could be quite different from the instrument used if the rank order of effective teachers is desired.

There are seven easily identifiable rating or merit rating systems in common use. Each has its advantages and disadvantages even when being used in the most favorable situation. They include:

> Chart System
> Graphic Rating Scale System
> Order of Merit System
> Paired Comparisons System
> Forced-Choice System
> Differentiated Use of Teacher Competence
> Qualitative Description with Anecdotal Illustrations

CHART SYSTEM

This system includes a check list of traits, statements, or questions which characterize job performance. The rater or supervisor merely checks off those qualities which characterize the job performance of the individual. The chief advantage of this system is its simplicity. It is easy to use, and the results are easy to interpret. The qualities are either checked off if present or left blank if absent. The score is the total number of items checked. Obviously, the value of this scale is largely determined by the merit and applicability of the statements.

As usually employed, the chart system does not recognize the quality of any of the traits possessed; neither does it indicate any relative value for them. For example, is a "well-modulated voice" as important to teaching effectiveness as "impartiality"? Or, is an impartial teacher 100 per cent impartial? Some chart systems attempt to minimize these weaknesses through scoring variations; degree of possession is indicated roughly by using the numbers 1, 2, or 3; and specific weights are assigned to each trait.

The use of the chart system in merit rating is declining, primarily because better instruments have been developed and are now available.

GRAPHIC RATING SCALE SYSTEM

This system is an extension of the chart system. A rating scale has been added to provide a score, or a score and a profile, for each person rated. The addition to this scale of a section which shows whether the rater had ample opportunity to observe the person results in a much improved instrument. (See Fig. 18.) Easy to administer, it is probably the most popular system in use today. This system consists of a list of characteristics, each accompanied by a four- or five-point scale ranging from poor to excellent. The traits to be rated are usually described in some detail, as are the various points on the scale. The chief advantages of the scale are that it is simple to interpret, easy to use, and comprehensive. Good samples are illustrated in Figs. 18 and 19.

Weaknesses of the graphic scale system result primarily from the rater's fallibility. Supervisors appear to have a reluctance to rate anyone unfavorably and hesitate to use the lower end of the scale. There is also a tendency of supervisors to rate an individual at a similar level for all traits; a generally good man receives a high rating in all traits whereas a poor worker receives a poor rating in all traits. This is identified as the "halo" effect. It appears that the only satisfactory way to overcome this deficiency lies in training the rater to observe individual traits apart from the total pattern of the individual.

ORDER OF MERIT SYSTEM

Under this system the supervisor lists each person in rank order for each of the traits which are being measured. Each individual is ranked only with respect to all other persons being rated. His score on each trait is the number of his position on the list. A total score or rank is determined by his average under all traits measured. This system is simple, easy to administer, and an effective method of determining the composite rank order of a small group. Its use is questionable because the score does not indicate actual individual worth, except in that one is better than others, and because there is no indication of the degree of difference that exists between those rated.

PAIRED COMPARISONS SYSTEM

This system is a standard psychological method for determining rank order within a group. The name of each person is paired with that of each other person in the group. The supervisor checks the name of the better person of each pair. Simple tabulation of the checks places each individual in a rank order. Extension of this system into a large number of traits or a large number of persons soon makes it unwieldy. For example, the rating of a group of 20 persons requires judgment of 190 pairs; the rating of 50 persons increases the total judgments to 1225 pairs. This system shares the weaknesses inherent in the order of merit system previously mentioned.

FORCED-CHOICE SYSTEM

This system was developed by the Personnel Research Section of the Adjutant General's Office during World War II.[18] It is one of the newest and most promising systems because it tends to eliminate the three most serious defects of rating—favoritism, the lenient tendency, and the "halo" effect.

The initial scale used by the Army contained a number of groups of descriptive words and phrases. Each group contained two complimentary words or phrases which research had proven to be equally desirable to raters; each group also included two unfavorable words or phrases which research determined were equally avoided by raters. The supervisor was required to check the word or phrases that *best* described and those that *least* described the officer being rated. Only half of the *favorable* items make the dis-

[18] E. Donald Sisson, "Forced Choice—The New Army Rating," *Personnel Psychology*, vol. I, no. 3 (1948), pp. 365-381.

UNIVERSITY OF NORTH CAROLINA

School of Education

PERSONALITY RATING SCALE
—Confidential—

Name_____Date_____

Please indicate your judgment by checking (X) on the line at the point which most nearly records your opinion about this person. The descriptive words are only suggestive of the general characteristics to be considered. Please use the space "Remarks" for a paragraph description of your impression of this person as a prospective teacher.

1. APPEARANCE

Opportunity to Observe Person

Very pleasing	Attractive	Passable	Careless	Slovenly	Extensive	Limited	None

2. DEPENDABILITY

Wholly reliable	Usually dependable	Dependable in routine matters	Requires follow-up	Irresponsible	Extensive	Limited	None

3. INDUSTRY

Completes task promptly with enthusiasm	Usually alert	Ploddingly industrious	Starts but often does not finish task	Lazy and indifferent	Extensive	Limited	None

4. COOPERATION

Constructively cooperative	Works fairly well with others	Passive cooperation	A solo performer	Causes friction	Extensive	Limited	None

5. INITIATIVE

Proposes and develops original ideas	Self reliant in performance of assignment	Capable in routine matters	Depends upon others for all ideas	Requires detailed instruction	Extensive	Limited	None

6. LEADERSHIP

Recognized by group as leader	Group generally accepts leadership	Can lead in easy situations	Ineffective as a leader	Develops antagonism	Extensive	Limited	None

7. EMOTIONAL CONTROL

Well poised and competent under strain	Normally self-controlled	Occasionally loses self-control	Easily annoyed by little things	Constantly upset	Extensive	Limited	None

8. SENSE OF HUMOR

Appreciates and understands place of humor	Can sense an amusing situation quickly	Can usually take advantage of an amusing incident	Can occasionally recognize a humorous situation	Does not respond to any amusing situation	Extensive	Limited	None

9. RESOURCEFULNESS

Effective in difficult situation	Alert but sometimes ineffective	Reasonable skill in meeting situations	Difficulty in adjustment	Helpless without complete details	Extensive	Limited	None

10. SOCIAL ACCEPTABILITY

Sought by others	Well liked by others	Unnoticed by others	Tolerated by others	Avoided by others	Extensive	Limited	None

Remarks:_____

_____

_____

Date_____Signed_____

Position_____

Please return to Teachers' Placement Bureau, Peabody.

Figure 18. Example of Graphic Rating Scale: I

Reproduced with the permission of Guy B. Phillips, Professor of Education at the University of North Carolina, who developed this instrument for use by the Teachers' Placement Bureau, in co-operation with a group of educators at the University of Chicago.

NEWTON PUBLIC SCHOOLS
REPORT OF INTERVIEW

Candidate ....Date of Birth..............................

College ....Degree....................Year..............

Graduate School ....Degree....................Year..............

Place of Internship ....Grade and/or
                    School   Town   State   ......Subject ....

Present Position ....
                    Grade and Subject   School   Place

Position Desired ....

Interviewed by ....

Date ....

Series............

——————————————— Do Not Write Below This Line ———————————————

Figure 19. *Example of Graphic Rating Scale: II*

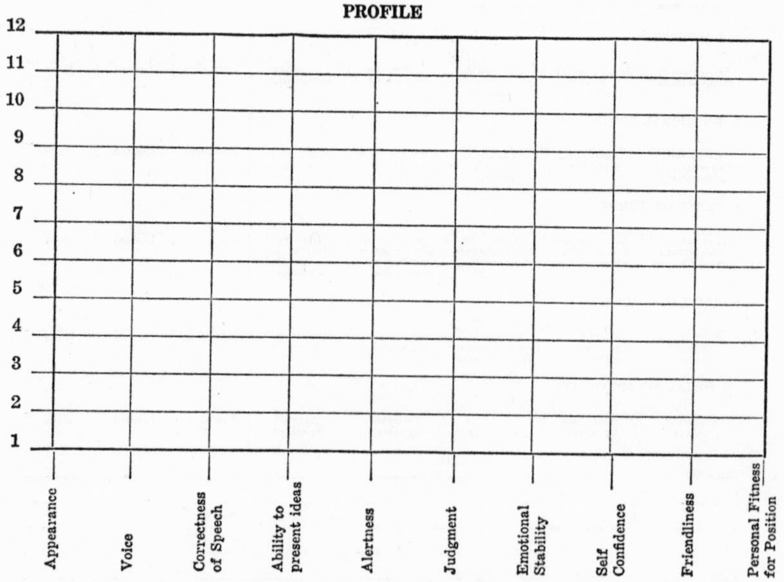

Summary of Candidate's Qualifications, Public Schools, Newton, Massachusetts

This instrument, appearing in its entirety on pages 420-426, is reproduced with the

INSTRUCTIONS: Ask yourself how this applicant compares with others who have had similar length of experience. Consider whether his voice, appearance, etc., would be liabilities or assets. Rate him by making a check (√) at that point on each scale where, in your judgment, the applicant stands. Rate the following traits by checking the appropriate point on the scale which follows each question:

1. APPEARANCE. What sort of first impression does he make? Does he look like a healthy and energetic person? Has he bodily or facial characteristics which might seriously hamper him? Is he well-groomed or slovenly? Attractive or unattractive in appearance?

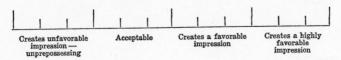

Creates unfavorable impression — unprepossessing	Acceptable	Creates a favorable impression	Creates a highly favorable impression

2. VOICE. Is the applicant's voice irritating or pleasant? Can you easily hear what he says? Does he mumble or talk with an accent which offends or baffles the listener? Is his speech clear and distinct, his voice so well-modulated that it is a valuable asset?

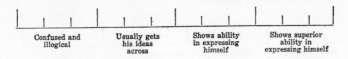

Irritating or indistinct	Understandable but unpleasant	Definitely pleasant or distinct	Exceptionally clear and pleasing

3. CORRECTNESS OF SPEECH. Does he speak grammatically correct English or does he make frequent grammatical errors? Is his choice of words accurate?

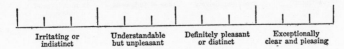

Frequent grammatical errors	Occasional grammatical errors	Free of grammatical errors	Exceptional choice of words

4. ABILITY TO PRESENT IDEAS. Does he speak logically and convincingly? Or does he tend to be vague, confused, or illogical?

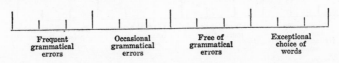

Confused and illogical	Usually gets his ideas across	Shows ability in expressing himself	Shows superior ability in expressing himself

J–2

permission of the Newton (Massachusetts) Schools and of the New England Development Council, Cambridge 38, Massachusetts, who reproduced the original in its publication, *Teacher Competence and Its Relation to Salary*, under the editorship of David V. Tiedeman, 1956.

5. ALERTNESS. How readily does he grasp the meaning of a question? Is he slow to comprehend obvious points? Does he understand quickly, even though the idea is new, involved or difficult?

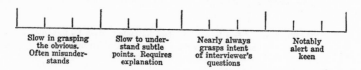

| Slow in grasping the obvious. Often misunderstands | Slow to understand subtle points. Requires explanation | Nearly always grasps intent of interviewer's questions | Notably alert and keen |

6. JUDGMENT. Does he impress you as a person whose judgment would be dependable even under stress? Is he hasty, erratic or emotional? Is he biased?

| Notably lacking in balance and restraint | Shows some tendency to react impulsively | Gives reassuring evidence of soundness of judgment | Inspires unusual confidence in soundness of judgment |

7. EMOTIONAL STABILITY. How well poised is he? Does he seem touchy, sensitive to criticism, easily upset? Is he easily irritated? Is he impatient?

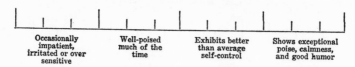

| Occasionally impatient, irritated or over sensitive | Well-poised much of the time | Exhibits better than average self-control | Shows exceptional poise, calmness, and good humor |

8. SELF-CONFIDENCE. Does he seem to be uncertain of himself, hesitant, lacking in assurance? Is he self-confident and assured?

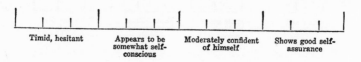

| Timid, hesitant | Appears to be somewhat self-conscious | Moderately confident of himself | Shows good self-assurance |

9. FRIENDLINESS. Is he a friendly, likeable person? Will his colleagues and students be drawn to him? Is he retiring or unfriendly?

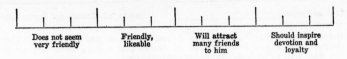

| Does not seem very friendly | Friendly, likeable | Will attract many friends to him | Should inspire devotion and loyalty |

10. PERSONAL FITNESS FOR THE POSITION. On the basis of this interview, how do you rate this applicant's suitability for a position in the Newton Public Schools? *It is assumed, of course, that later on you may consult other sources of information about him which may or may not alter your present judgment as to his suitability.*

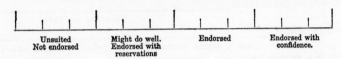

| Unsuited Not endorsed | Might do well. Endorsed with reservations | Endorsed | Endorsed with confidence. |

COMMENTS.

ACTIVITIES SHEET

Name_____   Date_____

College(s) attended_____   Years of Teaching Experience____

Please check those activities listed below in which you have participated. In the appropriate space beside each of those you check, describe briefly the nature and the extent of your participation.

__CLASS OFFICE(S) HELD-HIGH SCHOOL_____
                       (Which, when?)

__CLASS OFFICE(S) HELD-COLLEGE_____
                       (Which, when?)

__STUDENT GOVERNMENT-H.S._____
                       (Member, officer)

__STUDENT GOVERNMENT-COLLEGE_____
                       (Member, officer)

__HIGH SCHOOL HONORS_____
          (Nat'l Honor Society, class valedictorian, etc.)

__SCHOLASTIC & PROFESSIONAL HON. SOCIETIES_____
               (Kappa Delta Pi, Phi Beta Kappa,etc.)

__OTHER COLLEGE DISTINCTIONS RECEIVED_____
               (Who's Who in American Colleges, etc.)

__CLUBS-HIGH SCHOOL_____
          (Member, officer, special contributions)

__CLUBS-COLLEGE_____
          (Member, officer, special contributions)

__DEBATING_____
           (Judging, participant, courses, etc.)

__DRAMATICS_____
          (School, college, summer theatre, etc.)

__PUBLIC SPEAKING_____
      (Occasion & approximate number of largest group addressed)

__HIGH SCHOOL PUBLICATIONS_____
           (Editor, reporter, other specialty)

__COLLEGE PUBLICATIONS_____
           (Editor, reporter, other specialty)

__WRITING_____
     (For publications, where? - Nature and extent)

__BAND_____
    (Instrument, high school, college, etc.)

__CHOIR_____
                    (High school, college, other)

__CHORUS_____
                    (High school, college, number of years, etc.)

__GLEE CLUB_____
                    (High school, college, soloist, etc.)

__MUSIC - PIANO_____
                    (Play for assemblies, for classroom, lessons)

__ORCHESTRA_____
                    (Instrument, high school, college, etc.)

__COMMITTEE CHAIRMANSHIP - COLLEGE_____
                                        (List)

__PROFESSIONAL ORGANIZATIONS_____
                    (Future Teachers of America, A.C.E., N.E.A., etc.)

__EDUCATIONAL OR STUDENT CONFERENCES_____
                                (Where? Your role)

__CIVIC ACTIVITIES_____
                    (List those in which you hold membership. Officer?)

__PARENT-TEACHER ASSOCIATION_____
                            (Member, officer, visitor)

__ATHLETICS - H.S._____
                            (Team(s), positions, letter awards, etc.)

__ATHLETICS - COLLEGE_____
                            (Team(s), positions, letter awards, etc.)

__COACHING_____
                    (List sports you could coach)

__OFFICIATING_____
                    (List sports you could officiate as a "certified" official)

__SWIMMING INSTRUCTOR'S CERTIFICATE_____

__RED CROSS LIFE SAVING CERTIFICATE_____

__CAMPING_____
                    (Where? How many seasons? When?)

__CAMP COUNSELING_____
                    (Specialty. Where? When? How many seasons?)

__LEADERSHIP EXPERIENCE_____
                    (Scouts, Cubs, Brownies, Campfire Girls, etc.)

J-6

__SCOUTING_____
                     (How long? Highest rank attained)

__PLAYGROUND WORK_____
                 (Supervisor, Instructor, how long? Specialty)

__SETTLEMENT HOUSE WORK_____
                       (Where? When? Your role)

__TRAVEL_____
            (Farthest distance from home. When? How long away?)

__DRIVE CAR_____
                     (Sometimes, frequently)

__FLYING_____
                 (Passenger, pilot, navigator, etc.)

__MOUNTAIN CLIMBING_____
                 (When? Where? Once, frequently)

Include other activities in which you have participated.

crimination between a good and a poor officer; only these items are counted in the score. Through research and experimentation the choices presented have been proved to be equally desirable (or avoided) by raters; yet, research also showed that only one-fourth of the choices actually differentiated the good officer from the poor. The rater, of course, had and has no way of determining which items enter into the score. Industry is now using a variation of this system. Fig. 20 illustrates one of the blanks used by the armed forces.

The most interesting feature of this forced-choice system for educational supervisors and administrators is the questions it might raise relative to the traits listed on typical teacher rating blanks. For example, do they really differentiate between good and poor traits, between good teaching and ineffective teaching?

QUALITATIVE DESCRIPTION WITH ANECDOTAL ILLUSTRATIONS

This type of evaluation of teachers and teaching is perhaps the oldest; it is still the kind most generally in use. It got its start with one administrator's writing to another concerning the teaching promise of a teacher who applied for a job. As a rating instrument, it has been improved markedly by the use of illustrations of teaching effectiveness or ineffectiveness in certain situations. A modern example of a blank for this type of evaluation is shown in Fig. 21.

DIFFERENTIATED USE OF TEACHER COMPETENCE

Perhaps this newest type of rating makes the most sense. Recent experiments have sought to discover ways in which the professional skills of teachers could be utilized more effectively to the benefit of both children and those engaged in instruction.[19] To accomplish this objective, efforts are directed toward differentiating

[19] Lindley J. Stiles, "Individual and Team Teaching," *Wisconsin Journal of Education*, vol. 92 (January, 1960), pp. 7-11 and 13; R. H. Brown, "Three Experiments in Staff Utilization at Urbana," *The Bulletin of the National Association of Secondary School Principals*, vol. 43 (January, 1959), pp. 255-256; W. L. Cooper, "Staff Utilization Studies in J. Sterling Morton High School and Junior College, Cicero, Illinois," *The Bulletin of the National Association of Secondary School Principals*, vol. 43 (January, 1959), pp. 247-248.

Note: the January issues of *The Bulletin of the National Association of Secondary School Principals* for the years 1958, 1959, and 1960 presented reports of experiments in staff utilization.

PAIRS   OR   TETRADS

PAIRS

FOR RATER ONLY. For each pair of words or phases make a heavy X opposite the one that is the MORE DESCRIPTIVE of the rated officer.

1
A. Assigns men properly
B. Keeps his word

8
A. Maintains strict discipline
B. Good educational background

2
A. Courageous
B. Respected by his subordinates

9
A. Can select and define major objectives
B. Thorough knowledge of his own branch

3
A. Willing to take a chance
B. Has physical endurance

10
A. Temperate in his habits
B. Self-confident

4
A. Conscientious
B. Takes action to correct faulty performance

11
A. Is just
B. Can get subordinates to attempt the impossible

5
A. People seek his advice in personal matters
B. Knows his subordinates

12
A. Has a broad grasp of the problems
B. Has foresight

6
A. Alert
B. Has full knowledge of his job

13
A. Vigorous
B. Truthful

7
A. Thoughtful planner
B. Supports actions of subordinates

14
A. Tenacious
B. Makes practicable suggestions

TETRADS

This section consists of sets of phrases which describe characteristics related to proficiency on the job. Consider each set and decide which phrase is MOST DESCRIPTIVE of the officer being rated, and which phrase is LEAST DESCRIPTIVE of the officer. Judge the sets independently — it is not necessary to be consistent as you are describing the officer, not evaluating him. Blacken in the space to the right of the MOST DESCRIPTIVE and LEAST DESCRIPTIVE phrases in the appropriate column.

1
A. Becomes dogmatic about his authority.
B. Careless & slipshod in attention to duty.
C. No one ever doubts his ability.
D. Well-grounded in all phases of Army life.

4
A. Always criticizes, never praises.
B. Carries out orders by "passing the buck."
C. Knows his job and performs it well.
D. Plays no favorites.

2
A. Follows closely directions of higher echelons.
B. Inclined to "gold-brick."
C. Criticizes unnecessarily.
D. Willing to accept responsibility.

5
A. Constantly striving for new knowledge and ideas.
B. Businesslike.
C. Apparently not physically fit.
D. Fails to use good judgment.

3
A. A go-getter who always does a good job.
B. Cool under all circumstances.
C. Doesn't listen to suggestions.
D. Drives instead of leads.

6
A. Cannot assume responsibility.
B. Knows how and when to delegate authority.
C. Offers suggestions.
D. Too easily changes his ideas.

Forced-choice phrases may be assembled in pairs or tetrads.

Figure 20. Examples of Forced-Choice System

From *Army Personnel Tests and Measurement*, TM 12-.60, Department of the Army (April, 1953). Reproduced by permission of the Department of the Army.

UNIVERSITY OF NORTH CAROLINA

School of Education

CONFIDENTIAL STUDENT REFERENCE FORM

This blank with the names filled in is to be handed *by the Applicant* to an instructor qualified to speak of the applicant's character and the quality of work done.

Applicant's Name _____ Address_____

Instructor's Name _____ Address_____

The statement furnished below should include opinions as to the applicant's apparent fitness to teach, e.g. personality, disposition, character, qualities of leadership, etc., as well as intellectual ability. This statement will not be shown except to officials seeking teachers.

Here please give three (3) descriptions of success—or failure—in an actual situation:

Situation 1:

Situation 2:

Situation 3:

Signature _____ Department_____

Date_____

Please return to Teachers' Placement Bureau, Peabody.

Figure 21. Qualitative Description Type of Scale, with Illustrations

Reproduced with the permission of Guy B. Phillips, Professor of Education at the University of North Carolina, who developed this instrument for use by the Teachers' Placement Bureau, in co-operation with a group of educators at the University of Chicago. It has been enlarged by the addition of "Situations 1, 2, and 3."

the various operations involved in teaching and organizing the use of the instructional skills of teachers to permit each to be performed at optimum efficiency. The vehicle employed is coming to be called the instructional team. It typically includes non-certified personnel, for example, instructional secretaries, lay readers, and aides, as well as various levels of professional competence of teachers.

By differentiating the skills and functions of teaching, learners have the benefit of maximum help in each phase of their study. For instance, in the elementary school, an instructional team brings to children specialists in science, foreign language, art, music, physical education, reading, arithmetic, and social studies. Yet such differentiated instructional competence is made available within the framework of the self-contained classroom—as far as the student learning group is concerned—without the negative features of the departmentalized structure. In secondary schools, such experiments seek to provide students with specialists in aspects of a subject, for example, creative writing, appreciation of poetry in English, and differentiated help in terms of individual differences at a given time. Such arrangements involve several teachers, with complementing professsional competencies, working with a total of 150 to 200 pupils in contrast to one teacher per class as is typical of the traditional departmentalized system in secondary schools. Some phases of the work are offered in large group sections; others to small classes or to individual pupils. The teacher-time saved when one teaches as many as 150 students at once, in a lesson that is appropriate for large-group instruction, makes possible the provision of assistance to other students in numbers much smaller than the traditional sized classes.

Because the instructional team with its differentiated professional competencies makes possible the recognition of ranges of professional abilities—from intern to master teacher—it has been envisioned as one means by which professional maturity and competence in teaching can be recognized and rewarded as it develops. In effect, such proposals are based on the premise that there should exist means by which teachers can be promoted within the ranks of teaching itself.

THE NATIONAL TEACHER EXAMINATIONS AS A
BASIS FOR CERTIFICATION AND PROMOTION

The issuance of teaching certificates and the employment of teachers on the basis of a state-wide or local system of examinations characterized a long period in our educational history. The movement toward state certification and acceptance of college credits as a basis both for certification and employment was generally accepted as a professional advance. However, some communities, among them quite a few with preferred salary schedules, continued use of tests for teacher selection, promotion, and rating.

In conjunction with the growing emphasis on measurement in the second and third decades of this century, many standardized examinations purporting to measure teacher ability or to predict teaching success were published. These tests lacked facility for use as instruments of selection, primarily because they were too generally available and national norms were not available.

In 1940, the American Council on Education administered the first National Teacher Examination which was specifically designed and recommended as one criterion for the selection of teachers. These advantages were claimed for it: (1) nationwide norms and year-to-year comparability of scores were to be assured; (2) local communities would be relieved of the cost and time burden inherent in their testing process; and (3) the variability of intellectual and cultural standards of training institutions would become evident.[20] Since then, surprisingly little criticism of this examination has appeared in professional literature.[21] This is probably the result of (1) the extreme care which has been taken to maintain these examinations as confidential and to construct a complete revision annually and (2) the insistence of the American Council on Education that this examination be used as only one criterion in the *selection* of teachers.

The Council in 1949 suggested and provided directions for a community to develop local norms which would enable the examination to be more directly related to its specific school program. South Carolina, after an extensive study, made the examination an integral part of their certification and salary system in 1945. The Council also developed a similar examination for the selection of administrators and supervisors in 1948. A Teacher Education Examination Program (TEEP) was added in the 1950's to serve higher institutions offering teacher education in accredited programs. In 1959-1960 the Council administered these types of tests for states, counties, towns, and colleges to thousands of persons.[22]

[20] Ben D. Wood, "National Teacher Examinations," *Childhood Education,* vol. XVIII (January, 1942), pp. 227-230.

[21] Two critical articles that may interest the student are W. D. Anderson, "National Teacher Examination: A Criticism," *Childhood Education,* vol. XVIII (December, 1941), pp. 179-181; and John R. Emens, "National Teachers Examination," *Nation's Schools,* vol. XXXIX (February, 1947), p. 47.

[22] Those interested in the development and types of uses of national teacher examinations should read *The National Teacher Examinations: Handbook for School and College Officials* and *Teacher Education Examination Program* (TEEP), both published annually by Educational Testing Service, Princeton, N. J.; and Oscar K. Buros, ed., *The Fifth Mental Measurements Yearbook,* pp. 631-640 (Highland Park, N. J.: The Gryphon Press, 1960), for comments on pros and cons of their use, as well as concerning their validity and reliability. The Educational Testing Service is the official agency entrusted with the administration of these tests each year.

The National Teacher Examination is at present the only comprehensive examination of its type and scope available. It is constructed to evaluate and provide comparable examination scores in the areas of intelligence, cultural background, awareness of current social problems, professional educational information, and mastery of selected academic subjects. It makes no claim to evaluating any other factors of probable teaching success. In a local, state-wide, or national program of teacher selection, assignment, or review of qualifications prior to tenure appointment, the examination possesses certain strengths:

1. It can supplement college credentials by providing a measure of achievement in professional areas.
2. It can measure the general background and educational development, regardless of the formal course work taken.
3. It can provide consistent standards for comparision in specific areas and over periods of time.
4. For purposes of directing professional growth, it can locate the specific areas of weakness.
5. Results, reported as scaled scores, can be compared one year with another and with current national norms; or local norms can be developed.
6. Since it is administered nationally, examined personnel can make their scores available to prospective employers anywhere.

Weaknesses, actual and potential, are inherent in any man-made device. Any nationally administered pencil-and-paper examination would inherit many. These are some weaknesses of the National Teacher Examination that have been emphasized:

1. *It can be misinterpreted.* A high score does not mean high teaching effectiveness. The examination measures only academic backgrounds and intelligence.
2. *It can perpetuate a very erroneous idea.* Teacher competence cannot be measured by a paper-and-pencil test. A great gulf exists between the acquisition of knowledge and its successful application.
3. *It can be misused.* Using an examination as the sole standard for teacher selection or using it as an instrument of teacher elimination without recourse to other indications of teaching potential would not be considering the limits inherent in examinations.
4. *It can threaten development of improved teacher preparation programs.* Teacher education institutions must have freedom to experiment to improve their programs. The objective of teacher training

institutions should be "better teachers," not necessarily higher scores on achievement tests.

Predicting or measuring teaching effectiveness cannot be done solely on the basis of examinations. This must be emphasized. An examination can be a valuable tool for diagnosis and *one* criterion of evaluation whether the purpose be selection or rating. It should never be the sole or even the most important standard. For teacher rating, particularly, a direct means of checking actual accomplishment has to be used.

Problems for Individual Study and Class Discussion

1. List as many traits as you can which have a bearing upon a teacher's success.
2. Can a supervisor rate a teacher objectively? Or will subjective opinion enter into the procedure, regardless of the type of rating scale or instrument which is used? Support your position.
3. If the pupils of Teacher A in grade 6 consistently rank well upon the items in a standard achievement test, can you conclude that A is a superior teacher? Explain.
4. What are the values in a self-rating scale for teachers? Are there any weaknesses? If so, what are they?
5. Why should any teacher object to being evaluated or rated in regard to his teaching effectiveness? Does not the teacher evaluate, or rate the pupils on their performance and achievement? Give evidence to support your point of view.
6. Does merit rating really work in practice? Trace the merit rating system employed by the Civil Service of the U. S. Government.
7. Make out a graphic rating scale for examination and discussion at your regular March meeting with your teachers.
8. List some of the advantages and some of the disadvantages of the use of such instruments as the National Teacher Examinations.
9. Should a man teacher of promise with a good record be paid more than a woman teacher of like promise with a good record? Defend your stand.
10. Can pupils give valuable assistance in assessing the value and merit of a teacher, or not? Support your position.

Note: Many school systems are using or have employed merit rating plans recently. Other systems, like the states of North Carolina and Utah, have made extensive studies of merit rating over a period of years. One region, New England, completed a nine-year study in 1956, *Teacher Competence and Its Relation to Salary*, already referred to in the body of this chapter; its School Development Council is still at work on the problem, with its address at Spaulding House, Cambridge 38, Massachusetts. The interested student can secure a fairly accurate list of school systems employing merit rating plans from this New England School Development Council; from the National School Boards Association, Evanston, Illinois, which fell heir to all of the research publications of the National Council for Better Schools; and from the National Education Association, Washington, through its Research Division, and especially from its Steering Committee on the Joint Project for Study of Teacher Competence, established in 1960 by the American Association of School Administrators, the Department of Classroom Teachers, and the National School Boards Association.

Additional Selected References for Problem or Unit Study

Ashman, M., "Teachers in Summit, N. J. Say Merit Pay Works," *School Management*, vol. IV, No. 4, (April, 1960), pp. 69-73, 142, 144-145.

Beecher, D. E., *The Evaluation of Teaching* (Syracuse: Syracuse University Press, 1954), *passim.*

Boardman, C. W., Douglass, H. R., and Bent, R. K., *Democratic Supervision in Secondary Schools* (Boston: Houghton Mifflin Company, 1953), chs. X, XXI.

Brickman, Benjamin, "Rewarding the Superior Teacher," *School and Society*, vol. 77 (September, 1959), pp. 356-358.

Burton, W. H., and Brueckner, L. J., *Supervision: A Social Process* (New York: Appleton-Century-Crofts, Inc., 1955), ch. XI.

California Journal of Secondary Education, vol. XXXV (April, 1960) has a comprehensive symposium on "The Constructive Use of Teacher Talents," pp. 232-270. (Team teaching)

Chandler, B. J., "Merit Rating Not Detrimental to Morale," *The Nation's Schools*, vol. 61 (April, 1958), pp. 58-60.

Chandler, B. J., and Petty, P. V., *Personnel Management in School Administration* (Yonkers-on-Hudson: World Book Company, 1955), ch. IX.

The Education of Teachers: Certification, Official Report of the San Diego Conference, TEPS (Washington: National Education Association, 1960), pp. 79-199, and part III.

Elsbree, W. S., and McNally, H. J., *Elementary School Administration and Supervision*, 2nd ed. (New York: American Book Company, 1959), ch. X.

The High School Journal, "Merit Rating," vol. XLIII (May, 1960), *passim.*

Huggett, A. J., and Stinnett, T. M., *Professional Problems of Teachers* (New York: The Macmillan Company, 1956), chs. II, IV-VI.

Information on Merit Rating, Research Bulletin No. 59-1 (Raleigh, Box 350: North Carolina Education Association, October, 1959), *passim.*

The Journal of Teacher Education (June, 1957); issue is devoted almost entirely to the subject of merit rate salary schedules for teachers.

Kearney, N. C., *A Teacher's Professional Guide* (Englewood Cliffs, N. J.: Prentice-Hall, Inc., 1958), ch. IX.

Lieberman, M., *The Future of Public Education* (Chicago: University of Chicago Press, 1960), ch. XII.

Misner, Paul J., "The Merit Rating Issue," *Seven Studies* (Evanston, Ill.: National School Boards Association, Inc., 1958), pp. 42-55.

Moore, H. E., and Walters, N. B., *Personnel Administration in Education* (New York: Harper and Brothers, 1955), part II.

NEA Journal, vol. L (Jan., 1961), presents preliminary findings of national committee on "New Horizons in Teacher Education and Professional Standards," pp. 55-68.

NEA Research Bulletin, Washington, presents up-to-date information on merit rating from time to time; for example "Salary Provisions for Quality of Service," vol. XXXVIII, no. 4 (December, 1959), pp. 106-110.

NEA Research Division, Washington: *Special Memo: Quality-of-Service Recognition in Teachers' Salary Schedules* (July, 1956). A report on 556 school districts of 30,000 or more population.

New England School Development Council, 20 Oxford Street, Cambridge 38, *Teacher Competence and Its Relation to Salary* (July, 1956), *passim* (a nine-year study).

Phi Delta Kappan, vol. XLII (January, 1961), includes seven articles on merit rating and pay.

Review of Educational Research, vol. XXII (June, 1952), presents the first "Report of the Committee on the Criteria of Teacher Effectiveness" of the American Educational Research Association; vol. XXV (June, 1955) brings up to date "The Measurement and Prediction of Teaching Efficiency," pp. 261-269; and vol. XXVIII (June, 1958) adds new research on "The Measurement and Prediction of Teaching Efficiency," pp. 256-264.

Rogers, V. M., ed., *Merit Rating for Teachers?* (Syracuse: Syracuse University Press, 1959).

Ryans, D. G., *Characteristics of Teachers: Their Description, Comparison, and Appraisal* (Washington: American Council on Education, 1960), *passim.*

Thompkins, E., and Roe, V., *The Case for and Against Merit Rating: Digest of Significant References,* 1951-1956 (Washington, D. C.: Association of Secondary School Principals, June 1, 1956).

Utah School Merit Study Committee, Salt Lake City, 223 State Capitol, *Report and Recommendations,* Utah School Merit Study (1958), *passim.*

Vander Werf, L. S., *How to Evaluate Teachers and Teaching* (New York: Rinehart and Company, 1958), *passim.*

Wiles, K., *Supervision for Better Schools,* 2nd ed. (New York: Prentice-Hall, Inc., 1955), chs. XIII-XIV.

Woodring, P., *New Directions in Teacher Education* (New York: The Fund for the Advancement of Education, 1957), ch. IV.

Yeager, W. A., *Administration and the Teacher* (New York: Harper and Brothers, 1954), ch. XIV.

CHAPTER 21

A Look at the Future

of Supervision

THE FUTURE OF SUPERVISION is bright—and challenging. As supervision has slowly earned its way over the years, it has dealt more and more intensively with those problems which were considered fundamental to the effective in-service training of teachers and to the improvement of the teaching-learning situation. New emphasis has been placed also upon the development of the most desirable environment for learning for the child, upon teacher-pupil planning as a component part of this environment, upon co-operative teacher planning for improved teaching, and upon the availability of the supervisor as a competent resource person for the staff. What of the future, then? Does supervision face problems during the next quarter of a century that will differ much from these?

Yes, supervision faces some newer problems, and the solutions will require more extensive knowledge and different competencies of the supervisor. This chapter will attempt to identify these newer problems and to indicate some of the training that will be needed to make supervisors competent to meet them.

Newer Professional Problem Areas

Table 9 presents graphically these major problem areas and the information and competencies that the supervisor will need.

Table 9. Newer Problems of the Supervisor and Competencies Needed to Meet Them

Problems	Competencies
1. Mass media of communication: radio—TV—newsstand publications—newspapers	1. How to use these media through knowledge of policies and practices in other schools
2. Intergroup, intercultural, religious and racial problems	2. Information on experiments, materials, and practices; and ability to help develop impartial approach
3. Free curricular and instructional materials	3. Standards for analysis, and for grade levels, if usable
4. Teaching children and teachers by television	4. Information on successful experimental practices in teaching children and adults by TV
5. Crowded and overcrowded buildings	5. Information on 2-shift programs and on double sessions, and how organized
6. Co-operative reports to parents, that is, teacher and parent co-operatively assess pupil progress (teacher-parent conferences)	6. Knowledge of successful practices in this area
7. Teaching of controversial issues, and freedom in teaching	7. Ability to identify propaganda, to secure source and factual materials on each side, and to identify the issue(s)
8. Helping parents to understand what the school is trying to do	8. Facility as to when, where, and how the supervisor meets the public and the community
9. Role of supervisor in planning school buildings	9. Familiarity with blueprints and reading of specifications; visits to schools for ideas
10. Work experience programs in high school and their enlargement	10. Information about types of programs and learning how they operate by visitation
11. Analysis and understanding of attacks on public education	11. Familiarity with types, sources, and how other communities have met them
12. Lack of trained teachers	12. How to train these in service
13. Curriculum improvements by the individual teacher; system-wide curriculum improvements	13. Knowledge of newer methods and how to use them; skill in group processes and problem solving

(continued on next page)

Problems	Competencies
14. Addition of new subjects, such as home and family life education, consumer and economic education, driver training	14. Information on the subject area and practices in it
15. Effective use of newer specialists, such as health educators, speech teachers, social workers	15. Information on duties and responsibilities of school and of other agencies involved
16. How to supervise unit-and-activity teaching	16. Knowledge of this newer method, and skill in understanding each teacher's approach
17. Teacher-pupil planning	17. Mastery of this technique himself
18. Action research and other types of experimentation	18. Ability to carry out group research; knowledge of types
19. How to provide more adequately for the talented pupil	19. Information on current practices, grouping, types of programs

Problems Involving Groups Outside the School

CO-OPERATION WITH OUTSIDE AGENCIES
TO IMPROVE THE SCHOOL PROGRAM

Since 1900 it has been common for educational foundations of one kind or another to set aside funds for the specific purposes of improving school practices. Examples of these were the funds allocated by the Rockefeller Foundation to the Departments of Education of the Southern states from 1900 to the 1920's to stimulate the construction and supervision of public high schools in that region; by the Jeannes and Rosenwald Foundations for the improvement of education for Negroes in the South; and by the Peabody Fund for the erection of buildings at higher institutions to house and train teachers for the public schools. In the last quarter of a century, other subventions have been made; prominent among these have been the funds allocated by the General Education Board for the Studies by the Progressive Education Association of general education and the experimental Eight-Year Study; by the General Education Board and the regional accrediting associations for the Cooperative Study of Secondary School Standards; and by the W. K. Kellogg Foundation for experimental studies directed toward improving health education for children and the training of educational administrators.

Most of these foundation grants of funds have been made with these purposes in view: (1) to stimulate schools or institutions to experiment to improve school practices or conditions and (2) to place the responsibility, both fiscal and in policy, for permanent continuation of improved practices upon the schools, or institutions, or professional educational organizations which were involved. In addition to these subventions, professional educational groups have themselves allocated funds for special or experimental studies, or have sponsored new movements with which the modern supervisor has to work. At times, professional education groups have started an idea or experiment, and additional funds have been given by educational foundations to carry out the experiment, as, for example, the Southern Association's Co-operative Study in Elementary Education and the National Survey of Secondary Education.

Regardless of source of financial support, the supervisor has to work with one or another of these kinds of experimental groups from time to time. He should become familiar with groups such as the following, which have been active recently or are still active:

Associated Public School Systems, 525 W. 120th St., New York, 27, N. Y. A group of school systems from all sections of the country, banded together to promote and exchange promising practices and ideas. Their official publication is *Know-How,* published quarterly; in it and in their APSS Yearbooks are found many promising ideas for the supervisor. Since member schools swap publications, the sources of accounts of good practices are extremely wide on all kinds of problems.

Citizenship Education Project (1949-   ), Teachers College, Columbia University, New York, N. Y. The project identified, developed, and tested out resources to assist co-operating schools to improve their programs in citizenship education. A total of 150 schools took part in various sections of the country. The materials card file was a valuable resource contribution, primarily data and annotations of books, pamphlets, film and recordings, and sources of pertinent materials for grades 7-12. Among the latest contributions are *Resources of Citizenship: A Guide to the Selection of Teaching Materials* (1955), *Laboratory Practices in Citizenship: Learning Experiences in the Community* (1958), and *Building Better Programs in Citizenship* (1958). This project is being reorganized with the sponsorship of several universities in the country, and is now called the University Council for Citizenship Education. Their address is the same at Columbia University.

Committee for Education in Family Finance, 488 Madison Avenue, New York, N. Y. With financial aid from the Institute for Life Insurance, this group of educators is interested in promoting better economic education. It provides money and leadership for about a dozen workshops each summer in selected higher institutions; the workshop emphasizes how to give aid in managing the finances of the family, and produces teaching guides and units, some of which are published each year. The periodical is *Topics for Teachers*, which lists good practices and publications.

Co-operative Program in Educational Administration, originally subsidized by the W. K. Kellogg Foundation in 1948, and sponsored by the American Association of School Administrators, with the co-operation of the Department of Rural Education (both of the National Education Association), the National Council of State School Officers, and the National Conference of Professors of Educational Administration. Eight centers were established in colleges and universities in the various regions of the country. Their purpose was to develop better programs of preservice and in-service education for school administrators. They studied the definitions of the job, criteria for recruitment and selection, preservice and in-service programs, action research in the area of the superintendency, and development in skills in dealing with people. Many implications for the training of the supervisor as an educational leader came from this widespread study, which was reorganized first as the Committee for the Advancement of School Administration and is now known as the University Council on Educational Administration (UCEA), with headquarters at the Ohio State University.

Council for the Advancement of Secondary Education (CASE), established jointly by the National Association of Secondary School Principals (National Education Association), and the National Better Business Bureau (1954-   ). The Council tackled as its first project a Study on Economic Education. Four research studies were projected: (1) what adequate economic understandings an individual must have to understand newspapers, popular magazines, farm and labor journals; (2) a survey and analysis of economic textbooks and courses of study; (3) what important economic items should be included in the education of every youth; and (4) evaluation of a large list of these items. Main purpose of the study: to reach agreement upon the basic economic information upon which people build opinions and judgments.

Joint Council on Economic Education, 2 West 46th St., New York 36, N. Y. Sponsored by the Committee for Economic Development. Purpose: to give school personnel basic understandings of the American economic system and how it operates. Organized in 1949, it is a nonprofit, nonpartisan educational organization which helps to finance and carry on workshops on economic education. Many supervisors have been among the more than 10,000 persons who have attended some 200 workshops in many states since the Joint Council was organized. These workshops do prepare some resource units for teachers.

Metropolitan School Study Council, 525 West 120th St., New York 27, N. Y. Allied to the same group which started the Associated Public School Systems, this is the older body comprising membership primarily in the metropolitan area around New York City; most members come from Connecticut, New Jersey, and New York. Their publication is *Exchange,* published five times a year as a medium through which these school systems with similar problems swap ideas and practices.

National Citizens Council for Better Schools, 9 East 40th St., New York 16, N. Y. A group of men and women not connected with professional education formed this organization in 1949; plans were made to continue it after its charter expired in 1955. The objective was to get Americans to work themselves to solve their own school problems. There were also regional offices. The official organ for exchanging news of how communities work to solve their school problems was *Better Schools;* the Council also prepared good "guides" for the study of school problems. This Council went out of existence by June 30, 1960, but many of its reports and publications are still available through the National School Boards Association. Its main contribution is in the existence of many state and regional councils, such as the New England School Development Council and the Educational Research Council of Greater Cleveland.

National School Boards Association: A Federation of State Associations, 1940 Sheridan Road, Evanston, Ill. Their purposes include studies of the educational programs of the different states, swapping of information, and work for the most effective organization and administration of schools. Their annual Convention Yearbook summarizes the progress of each state organization, and their regular publication is *School Boards,* a monthly. Since supervision can be either encouraged or discouraged by school boards, the supervisor should keep abreast of this movement in his state.

CO-OPERATION BETWEEN THE PUBLIC AND
SCHOOL PERSONNEL IN EVALUATION OF THE SCHOOL

Since 1940 there has been a rapid development of good instruments for evaluating a school's instructional program. Likewise, there has been a remarkable growth of the movement for schools and the public (the community) to study and evaluate their schools co-operatively. Some of these instruments also include evaluation of many other aspects of a school or system, such as administration, school buildings, support and control, instructional staff, supplies and equipment, and special school services.

The supervisor's main concern here is with the curriculum, the instructional program of the school. In any evaluation of a school's program two principles must be kept constantly in view: (1) The school which is to be evaluated must state *its purposes* for its curriculum for children and (2) All appraisals must be made in terms of *how well* the school is succeeding in carrying out those purposes.

The publications listed below are good samples of the types of instruments that have been developed for use by both school personnel and the public. They furnish a major resource when the supervisor is called upon to help in evaluating the school program; in fact, he should encourage the staff and the community to carry out such an evaluation from time to time.

Baker, James F., *Elementary Evaluative Criteria* (Boston 15: Boston University, 1953). Patterned in general after the *Evaluative Criteria*, 1940 and 1960 editions, it has a statement of guiding principles (purposes) checklist and evaluation items, and summaries for all aspects of the curriculum; library and guidance services; school plant; staff; and administration.

Evaluative Criteria, 1960 ed., National Study of Secondary School Evaluation, 1785 Massachusetts Avenue, N. W., Washington 6, D. C. This revision of the first edition (1940) includes extensive checklists and evaluations based on these aspects after the philosophy of the school has been set forth concerning the needs of youth in a community: Program of studies, including all subject-matter areas and the core program; pupil activity program; library services; school plant; administration and staff; and pupil population and school community.

Hamlin, Herbert M., *Citizen's Committees in the Public Schools* (Danville, Ill.: Interstate Printing Company, 1952). Sets forth promising ways to channel citizen participation in planning in public schools, including types of organization and activities.

Southern Association, Commission on Research and Service, *Evaluating the Elementary School: A Guide for Co-operative Study* (Atlanta: Southern Association, 316 Peachtree Street, N. E., 1951). Includes viewpoint and functions or aims of the school, program, resources and services, and planning in the school. Wise use is made of provisions for describing practices and for giving examples of situations and needs.

Sumption, Merle R., *How to Conduct a Citizens' School Survey* (Englewood Cliffs, N. J.: Prentice-Hall, Inc., 1952). Illustrates how a community can set up and carry out a survey that will be of use to its school board in a long-range program. To be studied are the community, child population, financial ability of the district, school housing, planning the program, and how to maintain good public relations.

Thomas, Maurice J., *A Guide for Action: Improving Public Education Through Citizen Participation* (Pittsburgh: University of Pittsburgh Press, 1954). Prepared especially for use by lay committees. It has five checklists on: curriculum; personnel; organization, administration and finance programs, school plant, and maintenance program. A feature of this instrument is its simplicity—it can be used effectively by citizens of limited educational background.

Yauch, Wilbur A., *How Good Is Your School?* (New York: Harper and Brothers, 1951). This is a handbook primarily to help parents judge the quality of their school and how to make it better. A checklist in chapter XV could be used by any parent in a visit to the school.

Supervision as a Career

Since supervision has now come of age in the educational system, the next decades will see excellent opportunities for careers in supervision for well-trained, experienced people. Who will be the supervisor in 1960? In 1970? What training will be required of him? What measures are being taken to educate the supervisor adequately for his task? What kind of person becomes a supervisor? What kind of person should become a supervisor? Is any pattern emerging for the education of supervisors? Are the professional requirements of large cities concerning the education of their supervisors resulting in any trends in the professional preparation of supervisors?

PREPARATION OF SUPERVISORS

Starting with the *status quo*, these are findings from a survey made of certification requirements of the forty-eight states in 1954.[1] Supervisors in 34 states must have special certificates. Only four states now issue a general supervisor's certificate. The typical supervisors' certificates are the elementary, the secondary, and the special subject certificate.

Thirteen states require a supervisor to have a master's degree, with valid teacher's certificate, special courses in supervision, and from three to five years of teaching experience. Thirteen states require from 8 to 30 semester hours of graduate work, special preparation in supervision, a valid teacher's certificate, and from two to five years experience in teaching. Eight states require academic training and experience in wide variety. From two to as much as fifteen semester hours of graduate work is required among these states, including special preparation in supervision. In some of the states,

[1] Virginia Richard, "Certification Requirements for Supervisors in the United States," *Educational Leadership*, vol. XII (December, 1954), pp. 170-175. *Cf.* also Southern States Work Conference, *Educational Supervision: A Leadership Service* (Tallahassee: Florida State Department of Education, 1955); and National Education Association, *A Manual on Certification Requirements* (Washington, D. C.), an annual publication for school personnel.

if one has a valid teaching certificate and the requisite additional training, he can be appointed as a supervisor; in others more education in supervision and more teaching experience are necessary.

The special preparation which is generally required in the area of supervision includes courses in school administration and organization; scope, purposes, and practices in supervision; school curriculum; child growth and development; evaluation of instruction; and courses on the work and program of the school level on which one is to supervise, such as work in elementary education or in secondary education.

Most states emphasize that the teaching or administrative experience which is required must have been completed within the last five years. Some states require some administrative or supervisory cadetship of candidates for the certificate.

In terms of degrees and graduate study, the well-prepared supervisor would have to have a bachelor's degree, a teacher's certificate valid on the grade or subject level which he is to supervise, at least three or more years of teaching experience, and to have completed a well-balanced graduate degree program planned especially to meet the needs of supervisors and administrators. In this program, some actual internship or field experience in a supervisory situation would be desirable and valuable.

QUALIFICATIONS OF SUCCESSFUL SUPERVISORS

Heading the list is the leadership ability of the supervisor; he is now the leader of his teachers, as well as the main teacher educator. He has to be able to do things *for* and *with* teachers for the improvement of the program. Another important qualification is the supervisor's power of persuasion—the supervisor who can give a teacher the idea that he is creating power with other people is a persuasive success. A well-balanced, sound philosophy of life and of education is another characteristic of the effective supervisor; he is susceptible to change if the change is orderly and called for by changing conditions or circumstances. The good prospect for training for a supervisory position is not markedly different from the good, effective teacher, except in perhaps one respect, namely, he expects to go into supervision and the position of supervision has a prestige of a highly professional nature in his mind. He also feels secure in his work and in his present position. Because of that feeling of security, he does not feel compelled to fight for prestige or respect; he has those assets already and can spend his time acquiring other competencies that he needs. He is able to identify the new knowledge or the new skill that he needs, because he has learned to meet failure, to learn from it, and to adjust to what he can accomplish.

In the realm of human relations, the prospective supervisor should have an understanding of the need of each member of the school personnel to be successful in some effort. As each member of the staff is made to feel that his effort is creative, or that he has made a real contribution, so does the supervisor succeed in creating and releasing power in the group. In this manner new status is acquired by each one from time to time; and as each teacher acquires new status steadily, he tends to lend a helping hand to others in their efforts to acquire status and a sense of security.

School personnel frequently overlook one qualification that a good supervisor must possess today, namely, an insatiable desire ever to learn new things, new skills, new information, new methods. The effective supervisor is ever learning; as a matter of fact, you can seldom mention any new methods or facts and find him entirely ignorant of them.

TYPES OF SUPERVISORY ORGANIZATION AND PERSONNEL

Attention has been directed several times in this volume to the developing trend in combining the two offices of supervisor and curriculum co-ordinator in a school system into one office, marked by some such title as director of instruction, or co-ordinator of instruction and supervision. Indications point to a continuation of this trend, since curriculum improvement and the improvement of instruction are so closely interrelated. Indications also point to the eventual requirement of a doctor's degree for these positions.

Another newer practice that promises to grow is that of state consultative services in the field of supervision. The National Council of Chief State School Officers has been working steadily for some years on the basic premise that the chief responsibility of state departments of education consists of leadership functions. In line with this concept, supervisory staffs in state departments have been steadily changing from direct observation of individual teachers to the use of their personnel and resources with school systems as consultative services. For example, when an elementary super-visor goes out now from the state department, he serves upon invita-tion as a consultant and resource person to an elementary school principal and to the principal's local supervisor and teachers, or to the elementary principals and supervisors in a whole system. The main emphasis in the supervisor's work has changed from working with or teaching individual teachers to planning, consulting with, and helping supervisors and principals in their programs. This change makes it imperative that state departments obtain and hold extremely well-qualified people for this important task. More and more, the personnel of these consultative divisions are acquiring the doctor's degree to prepare themselves adequately for this new kind of work.

There seems little indication that there will be much change in the future in the kinds of supervisory personnel that the schools will demand and employ. The general supervisor in the elementary school, the high school supervisor, the department head, the special high school supervisor, and the principal or assistant principal will probably continue to perform major supervisory functions. For example, Kentucky recently instituted a new Foundation Program for its public schools, under which its principals' salaries were to be raised; but provisions were made by the State Department of Edu-cation for "principal" to be defined as one who spent at least half of his time in the supervision of instruction. The chances are that for some time to come the principal will continue to act in the dual role of both administrator and supervisor, as he has in the past in various sections of the country.

Research and Experimentation

In the critical years ahead for education, supervisors, adminis-trators, and teachers will be forced to experiment in order to give an adequate educational program to the large increase in enrollment. In doing so, they should retain the "open mind." When some per-son or some system wants to experiment, experimentation should be encouraged under conditions that will not harm the pupil and with purposes of the experiment clearly defined so that the results of the experimentation can be assessed.

For example, the St. Paul school system experimented for a

number of years with "resource teachers." How was the experiment set up? Who were these resource teachers, and how did they work? How effectively or ineffectively did the plan work? What are implications from their experiment for the use of resource teachers in other schools? What significance did the experiment have for supervision? In like manner, study and final assessment are yet to be made of the experiment with the use of "teacher aids" in Bay City, Michigan, and other public school systems. The time is perhaps not far off when controlled experimentation will have to be conducted in regard to the use for periods of time of Future Teachers of America high school members as aids to teachers in the upper elementary grades.

Other Demands upon the Supervisor of the Future

This account should not be closed without pinpointing some of the knowledges and skills which the supervisor of the future must possess, even though some of us in the past may have gotten along without them. He will have to learn how to supervise student or cadet teaching, as this apprenticeship becomes universal in preservice teacher education. He will have to learn how to get along more satisfactorily with women, since, after all, most teachers are women. Further, he will be dealing with approximately 65 per cent married teachers, as compared to the 30-40 per cent formerly. One of his big tasks will be to help the new teacher to lead discussions and to learn how to be chairman of a group. He will also have a major job in helping the beginning teacher who married just after she finished college, devoted herself to rearing a family for ten years before she taught, and is starting to teach now that all of her children are in school. Another responsibility with new teachers pertains to being prepared to advise them about further in-service teaching or graduate work.

Another group of responsibilities involves community contacts. When and how does the supervisor carry on public relations with the community? Meet parents? Get out notices or bulletins? Maintain lines of communication with community organizations and clubs? Learn to use community resources more effectively in the instructional program?

Other supervisory problems are: (1) how to help teachers with their sense of values, in their decision-making, and in their development of good tastes, (2) how to aid teachers in gaining more information on teachers' organizations, including teachers' unions and co-operatives, (3) where and how to obtain adequate information on school laws and how they operate in the state, (4) how to help teachers to improve oral reading and expression, (5) what material and information to include in a handbook for teachers, and what to leave out, or when to leave off such a handbook entirely, and (6) how to learn the differences, if any, between duties and responsibilities of supervisors in city schools and in county schools, in urban as compared to rural situations.

Perhaps there are three ground rules that the supervisor should operate under at all times. First, the teaching profession has come a long way—from the teacher as judge, disciplinarian, and oracle to the teacher as constructive, creative guide of children and youth. Secondly, real teaching is exciting, and the supervisor should never do anything to a teacher to prevent its being so. In the third place, there are several unmistakable signs by which the supervisor can tell when he is becoming complacent—which is the beginning of the end of his effectiveness. These signs are:

When he begins to know all of the answers.

When he sits in his office more than he is at work outside of it.

When he thinks of something else while a teacher is telling him his problem.

When he begins to think that children are worse today than they used to be.

When he becomes allergic to any change in his habits or schedule.

When he blames the poor morale or inadequate program of the school upon someone else.

When he fails to keep up with new ideas in education.

When he becomes sloppy in his dress and appearance.

When he feels that his importance has been overlooked.

When the page of a book or a report becomes more interesting than the face of a child.

Problems for Individual Study and Class Discussion

1. If you are going to train as a supervisor of the junior high school, should you have teaching experience on both high school and elementary school levels, or not? Support your point of view.
2. Write out some standards to use in co-operative school-community planning for the curriculum.
3. To make the school a "community" school, it is necessary to define the "community." Just what is a community?
4. Next year the State High School Division of Instructional Service, at your request, is going to evaluate your secondary school. As high school supervisor, what steps should you and your staff take this year to prepare for this evaluation by this outside group?
5. Why would a highly successful teacher desire to change schools after a short period of time? Would you try to discover her reasons for leaving or let her go? Explain.
6. If you wanted to install a new and radically different program in your school, how much time would be required for teachers, parents, and pupils to become thoroughly familiar with its purposes before you and your staff put it into operation? Explain.
7. Will the supervisor of the future have to have many of the competencies and knowledges of a good school librarian? Explain.
8. What is the supervisor's role in school building planning? List the areas and aspects of the new building in regard to which you would call upon your staff for help and guidance.
9. List the duties and responsibilities of supervisors in one column. Then star (°) those duties with which a rural supervisor would have much more concern than a city supervisor.
10. Your principal calls you in for consultation concerning a new teacher who was a failure in his first year in a neighboring school. He wishes you to interview this man, since he feels that he may have potential abilities that will make him a good teacher. How would you plan for this conference?
11. What should be the role of the supervisor toward cadet or practice teachers in the school system? What special problems does their presence pose for the supervisor?
12. Give your opinion of unionization of teachers. When teachers organize for professional betterment, what stand on the issue ought the supervisor to take?

Additional Selected References for Problem or Unit Study

Adkins, E. P., ed., *Television in Teacher Education* (Washington: American Association of Colleges of Teacher Education, National Education Association, 1960), *passim*.

American Association of School Admiinstrators, Thirty-fifth Yearbook, *The Superintendent as Instructional Leader* (Washington: National Education Association, 1957), *passim.*

Association for Supervision and Curriculum Development, 1960 Yearbook, *Leadership for Improving Instruction* (Washington: National Education Association, 1960), chs. I-IV, VII; 1961 Yearbook, *Balance in the Curriculum* (Washington: National Education Association, 1961), *passim;* and Snyder, E. R. (ed.), *The Self-Contained Classroom* (Washington: National Education Association, 1960), *passim.*

The Bulletin of the National Association of Secondary School Principals has a whole issue on "Public Relations for the American High School," vol. XLIV (September, 1960), and "Seeking Improved Learning Opportunities: Fourth Report on Staff Utilization Studies," vol. XLV (Jan., 1961).

Burton, W. H., and Brueckner, L. J., *Supervision: A Social Process* (New York: Appleton-Century-Crofts, Inc., 1955), ch. XVIII.

California Journal of Secondary Education, a symposium on "The High School and the American Public: A Search for Quality," vol. XXXV (October, 1960), pp. 360-399, and "The Educational Program in the New Decade," vol. XXXVI (Feb., 1961), pp. 95-127. (This publication changed its name in 1961 to *Journal of Secondary Education.*)

Campbell, R. F., and Ramseyer, J. A., *The Dynamics of School-Community Relationships* (New York: Allyn and Bacon, 1955), *passim.*

Conant, J. B., *The Child, the Parent, and the State* (Cambridge, Mass.: Harvard University Press, 1959), *passim.*

Corbally, J. E., Jr., *et al., Educational Administration: The Secondary School* (Boston: Allyn and Bacon, 1961), chs. XI-XII.

Cramer, R. V., and Domian, O. E., *Administration and Supervision in the Elementary School* (New York: Harper and Brothers, 1960), ch. XVI.

Cronin, J. M., "What's All This About 'Teacher Aides'?" *California Journal of Secondary Education,* vol. XXXIV (November, 1959), pp. 390-397.

Crosby, M., *Supervision as Co-operative Action* (New York: Appleton-Century-Crofts, Inc., 1957), section V.

Department of Elementary School Principals, *The Elementary School Principalship: A Research Study,* Thirty-seventh Yearbook (Washington, D. C.: National Education Association, 1958), chs. I-II, X, XII.

The Education of Teachers: Certification, National Commission on Teacher Preparation and Professional Standards (Washington: National Education Association, 1961), parts III, IV, and V.

Educational Leadership examines the modern concepts of supervision and presents various aspects in symposia from time to time.

Ehlers, H., ed., *Crucial Issues in Education: An Anthology,* rev. ed. (New York: Henry Holt and Company, Inc., 1959), *passim.*

Everett, Samuel (ed.), *Programs for the Gifted: A Case Book in Secondary Education* (New York: Harper and Brothers, 1960), *passim.*

Fund for the Advancement of Education, 477 Madison Avenue, New York 22,

New Directions in Teacher Education, by Paul Woodring (1957); *They Went to College Early,* Evaluation Report No. 2 (1957).

Gauerke, W. E., *Legal and Ethical Responsibiilties of School Personnel* (Englewood Cliffs, N. J.: Prentice-Hall, Inc., 1959), *passim.*

Hicks, H. J., *Educational Supervision in Principle and Practice* (New York: The Ronald Press Company, 1960), ch. XIV.

The High School Journal presents a symposium on "Teaching Aids in the Secondary School," vol. XLIV (Nov., 1960), pp. 34-94.

Hill, C. M., director, *Teaching Fellows,* The Yale-Fairfield Study of Elementary Teaching (New Haven: Yale University, May, 1960).

Huggett, A. J., and Stinnett, T. M., *Professional Problems of Teachers* (New York: The Macmillan Company, 1956), chs. XV-XVI.

Hullfish, H. G., and Smith, P. G., *Reflective Thinking: The Method of Education* (New York: Dodd, Mead and Company, 1961), *passim.*

Irey, J. E., Jr., and Godbold, B. D., "MPATI: Breakthrough in Educational Television," *Phi Delta Kappan,* vol. XLII (Feb., 1961), pp. 192-196.

Kearney, N. C., *A Teacher's Professional Guide* (Englewood Cliffs, N. J.: Prentice-Hall, Inc., 1958), chs. V, X, and XVII, resource teachers, pp. 87-88.

Law and The School Superintendent, Vol. I, "Legal Problems of Education Series," R. L. Drury, ed. (Cincinnati: The W. H. Anderson Company, 1958), *passim.*

Lawler, M., *Curriculum Consultants at Work* (New York: Teachers College, Columbia University, 1958), *passim.*

Lumsdaine, A. A., and Glaser, R., *Teaching Machines and Programmed Learning* (Washington: Department of Audio-Visual Instruction, National Education Association, 1960), *passim.*

McNally, H. J., and Passow, A. H., and associates, *Improving the Quality of Public School Programs: Approaches to Curriculum Development* (New York: Teachers College, Columbia University, 1960), *passim.*

Morse, A. D., *Schools of Tomorrow—Today! A Report on Educational Experiments* (Garden City: Doubleday and Company, 1960), *passim.*

NEA Journal has a long section on "Your Child's Intelligence," vol. L (Jan., 1961), pp. 34-48.

National Society for the Study of Education, *In-Service Education,* Fifty-sixth Yearbook, Part I; *Education for the Gifted,* Fifty-seventh Yearbook, Part II; *Social Forces Influencing American Education,* Sixtieth Yearbook, Part II (Chicago: University of Chicago Press, 1957, 1958, and 1961 respectively).

Ohio Association for Supervision and Curriculum Development, Research Committee, *The Role of the Supervisor in Ohio's Schools* (Columbus 15: The Ohio Education Association, 1957).

Packard, V., *The Waste Makers* (New York: David McKay Company, Inc., 1960). A book about the commercialism of almost every part of American life, and suggestions to the common consumer for his education.

Remmlein, M. K., and others, "Economic, Legal, and Social Status of Teachers," *Review of Educational Research*, "Teacher Personnel," vol. XXVIII (June, 1958), pp. 242-255.

Reutter, E. E., Jr., *Schools and the Law* (New York: Oceana Publications, Inc., 1960), *passim*.

Root, E. M., *Brainwashing in the High Schools* (New York: Devin-Adair Company, Inc., 1958). A point of view on censorship of school textbooks.

School Management, "How to Improve Instruction with Teaching Teams," vol. IV, no. 11 (November, 1960), pp. 50-54.

Scott, C. W., and others, *The Great Debate: Our Schools in Crisis* (Englewood Cliffs, N. J.: Prentice-Hall, Inc., 1959), *passim*.

Strang, R., *Helping Your Gifted Child* (New York: E. P. Dutton and Company, Inc., 1960), *passim*.

Tarbet, Donald G., *Television and Our Schools* (New York: The Ronald Press Company, 1961), *passim*.

U. S. Department of Health, Education and Welfare, Bulletin 1955, No. 11, *Supervision in Rural Schools*, by Jane Franseth (Washington, D. C.: U. S. Government Printing Office).

Wey, H., and Corey, J., *Action Patterns in School Desegregation: A Guidebook* (Bloomington, Ind.: Phi Delta Kappan, 1959).

"What Teachers Say About Better Use of Their Time," *School Management*, vol. IV, no. 5 (May, 1960), pp. 63-66, 130, 132.

Woodring, P., *A Fourth of a Nation* (New York: McGraw-Hill Book Company, Inc., 1957), chs. IV-V.

Zirbes, L., *Challenges to Educational Advance* (Columbus: Bureau of Educational Research, The Ohio State University, 1960), *passim*.

Appendix

ANNOTATED LIST OF COMPANIES AND OR-
GANIZATIONS WHICH SUPPLY TEACH-
ING MATERIALS AND EQUIPMENT FOR
SCHOOLS

(ALPHABETICALLY ARRANGED)

Allied Youth, Inc., 1709 M St., N. W., Washington 6, D. C. Material on alcohol education.

Allyn and Bacon, Englewood Cliffs, N. J. School textbooks.

American Association of School Administrators, 1201 Sixteenth St., N. W., Washington 6, D. C. Professional materials of wide range on administrative aspects.

American Automobile Association, 1712 G St. N. W., Washington, D. C. Traffic, automobile, safety education, and driving materials.

American Book Company, 55 Fifth Ave., New York 3, N. Y. Textbooks, and professional books, records for modern language study.

American Cancer Society, Inc., 521 W. 57th St., New York, N. Y. Health education materials nd services.

American Council on Education, 1785 Massachusetts Ave., N. W., Washington 6, D. C. Intergroup and guidance studies, professional books and reports.

American Crayon Company, 1706 Hayes Ave., Sandusky, Ohio. Chalks, crayons, colors, books.

American Education Publications, Columbus, Ohio. Weekly readers and current events papers for grades 1-12, textbooks.

American Library Association, 50 E. Huron St., Chicago 11, Ill. Books, pamphlets, filmstrips, records of children's stories.

American Medical Association, 535 N. Dearborn St., Chicago 10, Ill. Health publications and information.

American Newspaper Publishers Association, 750 3rd Ave., New York 17, N. Y. Information on newspapers.

American School Publishing Company, 470 Park Ave. S., New York 16, N. Y. Data on school construction, equipment.

American Technical Society, 848 E. 5th St., Chicago 37, Ill. Books on agriculture, technical aspects, and teacher training.

Americana Corporation, 4606 East-West Highway, Washington 14, D. C. Encyclopedias.

Appleton-Century-Crofts, Inc., 35 W. 32nd St., New York 1, N. Y. Professional, reference, and supplementary books.

Associated Publishers, Inc., 1538 Ninth St., N. W., Washington 1, D. C. Books on the Negro.

Association of American Railroads, Transportation Bldg., Washington 6, D. C. Teaching aids on railroad transportation.

Association for Childhood Educational International, 3615 Wisconsin Ave., N. W., Washington 6, D. C. Professional books, pamphlets, booklists, and teaching aids.

Association Films, Inc., 347 Madison Ave., New York 17, N. Y. Distributor, free-loan, and rental films.

Atlantic Monthly Company, 8 Arlington St., Boston 16, Mass. Reading speed and comprehension materials, student editions.

A. S. Barnes and Company, 11 E. 36th St., New York 16, N. Y. Sports guides, physical education and record books.

Bausch and Lomb Optical Company, 635 St. Paul St., Rochester, N. Y. Scientific instruments and equipment, projectors of various kinds.

Beckley-Cardy Company, 1900 N. Narragansett St., Chicago 39, Ill. Books, teaching materials, equipment, and supplies.

Bellman Publishing Company, Box 172, Cambridge 38, Mass. Books and pamphlets on careers and vocations and on choosing a college, on fellowships, scholarships and loans.

Charles A. Bennett Company, Inc. (formerly Manual Arts Press), 237 N. Monroe St., Peoria 3, Ill. Books on shop, home economics, and art; filmstrips.

Binney and Smith Company, Inc., 380 Madison Avenue, New York, N. Y. Crayons, chalks, water colors, paste.

Bobbs-Merrill Company, Inc., 1720 E. 38th St., Indianapolis 6, Ind. Texts, and reference and supplementary books.

Stanley Bowmar Company, Inc., 12 Cleveland Ave., Valhalla, N. Y. Aids to visual education.

Boy Scouts of America, New Brunswick, N. J. Boy Scout school and P.T.A. material.

William C. Brown Company, 135 S. Locust St., Dubuque, Iowa. Professional books.

Bruce Publishing Company, 2642 University Ave., St. Paul 14, Minn. Schoolbooks, mostly in vocational and science fields.

Burgess Publishing Company, 426-428 S. 6th St., Minneapolis 15, Minn. Books mostly in agriculture and sciences.

California Test Bureau, 5916 Hollywood Blvd., Los Angeles 28, Calif. Tests of all kinds.

Center for Safety Education, New York University, Washington Sq., New York, N. Y. Safety books, tests, and printed materials.

University of Chicago Press, 5750 Ellis Ave., Hyde Park Station, Chicago 37, Ill. Professional books, reports on reading conferences.

Child Craft Division of Smith Cabinet Manufacturing Company, Inc., 112 W. 34th St., New York, N. Y. Kindergarten and childhood education materials.

Child Study Association of America, Inc., 132 E. 74th St., New York 21, N. Y. Materials on child growth and development.

Citizenship Education Project, Teachers College, Columbia University, New York 27, N. Y. Materials on citizenship education.

F. E. Compton and Company, 1000 N. Dearborn St., Chicago 10, Ill. Encyclopedias.

Consumers Union of the United States, Inc., 256 Washington Ave., Mount Vernon, N. Y. Consumer education reports.

Continental Press, The, Elizabethtown, Pa. Workbooks and activity units (preprinted masters for liquid duplicators).

Coronet Instructional Films, 65 E. South Water St., Chicago 1, Ill. Teaching films for all grades and subjects.

George F. Cram Company, Inc., 730 E. Washington St., Indianapolis 7, Ind. Maps, globes, charts, atlases, outline maps.

Creative Crafts Publications, Hartland, Mich.

Creative Playthings, Inc., 405 Lexington Ave., New York, N. Y. Tools and play equipment for preschool, kindergarten, and primary grades.

Arthur C. Croft Publications, 100 Garfield Ave., New London, Conn. Professional development program, including professional guides or kits for supervisors, teachers, principals, and administrators, each published monthly or twice a month.

Thomas Y. Crowell Company, 432 Park Ave. S., New York 16, N. Y. Textbooks, reference books.

Da-Lite Screen Company, Inc., Road 15, North Warsaw, Ind. Projection screens.

Delmar Publishers, Inc., Mountain View Ave., Albany, N. Y. Materials for industrial arts and vocational courses.

Denoyer-Geppert Company, 5235 Ravenswood Ave., Chicago 40, Ill. Maps, globes, charts, atlases, pictures, models, specimens for geography, history, biology, nature study, and health and hygiene.

Department of Elementary School Principals, National Education Association, 1201 Sixteenth St., N. W., Washington 6, D. C. Professional teaching materials on elementary education.

Department of Rural Education, National Education Association, 1201 Sixteenth St., N. W., Washington 6, D. C. Materials for teachers and administrators.

Dodd, Mead and Company, Inc., 432 Park Ave. S., New York 16, N. Y. Children's books, professional books, textbooks, language tapes.

Doubleday and Company, Inc., 575 Madison Ave., New York 22, N. Y. Books.

E. P. Dutton and Company, Inc., 300 Park Ave. S., New York 10, N. Y. Books for boys and girls.

Economy Company, The, 24 W. Park Place, Oklahoma City, Okla. Textbooks and workbooks.

Educational Directories, Inc., 1124 Greenleaf Ave., Wilmette, Ill. Patterson's Source Guide for Educational Materials and Equipment. An annual.

Educational Map and Chart Service, Inc., Syracuse, Ind. Charts on teaching democracy.

Educational Publishers, Inc., 720 Washington Ave., S. E., Minneapolis, Minn. Educational tests of various kinds and professional books.

Educational Publishing Corporation, 23 Leroy Ave., Darien, Conn. Monthly magazines, teaching materials, books.

Educational Recording Services, Los Angeles 45, Calif. Educational recordings for professional meetings and for teaching.

Educational Test Bureau, Educational Publishers, Inc., 720 Washington Ave., Minneapolis 14, Minn. Standardized tests and scales, professional books.

Educational Testing Service, 20 Nassau St., Princeton, N. J. Testing programs for high schools and colleges.

EMC Recordings Corporation, 806 E. 7th St., St. Paul 6, Minn. Tape recordings for Latin, French, Spanish, and German teachers.

Encyclopedia Britannica Films, Inc., 1123 Central Ave., Wilmette, Ill. Films and slides for all grades.

Encyclopedia Britannica, Inc., 425 N. Michigan Ave., Chicago 11, Ill. Reference materials, encyclopedias.

Extra-Curricular Publishing Company, Keokuk, Iowa. Information and materials.

Eye Gate House, Inc., 146-01 Archer Ave., Jamaica, N. Y. Filmstrip producers.

Field Enterprises Educational Corporation (publishers of World Book Encyclopedia), 510 Merchandise Mart Plaza, Chicago 54, Ill. Also films and list of sources of free and inexpensive teaching materials.

Follett Publishing Company, 1010 W. Washington Blvd., Chicago 7, Ill. Educational books and materials.

Foreign Policy Association, National Headquarters, 345 E. 46th St., New York 17, N. Y. Materials on national and international affairs.

French Government Tourist Bureau, 610 Fifth Ave., New York, N. Y.

Garrard Press, 510-522 Hickory St., Champaign, Ill. Materials on reading and professional books.

General Mills, Inc., 9200 Wayzata Blvd., Minneapolis, Minn. Teaching aids for nutrition and health education; films; panels, filmstrips, and illustrated booklets.

Ginn and Company, Statler Bldg., Back Bay P. O. 191, Boston 17, Mass. Textbooks and professional books.

Girl Scouts of the United States of America, 830 3rd Ave., New York 22, N. Y. Information and materials.

Globe Book Company, Inc., 175 Fifth Ave., New York 10, N. Y. Books for school libraries, supplementary and remedial reading purposes.

Grolier Society, Inc., 575 Lexington Ave., New York 22, N. Y. Encyclopedias.

Hagstrom Map Company, 311 Broadway, New York 7, N. Y. Picture maps for all grades, historical and literary.

E. M. Hale and Company, 1201 S. Hastings Way, Eau Claire, Wisc. Books.

C. S. Hammond and Company, Inc., 515 Valley St., Maplewood, N. J. Textbooks, maps, atlases, globes.

Harcourt, Brace & World, Inc., 750 3rd Ave., New York 17, N. Y. Books of all sorts for schools.

Harper and Brothers, 49 E. 33rd St., New York 16, N. Y. Books of all kinds for schools, and professional books for teachers.

D. C. Heath and Company, 285 Columbus Ave., Boston 16, Mass. School and college textbooks.

Historical Publishing Company, Monroe, Mich. History and geography loose-leaf outline maps.

Holiday House, 8 W. 13th St., New York 11, N. Y. Books for young people.

Holt, Rinehart and Winston, Inc., 383 Madison Ave., New York 17, N. Y. Textbooks, professional books.

Houghton Mifflin Company, 2 Park St., Boston 7, Mass. Textbooks, professional books.

Information Classroom Picture Publishers, 40 Ionia Ave., N. W., Grand Rapids 2, Mich. Pictures, prints.

Institute of Life Insurance, 488 Madison Ave., New York 22, N. Y. Classroom units and visual aids.

Iroquois Publishing Company, Inc., 1300 Alum Creek Drive, Columbus 16, Ohio. Textbooks and teaching devices.

Jam Handy Organization, The, 2821 E. Grand Blvd., Detroit 11, Mich. Filmstrips and motion pictures.

Judy Publishing Company, The, 2517 Michigan Ave., Chicago 16, Ill. Manipulative materials for language arts, social studies, arithmetic, science.

Keystone View Company, Meadville, Pa. Visual aid equipment, slides, tachistoscopic service, stereoscopes, and stereographs.

Laidlaw Brothers, Inc., Thatcher and Madison St., River Forest, Ill. Textbooks and educational materials.

Linguaphone Institute, 30 Rockefeller Plaza, New York 20, N. Y. Language recordings, foreign and English.

Little, Brown and Company, 34 Beacon St., Boston 6, Mass. Books, desk maps.

Living Language Course, 100 Ave. of the Americas, New York 3, N. Y. Recorded lessons in French, Spanish, Italian, or German.

Longmans, Green and Company, Inc., 119 W. 40th St., New York 18, N. Y. Professional and scientific books.

Lyons and Carnahan, 2500 Prairie Ave., Chicago 16, Ill. Texts, reference books.

The Macmillan Company, 60 Fifth Ave., New York 11, N. Y. Textbooks, reference and professional books.

Mahnke Productions, Carl F., 215 E. 3rd St., Des Moines, Iowa. Sound films and film strips.

Martin and Murray Company, Inc., RCA Bldg., 30 Rockefeller Plaza, New York 20, N. Y. Dictionaries and encyclopedias.

Mayfair Agency, The, 32 N. Van Brant St., Englewood, N. J. Magazine subscription house for libraries.

The McCormick-Mathers Publishing Company, Inc., Box 2212, 1440 E. English St., Wichita 1, Kan. School textbooks and workbooks.

McGraw-Hill Company, Inc., 330 W. 42nd St., New York 36, N. Y. Texts, professional books, and teacher-training films.

McKinley Publishing Company, 809 N. 19th St., Philadelphia, Pa. Outline and desk maps.

McKnight and McKnight Publishing Company, U. S. Rte. 66 and Towanda Ave., Bloomington, Ill. Books on guidance and industrial arts.

Charles E. Merrill Books, Inc., 1300 Alum Creek Drive, Columbus 16, Ohio (see American Education Publications).

Metropolitan Life Insurance Company, 1 Madison Ave., New York 10, N. Y. School health materials.

Milton Bradley Company, Springfield, Mass. Art, kindergarten, educational supplies and equipment.

Models of Industry, Inc., 2100 Fifth St., Berkeley 2, Calif. Kits for learning to make by doing.

Modern Talking Picture Service, Inc., 3 E. 54th St., New York, N. Y. Free educational motion pictures.

National Association for Mental Health, 10 Columbus Circle, New York 19, N. Y. Mental health publications and audio-visual aids.

National Association of Secondary School Principals, 1201 Sixteenth St., N. W., Washington 6, D. C. Consumer education, civic education, and professional high school publications.

National Audio-visual Association, Don White, Executive Vice President, Box 337, Fairfax, Va. Publishes the *Audio-Visual Equipment Directory*, a guide to recent models of audio-visual equipment; projectors, reproducers, recorders, and accessories.

National Coal Association, 1130 17th St., N. W., Washington, D. C. Free teaching materials on the coal industry.

National Congress of Parents and Teachers, 700 N. Rush St., Chicago 11, Ill. Publications.

National Council for the Social Studies, 1201 Sixteenth St., N. W., Washington 6, D. C. Materials, units, professional publications on teaching of social studies.

National Council of Teachers of English, 704 S. Sixth St., Champaign, Ill. (address of the council's secretary). Materials on teaching of English and professional publications.

National Education Association, 1201 Sixteenth St., N. W., Washington 6, D. C. Materials and publications on teachers, teaching, teaching areas, and publications of its various departments.

National Forum Foundation for American Education, Inc., 407 S. Dearborn St., Chicago 5, Ill. Guidance and curriculum materials, grades 7-12.

National Foundation for Infantile Paralysis, 1 E. 54th St., New York, N. Y. Publications, posters, films, and filmstrips.

National Geographic Society, 16 and M Sts., N. W., Washington 6, D. C. Magazine, bulletins, and wall maps.

National Safety Council, 425 N. Michigan Ave., Chicago 11, Ill. Materials, publications, and supplies.

W. W. Norton and Company, Inc., 55 Fifth Ave., New York, N. Y. Professional books.

A. J. Nystrom and Company, 3333 Elston Ave., Chicago 18, Ill. Maps, globes, charts and materials for use in geography, history, social studies, and science.

F. A. Owen Publishing Company, Dansville, N. Y. *The Instructor,* pictures and prints, and aids for teachers and schools.

A. N. Palmer Company, 55 Fifth Ave., New York 3, N. Y. Penmanship textbooks and materials.

Parents Magazine Educational Press, Inc., 52 Vanderbilt Ave., New York 17, N. Y. Children's magazine.

Philosophical Library, Inc., 15 E. 40th St., New York 16, N. Y. Professional books.

Plymouth Press, The, 2921 W. 63rd St., Chicago 29, Ill. Seatwork, reading, and arithmetic devices for primary grades.

Pocket Books, Inc., 630 Fifth Ave., New York 20, N. Y. Pocket books.

Popular Science Publishing Company, 355 Lexington Ave., New York 17, N. Y. Filmstrips and disks.

Prentice-Hall, Inc., Englewood Cliffs, N. J. Professional books, textbooks.

Psychological Corporation, The, 304 E. 45th St., New York, N. Y. Tests of various kinds.

Public Affairs Committee, Inc., 22 E. 38th St., New York 16, N. Y. Pamphlets on public affairs.

Public School Publishing Company, 500-512 N. East St., Bloomington, Ill. Educational test materials.

Radio Corporation of America, Camden, N. J. Audio-visual products.

Rand McNally and Company, 8255 North Central, Skokie, Ill. School textbooks, maps, globes, atlases.

Random House, 457 Madison Ave., New York 22, N. Y. Landmark Books and enrichment records based on them for young readers.

Readers Digest Services, Inc., Educational Division, Pleasantville, N. Y. Educational edition of the *Readers Digest* and *Reading Skill Builder* series at middle grade levels.

Ronald Press Company, 15 E. 26th St., New York 10, N. Y. Reference, commercial education, and professional books.

Row, Peterson and Company, 2500 Crawford Ave., Evanston, Ill. School textbooks, pamphlet series, and professional books.

W. B. Saunders Company, 218 W. Washington Sq., Philadelphia 5, Pa. Physical education books.

Scholastic Magazines, 33 W. 42nd St., New York 36, N. Y. Weekly student magazines edited for classroom use; professional magazines for educators.

School Thrift, Inc., 326 S. Broadway, Yonkers, N. Y. School savings, service, and supplies.

"Science Kit," Box 69, Tonawanda, N. Y. Portable elementary science laboratories.

Science Research Associates, Inc., 57 W. Grand Ave., Chicago 10, Ill. Testing guidance and reading improvement materials; professional books.

Science Service, 1719 N St., N. W., Washington 6, D. C. Science materials and publications.

Scott, Foresman and Company, 433 E. Erie St., Chicago 11, Ill. School textbooks and workbooks, remedial reading materials, professional books on special aspects.

William R. Scott, Inc., Young Scott Books, 8 W. 13th St., New York 11, N. Y. Children's books.

Silver Burdett Company, Park Ave. and Columbia Rd., Morristown, N. J. Textbooks, music records, filmstrips.

The L. W. Singer Company, Inc., 249-259 W. Erie Blvd., Syracuse 2, N. Y. Textbooks for schools.

Soil Conservation Service, Department of the Interior, Washington, D. C. Bulletins and audio-visual materials.

Southwestern Publishing Company, 5101 Madison Rd., Cincinnati 27, Ohio. School textbooks and lists of visual aids and free or inexpensive materials in business education.

The Stackpole Company, Cameron and Kelker Sts., Telegraph Press Bldg., Harrisburg, Pa. Professional books.

Stanwix House, Inc., 3020 Chartiers Ave., Pittsburgh, Pa. Large-type edition publications for visually handicapped.

State University of Iowa, Bureau of Educational Research and Service, Iowa City, Iowa. Education research studies, bulletins and tests.

The Steck Company, 9th and Lavaca Sts., Austin 61, Texas. Music, library, and supplementary books.

R. H. Stone Products, 9225 Grand River St., Detroit, Mich. Mor-Pla jumbo blox.

Syracuse University Press, 920 Irving Ave., Syracuse 10, N. Y. Books on Russia and communism; guidance bibliographies.

Teaching Film Custodians, Inc., 25 W. 43rd St., New York, N. Y. Educational motion pictures.

United States Department of Agriculture, Washington, D. C. Materials, bulletins, and audio-visual materials.

United States Government Printing Office, Washington 25, D. C. Ordering service for all materials of Federal government for which a charge is made.

United States Office of Education, Department of Health, Education and Welfare, Washington 26, D. C. Materials for administrators and teachers.

United States Treasury Department, Savings Bonds Division—Education Section, Washington 25, D. C. Free teaching aids.

United World Films, Inc., 1445 Park Ave., New York 29, N. Y. Education films and filmstrips.

D. Van Nostrand Company, Inc., 120 Alexander St., Princeton, N. J. School texts, especially science.

Weber, Costello Company, 12 and McKinley Sts., Chicago Heights, Ill. Globes, wall and outline maps.

Webster Publishing Company, 1154 Reco Ave., St. Louis 26, Mo. School textbooks, workbooks and tests.

W. M. Welch Manufacturing Company, 1515 Sedgwick St., Chicago 10, Ill. Scientific school supplies.

Albert Whitman and Company, 560 W. Lake St., Chicago 6, Ill. Supplementary reading books, remedial reading and sightsaving books.

John Wiley and Sons, Inc., 440 Park Ave. S., New York 16, N. Y. Professional books.

H. W. Wilson Company, 950-972 University Ave., New York 52, N. Y. Library reference books and catalogs.

Zaner-Bloser Company, The, 612 N. Park St., Columbus 8, Ohio. Handwriting books and supplies.

INDEX